SURVEY OF
CRIMINAL LAW

The West Paralegal Series

Your options keep growing with West Publishing.
Each year our list continues to offer you more options for every course, new or existing, and on-the-job reference materials. We now have over 140 titles from which to choose.

We are pleased to offer books in the following subject areas:

Administrative Law
Alternative Dispute Resolution
Bankruptcy
Business Organizations/Corporations
Civil Litigation and Procedure
CLA Exam Preparation
Client Accounting
Computer in the Law Office
Constitutional Law
Contract Law
Criminal Law and Procedure
Document Preparation
Environmental Law
Ethics

Family Law
Federal Taxation
Intellectual Property
Introduction to Law
Introduction to Paralegalism
Law Office Management
Law Office Procedures
Legal Research, Writing, and Analysis
Legal Terminology
Paralegal Employment
Real Estate Law
Reference Materials
Torts and Personal Injury Law
Will, Trusts, and Estate Administration

You will find unparalleled, practical teaching support.
Each text is enhanced by instructor and student supplements to ensure the best learning experience possible to prepare for this field. We also offer custom publishing and other benefits such as West's Student Achievement Award. In addition, our sales representatives are ready to provide you with needed and dependable service.

We want to hear from you.
The most important factor in improving the quality of our paralegal texts and teaching packages is active feedback from educators in the field. If you have a question, concern, or observation about any of our materials or you have written a proposal or manuscript, we want to hear from you. Please do not hesitate to contact your local representative or write us at the following address:

West Paralegal Series, 3 Columbia Circle, P.O. Box 15015, Albany, NY 12212-5015.

For additional information point your browser to
http://www.westlegalstudies.com and **http://www.delmar.com**

West Legal Studies — *Your Paralegal Publisher*
an imprint of Delmar Publishers

an International Thomson Publishing company

Felony Murder
vs
Involuntary Manslaughter

SURVEY OF
CRIMINAL LAW

Second Edition

Daniel E. Hall

WEST LEGAL STUDIES

an International Thomson Publishing company I(T)P®

Albany • Bonn • Boston • Cincinnati • Detroit • London • Madrid
Melbourne • Mexico City • Minneapolis/St. Paul • New York • Pacific Grove
Paris • San Francisco • Singapore • Tokyo • Toronto • Washington

NOTICE TO THE READER

Cover design: Linda DeMasi

Background by: Jennifer McGlaughlin

Delmar Staff:
Acquisitions Editor: Christopher Anzalone
Developmental Editor: Jeffrey D. Litton
Project Editors: Eugenia L. Orlandi

Production Coordinator: Jennifer Gaines
Art/Design Coordinator: Douglas J. Hyldelund

COPYRIGHT © 1997
By West Legal Studies
an imprint of Delmar Publishers
a division of International Thomson Publishing

The ITP logo is a trademark under license.
Printed in the United States of America

For more information, contact:

Delmar Publishers
3 Columbia Circle , Box 15015
Albany, New York 12212-5015

International Thomson Publishing Europe
Berkshire House
168-173 High Holborn
London, WC1V 7AA
United Kingdom

Nelson ITP, Australia
102 Dodds Street
South Melbourne,
Victoria, 3205 Australia

Nelson Canada
1120 Birchmont Road
Scarborough, Ontario
M1K 5G4, Canada

International Thomson Publishing France
Tour Maine-Montparnasse
33 Avenue du Maine
75755 Paris Cedex 15, France

International Thomson Editores
Seneca 53
Colonia Polanco
11560 Mexico D. F. Mexico

International Thomson Publishing GmbH
Königswinterer Strasße 418
53227 Bonn
Germany

International Thomson Publishing Asia
60 Albert Street
#15-01 Albert Complex
Singapore 189969

International Thomson Publishing Japan
Hirakawa-cho Kyowa Building, 3F
2-2-1 Hirakawa-cho, Chiyoda-ku,
Tokyo 102, Japan

ITE Spain/ Paraninfo
Calle Magallanes, 25
28015-Madrid, Espana

5 6 7 8 9 10 XXX 03 02

Library of Congress Cataloging-in-Publication Data
Hall, Daniel (Daniel E.)
    Survey of criminal law/Daniel E. Hall. — 2nd ed.
        p. cm.
    Includes index.
    ISBN 0-8273-7570-0
    1. Criminal law—United States.   2.. Legal assistants— United
States—Handbooks, manuals, etc.   I. Title.
KF9219.3.H323 1997
345.73—dc20
[347.305]
                                                        95-49170
                                                        CIP

DEDICATION

To Stace

CONTENTS

CHAPTER 3:   The Two Essential Elements   53

CHAPTER 4:   Crimes Against the Person   90

CHAPTER 5:   Crimes Against Property and Habitation   132

CHAPTER 7:   Parties and Inchoate Offenses   196

CHAPTER 8:   Factual and Statutory Defenses   209

CHAPTER 9:   Constitutional Defenses   237

APPENDICES

PREFACE

The field of criminal law is dynamic. Recent years have been host to significant movements and changes in this field. State legislatures have acted quickly and with considerable consistency in regard to victims' rights, stalking, and racially motivated crimes. The introduction of AIDS into the life of America has meant the introduction of AIDS to the law. Although AIDS has not presented new issues to criminal law, it has caused issues that preexisted it to surface in different, and often dramatic, ways. Courts continue to adapt the law to meet these, and other, new challenges.

In the past ten years, the Supreme Court has revisited issues, and in some cases, revisited them again. *Blockburger* was the law, then it was not, and then it was again. Victim impact evidence was a part of sentencing in many states until the Court invalidated its use in *Booth v. Maryland* in 1987. Then, only four years later, in *Payne v. Tennessee,* the Court reopened the door to victim impact evidence. Several other decisions of the Court have represented either a retreat or a divergence from prior jurisprudence.

Until recently, litigants looked almost exclusively to federal law for protection of individual rights. We are witnessing, however, a small revolution, or a rebirth, in state constitutional law. This edition includes a discussion of the importance of state constitutionalism in the preservation of individual rights.

Survey of Criminal Law reflects the law as it exists in 1995. I have remained true to the format and methods used in the first edition. Several new cases have been included, but, as before, the text stands alone. As before, cases have been heavily edited, and citations omitted, for improved utility and comprehensibility.

Several additions have been made to this edition. The respective powers and jurisdictions of the federal and state governments have been better defined. The section discussing the role of administrative agencies in criminal law has been entirely rewritten to make this somewhat dense subject more understandable to the undergraduate student.

Stalking, hate crimes, and civil rights crimes have been added. AIDS and the problems it poses to criminal law are discussed through both a sidebar and a case on factual impossibility. Also, a new section on environmental crimes has been added.

The old chapter on defenses has been split into two, one covering statutory and factual defenses, and the other constitutional defenses. The sections on constitutional defenses have been expanded to include discussions of due process, privacy, and the exercise of religion.

Several new sidebars contain relevant or tangential material intended to pique students' interest in the subject. Serial and mass killing, physician-assisted suicide, and computers and crime are examples.

I extend appreciation to Della Smith for research assistance and to the reviewers for their thoughtful comments, suggestions, and criticisms. Many of the changes found in the second edition are the result of their reviews. However, I take full responsibility for all omissions and errors. I also thank all on the Delmar staff who were involved in the production, publication, and promotion of this book. Finally, I invite everyone who has used this text, whether as an educator or student, to make suggestions for improvement.

Daniel E. Hall

TABLE OF CASES

CHAPTER 1

INTRODUCTION TO THE LEGAL SYSTEM OF THE UNITED STATES

CHAPTER OUTLINE   Federalism

Separation of Powers

The Structure of the Court System

The Duties and Powers of the
     Judicial Branch

Comparing Civil Law and Criminal
     Law

Federalism

Before one can undertake learning criminal law or criminal procedure, a basic understanding of the legal system of the United States is necessary. This can be a complex task, as criminal law and procedure are significantly influenced by federal and state constitutional law, the common law, and statutory law at both the federal and state levels. It will be easier to understand how these areas of law affect criminal law if we first explore the basic structure of American government.

The United States is divided into two sovereign forms of government—the government of the United States and the governments of the many states. This division of power is commonly known as **federalism**. It is also common to refer to this division as the vertical division of power, as the national government rests above the state governments in hierarchy. The framers of the Constitution of the United States established these two levels of government in an attempt to prevent the centralization of power, that is, too much power being vested in one group. The belief that "absolute power corrupts absolutely" was the catalyst for the division of governmental power.

SIDEBAR

At trial, a *sidebar* is a meeting between the judge and the attorneys, at the judge's bench, outside the hearing of the jury. Sidebars are used to discuss issues that the jury is not permitted to hear. In this text, sidebars will appear periodically. These features contain information relevant to the subject being studied.

In theory, the national government, commonly referred to as the *federal government,* and the state governments each possess authority over citizens, as well as over particular policy areas, free from the interference of the other government (dual sovereignty).

Determining what powers belong to the national government, as opposed to the states, is not always an easy task. The framers of the Constitution intended to establish a limited national government. That is, most of governmental powers were to reside in the states, with the national government being limited to the powers expressly delegated to it in the federal Constitution. This principle is found in the Tenth Amendment, which reads, "The powers not delegated to the United States by the Constitution, nor prohibited to it by the States, are reserved to the States respectively, or the people."

BALLENTINE'S
---

federalism   The system by which the states of the United States relate to each other and to the federal government.

What powers are delegated to the United States by the Constitution? There are several, including, but not limited to the power:

1. To coin money, punish counterfeiters, and fix standards of weights and measures.
2. To establish a post office and post roads.
3. To promote the arts.
4. To punish piracy and other crimes on the high seas.
5. To declare war and raise armies.
6. To conduct diplomacy and foreign affairs.
7. To regulate interstate and foreign commerce.
8. To make laws necessary and proper for carrying into execution other powers expressly granted in the Constitution.

The last two of these powers—the regulation of interstate commerce and the making of all necessary and proper laws—have proven to be significant sources of federal power. Also important is the Supremacy Clause of Article VI, which provides that

> This Constitution, and the Laws of the United States which shall be made in Pursuance thereof; and all Treaties made, or which shall be made, under the Authority of the United States, shall be the supreme Law of the Land; and the Judges in every State shall be bound thereby, any Thing in the Constitution or Laws of any State to the Contrary notwithstanding.

Simply stated, the Supremacy Clause declares national law, if valid, to be a higher form of law than state law. Of course, if the national government attempts to regulate an area belonging to the states, its law is invalid and the state law is controlling. But if the national government possesses **jurisdiction** and a state enacts a conflicting law, the state law is invalid. This is not a common issue in criminal law, because state and federal laws rarely conflict; rather, they are more likely to be parallel or complementary. In such cases, a state and federal government have **concurrent jurisdiction** (see Figure 1-1).

Keep in mind that the United States Constitution is the highest form of law in the land. It is the national constitution that establishes the structure of our government. You will learn later the various duties

---

—BALLENTINE'S—

jurisdiction   In a general sense, the right of a court to adjudicate lawsuits of a certain kind. In a specific sense, the right of a court to determine a particular case; ... the power of the court over the subject matter of, or the property involved in, the case at bar. In a geographical sense, the power of a court to hear cases only within a specific territorial area.

concurrent jurisdiction   Two or more courts having the power to adjudicate the same class of cases or the same matter.

Figure 1-1
Federal and State
Criminal Jurisdiction

STATE JURISDICTION	CONCURRENT JURISDICTION	NATIONAL JURISDICTION
1. States may regulate for the health, safety, and morals of their citizens	1. Those acts that fall into both federal and state jurisdictions	1. Crimes that are interstate in character
2. Those acts that involve a state government, its officials and property		2. Crimes involving the government of the United States, including its officials and property
Example: murder; rape; theft; driving under the influence of a drug; gambling	Example: Bank robbery of a federally insured institution	Example: Murder of a federal official or murder on federal land; interstate transportation of illegal item; interstate flight of a felon

of the judicial branch of government. One duty is the interpretation (determining what written law means) of statutes and constitutions. The highest court in the United States is the United States Supreme Court; as such, that Court is the final word on what powers are exclusively federal or state, or concurrently held. However, once the Supreme Court decides that an issue is exclusively under the control of state governments, then each state has the final word on that issue.

During the past 200 years, the Supreme Court has differed in its approach to federalism. Two general approaches can be identified, though. *Dual federalism* refers to an approach under which the states and federal government are viewed as coequals. Under this approach, the Tenth

Amendment is interpreted broadly and the Commerce Clause and the Necessary and Proper Clause are read narrowly. The Tenth Amendment is interpreted as an independent source of state powers, staking out policy areas within which the national government cannot encroach.

Another theory, *cooperative federalism*, asserts that the national government is supreme. Under this approach, the Commerce and Necessary and Proper Clauses are construed broadly. The Tenth Amendment becomes a truism, that is, it reserves to the states only those powers the national government does not possess.

Another characteristic of cooperative federalism is increased interaction between the states and federal government (and local forms of government) in an effort to effectively regulate and administer laws and programs. This aspect of cooperative federalism is a product of the political branches, the executive and legislative. The increased cooperation between state and federal law enforcement agencies to fight the war against drugs during the 1980s and early 1990s is a good example of cooperative federalism.

The Court has vacillated between the two approaches, and the current approach is cooperative federalism. This is not to say that the states are powerless. In fact, one policy area over which the states have maintained considerable control is criminal law. More than 90 percent of all crimes fall within the jurisdiction of the states, not the federal government. However, the sphere of federal government power in criminal law is increasing. This is because more acts are taken in, or are committed using an item that has traveled in, interstate commerce. Acts that have traditionally been state-law crimes may today be federal crimes as well, if there is an interstate component to the act. For example, carjacking, which is the state crime of robbery, if committed with a gun that has travelled in interstate commerce, is also a federal crime.

Regardless of the expansion of federal jurisdiction, most crimes continue to fall within the exclusive jurisdiction of the states. This is because one of the responsibilities of the states is to regulate for the health and safety of its citizens. This known as the **police power**. Most murders, rapes, and thefts are state-law crimes. A few policy areas belong exclusively to the federal government. Punishing counterfeiters is an example.

Many crimes fall within the jurisdiction of both state and federal governments. In these situations, state and federal authorities share jurisdiction to bring charges against the accused. Drug dealers are subject to federal law if they transport or sell drugs in interstate commerce and are also subject to the laws of the states where the transaction occurred. Robbing a federally insured bank, interstate transportation of a crime

---

BALLENTINE'S

police power   The power of government to make and enforce laws and regulations necessary to maintain and enhance the public welfare and to prevent individuals from violating the rights of others.

victim, and violating a person's civil rights (i.e., police brutality) are other examples. Which government will bring charges in these situations is more a political question than a legal one. It is not a violation of double jeopardy for an individual to be tried and punished by both federal and state governments, even for the same act.

Note that local governments have not been mentioned so far. This is because the Constitution does not recognize the existence of local governments. However, state constitutions and laws establish local forms of government, such as counties, cities, and districts. These local entities are often empowered by state law with limited authority to create criminal law. These laws, usually in the form of ordinances, are discussed in Chapter 2.

The result of this division of power is that the states (as well as other jurisdictions, such as the District of Columbia), the federal government, and local governments each have a separate set of criminal laws. For this reason, you must keep in mind that the principles you will learn from this book are general in nature. It would be both impossible and pointless to teach the specific laws of each jurisdiction of the United States.

Separation of Powers

Another division of governmental power is known as **separation of powers**. This is the division of governmental power into three branches, the executive, legislative, and judicial, making a horizontal division of power, just as federalism is the vertical division. (See Figure 1-2.) Each branch is delegated certain functions that the other two may not encroach upon. The executive branch consists of the president of the United States, the president's staff, and the various administrative agencies that the president oversees. Generally, it is the duty of the executive branch to enforce the laws of the national government. In criminal law, the executive branch investigates alleged violations of the law, gathers the evidence necessary to prove that a violation has occurred, and brings violators before the judicial branch for disposition. The president does this through the various federal law enforcement and administrative agencies.

The legislative branch consists of the United States Congress, which creates the laws of the United States. Congressionally created laws are

---

BALLENTINE'S

separation of powers   A fundamental principle of the Constitution, which gives exclusive power to the legislative branch to make the law, exclusive power to the executive branch to administer it, and exclusive power to the judicial branch to enforce it. The authors of the Constitution believed that the separation of powers would make abuse of power less likely.

	LEGISLATIVE BRANCH	EXECUTIVE BRANCH	JUDICIAL BRANCH
The Government of the United States (Federal Government)	United States Congress	President of the United States	Federal Courts
State Governments	State Legislatures	Governors	State Courts

Figure 1-2 Division of Governmental Power

known as **statutes**. Finally, the judicial branch comprises the various federal courts of the land. That branch is charged with the administration of justice. A more comprehensive discussion of the judicial branch follows later in this chapter.

In a further attempt to diffuse governmental power, the framers designed a system of checks and balances that prevents any one branch from exclusively controlling a function. Several checks can be found in the Constitution.

For example, Congress is responsible for making the law. This function is checked by the president, who may veto legislation. The president is then checked by Congress, which may override a veto with a two-thirds majority. The president is responsible for conducting foreign affairs and making treaties, and is the Commander-in-Chief of the military. Congress, however, must approve treaties and declare war, and it establishes the rules that regulate the military.

Through the power of judicial review, the judiciary may invalidate actions of the president or Congress that violate the Constitution. In contrast, the political branches select federal judges through the nomination (president) and confirmation (Senate) process. Unpopular judicial decisions may be changed either by statute, if the issue is one of statutory interpretation, or by constitutional amendment, if the issue is one of constitutional interpretation.

Keep in mind that two levels of government exist, excluding local entities. Even though the United States Constitution does not establish three branches of government for the many states (the United States Constitution only designs the structure of the federal government), all state constitutions do, in varying forms, model the federal constitution. The result is a two-tiered system with each tier split into three parts.

────────────── BALLENTINE'S ──────────────

statute   A law enacted by a legislature; an act.

What should be gleaned from this is that the legislatures are responsible for defining what acts are criminal, what process must be used to assure that a wrongdoer answers for an act, and what punishment should be imposed for the act.

It is the duty of the executive branch to enforce and implement the laws created by the legislature, as well as to enforce the orders of courts. For example, if a state legislature prohibits the sale of alcohol on Sundays, it is the duty of the appropriate state law enforcement agencies, such as the police or alcohol, firearm, and tobacco agents, to investigate suspected violations and take whatever lawful action is necessary to bring violators to justice. Law enforcement, in the criminal law context, is accomplished through law enforcement agencies and prosecutorial agencies. At the federal level, there are many law enforcement agencies. The Federal Bureau of Investigation, Drug Enforcement Administration, United States Marshal Service, and Department of the Treasury name only a few. State law enforcement agencies include state departments of investigation, state police departments, and local police departments. These and other enforcement agencies are responsible for investigating criminal conduct and for gathering evidence to prove that a criminal violation has occurred. When the law enforcement agency has completed its investigation, the case is turned over to a prosecutor. The prosecutor is the attorney responsible for representing the people. The prosecutor files the formal criminal charge, or conducts a grand jury, and then sees the prosecution through to fruition. In the federal system, the prosecutor is called a United States Attorney. In the states and localities, prosecutors are known as district attorneys, county attorneys, state attorneys, city attorneys, or, simply, prosecutors.

Finally, the judicial branch is charged with the administration of justice. The courts become involved after the executive branch has arrested or accused an individual of a crime. This is explored further in the next section of this chapter. Lawyers, legal assistants, and law enforcement officials are likely to have significant contacts with state and federal courts; therefore, it is important to understand the structure of the court system.

The Structure of the Court System

Within the federal and state judiciaries, a hierarchy of courts exists. All state court systems, as well as the federal court system, have at least two types of courts, trial courts and appellate courts. However, each state is free to structure its judiciary in any manner; hence, significant variation is found in the different court systems. What follows are general principles that apply to all states and the federal system.

Trial courts are what most people envision when they think of courts. Trial courts are where a case begins, where witnesses are heard and evidence is presented, often to a jury as well as to a judge. In the federal system, trial courts are known as United States District Courts. The United States is divided up into 94 judicial districts, using state boundaries to establish district limits. Each state constitutes at least one district, although larger states are divided into several districts. For example, Kansas has only one district, and the federal trial court located in Kansas is known as the United States District Court for the District of Kansas. California, in contrast, is made up of four districts, the Northern, Eastern, Central, and Southern Districts of California.

State trial courts are known by various names, such as district, superior, county, and circuit courts. Despite variations in name, these courts are very similar.

SIDEBAR

The court system is actually many court systems comprised of the federal system and the many state systems. As of 1990, there were 28,658 state court judges in the United States sitting in 15,642 state courts. By 1988, there were 280 bankruptcy judges, 284 magistrates, 575 district judges, 168 circuit judges, and 9 Supreme Court Justices.

Source of state statistics: Judicial Council of California, National Center for State Courts.

Source of federal statistics: R. Katzmann, *Judges and Legislators* (Washington, D.C.: Brookings, 1988), at 60.

Appellate courts review the decisions and actions of trial courts (or lower appellate courts, as discussed later) for error. These courts do not conduct trials, but review the **record** from the trial court and examine it for mistakes, known as trial court error. Usually, appellate courts will hear argument from the attorneys involved in the case under review, but witnesses are not heard nor other evidence submitted. After the appellate court has reviewed the record and examined it for error, it renders an opinion. An appellate court can reverse, affirm, or remand the lower court decision. To *reverse* is to determine that the court below has rendered a wrong decision and to change that decision. When an appellate court affirms a lower court, it is approving the decision made and leaving it unchanged.

————————————BALLENTINE'S————————————

trial court   A court that hears and determines a case initially, as opposed to an appellate court; a court of general jurisdiction.

appellate court   A higher court to which an appeal is taken from a lower court.

record on appeal   The papers a trial court transmits to the appellate court, on the basis of which the appellate court decides the appeal. The record on appeal includes the pleadings, all motions made before the trial court, the official transcript, and the judgment or order appealed from.

In some cases an appellate court will remand the case to the lower court. A *remand* is an order that the case be returned to the lower court and that some action be taken by the judge when the case is returned. Often this will involve conducting a new trial. For example, if an appellate court decides that a judge took an action that prevented a criminal defendant from having a fair trial, and the defendant was convicted, an appellate court may reverse the conviction and remand the case to the trial court for a new trial with instructions that the judge not act in a similar manner.

In the federal system and many states, there are two levels of appellate courts, an intermediate and highest level. The intermediate level courts in the federal system are the United States Courts of Appeal.[1] There are eleven judicial circuits in the United States, with one court of appeal in each circuit. Additionally, there is a court of appeal for Washington, D.C. and for the Federal Circuit. Therefore, there are thirteen United States Courts of Appeal in total (see Figure 1-3). Appeals from the district courts are taken to the circuit courts. The highest court in the country is the United States Supreme Court. Appeals from the circuit courts are taken to the Supreme Court. Also, appeals of federal issues from state supreme courts are taken to the United States Supreme Court. Although appeal to a circuit court or a state supreme court is generally a right anyone has, the Supreme Court is not required to hear most appeals, and it does not. In recent years the Supreme Court has denied review of approximately 97 percent of the cases appealed.[2] Therefore, the circuit courts are often a defendant's last chance to have his or her case heard.

Many states also have intermediate-level appellate courts, as well as a high court, although a few states have only one appellate court. Most states call the high court the supreme court of that state and the intermediate level court the court of appeals. An exception is New York, which has named its highest court the Court of Appeals of New York and its lower-level courts supreme courts.

In states that have only one appellate court, appeals are taken directly to that court. New Hampshire is such a state, so appeals from New Hampshire's trial courts are taken directly to the Supreme Court of New Hampshire. Note that in most instances a first appeal is an appeal of right. That means that one has a right to appeal, and the appellate court is required to hear the case. However, second appeals are generally not appeals of right, unless state law has provided otherwise. To have a case heard by the United States Supreme Court and most state supreme courts, the person appealing must seek *certiorari*, an order from an appellate court to the lower court requiring the record to be

---
BALLENTINE'S

certiorari (Latin) A writ issued by a higher court to a lower court requiring the certification of the record in a particular case so that the higher court can review the record and correct any actions taken in the case which are not in accordance with the law. The Supreme Court of the United States uses the writ of certiorari to select the state court cases it is willing to review. Commonly referred to as "cert."

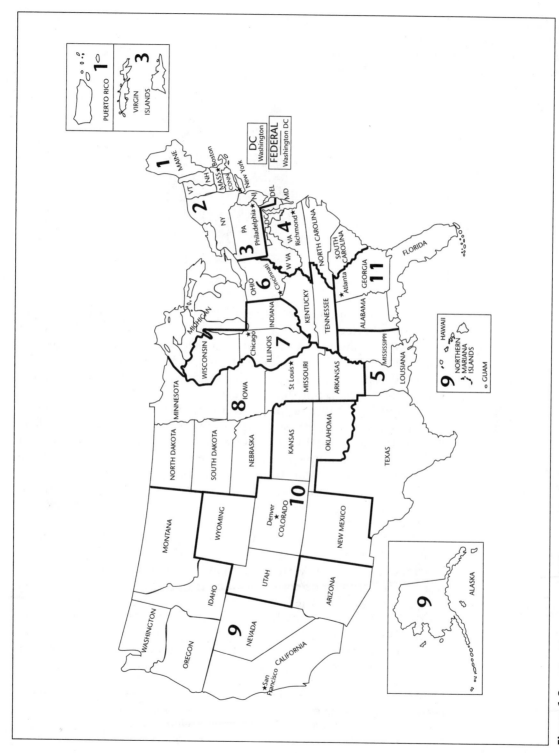

Figure 1-3 The Thirteen Federal Judicial Circuits

Stenographs are one method of recording hearings and trials. These machines are used by court reporters.

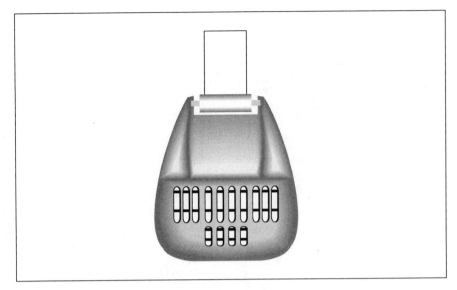

sent to the higher court for review. When "cert." is granted, the appellate court will hear the appeal, and when certiorari is denied it will not.

Finally, be aware that a number of **inferior courts** exist. These are courts that fall under trial courts in hierarchy. As such, appeals from these courts do not usually go to the intermediate level appellate courts, as described earlier, but to the trial-level court first. Municipal courts, police courts, and justices of the peace are examples of inferior courts. An appeal from one of these courts is initially heard by a state trial-level court before an appeal is taken to a state appellate court. The federal system also has inferior courts. The United States Bankruptcy Courts are inferior courts, as appeals from the decisions of these courts go to the district courts, in most cases, and not to the courts of appeals. Only after the trial court has rendered its decision may an appeal be taken to an appellate court.

Most inferior courts in the state system are not **courts of record**. No tape recording or stenographic recording of the trial or hearing at the inferior court is made. As such, when an appeal is taken to the trial level court, it is normally *de novo*. This means that the trial-level court conducts a new trial, rather than reviewing a record as most appellate courts do. This is necessary because there is no record to review, because the inferior court is not a court of record. Federal district courts do not conduct new trials, as all federal courts, including bankruptcy courts, are courts of record. State inferior courts have limited jurisdiction; for

---

BALLENTINE'S

inferior court   1. A court of original jurisdiction, as distinguished from an appellate court; a trial court. 2. A court of limited jurisdiction.

court of record   Generally, another term for trial court.

example, municipal courts usually hear municipal ordinance violations and only minor state law violations. The amount of money that a person may be fined and the amount of time that a defendant may be sentenced to serve in jail are also limited. Generally, no juries are used at the inferior court level.

Figure 1-4 is a basic diagram of the federal and state court systems. The appellate routes are indicated by lines drawn from one court to another. Later in this book you will learn how the appeals process works and how the federal and state systems interact in criminal law. Note where this diagram is located so that you may refer to it later.

Figure 1-4
State and Federal
Court Structures

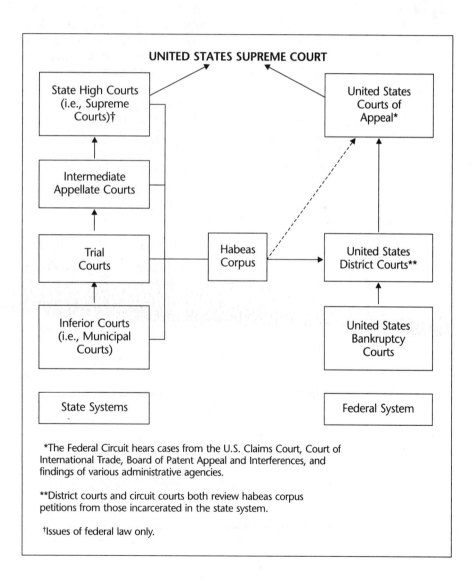

UNITED STATES SUPREME COURT

State High Courts (i.e., Supreme Courts)†

United States Courts of Appeal*

Intermediate Appellate Courts

Trial Courts

Habeas Corpus

United States District Courts**

Inferior Courts (i.e., Municipal Courts)

United States Bankruptcy Courts

State Systems

Federal System

*The Federal Circuit hears cases from the U.S. Claims Court, Court of International Trade, Board of Patent Appeal and Interferences, and findings of various administrative agencies.

**District courts and circuit courts both review habeas corpus petitions from those incarcerated in the state system.

†Issues of federal law only.

Most state trial courts are known as **courts of general jurisdiction.** Courts of general jurisdiction possess the authority to hear a broad range of cases, including civil law as well as criminal. In contrast, **courts of limited jurisdiction** hear only specific types of cases. You have already been introduced to one limited jurisdiction court, municipal courts. Inferior courts, such as municipal courts, are always courts of limited jurisdiction. Some states employ systems that have specialized trial courts to handle domestic, civil, or criminal cases. These may be in the form of a separate court (e.g., Criminal Court of Harp County), or may be a division of a trial court (e.g., Superior Court of Harp County, Criminal Division). Appellate courts may also be limited in jurisdiction to a particular area of law, such as the Oklahoma Court of Criminal Appeals.

The federal government also has special courts. As previously mentioned, a nationwide system of bankruptcy courts is administered by the national government. In addition, the United States Claims Court, Tax Court, and Court of International Trade are part of the federal judiciary, and each have a specific area of law over which they may exercise jurisdiction. Often those cases over which they have jurisdiction are exclusive of district courts. However, the jurisdiction of those courts is outside the scope of this book, as they deal only with civil law. Criminal cases in federal court are heard by district courts, and criminal appeals are heard by the United States Courts of Appeals.

The Duties and Powers of the Judicial Branch

Of the three branches of government, attorneys and paralegals have the most interaction with the judicial branch. For that reason, we single out the judicial branch for a more extensive examination of its functions.

First, it must be emphasized that all courts, local, state, and federal, are bound by the United States Constitution. The effect of this is that all courts have a duty to apply federal constitutional law. This is important in criminal law because it allows defendants to assert their United States

---

—————————————BALLENTINE'S—————————————

court of general jurisdiction   Generally, another term for trial court; that is, a court having jurisdiction to try all classes of civil and criminal cases except those which can be heard only by a court of limited jurisdiction.

court of limited jurisdiction   A court whose jurisdiction is limited to civil cases of a certain type ... or which involve a limited amount of money ... , or whose jurisdiction in criminal cases is confined to petty offenses and preliminary hearings ... . A court of limited jurisdiction is sometimes called a court of special jurisdiction.

constitutional claims and defenses in state court, where most criminal cases are heard. Of course, defendants may also assert applicable state defenses as well.

As previously stated, the judicial branch is charged with the administration of justice. The courts administer justice by acting as the conduit for dispute resolution. The courts are the place where civil and criminal disputes are resolved, if the parties cannot reach a resolution themselves. In an effort to resolve disputes, courts must apply the laws of the land. To apply the law, judges must **interpret** the legislation and constitutions of the nation. To *interpret* means to read the law in an attempt to understand its meaning. This nation's courts are the final word in declaring the meaning of written law. If a court interprets a statute's meaning contrary to the intent of a legislature, then the legislature may later rewrite the statute to make its intent more clear. This has the effect of "reversing" the judicial interpretation of the statute. The process is much more difficult if a legislature desires to change a judicial interpretation of a constitution. At the national level, the Constitution has been amended twenty-six times. The amendment process is found in Article V of the Constitution and requires not only action by the federal legislature but also action by the states. To amend a constitution is simply a more cumbersome and time-consuming endeavor than amending legislation.

The judicial branch is independent from the other two branches of government. Often people think of the courts as enforcers of the law. Though this is true in a sense, it is untrue in that the judicial branch does not work with the executive branch in an attempt to achieve criminal convictions. It is the duty of the courts of this nation to remain neutral and apply the laws in a fair and impartial manner. The United States Constitution establishes a judiciary system that is shielded from interference from the other two branches. For example, the Constitution prohibits Congress from reducing the pay of federal judges after they are appointed. This prevents Congress from coercing the courts into action under the threat of no pay. The Constitution also provides for lifetime appointments of federal judges, thereby keeping the judicial branch from being influenced by political concerns, which may cause judges to ignore the law and make decisions based on what is best for their political careers. Judicial independence permits courts to make decisions that are disadvantageous to the government, but required by law, without fear of retribution from the other two branches.

The need for an independent judiciary is most important when considering the power of **judicial review**. Judicial review is a power

---

BALLENTINE'S

interpret To construe; to explain; to draw out meaning.
judicial review Review by an appellate court of a determination by a lower court.

held by the judicial branch, which permits it to review the actions of the executive and legislative branches and of the states and declare acts that are in violation of the Constitution void. Hamilton wrote of the power of judicial review, and of the importance of an independent judiciary, in the *Federalist Papers,* where he stated:

> Permanency in office frees the judges from political pressures and prevents invasions on judicial power by the president and Congress.
>
> * * *
>
> The Constitution imposes certain restrictions on the Congress designed to protect individual liberties, but unless the courts are independent and have the power to declare the laws in violation of the Constitution null and void these protections amount to nothing. The power of the Supreme Court to declare laws unconstitutional leads some to assume that the judicial branch will be superior to the legislative branch. Let us look at this argument.
>
> Only the Constitution is *fundamental* law; the Constitution establishes the principles and structure of the government. [To a]rgue that the Constitution is not superior to the laws suggests that the *representatives of the people* are superior *to the people* and that the Constitution is inferior to the government it gave birth to. The courts are the arbiters between the legislative branch and the people; the courts are to interpret the laws and prevent the legislative branch from exceeding the powers granted it. The courts must not only place the Constitution higher than the laws passed by Congress, they must also place the intentions of the people ahead of the intentions of the representatives ... [emphasis in original].

The landmark case dealing with judicial review is *Marbury v. Madison,* 1 Cranch 137, 2 L. Ed. 60 (1803). Chief Justice Marshall wrote the opinion for the Court and determined that, although the Constitution does not contain explicit language providing for the power of judicial review, Article III of the Constitution implicitly endows the power in the judiciary. It is now well established that courts possess the authority to review the actions of the executive and legislative branches and to declare any law, command, or other action void if such violates the United States Constitution. The power is held by both state and federal courts. Any state or federal law that violates the United States Constitution may be struck down by either federal or state courts. Of course, state laws that violate state constitutions may be stricken for the same reason.

The power to invalidate statutes is rarely used, for two reasons. First, the judiciary is aware of how awesome the power is, and this causes courts to be reluctant to use it. Second, many rules of statutory constructions exist, which have the effect of preserving legislation. For example, if two possible interpretations of a statute are possible, one that violates the Constitution and one that does not, one rule of statutory construction requires that the statute be construed so that it is consistent with the Constitution. Although rarely done, statutes are occasionally determined invalid. In the chapter on defenses, you will learn many constitutional constraints on government behavior. These defenses often rely on the power of the judiciary to invalidate statutes or police conduct to give them teeth.

Comparing Civil Law and Criminal Law

The difference between civil law and criminal law appears obvious, and great differences do exist. Yet, most students are surprised at the similarities that can be found.

The source of most of the dissimilarities between criminal law and civil law is the differing objectives of the two. The purpose of criminal law is twofold. First, it is intended to prevent behavior that society has determined to be undesirable. A second purpose of criminal law is to punish those who take the acts deemed undesirable by society. Arguably, there is only one purpose, to prevent antisocial behavior. Under this theory, punishment is only used as a tool to achieve the primary goal of preventing antisocial behavior. In any event, prevention and punishment are essential reasons why we have criminal law and a criminal justice system.

In contrast, civil law has as its primary purpose the compensation of those injured by someone else's behavior. It is argued that the real purpose of civil law is the same as that of criminal law. By allowing lawsuits against individuals who have behaved in a manner not consistent with society's rules, civil law actually acts to prevent undesirable behavior. However, prevention of bad behavior may be more the consequence of civil law than the purpose. To understand this you must know something about civil law.

Many definitions of civil law exist. The *American Heritage Dictionary of the English Language* (1980) defines it as "The body of law dealing with the rights of private citizens." *Black's Law Dictionary*, Fifth Edition (1979) defines civil law as "Laws concerned with civil or private rights and remedies, as contrasted with criminal laws." This author prefers a negative definition similar to the latter, such as, all law except that which is criminal law. Whatever definition you accept, many areas of law fall under the umbrella of civil law. Two of the largest categories of civil law are contract law and tort law.

Contract law is a branch of civil law that deals with agreements between two or more parties. You probably have already entered into a contract. Apartment leases, credit card agreements, and book-of-the-month club agreements are all contracts. To have a **contract**, two or more people must agree to behave in a specific manner. Generally, there must be mutuality of consideration for an agreement to be enforceable. That is, all the parties must both acquire a benefit and suffer a detriment. For example, when you agree to lease an apartment, you gain the use of the apartment during the lease period and your landlord loses the right to use the property. The flip side is that the landlord gets your money, in the form of rent, and you lose the value of that rent. You promise to pay rent at a specified time, and the landlord promises to give you the use of the premises during the rental period. In contract law, the duties and obligations of the parties are created by the parties themselves and appear in the form of a contract. If you violate your obligation to your landlord under the contract (i.e., you move out earlier than the contract allows), you have committed a civil wrong called a breach of contract. The landlord may sue you for your breach and receive **damages**. *Damages* are monetary compensation for loss.

Tort law is a branch of civil law that is concerned with civil wrongs, but not contract actions. We have all seen television ads for personal injury attorneys. These attorneys are practicing in the tort law area. A civil wrong, other than a breach of contract, is known as a **tort**. Torts are different from contracts in that the duty owed another party in contract law is created by the parties through their agreement. In tort law, the duty is imposed by the law. For example, at a party you are struck and injured by a beer bottle heaved by an intoxicated partier: a tort has been committed. The partier is known as a *tortfeasor*, which is the term used to describe one who commits a tort. Yet, why does that partier owe you a duty to not strike you with a flying beer bottle? You have not entered into a contract with the partier whereby he has promised not to harm you in this manner. The answer is that the law imposes the duty to act with caution when it is possible to injure another or cause injury

---
BALLENTINE'S
---

contract   An agreement entered into, for adequate consideration, to do, or refrain from doing, a particular thing. The Uniform Commercial Code defines a contract as the total legal obligation resulting from the parties' agreement. In addition to adequate consideration, the transaction must involve an undertaking that is legal to perform, and there must be mutuality of agreement and obligation between at least two competent parties.

damages   The sum of money that may be recovered in the courts as financial reparation for an injury or wrong suffered as a result of breach of contract or a tortious act.

tort   A wrong involving a breach of duty and resulting in an injury to the person or property of another. A tort is distinguished from a breach of contract in that a tort is a violation of a duty established by law, whereas a breach of contract results from a failure to meet an obligation created by the agreement of the parties. Although the same act may be both a crime and a tort, the crime is an offense against the public which is prosecuted by the state in a criminal action; the tort is a private wrong that must be pursued by the injured party in a civil action.

to another's property. This duty is imposed upon all people at all times. The law requires that we all act reasonably when conducting our lives.

When a person fails to act reasonably and unintentionally injures another, that person is responsible for a **negligent** tort. Automobile accidents and medical malpractice are examples of negligent torts. When a person injures another intentionally, an **intentional** tort has occurred. Many intentional torts are also crimes, and this is an area where civil law and criminal law have much in common. If at that fraternity party you make a partier angry, and as a result he intentionally strikes you with the bottle, then he has committed both a crime and an intentional tort. Although criminal law may impose a jail sentence (or other punitive measures), tort law normally seeks only to compensate you for your injury. So, if you suffered $1,000 in medical bills to repair your broken nose, you would be entitled to that amount, but the partier cannot be sentenced to jail or otherwise be punished within the civil tort action. A separate criminal charge may be filed by the government.

The final type of tort is the **strict liability** tort. In these situations liability exists even though the tortfeasor acted with extreme caution and did not intend to cause harm. An example of a strict liability tort is blasting. Whenever a mining or demolition company uses blasting, it is liable for any injuries or damages it has caused to property, even if the company exercised extreme caution.

Damages that are awarded (won) in a lawsuit to compensate a party for actual loss are **compensatory damages**. Compensatory damages do just what the name states—compensate the injured party. However, another type of damages exists, **punitive damages**. Contrary to what you have learned so far, punitive damages are awarded in civil suits and are intended to prevent undesirable behavior by punishing those who commit outrageous acts. Punitive damages are often requested by plaintiffs in

---

BALLENTINE'S

---

negligence   The failure to do something that a reasonable person would do in the same circumstances, or the doing of something a reasonable person would not do. Negligence is a wrong generally characterized by carelessness, inattentiveness, and neglectfulness rather than by a positive intent to cause injury.

intentional   Done with intent or with an intention; knowingly.

strict liability   Liability for an injury whether or not there is fault or negligence; absolute liability.

compensatory damages   Damages recoverable in a lawsuit for loss or injury suffered by the plaintiff as a result of the defendant's conduct. Also called actual damages, they may include expenses, loss of time, reduced earning capacity, bodily injury, and mental anguish.

punitive damages   Damages that are awarded over and above compensatory damages or actual damages because of the wanton, reckless, or malicious nature of the wrong done by the plaintiff. Such damages bear no relation to the plaintiff's actual loss and are often called exemplary damages, because their purpose is to make an example of the plaintiff to discourage others from engaging in the same kind of conduct in the future.

lawsuits, but are rarely awarded. Do not worry if the idea of punitive damages confuses you because it appears to be a criminal law concept. They are penal in nature and many lawyers argue that punitives should not be allowed because a person can end up punished twice, once when convicted and sentenced by a criminal court and again by a civil court if punitives are awarded. Yet, punitive damages have been upheld in most instances by the Supreme Court. A note of caution: Do not get the concept of punitive damages mixed up with restitution or fines, which are discussed in the chapter on punishment.

Finally, a few other differences between criminal law and civil law should be mentioned. First, in civil law the person who brings the lawsuit (the plaintiff) is the person who was injured. For example, you go to the grocery store to do your shopping and request the assistance of a checkout person who recently was divorced from a spouse who looks very much like you. The checker immediately becomes enraged and vents all of his anger for his ex-wife on you by striking you with a box of cereal, which he was checking. He has committed a possible assault and battery in both tort law (these are intentional torts) and criminal law. However, in tort law you must sue the checker yourself to recover any losses you suffer.

This is not true in criminal law. The government, whether national, state, or local, is always the party that files criminal charges. Often you will hear people say that they have filed criminal charges against someone. This is not true. What they have usually done is file a complaint; the government determines whether criminal charges are to be filed. This is because a violation of criminal law is characterized as an attack on the citizens of a state (or the federal government), and, as such, a violation of public, not private, law. Because it is public, the decision to file, or not file, is made by a public official, the prosecutor. So, in our example, you have to contact either the police or your local prosecutor to have a criminal action brought against the checker. Civil cases are entitled Citizen v. Citizen; in criminal law, it is Government (i.e., State of Montana) v. Citizen. In some jurisdictions criminal actions are brought under the name of the people. This is done in New York, where criminal cases are entitled The People of the State of New York v. Citizen.

There is no difference between a criminal action brought in the name of the state and a criminal action brought in the name of the people of a state. All prosecutions at the national level are brought by the United States of America. Note that governments may become involved in civil disputes. For example, if the state of South Dakota enters into a contract with a person, and a dispute concerning that contract arises, the suit will either be Citizen v. South Dakota or South Dakota v. Citizen.

SIDEBAR   ABOUT CASE NAMES, TITLES AND CAPTIONS Cases filed with courts are given a case title, also known as a case name. The title consists of the parties to the action. In civil cases the title is citizen v. citizen, for example, Joe Smith v. Anna Smith. In criminal actions the tile is the government v. citizen. For example, United States of America v. Joe Smith or State of New Mexico v. Anna Smith.

Cases also have captions. The caption appears at the top of the title page of all documents filed with a court and includes the case name, the court name, the case number, and the name of the document being filed with the court. The illustration in Figure 1-5 is an example of a caption.

FIGURE 1-5
Simple Caption—
Criminal Case and
Civil Case

IN THE UNITED STATES DISTRICT COURT FOR
THE DISTRICT OF MARYLAND
NORTHERN DIVISION

UNITED STATES OF AMERICA)
_____ Plaintiff,)
)
v.) CASE NO. _____
)
JOHN D. CRIMINAL,)
_____ Defendant)

IN THE UNITED STATES DISTRICT COURT FOR
THE DISTRICT OF MARYLAND
NORTHERN DIVISION

JOHN I. CITIZEN)
_____ Plaintiff,)
)
v.) CASE NO. _____
)
JANE Q. SMITH)
_____ Defendant)

The two fields also differ in what is required to have a successful case. In civil law one must show actual injury to win. If, in our example the box of cereal missed your head and you suffered no injury (damages), you would not have a civil suit. However, a criminal action for assault or battery may still be brought, as no injury is required in criminal law. This is because the purpose of criminal law is to prevent this type of conduct, not to compensate for actual injuries. To turn this around, there are many instances in which a person's negligence could be subject to a civil cause of action, but not to a criminal action. If a person accidently strikes another during a game of golf with a golf ball, causing injury, the injured party may sue for the concussion received, but no purpose would be served by prosecuting the individual who hit the ball. No deterrent effect is achieved, as there was no intent to cause the injury. In most cases, society has made the determination (through its criminal laws) that a greater amount of **culpability** should be required for criminal liability than for civil. Criminal law is usually more concerned with the immorality of an act than is tort law. This is consistent with the goals of the two disciplines, as it is easier to prevent intentional acts than accidental ones. These concepts will be discussed later in the chapter on mens rea.

Review Questions

1. What is the primary duty of the executive branch of government in criminal law?

2. Define the phrase "court of record."

3. Define jurisdiction and differentiate between a court of general jurisdiction and a court of limited jurisdiction.

4. What are the goals of criminal law? Civil law?

5. Who may file a civil suit? A criminal suit? How are these different?

6. What are compensatory damages? Punitives?

7. Should punitive damages be permitted in civil law? Explain your position.

8. Define culpability.

Review Problems

1. In 1973 the United States Supreme Court handed down the famous case, *Roe v. Wade*, 410 U.S. 113 (1973), wherein the Court determined that the decision to have an abortion is a private decision that is protected from government intervention, in some circumstances, by the United States Constitution. Suppose that a state legislature passes legislation (a state statute) that attempts to reverse the *Roe* decision by prohibiting all abortions in that state. Which is controlling in that state, the statute or the decision of the United States Supreme Court? Explain your answer.

------------------------------BALLENTINE'S------------------------------

culpable   Blameworthy; blamable; responsible; at fault.

2. Same facts as in problem 1, except the state supreme court has determined that the state constitution protects the life of fetuses from abortion, except when the life of the mother is endangered. Which is controlling when a mother seeks to have an abortion and her life is not endangered to any greater amount than the average pregnancy, the state constitutional provision protecting fetuses or the decision of the United States Supreme Court? Explain your answer.

3. Assume that the United States Supreme Court has previously determined that regulation of traffic on county roads is a power reserved exclusively for the states. In reaction to this opinion, the United States Congress enacts a statute providing that the regulation of county roads will be within power of the United States Congress from that date forward. Your law office represents a client who is charged with violating the federal statute that prohibits driving on all roads while intoxicated. Do you have a defense? If so, explain.

Notes

1   28 U.S.C. § 41 *et seq.*

2   According to the Office of the Deputy Clerk, Supreme Court of the United States, there were 6,232 cases on the Supreme Court docket in 1994. The Court granted review and rendered decisions in 104 cases, 1.5% of the total.

CHAPTER 2

INTRODUCTION TO CRIMINAL LAW

The Distinction Between Criminal Law and Criminal Procedure

In all areas of legal study, a distinction is made between substance and procedure. Substantive law defines rights and obligations. Procedural law establishes the methods used to enforce legal rights and obligations. The substance of tort law tells you what a tort is and what damages an injured party is entitled to recover from a lawsuit. Substantive contract law defines what a contract is, tells us whether it must be in writing to be enforceable, who must sign it, what the penalty for breach is, and other such information. The field of civil procedure sets rules for how to bring the substance of the law before a court for resolution of a claim. To decide that a client has an injury that can be compensated under the law is a substantive decision. The question then becomes how this injured client gets the compensation to which he or she is entitled. This is the procedural question. Procedural law tells you how to file a lawsuit, where to file, when to file, and how to prosecute the claim. Such is the case for criminal law and procedure.

Criminal law, as a field of law, defines what constitutes a crime. It establishes what conduct is prohibited and what punishment can be imposed for violating its mandates. Criminal law establishes what degree of intent is required for criminal liability. In addition, criminal law sets out the defenses to criminal charges that may be asserted. Alibi, insanity, and the like are defenses and fall under the umbrella of criminal law.

Criminal procedure puts substantive criminal law into action. It is concerned with the procedures used to bring criminals to justice, beginning with police investigation and continuing throughout the process of administering justice. When and under what conditions may a person be arrested? How and where must the criminal charge be filed? When can the police conduct a search? How does the accused assert a defense? How long can a person be held in custody by the police without charges being filed? How long after charges are filed does the accused have to wait before a trial is held? These are all examples of questions that criminal procedure deals with. Do not worry if you cannot always distinguish between a procedural question and a substantive one. There is considerable overlap between the two concepts.

The first half of this text is devoted to criminal law and the latter half to criminal procedure. In the remainder of the book, the phrase

---
BALLENTINE'S

criminal law Branch of the law that specifies what conduct constitutes crime and establishes appropriate punishments for such conduct.

criminal procedure The rules of procedure by which criminal prosecutions are governed.

"criminal law" is used often. This, in most cases, refers to general criminal law, including both substantive criminal law and criminal procedure.

The Power of Government to Regulate Behavior

Freedom and liberty are two concepts that pervade the American political being. Most of us have learned that the longing for freedom of religious thought caused the English Puritan emigration from England to what was to become Plymouth, Massachusetts, in 1620. Later, the desire for freedom from the oppressive crown of England was the catalyst for the Declaration of Independence and the American Revolution. Finally, the fear that all governments tend to abuse their power led to the creation of a constitution that contains specific limits on governmental power and specific protections of individual rights. But what exactly is freedom? Liberty?

Freedom generally means the ability to act without interference. In a political and legal sense, it means the ability to act free from the interference of government. However, even in the most free societies personal behavior is limited. This is because the actions of every member of society has the potential, at times, to affect other members. The total absence of government is anarchy, but few people believe that freedom results from anarchy. Without government, there would be little control over behavior. No system would exist to punish those who intentionally injure others. No system would exist to allow someone injured by the negligence of another to recover his or her losses. There would be no deterrence to wrongful behavior, other than fear of retribution from the victim. The strong and cunning would prey on the weak and unintelligent; the licentious on the decent. Although it is true that to live in such a world would be living free from government interference, it cannot be reasonably considered freedom. If women are in constant fear of sexual assault, they are not free. If people are hesitant to own property for fear of it being taken by others, they are not totally free. To prevent anarchy, people establish governments. The people then vest their governments with certain authorities and powers, so that the government can control the behavior of all people.

The forefathers of the United States did this when they met in Philadelphia to draft the Constitution of the United States. Some characterize the relationship between a democratic form of government and its people as a contract. The people give up some freedoms in an effort to secure other freedoms. The preamble to the United States Constitution recognizes this principle. It states "We, the People of the United

States, in order to form a more perfect union, establish justice, insure domestic tranquility, provide for the common defense, promote the general welfare, and secure the blessings of liberty to ourselves and our posterity, do ordain and establish this Constitution for the United States of America." The concept is also found in the Declaration of Independence, where Thomas Jefferson penned "that all Men are created equal, that they are endowed by their Creator with certain unalienable Rights, that among these are Life, Liberty, and the Pursuit of Happiness—That to secure these Rights, Governments are instituted among Men, deriving their just Powers from the Consent of the Governed."

So the contract is formed. The people are to receive the benefits of an organized, fair government. The government is to establish laws designed to protect the people from one another and from other nations. In exchange, the people agree to comply with the laws created by their government. Some would argue that the duty extends to require the people to participate in the activities of the government. You have probably heard people speak of a "duty" to vote. Clearly, this is the rationale for requiring individuals to sit as jurors.

Every government is different. Some governments permit little or no political participation by the people. Others permit more. In those nations where the people are active participants, the rights and duties of individuals can vary significantly. This is because values are very different from culture to culture. Hence, what one society believes to be an important freedom and protects from government interference may not be so valued by other societies.

In nearly all nations, however, governmental involvement in the affairs of people is continually increasing. This is due in part to the fact that people are less independent, that is, that members of society now depend on one another to provide goods and services that were once commonly self-provided. In addition, the staggering increase in world population has caused people to have much more contact with each other than they did 100 years ago. The greater the population, contact between, and dependence of people on one another, the greater the number of conflicts that will arise requiring government intervention. As the population and dependence of people increase, so does the likelihood that one person's action may affect another. A person who lives alone in a forest far from other people can scream loudly in the middle of the night without bothering anyone. He or she could dispose of trash in any manner desired. If that same person lived in the middle of a city, the scream could wake people, and the improper disposal of trash could cause the spread of disease, as well as create an unpleasant environment. As the number of contacts between members of a society increases, so does the number of conflicts requiring government intervention. Even if the parties involved do not desire legal intervention to resolve their conflict, society will sometimes intervene through its government to prevent unacceptable behavior. For example, society has decided that duels are not an acceptable method of resolving disputes, even if two individuals wish to use this method. The government will try to prevent such behavior from occurring. If the duel is not discovered until after the fact, then the parties involved may be punished for participating.

As the need for government involvement in the private lives of citizens increases, it becomes more difficult to protect individual rights, also known as **civil liberties**. Although we the people have bestowed upon our government certain powers which have the effect of limiting our behavior, we have also specifically created "civil rights," which the government may not encroach upon. Many of these rights are contained in the first ten amendments to our Constitution, which are commonly known as the **Bill of Rights**. As the world becomes more populated and complex, the balance between permissible government involvement in the private lives of its citizens and impermissible encroachment upon those citizens' civil liberties becomes harder to maintain. As that line becomes thinner, the duty of the defense lawyer and legal assistant to be zealous in preparation of their defenses increases.

As previously discussed, the attempt to control people's behavior is achieved through both civil law and criminal law. Generally, society reserves only those acts that are perceived as serious moral wrongs or extremely dangerous for sanction under criminal law. Those acts that are accidental or are not serious breaches of moral duty are usually not criminal, but may lead to civil liability. Thoughts about what acts should be considered under each category are very subjective and often change because a problem intensifies or because the public perceives an increased problem, even though the situation may not be any different than years before.

For example, the 1980s saw an increased effort to stop people from driving while under the influence of alcohol. Many states enacted new laws increasing the penalty for violating their D.U.I. statutes. In addition, a few states limited police discretion by requiring that violators be arrested. The practice once exercised by many police departments of taking drunk drivers home was stopped by legislative command. At one time, it can be argued that civil law was as much of a deterrent to driving under the influence as was criminal. Fear of civil liability for causing property damage or personal liability was as great as fear of criminal liability, because of the inconsistent and often minor penalties which followed convictions for driving under the influence. However, as public concern over alcohol-related automobile accidents increased, the focus

---
BALLENTINE'S
---

civil liberties   Political liberties guaranteed by the Constitution and, in particular, by the Bill of Rights, especially the First Amendment.

Bill of Rights   The first 10 amendments to the United States Constitution. The Bill of Rights is the portion of the Constitution that sets forth the rights which are the fundamental principles of the United States and the foundation of American citizenship.

turned to criminal law to prevent such behavior. Increased penalties, consistent arrest policies, and mandatory alcohol treatment for those convicted are now common. The extensive media coverage that particular cases have received, such as the Larry Mahoney accident,[1] have increased the public awareness that one who drives while intoxicated risks arrest, conviction, and punishment, as well as civil liability for injuries to property and person. What this example teaches is that society determines what acts will be treated as criminal based on public perceptions of morality, the importance of deterrence, and the danger posed to the public by the acts in question. Do not forget that criminal acts are often the subject of civil suits. This is not always true, as you learned in Chapter 1, when the general purposes of civil law and criminal law were discussed.

The Purposes of Punishing Criminal Law Violators

You have already learned that the general goal of criminal law is to prevent behavior determined by society to be undesirable. The criminal justice system uses punishment as a prevention tool. Many theories support punishing criminal law violators. Although some people focus on one theory and use it as the basis for punishment, a more accurate approach, in this author's opinion, is to recognize that many theories have merit and that when a legislature establishes the range of punishment applicable to a particular crime, many theories were involved in motivating individual legislators. It is unlikely that every member of a legislature will be motivated by the same objective. It is also unlikely that an individual legislator will be motivated by one theory only. Rather, all of the following objectives influence legislative decision making to some degree.

Specific and General Deterrence

Specific deterrence seeks to **deter** individuals already convicted of crimes from committing crimes in the future. It is a negative reward theory. By punishing Mr. X for today's crime, we teach him that he will be disciplined for future criminal behavior. The arrest and conviction of an individual show that individual that society has the capability to detect crime and is willing to punish those who commit crimes.

BALLENTINE'S
---

deter   To discourage; to prevent from acting.

General deterrence attempts to deter all members of society from engaging in criminal activity. In theory, when the public observes Mr. X being punished for his actions, the public is deterred from behaving similarly for fear of the same punishment. Of course, individuals will react differently to the knowledge of Mr. X's punishment. Individuals weigh the risk of being caught and the level of punishment against the benefit of committing the crime. All people do this at one time or another. Have you ever intentionally run a stoplight? Jaywalked? If so, you have made the decision to violate the law. Neither crime involves a severe penalty. That fact, in addition to the likelihood of not being discovered by law enforcement agents, probably affected your decision. Presumably, if conviction of either crime was punished by incarceration (time in jail), then the deterrent effect would be greater. Would you be as likely to jaywalk if you knew that you could spend time in jail for such an act? Some people would; others would not. It is safe to assume, however, that as the punishment increases, so does compliance. However, one author observed that it is not as effective to increase the punishment as it is to increase the likelihood of being punished.[2] It is unknown how much either of these factors influences behavior, but it is generally accepted that they both do.

Incapacitation

Incapacitation, also referred to as restraint, is the third purpose of criminal punishment. Incapacitation does not seek to deter criminal conduct by influencing people's choices, but prevents criminal conduct by restraining those who have committed crimes. Criminals who are restrained in jail or prison, or in the extreme, executed, are incapable of causing harm to the general public. This theory is often the rationale for long-term imprisonment of individuals who are believed to be beyond rehabilitation. It is also promoted by those who lack faith in rehabilitation and feel that all criminals should be removed from society to prevent the chance of repetition.

Crimes that are caused by mental disease or occur in a moment of passion are not affected by deterrence theories, because the individual does not have the opportunity to consider the punishment that will be inflicted for committing the crime before it is committed. Deterrence theories are effective only for individuals who are sufficiently intelligent to understand the consequences of their actions, who are sane enough to understand the consequences of their actions, and who are not laboring under such uncontrollable feelings that an understanding that they may be punished is lost.

Rehabilitation

Rehabilitation is another purpose of punishing criminals. The theory of rehabilitation is that if the criminal is subjected to educational and vocational programs, treatment and counseling, and other measures, it is possible to alter the individual's behavior to conform to societal norms. Another author noted that:

> To the extent that crime is caused by elements of the offender's personality, educational defects, lack of work skills, and the like, we should be able to prevent him from committing more crimes by training, medical and psychiatric help, and guidance into law-abiding patterns of behavior. Strictly speaking, rehabilitation is not "punishment," but help to the offender. However, since this kind of help is frequently provided while the subject is in prison or at large on probation or parole under a sentence that carries some condemnation and some restriction of freedom, it is customary to list rehabilitation as one of the objects of a sentence in a criminal case.[3]

The concept of rehabilitation has come under considerable scrutiny in recent years, and the success of rehabilitative programs is questionable. However, the poor quality of prison rehabilitative programs may be the cause of the lack of success of these programs.

Retribution

Retribution, or societal vengeance, is the fifth purpose. Simply put, punishment through the criminal justice system is society's method of avenging a wrong. The idea that one who commits a wrong must be punished is an old one. The Old Testament speaks of an "eye for an eye." However, many people question the place of retribution in contemporary society. Is retribution consistent with American values? Jewish or Christian values? The question is actually moot, as there are few instances in which retribution stands alone as a reason for punishing someone who did not comply with the law. In most instances society's desire for revenge can be satisfied while fulfilling one of the other purposes of punishment, such as incapacitation.

It has also been asserted that public retribution prevents private retribution.[4] That is, when the victim (or anyone who might avenge a victim) of a crime knows that the offender has been punished, the victim's need to seek revenge is lessened or removed. Therefore, punishing those who harm others has the effect of promoting social order by preventing undesirable conduct by victims of crimes. Retribution in such instances has a deterrent effect, as victims of crimes are less likely to seek revenge. This is a good example of how the various purposes discussed are interrelated.

Finally, consider a sociological note. Do not become so focused on criminal law as a method of social control that you forget the many other methods of control that exist.

The criminal law is not, of course, the only weapon which society uses to prevent conduct which harms or threatens to harm these important interests of the public. Education, at home and at school, as to the types of conduct that society thinks good and bad, is an important weapon; religion, with its emphasis on distinguishing between good and evil conduct, is another. The human desire to acquire and keep the affection and respect of family, friends and associates no doubt has a great influence in deterring most people from conduct which is socially unacceptable. The civil side of the law, which forces one to pay damages for the harmful results which his undesirable conduct has caused to others, or which in inappropriate situations grants injunctions against bad conduct or orders the specific performance of good conduct, also plays a part in influencing behavior along desirable lines.[5]

Sources of Criminal Law

Criminal law is actually a body of many laws emanating from many sources. Today most American criminal law is a product of legislative enactment. That has not always been so. Further, administrative regulations now make up a much larger percentage of the criminal law than in the past. It is vital to successful legal research that you understand the sources of criminal law. As you read this section, you will begin to see why an understanding of the functions of the three branches of government is important to an understanding of all criminal law.

The Common Law

The oldest form of criminal law in the United States is the **common law**. The common law was developed in England and brought to the United States by the English colonists.

The common law, as it exists in this country, is of English origin. Founded on ancient local rules and customs and in feudal times, it began to evolve in the King's courts and was eventually molded into

---
BALLENTINE'S
---

common law   1. Law found in the decisions of the courts rather than in statutes; judge-made law. 2. English law adopted by the early American colonists, which is part of the United States' judicial heritage and forms the basis of much of its law today.

the viable principles through which it continues to operate. The common law migrated to this continent with the first English colonists, who claimed the system as their birthright; it continued in full force in the 13 original colonies until the American Revolution, at which time it was adopted by each of the states as well as the national government of the new nation.[6]

But what exactly is this common law? Simply stated, the common law is judge-made law. It is law that has been developed by the hands of the judges of both England and the United States. To comprehend how common law developed, you must understand the concepts of precedence and **stare decisis.** When a court renders a legal decision, that decision becomes binding on itself and its inferior courts, whenever the same issue arises again in the future. The decision of the court is known as a **precedent.** The principle that inferior courts will comply with that decision when the issue is raised in the future is known as "stare decisis et non quieta movera" (a Latin phrase meaning "stand by precedents and do not disturb settled points"). The Supreme Court of Indiana expressed its view of stare decisis:

> Under the doctrine of stare decisis, this Court adheres to a principle of law which has been firmly established. Important policy considerations militate in favor of continuity and predictability in the law. Therefore, we are reluctant to disturb long-standing precedent which involves salient issues. Precedent operates as a maxim for judicial restraint to prevent the unjustified reversal to a series of decisions merely because the composition of the court has changed.[7]

During the feudal years in England, there were few formal criminal laws. Rather, local customs and practices developed into rules that governed the behavior of people. The concepts of fairness, justice, and equity were the guiding principles behind these rules. Eventually the courts began to recognize these rules. With that recognition came judicial decisions enforcing them. As precedent, each of those decisions began to establish a body of law, both civil and criminal in nature. The whole of those decisions is known as the common law.

The common law, as frequently defined, includes those principles, usages, and rules of action applicable to the government and security

---

BALLENTINE'S

stare decisis (Latin) Means "standing by the decision." Stare decisis is the doctrine that judicial decisions stand as precedents for cases arising in the future. It is a fundamental policy of our law that, except in unusual circumstances, a court's determination on a point of law will be followed by courts of the same or lower rank in later cases presenting the same legal issue, even though different parties are involved and many years have elapsed.

precedent Prior decisions of the same court, or a higher court, which a judge must follow in deciding a subsequent case presenting similar facts and the same legal problem, even though different parties are involved and many years have elapsed.

of persons and property which do not rest for their authority upon any express or positive statute or other written declaration, but upon statements of principles found in the decisions of courts. The common law is inseparably identified with the decisions of the courts and can be determined only from such decisions in former cases bearing upon the subject under inquiry. As distinguished from statutory or written law, it embraces the great body of unwritten law founded upon general custom, usage, or common consent, and based upon natural justice or reason. It may otherwise be defined as custom long acquiesced in or sanctioned by immemorial usage and judicial decision … .

In a broader sense the common law is the system of rules and declarations of principles from which our judicial ideas and legal definitions are derived, and which are continually expanding. It is not a codification of exact or inflexible rules for human conduct, for the redress of injuries, or for protection against wrongs, but is rather the embodiment of broad and comprehensive unwritten principles, inspired by natural reason and an innate sense of justice, and adopted by common consent for the regulation and government of the affairs of men.[8]

As stated, the common law is fluid and dynamic, changing to meet societal values and expectations. As one court stated, "The common law of the land is based upon human experience in the unceasing effort of an enlightened people to ascertain what is right and just between men."[9]

What happened historically is that courts defined crimes, as there was usually no legislative enactment that determined what acts should be criminal. As time passed, established "common-law crimes" developed. First the courts determined what acts should be criminal, and then the specifics of each crime developed; that is, what exactly had to be proved to establish guilt, what defenses were available, and what punishment was appropriate for conviction. Although there is great similarity between the common laws of the many jurisdictions, differences exist because judicial decisions of one state are not binding precedents on other states and because customs and practices vary among communities. However, courts may look outside their jurisdictions for opinions to guide them in their decision making if no court in their jurisdiction has addressed the issue under consideration. Each state, as a separate and sovereign entity, has the power to decide whether to adopt the common law, in whole or in part, or to reject it.

Initially, the thirteen original states all adopted the common law. Most did so through their state constitutions. Today, only Louisiana has not adopted the common law in some form. However, for reasons you will learn later, approximately half of the states no longer recognize common-law crimes.[10] Even in those states, though, the civil common law and portions of the criminal common law (i.e., defenses to criminal charges) continue in force. Most states have expressly adopted the common law either by statute or constitutional authority. Many states adopted only parts of the common law.

Generally, there is no federal common law; rather, federal courts, in civil cases, apply the common law of the states in which they sit. For example, a United States district court in New Jersey will apply New Jersey common law. Even though this may appear strange to you, it is common practice for federal courts to apply state law. Further discussion of this topic is beyond the scope of this text.

Finally, be aware that common law has been modified and even abolished in some jurisdictions. The modifications to, and nullifications of, common law have come about in many different manners. In some instances, courts have decided that the common law must be changed to meet contemporary conditions. In extreme situations, parts of the common law have been totally abolished. Because legislatures are charged with the duty of making the laws, they have the final word, unless there is a state constitutional provision stating otherwise, on the status of the common law. Some legislatures have expressly given their judiciaries the authority to modify the common law, often with limitations. State legislatures are free to modify, partially abolish, or wholly abolish the common law as long as their own state constitution or the United States Constitution is not violated by so doing. The common law normally is inferior to legislation. This means that if a legislature acts in an area previously dealt with by common law, the new statute controls, absent a statement by the legislature to the contrary. For example, assume that under common law adultery was a crime in State Y. The legislature of State Y can change this by simply enacting a statute that provides that adultery is not criminal. The legislature may also amend the common law by continuing to recognize common-law adultery, but change the penalty for violation. If a state constitution, statute, or judicial decision has not abrogated the common law, presume that it continues in effect.

The Principle of Legality

The question of whether common-law crimes should continue to exist is debatable. Those who favor permitting common-law crimes claim that it permits courts to "fill in the gaps" left by the legislatures when those bodies either fail to foresee all potential crimes or simply forget to include a crime that was foreseen. You should question whether the judicial branch should be actively second-guessing or cleaning house for the legislative branch. There appears to be a separation of powers issue when the judicial branch begins to behave in such a manner. However, few people want intentionally dangerous or disruptive behavior not to be criminalized.

Those who oppose a common law of crimes point to the concept embodied in the phrase "nullum crimen sine lege," which means, "there is no crime if there is no statute." Similarly, "nulla poena sine lege" has come to mean that "there shall be no punishment if there is no statute." These concepts, when considered in concert, insist that the criminal law must be written, that the written law must exist at the time that the accused took the act in question, and that criminal laws be more precise than civil laws.[11] This is the *principle of legality.*

The legality principle is founded on the belief that all people are entitled to know, prior to taking an act, that an act is criminal and that punishment could result from such behavior. This is commonly referred to as *notice.* The idea is sensible, as it appears to be a rule consistent with general notions of fairness and justice. Does it appear fair to you to hold an individual criminally accountable for taking an act that he or she could not have known was prohibited? The legality principle remedies the notice problem by requiring that written law be the basis of criminal liability, not unwritten common law. Understand that the law imposes a duty on all people to be aware of written law; thus, all people are presumed to be aware of criminal prohibitions. The *Keeler* case discusses the legality principle.

KEELER v. SUPERIOR COURT
Supreme Court of California
2 Cal. 3d 619, 470 P.2d 617 (1970)

In this proceeding for writ of prohibition we are called upon to decide whether an unborn viable fetus is a "human being" within the meaning of the California statute defining murder. We conclude that the legislature did not intend such a meaning, and that for us to construe the statute to the contrary and apply it to this petitioner would exceed our judicial power and deny petitioner due process of law.

The evidence received at the preliminary examination may be summarized as follows: Petitioner and Teresa Keeler obtained an interlocutory decree of divorce on September 27, 1968. They had been married for sixteen years. Unknown to petitioner, Mrs. Keeler was then pregnant by one Ernest Vogt, whom she had met earlier that summer. She subsequently began living with Vogt in Stockton, but concealed the fact from petitioner. Petitioner was given custody of their two daughters, aged 12 and 13 years, and under the decree Mrs. Keeler had the right to take the girls on alternate weekends.

On February 23, 1969, Mrs. Keeler was driving on a narrow mountain road in Amador County after delivering the girls to their home. She met petitioner driving in the opposite direction; he blocked the road with his car, and she pulled over to the side. He walked to her vehicle and began speaking to her. He seemed calm, and she rolled down her window to hear him. He said, "I hear you're pregnant. If you are you had better stay away from the girls and from here." She did not reply, and he opened the car door; as she later testified, "He assisted me out of the car... [I]t wasn't rough at this time." Petitioner then looked at her abdomen and became "extremely upset." He said, "You sure are. I'm going to stomp it out of you." He pushed her against the car, shoved his knee into her abdomen, and struck her in the face with several blows. She fainted, and when she regained consciousness petitioner had departed.

Mrs. Keeler drove back to Stockton, and the police and medical assistance were summoned. She had suffered substantial facial injuries, as well as extensive bruising of the abdominal wall. A Caesarian section was performed, and the fetus was examined in utero. Its head was found to be severely fractured, and it was delivered stillborn. The pathologist gave as his opinion that the cause of death was skull fracture with consequent cerebral hemorrhaging, that death would be immediate, and that the injury could have been the result of force applied to the mother's abdomen. There was no air in the fetus' lungs, and the umbilical cord was intact. ...

The evidence was in conflict as to the estimated age of the fetus; the expert testimony on the point, however, concluded "with reasonable medical certainty" that the fetus had developed to the stage of viability, i.e., that in the event of premature birth on the date in question it would have had a 75 percent to 96 percent chance of survival.

An information was filed charging petitioner, in count I, with committing the crime of murder. . . .

Penal Code section 187 provides: "Murder is the unlawful killing of a human being, with malice aforethought." The dispositive question is whether the fetus which petitioner is accused of killing was, on February 23, 1969, a "human being" within the meaning of the statute. If it was not, petitioner cannot be charged with its "murder'. ...

* * *

We conclude that in declaring murder to be the unlawful and malicious killing of a "human being" the Legislature of 1850 intended that term to have the settled common law meaning of a person who had been born alive, and did not intend the act of feticide—as distinguished from abortion—to be an offense under the laws of California.

* * *

The People urge, however that the sciences of obstetrics and pediatrics have greatly progressed since 1872, to the point where with proper medical care a normally developed fetus prematurely born ... is "viable" ... since an unborn but viable fetus is now fully capable of independent life .... But we cannot join in the conclusion sought to be deduced: we cannot hold this petitioner to answer for murder by reason of his alleged act of killing an unborn—even though viable—fetus. To such a charge there are two insuperable obstacles, one "jurisdictional" and the other constitutional.

Penal Code section 6 declares in relevant part that "No act or omission" accomplished after the code has taken effect "is criminal or punishable, except as prescribed by this code ... ." This section embodies a fundamental principle of our tripartite

form of government, i.e., that subject to the constitutional prohibition against cruel and unusual punishment, the power to define crimes and fix penalties is vested exclusively in the legislative branch. Stated differently, there are no common law crimes in California. . . . In order that a public offense be committed, some statute, ordinance or regulation prior in time to the commission of the act, must denounce it.

* * *

Applying these rules to the case at bar, we would undoubtedly act in excess of the judicial power if we were to adopt the People's proposed construction of section 187. As we have shown, the Legislature has defined the crime of murder in California to apply only to the unlawful and malicious killing of one who has been born alive. We recognize that the killing of an unborn but viable fetus may be deemed by some to be an offense of similar nature and gravity; but as Chief Justice Marshall warned long ago, "It would be dangerous, indeed, to carry the principle, that a case which is within the reason or mischief of a statute, because it is of equal atrocity, or of kindred character, with those which are enumerated." ... Whether to thus extend liability for murder in California is a determination solely within the province of the Legislature. For a court to simply declare, by judicial fiat, that the time has now come to prosecute under section 187 one who kills an unborn but viable fetus would indeed be to rewrite the statute under the guise of construing it. ... to make it "a judicial function" ... "raises very serious questions concerning the principle of separation of powers."

The second obstacle to the proposed judicial enlargement of section 187 is the guarantee of due process of law. ...

The first essential of due process is fair warning of the act which is made punishable as a crime. "That the terms of a penal statute creating a new offense must be sufficiently explicit to inform those who are subject to it what conduct on their part will render them liable to its penalties, is a well-recognized requirement, consonant alike with ordinary notions of fair play and the settled rules of law."

Do not forget that *Keeler* is an opinion of the California Supreme Court; therefore, it is not the law of all the land. It is the law in California, though, and similar decisions have been made elsewhere.

HOW TO BRIEF A CASE Decisions of courts are often written and are called *judicial opinions* or cases. These cases are published in law reporters so they may be used as precedent. Many cases appear in this text for your education. Your instructor may also require that you read other cases, often from your jurisdiction. The cases included in your book have been edited, citations have been omitted, and legal issues not relevant to the subject discussed have been excised.

Most judicial opinions are written using a similar format. First, the name of the case appears with the name of the court, the cite (location where the case has been published), and the year. When the body of the case begins, the name of the judge, or judges, responsible for writing the opinion appears directly before the first paragraph. The opinion contains an introduction to the case, which normally gives you the procedural history of the case. This is followed by a summary of the facts that led to the dispute, the court's analysis of the law that applies to the case, and the court's conclusions and orders, if any.

Most opinions used here are from appellate courts, where many judges sit at one time. After the case is over, the judges vote on an outcome. The majority vote wins, and the opinion of the majority is written by one of those judges. If other judges in the majority wish to add to the majority opinion, they may write what is known as a *concurring opinion*. Concurring opinions appear after majority opinions in the law reporters. When a judge who was not in the majority feels strongly about his or her position, he or she may file a dissenting opinion, which appears after the concurring opinions, if any. Only the majority opinion is law, although concurring and dissenting opinions are often informative.

During your legal education you may be instructed to "brief" a case. Even if your instructor does not require you to brief cases, you may want to, as many students understand a case better after they have completed a brief. Here are suggestions for reading and understanding cases.

1. Read the case. On your first reading, do not take notes; simply attempt to get a feel for the case. Then read the case again and use the following suggested method of briefing.
2. State the *relevant* facts. Often cases read like little stories. You need to weed out the facts that have no bearing on the subject you are studying.
3. Identify the issues. *Issues* are the legal questions discussed by the court.
4. State the applicable rules, standards, or other law.
5. Summarize the court's decision and analysis. Why and how did the court reach its conclusion? Note whether the court affirmed, reversed, or remanded the case.

Also note that the court determined that the common law violates "ordinary notions of fair play" and that no warning or notice was given to Keeler that his act could be defined as murder. As the court noted, these requirements are embodied in the **Due Process Clauses** of the

United States Constitution and the constitutions of the many states. Due process, in both civil and criminal law, requires that individuals be put on notice of impending government action, be given an opportunity to be heard and to present evidence, and often the right to a jury trial. Due process is founded upon principles of fair play and justice. However, the United States Supreme Court has determined that states may, under some circumstances, use the common law to define criminal conduct. The court in *Keeler* based its decision on the California Constitution's Due Process Clause. You should remember that the California Supreme Court is the final word on California law, and *Keeler* teaches you that the California Constitution provides more protection than the United States Constitution in this regard. Still, the United States Constitution places limits on the use of the common law by the states to create crimes. This is done primarily through the Due Process Clause and the provision prohibiting ex post facto laws. You will learn more about the Due Process and Ex Post Facto clauses later in this book when we examine defenses to criminal charges. If states, such as California in the *Keeler* case, want to increase a defendant's rights beyond what the United States Constitution protects, they may through their own statutes or constitutions.

Other Uses of the Common Law

Even in those jurisdictions that have abandoned use of the common law to create crimes, the common law continues to be important for many reasons.

First, many statutes mirror the common law in language. That is, legislatures often simply codify the common law's criminal prohibitions. Hence, when a question arises concerning whether a particular act of a defendant is intended to fall under the intent of a criminal prohibition, the case law handed down prior to codification of the common law may continue to be helpful after codification. The result is that the crime remains the same, but the source of the prohibition has changed. It is also possible for a legislature to change only part of a common-law definition and leave the remainder the same. If so, prior case law may be helpful when considering the unaltered portion of the definition.

Second, legislatures occasionally enact a criminal prohibition without establishing the potential penalty for violation. In such cases courts

---

BALLENTINE'S

due process clause   Actually a reference to two due process clauses, one in the Fifth Amendment and one in the Fourteenth Amendment. The Fifth Amendment requires the federal government to accord "due process of law" to citizens of the United States; the Fourteenth Amendment imposes a similar requirement upon state governments.

will often look to the penalties applied to similar common law crimes for guidance.

Third, in addition to defining crimes, the common law established many procedures that were used to adjudicate criminal cases. These procedures most often dealt with criminal defenses. What defenses could be raised, as well as how and when, were often answered by the common law. For example, the various tests to determine if a defendant was sane when an alleged crime was committed were developed under the common law. If a legislature has not specifically changed these procedural rules, they remain in effect, even if the power of courts to create common-law crimes has been abolished.

Statutory Law

As you have already learned, the legislative branch is responsible for the creation of law. You have also learned that legislatures possess the authority to modify, abolish, or adopt the common law, in whole or in part. During the nineteenth century, the codification of criminal law began. This effectively displaced the role of the judiciary in defining crimes. Today, nearly all criminal law is found in criminal codes.

Although the power of the legislative branch to declare behavior criminal is significant, there are limits. The constitutions of the United States and of the many states contain limits on such state and federal authority. Most of these limits are found in the Bill of Rights. For example, the first amendment to the federal Constitution prohibits government from punishing an individual for exercising choice of religion. If a legislature does enact law that violates a constitutional provision, it is the duty of the judicial branch to declare the law void. This is the power of judicial review, previously discussed in Chapter 1. For now, you need only understand that legislatures do not have unlimited authority to create criminal law. Individual (civil) rights limit legislative power to make conduct criminal, and the judicial branch acts to protect individuals from unconstitutional legislation.

Ordinances

The written laws of municipalities are **ordinances**. Ordinances are enacted by city councils and commonly regulate zoning, building, construction, and related matters. Many cities have criminal ordinances

─────────────────BALLENTINE'S─────────────────

ordinances   A law of a municipal corporation; a local law enacted by a city council, town council, board of supervisors, or the like.

that mirror state statutes, only they apply to those acts that occur within the jurisdiction of the city. For example, many cities have assault and battery ordinances, just as their states have assault and battery statutes. Traffic and parking violations may also be criminal, although some cities pursue these as civil violations, which permits the state to pursue the criminal charge.

Ordinances may not conflict with state or federal law. Any ordinance that is inconsistent with higher law may be invalidated by a court. States limit the power of cities to punish for ordinance violations, and most city court trials are to the bench, not to a jury.

Administrative Law

It is likely that at some time in your life you have had to deal with an administrative agency. Agencies are governmental units, federal, state, and local, which administer the affairs of the government. Although often lumped together, there are actually two types of agencies, social welfare and regulatory. The two names reflect the purposes behind each type. Social welfare agencies put into effect government programs. For example, in Indiana the State Department of Public Welfare administers the distribution of public money to those deemed needy. In contrast, state medical licensing boards are regulatory, because their duty is to oversee and regulate the practice of medicine in the various states. Both regulatory and administrative agencies receive their power from the legislative branch.

Because legislatures do not possess the time or the expertise to write precise statutes, they often enact a statute that is very general and in that statute grant one or more administrative agencies the authority to make more precise laws. Just as legislative enactments are known as statutes (or codes), administrative laws are known as **regulations** or rules. The extent to which a legislature may delegate its law-making authority has been a continuing source of debate. It is argued that legislatures may not grant such an important legislative function to agencies. This is believed to be a violation of the principle of separation of powers, because agencies usually fall under the control of the executive branch, and the legislative branch is not permitted to delegate its powers to the executive branch, or vice versa.

SIDEBAR   FINDING ADMINISTRATIVE REGULATIONS Federal administrative rules are found in the Code of Federal Regulations (C.F.R.). New rules that have not yet been added to the C.F.R. may be found in the *Federal Register.* Each state has its counterpart

————————————BALLENTINE'S————————————

regulation   A rule having the force of law, promulgated by an administrative agency.

publications. For example, in Florida they are the Florida Administrative Code and the *Florida Administrative Weekly,* respectively.

Despite this, the United States Supreme Court has determined that agencies may create regulations which have the effect of law, including criminal prohibitions. The Court's opinion on how much authority may be given administrative agencies has undergone a few changes over the years. In 1911 the United States Supreme Court handed down the opinion in the *Grimaud* case.

UNITED STATES v. GRIMAUD
United States Supreme Court
220 U.S. 506 (1911)

The defendants were indicted for grazing sheep on the Sierra Forest Reserve without having obtained the permission required by the regulations adopted by the Secretary of Agriculture. They demurred on the ground that the Forest Reserve Act of 1891 was unconstitutional, in so far as it delegated to the Secretary of Agriculture power to make rules and regulations and made a violation thereof a penal offense.

* * *

From the various acts relating to the establishment and management of forest reservations it appears that they were intended "to improve and protect the forest and to secure favorable conditions to water flows." ... It was also declared that the Secretary "may make such rules and regulations and establish such service as will insure the objects of such reservation, namely, to regulate their occupancy and use to prevent the forests thereon from destruction; *and any violation of the provisions of this act or such* rules and regulations shall be punished," as is provided in [the statute].

Under these acts, therefore, any use of the reservations for grazing or other lawful purpose was required to be subject to the rules and regulations established by the Secretary of Agriculture. To pasture sheep and cattle on the reservation, at will and without restraint, might interfere seriously with the accomplishment of the purposes for which they were established. But a limited and regulated use for pasturage might not be inconsistent with the object sought to be attained by the statute. The determination of such questions, however, was a matter of administrative detail. What might be harmless in one forest might be harmful to another. What might be injurious at one stage of timber growth, or at one season of the year, might not be so at another.

In the nature of things it was impracticable for Congress to provide general regulations for these various and varying details of management. Each reservation had its peculiar and special features; and in authorizing the Secretary of Agriculture to meet these local conditions Congress was merely conferring administrative functions upon an agent, and not delegating to him legislative power.

* * *

It must be admitted that it is difficult to define the line which separates legislative power to make laws, from administrative authority to make regulations. This difficulty has often been recognized [as] referred to by Chief Justice Marshall ... : "It will not be contended that Congress can delegate to the courts, or to any other tribunals, powers which are strictly and exclusively legislative. But Congress may certainly delegate to others, powers which the legislature may rightfully exercise itself." What were these non-legislative powers which Congress could exercise but which might also be delegated to others was not determined, for he said: "The line has not been exactly drawn which separates those important subjects, which *must* be entirely regulated by the legislature itself, from those of less interest, in which a general provision may be made, and power given to those who are to act under such general provisions to fill up the details."

From the beginning of the Government various acts have been passed conferring upon the executive officers power to make rules and regulations — not for the government of their departments; but for administering the laws which did govern. None of these statutes could confer legislative power. But when Congress had legislated and indicated its will, it could give to those who were to act under such general provisions "power to fill up the details" by the establishment of administrative rules and regulations, the violation of which could be punished by fine or imprisonment fixed by Congress, or by penalties fixed by Congress or measured by the injury done.

* * *

It is true that there is no act of Congress which, in express terms, declares that it shall be unlawful to graze sheep on a forest reserve. But the statutes, from which we have quoted, declare, that the privilege of using reserves for "all proper and lawful purposes" is subject to the proviso that the person shall comply "with the rules and regulations covering such forest reservation." The same act makes it an offense to violate those regulations.

* * *

The Secretary of Agriculture could not make rules and regulations for any and every purpose. As to those here involved, they all regulate matters clearly indicated and authorized by Congress.

Grimaud is the law today. Agencies may be delegated penal rulemaking authority. However, the Supreme Court has said that although Congress may delegate to an agency the authority to make criminal laws, it may not delegate the responsibility of establishing penalties to an agency, with the possible exception of small fines. Congress must either set the precise penalty or set a range from which an agency can further determine the appropriate penalty.

An interesting question concerns how much guidance Congress must give an agency in its delegation. Because Congress is delegating its power to create law to an agency, it is expected to give the agency some guidance as to what it wants. This limits the discretion of the agency and prevents it from becoming a substitute legislature.[12] Normally, Congress must provide an intelligible principle or sufficient standards to guide an agency.[13] It takes little congressional guidance to satisfy these tests. Because of the special nature of criminal law (i.e., the deprivation to liberty than may result from a criminal conviction) defendants have argued that Congress must be more specific, or give an agency less discretion, when delegating the authority to create penal rules, as opposed to nonpenal rules. The Supreme Court refused to answer that question in *Touby v. United States*.

TOUBY v. UNITED STATES
United States Supreme Court
500 U.S. 160 (1991)

Petitioners were convicted of manufacturing and conspiring to manufacture "Euphoria," a drug temporarily designated as a schedule I controlled substance pursuant to § 201(h) of the Controlled Substances Act. We consider whether § 201(h) unconstitutionally delegates legislative power to the Attorney General and whether the Attorney General's subdelegation to the Drug Enforcement Administration (DEA) was authorized by statute. ...

[T]he Controlled Substances Act (Act) ... establishes five categories or "schedules" of controlled substances, the manufacture, possession, and distribution of which the Act regulates or prohibits. Violations involving schedule I substances carry the most severe penalties, as these substances are believed to pose the most serious threat to public safety. Relevant here, § 20l(a) of the Act authorizes the Attorney General to add or remove substances, or to move a substance from one schedule to another. ...

When adding a substance to a schedule, the Attorney General must follow specified procedures. First, the Attorney General must request a scientific and medical evaluation from the Secretary of Health and Human Services (HHS), together with a recommendation as to whether the substances should be controlled. A substance cannot be scheduled if the Secretary recommends against it. ... Second, the Attorney General must consider eight factors with respect to the substance, including its potential for abuse, scientific evidence of its pharmacological effect, its psychic or physiological dependence liability, and whether the substance is an immediate precursor of a substance already controlled. ... Third, the Attorney General must comply with notice-and-hearing provisions of the Administrative Procedure Act ... which permit comment by interested parties. ... In addition, the Act permits any aggrieved person to challenge the scheduling of a substance by the Attorney General in a court of appeals. ...

It takes time to comply with these procedural requirements. From the time when law enforcement officials identify a dangerous new drug, it typically takes 6 to 12 months to add it to one of the schedules. ... Drug traffickers were able to take advantage of this time gap by designing drugs that were similar in pharmacological effect to scheduled substances but differing slightly in chemical composition, so that existing schedules did not apply to them. These "designer drugs" were developed and widely marketed long before the Government was able to schedule them and initiate prosecutions. ...

To combat "designer drug" problem, Congress in 1984 amended the Act to create an expedited procedure by which the Attorney General can schedule a substance on a temporary basis when doing so is "necessary to avoid an imminent hazard to the public safety." ... Temporary scheduling under § 20l(h) allows the Attorney General to bypass, for a limited time, several of the requirements for permanent scheduling. The Attorney General need consider only three of the eight factors required for permanent scheduling. ... Rather than comply with the APA notice-and-hearing provisions, the Attorney General need provide only a 30-day notice of proposed scheduling in the Federal Register. ... Notice also must be transmitted to the Secretary of HHS, but the Secretary's prior approval of a proposed scheduling is not required. ... Finally ... an order to schedule a substance temporarily "is not subject to judicial review."

Because it has fewer procedural requirements, temporary scheduling enables the government to respond more quickly to the threat posed by dangerous new drugs. A temporary scheduling order can be issued 30 days after a new drug is identified, and the order remains valid for one year. During this 1-year period, the Attorney General presumably will initiate the permanent scheduling process ... .

The Attorney General promulgated regulations delegating to the DEA his powers under the Act, including the power to schedule controlled substances on a temporary basis. Pursuant to that delegation, the DEA Administrator issued an order scheduling ... "Euphoria" as a schedule I controlled substance. ...

While the temporary scheduling order was in effect, DEA agents, executing a valid search warrant, discovered a fully operational drug laboratory in Daniel and Lyrissa Touby's home. The Toubys were indicted for manufacturing and conspiring to manufacture Euphoria. They moved to dismiss the indictment on the grounds that § 201(h) unconstitutionally delegates legislative power to the attorney General. ... The United States District Court for the District of New Jersey denied the motion to dismiss ... and the Court of Appeals for the Third Circuit affirmed ... . We granted certiorari ... and now affirm.

The Constitution provides that "all legislative Powers herein granted shall be vested in a Congress of the United States." From this language the Court has derived the nondelegation doctrine: that Congress may not constitutionally delegate its legislative power to another Branch of government. "The nondelegation doctrine is rooted in the principle of separation of powers that underlies our tripartite system of Government." ...

We have long recognized that nondelegation does not prevent Congress from seeking assistance, within proper limits, from its coordinate Branches. ... Thus, Congress does not violate the Constitution merely because it legislates in broad terms, leaving a certain degree of discretion to executive or judicial actors. So long as Congress

"lay[s] down by legislative act an intelligible principle to which the person or body authorized to [act] is directed to conform, such legislative action is not a forbidden delegation of legislative power." ...

Petitioners wisely concede that Congress has set forth in § 201(h) an "intelligible principle" to constrain the Attorney General's discretion to schedule controlled substances on a temporary basis. ... Petitioners suggest, however, that something more than an "intelligible principle" is required when Congress authorizes another Branch to promulgate regulations that contemplate criminal sanctions. They contend that regulations of this sort pose a heightened risk to individual liberty and that Congress must therefore provide more specific guidance. Our cases are not entirely clear as to whether or not more specific guidance is in fact required. ... We need not resolve the issue today. We conclude that § 201(h) passes muster even if greater congressional specificity is required in the criminal context.

Although it features fewer procedural requirements than the permanent scheduling statute, § 201(h) meaningfully constrains the Attorney General's discretion to define criminal conduct. ...

It is clear that in § 201(h) and 202(b) Congress has placed multiple restrictions on the Attorney General's discretion to define criminal conduct. These restrictions satisfy the constitutional requirements of the nondelegation doctrine.

In conclusion, an agency may be delegated the authority to declare acts criminal. Congress must provide at least an "intelligible principle," and possibly more, when making this type of delegation. Congress may not delegate the authority to set a penalty to an agency, although it may allow the agency to set the penalty for a violation from within statutory guidelines.

Court Rules

Just as administrative agencies need the authority to "fill in the gaps" of legislation because statutes are not specific enough to satisfy all of an agency's needs, so do courts. The United States Congress and all of the state legislatures have enacted some form of statute establishing general rules of civil and criminal procedure. However, to fill in the gaps left by legislatures, courts adopt **court rules**, which also govern civil and criminal processes. Although court rules deal with procedural issues (such as service of process, limits on the length of briefs and memoranda, and timing of filing) and not substantive issues, they are important. Of course, court rules may not conflict with legislative mandates. If a rule does conflict with a statute, the statute is controlling. One exception to this rule may be when the statute is unconstitutional and the rule is a viable alternative, but discussion of that issue is best left to a course on constitutional law and judicial process.

Most court rules are drafted under the direction of the highest court of the state and either become effective by vote of the court or after being presented to the state legislature for ratification. In the federal system, the rules are drafted by the Judicial Conference under the direction of the Supreme Court and then presented to Congress. If Congress fails to act to nullify the rules, they become law. Of course, Congress may amend the rules at will. Many jurisdictions also have local rules, that is, rules created by local courts for practice in those courts. The rules cannot conflict with either statutes or higher court rules. In the federal system, district courts adopt local rules. Being familiar with the rules of the courts in your jurisdiction is imperative. If you are not, you may miss important deadlines, file incomplete documents, or have your filings stricken.

The Model Penal Code

On occasion the **Model Penal Code** will be referenced in this text. Actually entitled *Model Penal Code and Commentaries,* it was drafted by a group of individuals expert in criminal law while working for the American Law Institute, which is a private organization. The intent of the drafters of the Code was to draft a consistent, thoughtful code that could be recommended to the states for adoption. The code itself is not law until adopted and made into law by a legislature.

According to one source, by 1985 thirty-four states had "enacted widespread criminal-law revision and codification based on its provisions; fifteen hundred courts had cited its provisions and referred to its commentary."[14] The Model Penal Code has been included in this text,

---
BALLENTINE'S

rules of court   Rules promulgated by the court, governing procedure or practice before it.

Model Penal Code   A proposed criminal code prepared jointly by the Commission on Uniform State Laws and the American Law Institute.

in edited form, as Appendix B. You should refer to that as the Code is discussed in following chapters.

Constitutional Law

Finally, constitutional law is included in this list of sources of criminal law, not because it defines what conduct is criminal, but because of its significant impact on criminal law generally. In particular, the United States Constitution, primarily through the Bill of Rights, is responsible for establishing many of the rules governing criminal procedure. This has been especially true in the past few decades. You will become more aware of why this is true as you learn more about criminal law and procedure. Pay close attention to the dates of the cases included in this text; it is likely that many were handed down in your lifetime.

IMPORTANT DATES IN THE HISTORY OF THE
CONSTITUTION OF THE UNITED STATES

May 25, 1787	Constitutional Convention opens in Philadelphia.
September 17, 1787	Constitutional Convention closes, and Constitution is sent to the states for ratification.
December 6, 1787	Delaware is the first state to ratify the Constitution.
June 21, 1788	New Hampshire is the ninth state to ratify and thereby provides the requisite number of ratifying states to adopt the Constitution for the entire United States.
May 29, 1790	Rhode Island is the thirteenth (last) state to ratify the Constitution.
December 15, 1791	Bill of Rights is ratified.
July 28, 1868	Fourteenth Amendment is ratified.

Although it is common to associate the study of constitutional law with the study of the United States Constitution, do not forget that each state also has its own constitution with its own body of case law interpreting its meaning. Even though the dominant source for defending civil liberties has been the United States Constitution, it is possible that a shift to state constitutions will occur, as the current Supreme Court is expected to be more conservative on criminal issues, which means less likely to extend constitutional protections. Remember, the United States Constitution is the highest form of law, and the states may not decrease the individual protections secured by it. States may, however, increase civil liberties through state law. Most state constitutions mirror the federal constitution, often verbatim. In spite of this, state courts are free to interpret their constitutional provisions as providing more protection than their federal counterparts, even if identical in text.

SOURCES OF CRIMINAL LAW

Source	Comment
CONSTITUTIONS	The United States and every state have a constitution. The United States Constitution is the supreme law of the land. Amendment of the federal constitution requires action by both the states and United States Congress.
STATUTES	The written law created by legislatures, also known as codes. State statutes may not conflict with either their own constitution or the federal constitution. State statutes are also invalid if they conflict with other federal law, and the federal government has concurrent jurisdiction with the states. Statutes of the United States are invalid if they conflict with the United States Constitution or if they attempt to regulate outside federal jurisdiction. Legislatures may change statutes at will.
COMMON LAW	Law which evolved, as courts, through judicial opinions, recognized customs, and practices. Legislatures may alter, amend, or abolish the common law at will. In criminal law the common law is responsible for the creation of crimes and for establishing defenses to crimes.
REGULATIONS	Created by administrative agencies under a grant of authority from a legislative body. Regulations must be consistent with statutes and constitutions and may not exceed the legislative grant of power. The power to make rules and regulations is granted to "fill in the gaps" left by legislatures when drafting statutes.
ORDINANCES	Written law of local bodies, such as city councils. Must be consistent with all higher forms of law.
MODEL PENAL CODE	Written under the direction of the American Law Institute. It was drafted by experts in criminal law to be presented to the states for adoption. It is not law until a state has adopted it, in whole or part. More than half the states have adopted at least part of the Model Penal Code.
COURT RULES	Rules created by courts to manage their cases. Court rules are procedural and commonly establish deadlines, lengths of filings, etc. Court rules may not conflict with statutes or constitutions.

Review Questions

1. What are civil liberties? Give two examples of civil liberties that are protected by the Constitution of the United States.

2. What is the common law? How do the concepts of stare decisis and precedent relate to the common law?

3. The common law is different in every state. Why?

4. What does the Latin phrase "nullum crimen sine lege" translate to? Explain the significance of that phrase.

5. Explain how the common law can violate the principle of legality.

6. State three uses the common law has in criminal law in those jurisdictions that do not permit common-law creation of crimes.

7. What is the source of most criminal law today? Where does that law come from?

8. What is an ordinance?

9. What is a regulation?

10. What is a court rule?

11. Place the following sources of law in order of authority, beginning with the highest form of law and ending with the lowest. Notice that both state and federal sources of law are included: United States Code, state constitutions, federal administrative regulations, ordinances, United States Constitution, state administrative regulations, state statutes.

Review Problems

1. In theory, people can increase their "freedom" by establishing a government and relinquishing freedoms (civil liberties) to that government. Explain why this paradox is true.

2. List the various purposes for punishing criminal law violators.

3–6. Using your answers from question 2, determine if the goals of punishment can be achieved if prosecution is sought for the following acts:

3. John, having always wanted a guitar, stole one from a fellow student's room while that student was out.

4. Jack suffers from a physical disease of the mind that causes him to have violent episodes. Jack has no way of knowing when the episodes will occur. However, the disease is controllable with medication. Despite this, Jack often does not take the medicine, as he finds the injections painful and inconvenient. One day, when he had not taken the medicine, Jack had an episode and struck Mike, causing him personal injury.

5. Same facts as in question 4, except there is no treatment or medication that can control Jack's behavior. He was diagnosed as having the disease years prior to striking Mike and has caused such an injury before during a similar violent episode.

6. Unknown to Kevin, he is an epileptic. One day while he was driving his automobile, he suffered his first seizure. The seizure caused him to lose control of his car and strike a pedestrian, inflicting a fatal injury.

Notes

[1] In May, 1988, Larry Mahoney, while driving under the influence of alcohol, struck a school bus, causing it to burst into flames. At the time he hit the bus he was traveling in the wrong direction on an interstate highway. Twenty-four children and three adults died in the fire. On December 22, 1989, a Kentucky jury convicted Mr. Mahoney of second-degree manslaughter and other lesser offenses, and recommended that he be sentenced to sixteen years in prison.

[2] *See* E. Puttkammer, *Administration of Criminal Law,* 16–17 (1953).

[3] Schwartz and Goldstein, *Police Guidance Manuals* (University of Virginia Press, 1968), Manual No. 3, at 21–32, reprinted in *Cases, Materials, and Problems on the Advocacy and Administration of Criminal Justice* 173 by Harold Norris (unpublished manuscript available in the Detroit College of Law library).

[4] *See* Note, 78 *Colum. L. Rev.* 1249, 1247–59 (1978); LaFave and Scott, *Criminal Law* 26 (Hornbook Series, St. Paul: West, 1986).

[5] LaFave and Scott at 23.

[6] 15A Am. Jur. 2d *Common Law* 6 (1976).

[7] *Marsillett v. State,* 495 N.E.2d 699, 704 (Ind. 1986) (citations omitted).

[8] 15A Am. Jur. 2d *Common Law* 1 (1976).

[9] *Helms v. American Security Co.,* 22 N.E.2d 822 (Ind. 1986).

[10] T. Gardner, *Criminal Law: Principles and Cases,* 4th ed. (Criminal Justice Series; St. Paul: West, 1989).

[11] P. Robinson, *Fundamentals of Criminal Law* (Boston: Little, Brown, 1988).

[12] *See Schechter Poultry Corp. v. United States,* 295 U.S. 495 (1935).

[13] *See* D. Hall, *Administrative Law* ch. 2 (Lawyers Cooperative/Delmar, 1994).

[14] J. Samaha, *Criminal Law,* 3d ed. (St. Paul: West, 1990).

CHAPTER 3

THE TWO ESSENTIAL ELEMENTS

CHAPTER OUTLINE Mens Rea

Actus Reus

Mens Rea

Nearly every crime consists of two essential elements, the mental and the physical. This chapter begins by addressing the mental part and concludes by examining the physical.

It is common to distinguish between acts that are intentional and those that occur accidentally. Everyone has had an experience where they have caused injury to another person or another person's property accidentally. The fact that the injury was accidental and not intended often leads to a statement such as, "I'm sorry, I didn't mean to hurt you." In these situations people often feel a social obligation to pay for any injuries they have caused, or to assist the injured party in other ways, but probably do not expect to be punished criminally. As the late Supreme Court Justice Holmes stated, "Even a dog distinguishes between being stumbled over and being kicked." As this statement implies, to make such a distinction between accidental and intentional acts that injure others appears to be natural and consistent with common notions of fairness. The criminal law often models this theory; that is, people are often held accountable for intentional behavior and not for accidental, even though the consequences may be the same. However, this is not always so. Under some circumstances accidental behavior (negligent or reckless) may be the basis of criminal liability.

Mens rea is the mental part, the state of mind required to be criminally liable. It is often defined as "a guilty mind" or possessing a criminal intent. It is best defined as the state of mind required to be criminally liable for a certain act. It is sometimes the case that no intent whatsoever is required to be guilty of a crime, although most criminal laws require intent of some degree before criminal liability attaches to an act.

Mens rea is an important concept in criminal law. It is also a confusing one. This is in large part because of the inconsistency and lack of uniformity between criminal statutes and judicial decisions. One author found seventy-nine words and phrases in the United States Criminal Code used to describe mens rea.[1] Often when courts or legislatures use the same term they do so assuming different meanings for the term. For this reason, the drafters of the Model Penal Code attempted to establish uniform terms and definitions for those terms. The Model Penal Code

---

mens rea   An "answerable intent," i.e., an intent for which one is answerable; an evil intent; a guilty mind; a criminal intent. In combination with actus reus (a guilty or criminal act), mens rea is an essential element of any crime except regulatory crimes or strict liability crimes and some petty offenses and infractions. Mens rea may be inferred or presumed.

approach is examined later. First, you will learn how the common law treated mens rea.

Mens Rea and the Common Law

One principle under the common law was that there should be no crime if there was no act accompanied by a guilty mind. The Latin phrase that states this principle is "actus non facit reum nisi mens sit rea." Today, under some statutes, no intent is required to be guilty of a crime. Despite this, the principle that "only conscious wrongdoing constitutes crime is deeply rooted in our legal system and remains the rule, rather than the exception."[2]

Many terms have been used to describe a guilty mind. Malicious, mischievous, purposeful, unlawful, intentional, with specific intent, knowing, fraudulent, with an evil purpose, careless, willful, negligent and reckless are examples of terms and phrases used to describe the mental state required to prove guilt.

General, Specific, and Constructive Intent

One common distinction is between *general intent* and **specific intent**. The distinction turns on whether the defendant intended to cause the consequences of the act. If the defendant had a desire or purpose to cause the result of the act, then the defendant possessed specific intent. If the defendant only intended the act, and not the result of that act, then the defendant possessed general intent. For example, Don Defendant throws a large rock at Vern Victim, inflicting a fatal wound. If Defendant only intended to injure Victim, not kill him, then he possessed general intent. However, if Defendant threw the rock hoping it would kill Victim, then he possessed specific intent. The distinction between general and specific intent is often an important one, as many statutes require specific intent for a higher-level crime and general for a lower. In this example, many state statutes would allow Defendant to be charged with first-degree murder if he intended to kill Victim, but only second-degree murder if he only intended to injure Victim.

If a defendant intends to cause the result, then the fact that the means used to achieve the result are likely to fail is irrelevant. For example, assume Defendant desires to cause the death of Victim. One day,

---

BALLENTINE'S

specific intent   The intent to commit the very act with which the defendant has been charged. General criminal intent (mens rea) is an essential element of virtually all crimes. Specific intent is an additional requirement with respect to certain crimes.

while walking down a street, Defendant notices Victim far away. Defendant picks up a rock and hurls it toward Victim, hoping it will strike Victim and kill him, although because of the distance he does not expect the rock to strike its intended target. However, all those afternoons practicing his baseball pitch paid off, and the rock hit Victim in the head, killing him instantly. The fact that Defendant threw the rock with an intent to kill is enough to establish Defendant's specific intent. The fact that the act is unlikely to be successful is no defense.

Specific intent may also be proved, in some jurisdictions, by showing that the defendant possessed knowledge of a particular fact or illegality. This requirement of knowledge is known as **scienter**. In jurisdictions that require such knowledge, if an individual violates a criminal law while believing that the act engaged in is lawful, then specific intent is lacking, and only general intent can be proven.[3] Scienter often does not require proof of subjective knowledge (what was actually in the defendant's mind), but can be established if the prosecution can prove that the defendant should have known the fact in question.

Often without scienter no crime exists to punish. Consider the crime of receiving stolen property. If an individual received stolen property, but did so without knowledge that it was stolen, then no crime has been committed. For some crimes that require scienter, the absence of scienter may leave a general-intent crime. If a man strikes a person whom he believes is obstructing traffic, he has committed an assault. If he knew, or should have known, that the person was a police officer attempting to direct traffic, then he may be accountable for the higher crime of assault on a police officer. However, if the police officer was not wearing a uniform and did not announce himself as an officer, then the defendant is liable only for simple assault. Possession of burglary tools and obstruction of justice are also examples: the former requiring knowledge of the tools' character and the latter requiring knowledge of obstruction.

At common law, specific intent could be found in a third type of situation, whenever **constructive** intent could be proven. That is, although the defendant does not intend to cause the result, it is so likely to occur that the law treats the act as one of specific intent. If John fires a handgun at close range at Sally, aiming at her torso, and kills her as a result, it is possible that he could be charged with the specific-intent crime of first-degree murder, even though he only intended to injure her. This is because the possibility of killing someone under those circumstances is significant. However, this may not be true if he aimed at her leg and the weapon discharged improperly, causing the bullet

---

BALLENTINE'S

scienter   (Latin) Knowledge, particularly guilty knowledge; i.e., knowledge a person has that, as a matter of law, will result in his or her liability or guilt.

constructive   Inferred, implied, or presumed from the circumstances.

to strike her in the torso. This is because the likelihood of killing someone with a gunshot to the leg is much less than with a gunshot to the upper body. The bullet entered Victim's torso as a result of the malfunction of the gun; it was not Defendant's desire to shoot her in the upper body.

As to the amount of probability necessary to prove constructive intent, only "practical or substantial" probability is required, not absolute.[4]

Specific intent can be found in a fourth situation, whenever a defendant intends a result beyond the act taken. This refers to situations when a criminal act is uncompleted. For example, if a man attacks a woman intending to rape her, but she is able to free herself and escape, he may be charged with assault with intent to rape. To prove this charge, the prosecution must show that he assaulted the victim with the specific intent of raping her. Proving that the defendant had a specific intent to assault her is not enough to sustain the intent-to-rape charge, although it would justify a conviction for assault, a lesser crime. Another example is the crime of breaking and entering with the intent to burglarize. Again, the prosecution must prove that the defendant intended to steal from the home after the entry and did not complete the burglary for some reason. Proving that the defendant broke in and entered, but had no intent to steal, will support a conviction for breaking and entering, but not intent to commit burglary.

General intent is much easier to define, as it is simply the desire to act. In most situations, if the prosecution can show that a defendant intended to take the act prohibited, then general intent is proved. Generally, no desire to cause a particular consequence is required. So, if you fire a gun without a desire to kill someone, but the bullet does kill a person, you possess a general intent and may be prosecuted for a general-intent homicide.

Some jurisdictions require more than simply a desire to act to prove general intent. In those states some level of negligence must be proven. Consider the following two examples: Rural Defendant has lived on a farm for more than twenty years. Defendant's nearest neighbor is over three miles away, and Defendant routinely target shoots in his back yard. He has never encountered anyone in the area where he shoots, and everyone who lives in the community knows of his practice. One day, while target shooting, he accidently shoots and kills a trespasser he did not know was on his property. In the second example, Metro Defendant likes to hunt on weekends. One weekend Metro and his friend were hunting, and Metro lost sight of his friend. Eager to capture his first deer of the season, Metro fired into a bush in which he observed some movement. It was Metro's friend that was in the bush, and Metro's gunshot inflicted a fatal wound. In both examples the defendants had no desire to harm the individuals shot, and both possessed the intent to fire the weapon. A strict construction of general and specific intent results in both committing a general-intent murder, but not

JANET A. CARSON, Appellant

v.

UNITED STATES, Appellee
556 A.2d 1076, 1989 D.C.
App. LEXIS 57 (1989)

On June 4, 1985, Janet Carson arrived home from work at about 3:45 P.M. and was informed by one of her children that a fuse needed replacement. While looking for a fuse, appellant noticed that eight dollars were missing from her dresser drawer. She called her children—thirteen-year-old Cornell, six-year-old Everett, five-year-old Angelica and eight-year-old Charmaine Schmidt—to her bedroom; each child denied knowing anything about the missing money. At that point she went downstairs, and as she returned upstairs she picked up an electrical cord; she later testified that she routinely used the cord to discipline the children. She again asked the children about the missing money, and they again denied any knowledge of the money's disappearance. Appellant then whipped each of the children several times.

The next day at the school attended by Everett, Angelica, and Charmaine, school officials noticed marks and bruises on the children. Detective Harmon of the Metropolitan Police Department went to the school and took the three children to Children's Hospital. Everett's abrasions were cleaned and bandaged; the other two children received no treatment.

Appellant was subsequently charged with three counts of cruelty to children. ... [Ms. Carson was convicted and sentenced to thirty days on each count, which was suspended to one year's probation. She appealed the conviction and this is the opinion of the appellate court.]

Before considering appellant's claim that the evidence was insufficient to support her conviction, we must first determine the mens rea required for conviction under D.C. Code § 22–901. We conclude that the offense is a general intent crime, which also requires a showing of malice. ...

Section 22–901 provides in pertinent part:

> Any person who shall torture, cruelly beat, abuse, or otherwise willfully maltreat any child under the age of 18 years ... shall be deemed guilty of a misdemeanor, and, when convicted thereof, shall be subject to punishment by a fine of not more than $250, or by imprisonment for a term not exceeding 2 years, or both.

The [D.C. Jury Instructions] define the elements of the offense as follows:

1. That the defendant tortured, cruelly beat, abused or otherwise maltreated a child;
2. That at the time of the incident, the child was under the age of 18 years; and
3. That the defendant acted willfully, that is, with an evil intent or with bad purpose to maltreat the child. It is not enough that you find that the defendant exercised bad judgment or acted unreasonably. Rather, it is necessary that you find that the defendant was motivated by an evil intent or state of mind in committing the acts which constitute the offense.

* * *

Judicial interpretation of D.C. Code § 22–901 has been limited ... [T]he United States Court of Appeals for the District of Columbia held that the terms "abuse" and "willfully mistreat" as used in the statute "call for something worse than good intentions coupled with bad judgment," and incorporate "the requirement of an evil state of mind." ... The cases would seem to teach that cruelty to children is something more than a general intent crime and something less than a specific intent crime.

* * *

In other contexts, this court has equated the terms "evil intent" and "malice." This court has noted that a showing of bad or evil purpose is "necessary to distinguish the mental state required for malice-based offenses from that involved in crimes the conviction for which demands proof no more than general intent or criminal negligence." Thus, if cruelty to children requires proof of something more than general intent, that something more would seem to be malice.

* * *

Having determined the mens rea required for conviction of cruelty to children, we must now determine whether the government's proof was sufficient to establish the requisite mens rea in this case. Appellant concedes that the record supports the trial court's finding of general intent. However, she argues that the government failed to prove that she acted with malice. She argues that according to her undisputed testimony, she was motivated not by an evil intent, but rather by a "concern for [her] children's welfare and up-bringing." At first blush, the record supports her argument as to motivation.

The government argues, however, that to find malice "all that is required [is] a conscious disregard of a known and substantial risk of the harm ... ."

Malice is a rather slippery concept, not amenable to precise definition. ... Simply put, we believe that a parent acts with malice when a parent acts out of a desire to inflict pain rather than out of genuine effort to correct the child, or when the parent, in a genuine effort to correct the child, acts with a conscious disregard that serious harm will result.

* * *

In this case, appellant's testimony regarding her motive was not directly contradicted. The government relied basically on the nature of the wounds and the manner of the punishment to establish malice. The government introduced pictures of the injuries sustained by the children and also pointed to the ages of the children, and the fact that appellant used an electrical cord to whip the children as evidence that appellant acted with evil intent, or at least as evidence that appellant acted with a conscious disregard that serious harm (of the nature which would flow from an evil intent) would result.

From our perspective in this court, we cannot conclude that the evidence justifies the inference that appellant acted out of a desire to inflict pain. ...

The trial court also noted that appellant had "high standards" for her children—"she didn't want them to steal; she didn't want them to use drugs." The court found that appellant had worked hard to make a good life for herself and her children. She had left the welfare rolls and become a policewoman, "supporting all those children on her own." We echo the trial court's sentiment that appellant had a genuine and deep-felt love and concern for her children.

Further, we do not believe that the punishment was so excessive or the manner so egregious as to lead to the conclusion that appellant acted with a conscious disregard of the serious harm which would result. The mother testified that the whippings lasted perhaps a minute. As to the manner of discipline, reasonable people might disagree as to whether whipping with an electrical cord is in itself offensive or no more offensive than the use of commonly employed devices or methods used to exact discipline. We would only note that appellant testified that because the children were jumping around and that because she was eight months pregnant and therefore awkward, the cord made contact on the children's bodies where it otherwise may not have done so.

However, when the manner of punishment, the length of punishment, the nature of the injuries and the ages of the children are viewed as a whole, we cannot say that the trial court was plainly in error in concluding that appellant acted with conscious disregard of the harm which resulted. ...

Conviction AFFIRMED.

a specific. However, in some jurisdictions Rural may be free from liability because he appears to have been less reckless or negligent than Metro, who should have considered the possibility that it could have been his friend he was firing at.

This discussion has not exhausted the many definitions and distinctions that exist for specific and general intent. In the *Carson* case, it appears that the Court of Appeals for the District of Columbia has created a hybrid general-specific intent for the crime of cruelty to children.

Malum in Se and Malum Prohibitum

Often crimes are characterized as either malum in se or malum prohibitum. If a crime is inherently evil, it is malum in se. If a crime is not evil in itself, but is only criminal because declared so by a legislature, then it is malum prohibitum. Murder, rape, arson, and mayhem are examples of crimes which are malum in se. Failure to file your quarterly tax report or to get the proper building permit are both crimes malum prohibitum.

The distinction between malum in se and malum prohibitum is used throughout criminal law, but the importance of the distinction is in how it affects intent. Crimes malum in se are treated as requiring an evil intent, and crimes malum prohibitum are not. Some crimes may be both malum in se and malum prohibitum, depending upon the degree of violation. For example, speeding "a little over the limit may be malum prohibitum, but speeding at high speed malum in se."[5] Whether an act is malum prohibitum or in se often determines what crime may be charged. This usually revolves around the issue of foreseeability of harm. In the preceding example, speeding slightly over the limit is not likely to cause another's death, whereas racing through a city thirty miles over the speed limit can foreseeably cause a fatal accident. If while driving four miles over the speed limit the defendant strikes and kills a pedestrian who walks into the driver's path from behind another car, the act is likely to be determined malum prohibitum, and no resulting manslaughter charge will follow. However, the same may not be true if the driver is traveling thirty miles over the speed limit at the time the accident occurs.

Although some jurisdictions no longer distinguish between crimes malum in se and malum prohibitum, many still do. What crimes fall into each category is determined by judicial decision. Thus the case law in your jurisdiction must be researched to determine where the crime in question falls.

Transferred Intent

Whenever a person intends a harm, but because of bad aim or other cause the intended harm befalls another, the intent is transferred from the intended victim to the unintended victim. This is the doctrine of **transferred intent**. If John Defendant observes a neighbor burning the

---
BALLENTINE'S
---

transferred intent The doctrine that if a defendant who intends to injure ... one person unintentionally harms another, the intent is transferred to the person who is unintentionally harmed. This doctrine permits the defendant to be prosecuted as if he or she had intended to harm the person injured.

American flag and in anger shoots at him, missing him but killing William, the doctrine of transferred intent permits prosecution of Defendant as if he intended to kill William.

There are limits on the doctrine of transferred intent. First, the harm that actually results must be similar to the intended harm. If the harms are substantially different, then the intent does not transfer. For example, if A throws a baseball at B's window, hoping to break it, and the ball instead hits C in the head and kills him, it cannot be said that the intent to break the window transfers to C and that A can be punished for intentionally killing C. A may be criminally liable for a lesser crime, such as involuntary manslaughter, depending upon the amount of negligence involved, but he is not responsible for intentionally causing C's death.

A second limitation on the doctrine is that the transfer cannot increase the defendant's liability. Another way of stating this is that any defenses the defendant has against the intended victim are transferred to the unintended victim. For example, A shoots at B in self-defense, but hits C, inflicting a fatal wound. Because A had a valid defense if B had been killed by the shot, then A also has a defense as to C. In this case A has committed no crime. In some situations a defense may only limit a person's criminal liability to a lesser charge. You will learn later that certain defenses negate specific intent, but not general intent. One such defense is intoxication. Assault is a general-intent crime, whereas assault with an intent to kill is a specific-intent crime. Intoxication may be a defense to the higher assault with an intent to kill, but not assault. So, if A, while intoxicated, hurls a knife at B, but hits C, A may be charged with assault, because intoxication would be no defense if he hit B. A would have a defense against the specific intent crime of assault with intent to kill, so the same defense is available for harm to C.

Strict Liability

At the beginning of this chapter it was noted that some acts are criminal although no mens rea accompanies the prohibited act. These crimes are proven simply by showing that the act was committed, and no particular mental state has to be proved at all. This is **strict liability**, or liability without fault, and is an exception to the common-law requirement that there be both an evil mind and an evil act to have a crime. The term *strict liability* is not used in all jurisdictions. Further, the term also has a tort meaning. Do not confuse criminal liability without fault with tort strict liability. However, for convenience, the phrase "strict liability" is used in this text.

BALLENTINE'S
---

strict liability Liability for an injury whether or not there is fault or negligence; absolute liability. The law imposes strict liability in product liability cases.

Strict liability crimes usually are minor violations, punished by fines and not incarceration. However, strict liability is permitted for felonies and may be punished with incarceration.

Most traffic violations, such as running a stoplight and speeding, are examples of strict liability crimes. Statutory rape is treated as a strict liability crime in most states; therefore, the accused adult cannot claim that he or she had a mistaken belief that the minor was above the statutory age when the two had sexual intercourse. There are many other strict liability crimes in every state, and legislatures are increasingly using the strict liability standard when declaring acts illegal.

It is common for crimes that are malum prohibitum to be strict liability, whereas crimes malum in se usually require proof of some mental state. It is also generally true that violation of crimes malum prohibitum are not punished as severely as crimes malum in se.

Crimes with strict liability are often termed "public offenses" or "regulatory offenses." The term *regulatory* is often used because the criminal prohibition has either been established by an administrative agency through rulemaking, is enforced by an administrative agency, or is part of a comprehensive regulatory scheme established by a legislature.

In many cases, strict liability laws deal with potential, rather than actual, harms. For example, a murder statute can only be applied after someone has been murdered. However, many strict liability offenses deal with violations and no harm. For example, running a stoplight, speeding, or failing to have adequate fire extinguishers in your business may or may not result in an injury. Regardless of whether harm results, you are liable for the offense. This is considered regulatory because the purpose is to induce compliance (using the easy proof standard) with the law, rather than to punish for caused harm. Increased compliance is a result of an awareness by people that violation alone means liability; hence, they are more cautious and less likely to engage in the prohibited conduct. Of course, this argument can be made to justify making all crimes strict liability. The idea of not requiring any intent for acts to be criminal is contrary to American values of fairness and justice, and this is probably the reason why the strict liability standard has not been extended to all crimes.

Strict liability is only available for crimes defined by legislatures. With little restriction, legislatures may define an act as criminal without requiring proof of intent. However, in jurisdictions that continue to recognize common-law crimes, mens rea must be an element.

Many have alleged that liability without fault is violative of the Constitution, but the United States Supreme Court has upheld strict liability

---

BALLENTINE'S

strict liability crimes   Crimes or offenses in which mens rea or criminal intent is not an element. Such offenses include regulatory crimes, petty offenses, and infractions.

statutes in most instances.[6] Despite this, if a legislature declares that a crime that has traditionally required proof of specific intent or purpose has no mens rea requirement, the due process question should be raised. This is especially true if the crime can be punished with a significant jail sentence.

MORISSETTE
v.
UNITED STATES
342 U.S. 246 (1952)

The contention that an injury can amount to a crime only when inflicted by intention is no provincial or transient notion. It is universal and persistent in mature systems of law as belief in freedom of the human will and a consequent ability and duty of the normal individual to choose between good and evil. A relation between some mental element and punishment for a harmful act is almost as instinctive as the child's familiar exculpatory "But I didn't mean to," and has afforded the rational basis for a tardy and unfinished substitution of deterrence and reformation in place of retaliation and vengeance as the motivation for public prosecution. ...

Crime, as a compound concept, generally constituted only from concurrence of an evil-meaning mind with an evil-doing hand, was congenial to an intense individualism and took deep and early root in American soil. As the states codified the common law of crimes, even if their enactments were silent on the subject, their courts assumed that the omission did not signify disapproval of the principle but merely recognized that intent was so inherent in the idea of the offense that it required no statutory definition.

However, [some crimes fall into a] category of another character, with very different antecedents and origins. The crimes there involved depend on no mental element but consist only of forbidden acts or omissions. ... The industrial revolution multiplied the number of workmen exposed to injury from increasingly powerful and complex mechanisms, driven by freshly discovered sources of energy, requiring higher precautions by employers. Traffic of velocities, volumes and varieties unheard of came to subject the wayfarer to intolerable casualty risks if the owners and drivers were not to observe new cares and uniformities of conduct. Congestion of cities and crowding of quarters called for health and welfare regulations undreamed of in simpler times. Wide distribution of goods became an instrument of wide distribution of harm when those who dispersed food, drink, drugs, and even securities, did not comply with reasonable standards of quality, integrity, disclosure and care. Such dangers have engendered increasingly numerous and detailed regulations which heighten the duties of those in control of particular industries, trades, properties, or activities that affect public health, safety or welfare.

... Many violations of such regulations result in no direct or immediate injury to person or property but merely create the danger or probability of injury which the law seeks to minimize.

* * *

Stealing, larceny, and its variants and equivalents, were among the earliest offenses known to the law that existed before legislation [common law]. ... State courts of last resort, on whom fall the heaviest burden of interpreting criminal law in this country, have consistently retained the requirement of intent in larceny-type offenses. If any state has deviated, the exception has neither been called to our attention nor disclosed by our research.

We hold that the mere omission from [the conversion statute] of any mention of intent will not be construed as eliminating that element from the crimes denounced.

In the *Morissette* case, the defendant entered federal property, a military bombing range, and collected spent bomb casings, which had been on the site for years. The casings were exposed to the weather and were rusting when the defendant removed them. The defendant was charged with converting (stealing) the casings. The defendant was convicted at the trial level, and the United States Supreme Court reversed the conviction.

Strict Liability and Statutory Construction

The problem addressed by the Supreme Court in *Morissette* occurs often: What is the mens rea requirement when a statute does not provide for such? That decision depends on many factors. First, the **legislative history** of the statute may indicate whether the crime was intended to have a mens rea requirement or not. The statements of members of legislatures while debating the law (before it became law and was a bill), reports of committees of Congress, and other related materials may indicate whether the legislature intended a mens rea requirement. Second, courts look to whether the crime existed under the common law. If so, the mens rea used under the common law may be adopted by the court. Other factors include the seriousness of the harm to the public; mens rea standards for other related crimes; the punishment imposed upon conviction; the burden that would be placed on the prosecution if mens rea were required; and rules of statutory construction.

Generally, the greater the potential harm to the public and the more difficult it is for prosecution to prove mens rea, the more likely a court is to find that strict liability is to be imposed.[7] Although not a significant factor, the amount of penalty can play a role. The greater the penalty, the more likely that some intent will be read into the statute. Also, courts will look to other related statutes for guidance. If a state legislature has consistently required proof of intent for all crimes of larceny and theft, then if a new statute is enacted dealing with a particular theft (i.e., theft of computer information), and that law does not specify the mental state that must be proven, then the court will fill in the missing element with intent.

Finally, courts have rules that must be followed when interpreting a statute. These are known as *canons of* **statutory construction**. You previously learned one of these rules; that is, whenever a statute can be construed as either constitutional or unconstitutional, it must be read as constitutional. Some jurisdictions follow the rule, either by judicial rule

---

—————BALLENTINE'S—————

legislative history   Recorded events that provide a basis for determining the legislative intent underlying a statute enacted by a legislature. The records of legislative committee hearings and of debates on the floor of the legislature are among the sources for legislative history.

statutory construction   Determining the meaning of a statute.

(canon) or by statute, that if a criminal statute does not specifically impose strict liability, then the court is to impose a mens rea requirement. *Troiano* is a case from New York, a jurisdiction where such a rule is applied.

PEOPLE
v.
Alicia TROIANO
552 N.Y.S.2d 541, 1990
N.Y. Misc. LEXIS 90 (1990)

[Defendant was charged with having insufficient brakes on her car and the following facts were stipulated to by the parties:]

On May 1, 1987 at approximately 11:35 P.M. the defendant was involved in a two-car accident ... . Defendant was the owner and operator of a 1972 Oldsmobile station wagon ... . The driver of the other vehicle died as a result of injuries suffered in that accident. The decedent failed to yield the right of way at a stop sign at that intersection. The decedent's blood alcohol level was .10%. Both vehicles were impounded. The defendant's vehicle was inspected by Al Stern of Al's Towing Corporation and as a result of that inspection the instant charge was brought. [Mr. Stern testified that the defendant's right rear brake was insufficient under state law guidelines.]

The defendant testified that she had not experienced any problems with the braking system of the car. She did not hear any squeaks or other noises. She did not notice any leaking of brake fluid and was able to stop properly at a stop sign just minutes before the accident. Further, the car had been inspected in September, 1986 and had a proper inspection sticker affixed to the windshield.

The defense also called Mr. Troiano, defendant's husband, who had been employed as an automobile mechanic until 1983. Following Stern's inspection, Mr. Troiano towed the vehicle in question back to his house. He pulled off all four wheels and examined the brake shoes and lining and found the brake lining on the right rear wheel to be a little more than $1/16$ of an inch at its thinnest point and, consequently adequate.

* * *

[The statute] provides in pertinent part, "every motor vehicle, operated or driven on the highways of the State, shall be provided with adequate brakes ... ."

The court will first deal with the question of whether the statute is one of strict liability. The plain language of [the brake statute] does not require a mens rea or a culpable mental state as an element of the crime and in reliance thereon the People have made no attempt to make a prima facie showing that defendant knew or had reason to know of the defect.

"Culpable mental state" means intentional, knowing, reckless or criminally negligent conduct ... . If the commission of a particular offense or some material element thereof does not require a culpable mental state on the part of the actor, such an offense is one of "strict liability."

It is a well-known principle of statutory construction that absent the legislature's clear indication of an intent to impose strict liability, a statute should be construed to require mens rea. ... [The court determined that the defendant had to have had knowledge of the defect to be liable and that no such showing had been made. Accordingly, defendant's motion for dismissal was granted.]

Vicarious Liability

The term **vicarious liability** refers to situations in which one person is held accountable for the actions of another. Under vicarious liability, there is no requirement of mens rea, as there is for strict liability, and additionally there is no requirement for an act, at least not by the defendant. The person who is liable for the actions of another need not act, encourage another to act, or intend any harm at all. As is true with vicarious liability in tort law, this situation is most common between employers and employees.

Employers may be liable for the actions of their employees when criminal laws relating to the operation of the business are violated. For example, the owner of a business may be prosecuted for failure to comply with product safety regulations, even though that was a duty delegated to an employee and the owner had no knowledge that the products manufactured were substandard. Vicarious liability is often imposed on those who market food and drugs.[8] This is because of the significant public welfare interest in the quality of these products.

Corporate Liability

Corporate liability is a form of vicarious liability. Under the common law, corporations could not be convicted of crimes. However, this is no longer the law.

Corporations, partnerships, and other organizations can be held criminally accountable for the acts of their employees and agents. The agent must be working within the scope of his or her employment for the company to be liable. If an employee of Burger King strikes an enemy while on break in the parking lot of the store, the company is not liable for battery. However, if officers of a corporation send employees into a workplace knowing that it is dangerous and represent to the employees that it is safe, the company may be liable for battery to the employee, or even manslaughter, if death results.

The Model Penal Code provides for corporate liability when the agent is acting within the scope of employment. In addition, it must be shown that the corporation had a duty under the law to take some act, and the act was not done or the act taken by the agent was authorized, requested, commanded, performed, or recklessly tolerated by the board of directors or other high management.[9]

BALLENTINE'S
---

vicarious liability   Liability imposed upon a person because of the act or omission of another.

corporate liability   The liability of a corporation for the acts of its directors, officers, shareholders, agents, and employees.

Obviously, companies cannot be incarcerated, so fines are usually imposed. In some instances, **injunctions** may be imposed. Finally, note that corporate liability does not free the agent from criminal liability. In most cases the agent or employee remains criminally liable for his or her act.

Current Approaches to Mens Rea

The Model Penal Code and States of Mind

The drafters of the Model Penal Code chose to reject most of the common-law terms when they addressed mens rea. The result is that the Model Penal Code recognizes four states of mind: purposeful; knowing; reckless; and negligent (see Figure 3-1).[10]

To act **purposely**, a defendant must have a desire to cause the result. *Purposely* most closely equates with what the common law called specific intent.

To act **knowingly**, a defendant must be aware of the nature of the act and be practically certain that his or her conduct will cause a particular result, which is not the defendant's objective. The difference between purposeful acts and knowing acts is that to be purposeful, one must act intending to cause the particular result. To act knowingly, the defendant must be practically certain (nearly 100 percent positive) that the result will occur, but the defendant is not taking the act to cause that result. For example, if a legitimate moving company owner leases a van to an illegal drug dealer knowing that the van will be used to transport drugs across the country, then the owner has acted knowingly. He has not acted with purpose because it is not his objective to transport the contraband.

The third state of mind recognized by the Model Penal Code is **recklessness**. A person acts recklessly when he or she consciously disregards a substantial and unjustifiable risk that the result will occur. The difference between a knowing act and a reckless act is in the degree of risk. "A person acts 'knowingly' with respect to a result if he is nearly

---
BALLENTINE'S
---

injunction A court order that commands or prohibits some act or course of conduct. It is preventive in nature and designed to protect a plaintiff from irreparable injury to his or her property or property rights by prohibiting or commanding the doing of certain acts. ... [A] form of equitable relief.

purposely Intentionally; knowingly.

knowingly With knowledge; deliberately; consciously; intentionally. As used in the criminal law and applied to a criminal defendant, "knowingly" means that the accused possessed intent, a necessary element of most crimes; in other words, that he or she knew what he or she was doing and understood the probable results.

recklessness Indifference to consequences; indifference to the safety and rights of others. Recklessness implies conduct amounting to more than ordinary negligence.

Figure 3-1
Mens Rea under the
Model Penal Code

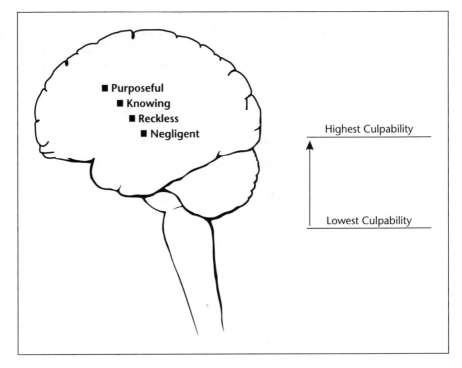

- ■ Purposeful
- ■ Knowing
- ■ Reckless
- ■ Negligent

Highest Culpability

Lowest Culpability

certain that his conduct will cause the result. If he is aware only of a substantial risk, he acts 'recklessly' with respect to the result."[11] The Code says that the risk taken must be one that involves a "gross deviation from the standard of conduct that a law-abiding person would observe in the actor's situation."[12]

The final state of mind is **negligence**. The definition of negligence is similar to recklessness; that is, there must be a "substantial and unjustifiable risk" taken by the defendant. However, a person acts negligently when there is no conscious awareness of the risk, when there should have been. To act recklessly one must take a risk that amounts to a "gross deviation from the standard of conduct that a law-abiding person would observe in the actor's situation." When a defendant has acted negligently, he or she has failed to perceive (be aware of) the risk altogether, and that failure is a gross deviation from a law-abiding person's standard.

—————————————————————BALLENTINE'S—————————

negligence   The failure to do something that a reasonable person would do in the same circumstances, or the doing of something a reasonable person would not do. Negligence is a wrong generally characterized by carelessness, inattentiveness, and neglectfulness rather than by a positive intent to cause injury.

Element Analysis

So far the discussion of culpable states of mind has been limited to one state of mind for each individual crime. For example, under the common law a specific intent to kill must be proven to establish first-degree murder. This was true of all offenses under the common law; that is, only one state of mind had to be shown. This was true even if the crime had many different elements.

Elements are the parts of a crime. The prosecution must prove all the elements of a crime beyond a reasonable doubt to gain a conviction. For example, the common-law elements of larceny were: (1) The taking and carrying away (2) personal property (3) of another (4) with an intent to steal. The prosecution has the burden of proving all four elements. If the prosecution fails to prove any element, the defendant must be acquitted. At common law, only one mental state had to be proved: intent to steal. Additionally, the prosecution had to show that the other four elements occurred without reference to mental state. This is known as offense analysis, as the entire offense is thought of as requiring one mental state.

The Model Penal Code, as well as some specific statutes, recognize that the various acts of a crime may involve differing mental states. As such, each element of a crime may have a different mens rea.[13]

Assume that state law prohibits: (1) Notary publics (2) from notarizing documents (3) of known blood relatives (4) of the third degree or closer (degrees define closeness of family relationship). Under the Code, the first two elements appear to require no mental state—just the act of a notary notarizing a document. Hence, it would be no defense for the notary to claim that he was signing the document as a witness and not as a notary. The third element requires specific knowledge that the person for whom he notarizes the document is a blood relative. If the notary can prove that there was no reason for him to have known of the relationship, then his knowledge is negated. The last element is likely to be treated as a negligence element. It would be a valid defense for the notary to show that he made a reasonable error as to the degree of the relationship, but not a defense if the error was unreasonable.

Proving Mens Rea

At trial the prosecution has the burden of establishing that the defendant possessed the required mental state when the act was committed. Proof of intent can be troublesome to prosecution, especially when the prosecution has to prove subjective intent. *Subjective intent* refers to the motives, intentions, and desires that were in the defendant's

---
BALLENTINE'S

element   A component or essential part of something.

mind at the time the act took place. Subjective intent is a defendant's actual intent.

Objective intent is not the defendant's actual intent; rather, it is a legal imposition upon the defendant of what he or she should have known or believed at the time the act occurred. Generally, the law imposes a reasonable person standard. That means that the defendant is expected to have known or believed what a reasonable person would have known at the time of the act. Objective intent is easier to prove than subjective intent. This is because the prosecution does not have to probe directly into a defendant's mind to prove that an intent to harm existed; rather, all that has to be shown is that the defendant should have known that the harm would result.

In most cases defendants do not admit to committing the acts in question. Even when defendants do admit to taking some acts, they commonly deny intent. For crimes that require intent, admission of the act is not enough to sustain a conviction. The question is, how does a prosecutor gain a conviction for a crime that requires a showing of intent when the defendant denies possessing the required intent? The answer is by using **inferences**.

An *inference* is a conclusion that a judge or jury is permitted to make after considering the facts of a case. Imagine that a man walks up to another man and strikes him in the head with a hammer, using great force in his swing. The wound is fatal, and the attacker is charged with first-degree murder. To sustain a first-degree murder charge in this jurisdiction, it must be shown that the man intended to cause the victim's death. The defendant disavows such intent, admitting only that he intended to hit and injure the victim. In such a case the jury would be permitted to infer the defendant's intent to kill the victim from the seriousness of the act. In a jurisdiction that uses the objective standard, the jury could conclude that a reasonable person would have known that the blow from a hammer would cause the victim's death, and the subjective intent of the defendant would not matter.

A **presumption** is a conclusion that must be made by a judge or jury. Most people have heard of the presumption of innocence in criminal law. This presumption is a *rebuttable presumption*. Rebuttable presumptions are conclusions that must be made by a judge or jury, unless

---
BALLENTINE'S
---

inference   That which may be reasoned from the evidence as being true or proven; a conclusion of fact.

presumption   A rule of law that, on the basis of reason and human experience, accords probative value to specific facts in evidence or draws a particular inference as to the existence of a fact that is not actually known but which arises from other facts that are known or proven. A presumption is distinguished from an inference in that a judge or jury may or may not, as it chooses, infer that a thing is true, whereas a presumption requires the inference to be drawn. Some presumptions are rebuttable; others are irrebuttable.

disproven by the facts. Hence, defendants are innocent until proven guilty. *Irrebuttable presumptions* are conclusions that must be made by the judge or jury and cannot be disproved. Regardless of what the evidence shows, an irrebuttable presumption stands as a fact.

Motive

The reason a person commits a crime is **motive.** More particularly, the reason that leads a person to a desired result or particular action is motive.

Motive is different from mens rea. Motive leads to mens rea. Motive is concerned with why people act. Mens rea, in contrast, is concerned with whether a person intended to act. For example, greed is a motive for many acts. A bank robber's motive for robbing a bank is greed (or even, possibly, the challenge). The robber's mens rea is neither greed nor the emotional thrill resulting from the risk; rather, it is the intent to take money using force or threat. Said another way, the robber's mens rea (intent) is used to satisfy his or her motive (greed).

Motive is not an element of crimes. Therefore, prosecutors do not have to prove motive to be successful in a prosecution. As a practical matter, however, the trier of fact will want to know why the defendant committed the alleged crime. In many crimes, the motive will be apparent. Greed is easily understood and is imputed by juries to accused thieves. In other crimes, such as murder, there may be no apparent motive, and the prosecutor must establish the defendant's reason for committing the crime. Was the murder motivated by greed (e.g., to gain an inheritance), or by passion (e.g., in revenge for infidelity), or some other emotion? Usually, the prosecutor will prove motive, but in a case in which the defendant has pleaded insanity, the defendant bears the burden of providing either that there was no motive (e.g., the defendant did not want this to happen, but a mental disease or defect made her do it), or that the motive was the product of insanity (e.g., he believed the decedent was Godzilla).

A bad motive does not make an otherwise lawful act criminal. Conversely, a good motive does not excuse the commission of a crime. The issue is simply whether the prosecution has proven, beyond a reasonable doubt, that all the elements of the crime were committed.

Motive plays a role at sentencing. A good motive may justify a mitigation of sentence, whereas a bad motive may act in the reverse.

In some instances, a good motive may prevent charges from being filed at all. Police and prosecutors do not pursue some cases, even though

---
BALLENTINE'S
---

motive   The reason that leads the mind to desire a result; that which leads the mind to engage in a criminal act; that which causes the mind to form intent; the reason for an intention.

a crime has been committed, when a person acted with good intentions. Conversely, law enforcement officials may pursue a case more passionately if the defendant acted from an evil motive.

Actus Reus

Earlier in this chapter you learned the Latin phrase "actus non facit reum nisi mens sit rea." The phrase expresses the common-law requirement that two essential elements must be present to have a crime: a guilty mind and a guilty act. **Actus reus** is the physical part of a crime; it is the act engaged in by the accused. An act is a physical movement. If Mrs. X shoots and kills Mrs. T, the act is pulling the trigger of the gun.

The Model Penal Code states that a "person is not guilty of an offense unless his liability is based on conduct that includes a voluntary act."[14]

Voluntariness

To be held criminally liable for one's actions, those actions must be voluntary. To be voluntary, an act must occur as a result of the actor's conscious choice. The person accused must have acted freely, or no liability attaches. The Model Penal Code requires that acts be voluntary and specifically lists the following as being involuntary:

1. reflexes and convulsions;
2. bodily movements during unconsciousness or sleep;
3. conduct during hypnosis or resulting from hypnotic suggestion; and
4. other movements that are not a product of the effort or determination of the actor.[15]

Do not confuse the concepts of mens rea and actus reus. All that is required to have an act is a choice by the defendant to act. No evil intent is required to have an act; that is a question of mens rea. Say that Jim chooses to swing his arm. As a result he hits Tom. What intent is required to prove battery and whether Jim possessed that intent are questions of mens rea. For actus reus, all that need be known is whether Jim voluntarily chose to swing his arm. His swing would be involuntary if Bill grabbed Jim's arm and moved it, causing it to strike Tom.

BALLENTINE'S
---

actus reus An "answerable act," i.e., an act for which one is answerable; a guilty act. In combination with mens rea ... , actus reus is an essential element of any crime.

In the *Cogdon* case, a woman was acquitted of murdering her daughter because it was determined that her acts were not voluntary.

KING
v.
COGDON
Supreme Court of Victoria (1950)[16]

Mrs. Cogdon was charged with the murder of her only child, a daughter called Pat, aged 19. Pat had for some time been receiving psychiatric treatment for a relatively minor neurotic condition of which, in her psychiatrist's opinion, she was now cured. Despite this, Mrs. Cogdon continued to worry unduly about her. Describing the relationship between Pat and her mother, Mr. Cogdon testified: "I don't think a mother could have thought any more of her daughter. I think she absolutely adored her." On the conscious level, there was no doubt [of] Mrs. Cogdon's deep attachment to her daughter.

To the charge of murdering Pat, Mrs. Cogdon pleaded not guilty. Her story, though somewhat bizarre, was not seriously challenged by the Crown, and led to her acquittal. She told how on the night before her daughter's death she had dreamt that their house was full of spiders and that these spiders were crawling all over Pat. In her sleep, Mrs. Cogdon left the bed she shared with her husband, went into Pat's room and awakened to find herself violently brushing at Pat's face, presumably to remove the spiders. This woke Pat. Mrs. Cogdon told her she was just tucking her in. At the trial, she testified that she still believed, as she had been told, that the occupants of a nearby house bred spiders as a hobby, preparing nests for them behind the pictures on their walls. It was these spiders that in her dreams had invaded their home and attacked Pat. There had also been a previous dream in which ghosts had sat at the end of Mrs. Cogdon's bed and she had said to them, "Well, you have come to take Pattie." It does not seem fanciful to accept the psychological explanation of these spiders and ghosts as the projections of Mrs. Cogdon's subconscious hostility towards her daughter; a hostility which was itself rooted in Mrs. Cogdon's own early life and marital relationship.

The morning after the spider dream she told her doctor of it. He gave her a sedative and, because of the dream and certain previous difficulties she had reported, discussed the possibility of psychiatric treatment. That evening Mrs. Cogdon suggested to her husband that he attend his lodge meeting, and asked Pat to come with her to the cinema. After he had gone Pat looked through the paper, not unusually found no tolerable programme, and said that as she was going out the next evening she thought she would rather go to bed early. Later while Pat was having a bath preparatory to retiring, Mrs. Cogdon went into her room, put a hot water bottle in the bed, turned back the bedclothes, and placed a glass of hot milk beside the bed ready for Pat. She then went to bed herself. There was some desultory conversation between them about the war in Korea, and just before she put out her light Pat called out to her mother, "Mum, don't be so silly worrying about the war, it's not on our front step yet."

Mrs. Cogdon went to sleep. She dreamt that "the war was all around the house," that the soldiers were in Pat's room, and that one soldier was on the bed attacking Pat. This is all of the dream that she could later recapture. Her first "waking" memory was of running from Pat's room, out of the house to the home of her sister who lived next door. When her sister opened the front door Mrs. Cogdon fell into her arms crying, "I think I've hurt Pattie."

In fact Mrs. Cogdon had, in her somnambulistic state, left her bed, fetched an axe from the woodheap, entered Pat's room, and struck her two accurate forceful blows on the head with the blade of the axe, thus killing her.

* * *

At all events the jury believed Mrs. Cogdon's story … [Mrs. Cogdon] was acquitted because the act of killing itself was not, in law, regarded as her act at all. …

No defense of insanity was raised in this case. If it had been, the analysis would have been different. In most jurisdictions one cannot claim lack of a voluntary act if insanity is also claimed. In those situations the rules of the insanity defense apply.[17] See Chapter 8 for a complete discussion of insanity as a defense.

Thoughts and Statements as Acts

Thoughts alone are not acts that can be made criminal. People may think evil thoughts, but if there is no act furthering such a thought, there is no crime.

Generally, people are also free to speak. The First Amendment to the United States Constitution protects freedom of speech. When the First Amendment applies, speech may not be made criminal. There are, however, limits to First Amendment protection of speech. Inciting riots, treason, solicitation, conspiracy, and causing imminent harm to others are examples of speech that may be prohibited. You will learn more about the First Amendment protection of speech later.

Personal Status as an Act

Generally, a person's status cannot be declared criminal. Illness, financial status, race, sex, and religion are examples of human conditions. Some conditions are directly related to illegal behavior. For example, being addicted to illegal narcotics is a condition that cannot be punished. This is because status is generally believed not to be an act. However, using and selling prohibited narcotics are acts and may be punished.

Vagrancy is one area over which there is a split in legal opinion. Some courts have held that vagrancy may be prohibited; others have determined that vagrancy is a condition and does not constitute a crime. One author noted that there is a "growing body of authority" holding such statutes unconstitutional.[18]

In *Robinson v. California*, 370 U.S. 660 (1962), the United States Supreme Court was called upon to review a California statute that made it a crime "either to use narcotics, or to be addicted to the use of narcotics." The Court reversed Robinson's conviction and in the opinion stated:

> This statute, therefore, is not one which punishes a person for the use of narcotics, for their purchase, sale or possession, or for antisocial or disorderly behavior resulting from their administration. It is not a law which even purports to provide or require medical treatment. Rather, we deal with a statute which makes the "status" of narcotic addiction a criminal offense, for which the offender may be prosecuted "at any time before he reforms." California has said that a person can be continuously guilty of this offense, whether or not he has ever used or

possessed any narcotics within the state, and whether or not he has been guilty of any antisocial behavior there.

It is unlikely that any State at this moment in history would attempt to make it a criminal offense for a person to be mentally ill, or a leper, or to be afflicted with a venereal disease. A State might determine that the general health and welfare require that the victims of these and other human afflictions be dealt with by compulsory treatment, involving quarantine, confinement, or sequestration. But, in the light of contemporary human knowledge, a law which made a criminal offense of such a disease would doubtless be universally thought of to be an infliction of cruel and unusual punishment in violation of the Eighth and Fourteenth Amendments. ...

We cannot but consider the statute before us as of the same category. ... We hold that a state law which imprisons a person thus afflicted as a criminal, even though he has never touched any narcotic drug within the State or been guilty of any irregular behavior there, inflicts a cruel and unusual punishment in violation of the Fourteenth Amendment. ...

Possession as an Act

Possession of certain items, such as narcotics, burglary tools or dangerous weapons, may be made criminal. Possession is not, strictly speaking, an act. Possession does not involve an active body movement; rather, possession is a passive state of being. Even so, most possession laws have been upheld.

Jurisdictions differ in what is required to prove possession. Some require that actual possession be shown, whereas others allow proof of constructive possession. Constructive possession is used to extend criminal liability to those who never exercised actual possession, but had dominion and control over the contraband. A person who is the owner and driver of a car may never possess the cocaine that his passenger is using, but the law says that the driver is in constructive possession because the dominion and control over the auto belong to the driver. In essence, the law imposes a duty on people to remove illegal items from the area over which they have dominion and control. Failure to comply with such a duty is treated as an act and can lead to criminal liability.

One problem with crimes of possession is the possibility of convicting people who had no knowledge of the existence of illegal items in an area under their dominion and control. An owner of a house has dominion and control over the guest room, but may not be aware that a guest has brought illegal items into the room. Most jurisdictions have remedied this problem by requiring knowledge of the presence of the goods. The Model Penal Code also uses such a test. The Code states that possession is an act as long as the "possessor knowingly procured or received the thing possessed or was aware of his control thereof for a sufficient period to have been able to terminate his possession."[19] Under the Code, possession can be actual or constructive. However, if constructive, the possessor must have known of the items for a period of time long enough to permit the possessor to terminate possession. So, if the owner of the house only discovered the cocaine minutes before the police arrived to search the premises, no possession could be found on the owner's behalf.

Finally, one person or many people can be in possession of items. Using the preceding example, assume that two or more people jointly owned the home in question. All of the owners could be liable, if it was determined that all had constructive possession and adequate time to remove the cocaine from the house. It is possible that fewer than all of the owners knew of the cocaine, and, as such, did not have constructive possession. Each person who is alleged to have dominion and control (constructive possession) must be examined individually, and separate decisions as to their individual liability must be made.

Omissions as Acts

Generally, only acts are prohibited by criminal law. Rarely does criminal law require a person to act. However, in some situations people have a duty to act, and failure to act is criminal. An **omission** is a failure to act when required to do so by criminal law.

It is often the case that a person who may have a moral duty to act does not have a legal duty to act. In most instances people do not have a legal duty to assist one another in times of need. It would not be criminal in most jurisdictions for an excellent swimmer to watch another drown. Nor would it be criminal to watch another walk into a dangerous situation, such as a bank robbery in progress, if the observer had no connection with the criminal event. There are exceptions to this rule. To be liable for a failure to act, a person must have a "duty" to act. The duty to act can come about in many different ways.

Duty Imposed by Statute

First, criminal statutes may impose a duty to act. The following are examples of duties imposed by statutes: businesses that store or dispose of toxic materials are required to file certain documents; taxpayers are required to file tax returns; and those involved in automobile accidents are required to stop at the scene of the accident.

Under the common law, in most instances, people had no duty to assist others whose lives were in danger. Today criminal statutes may impose liability for failure to assist someone in danger. A few states have

omission   Not doing something required by the law.

enactments that directly change the common-law rule and require people to assist others who are in danger. However, even in those jurisdictions, rescue need not be attempted if the rescuer's life would thereby be endangered.[20] Imposing criminal liability for not rescuing someone in danger of losing life or limb continues to be the exception and not the rule. However, no legal reason prevents all jurisdictions from requiring people to rescue one another when there is no danger associated with the rescue.

At common law, several exceptions to the "no duty to assist people in danger" rule evolved. Many of these are discussed in the following paragraphs. Bear in mind that many legislatures have codified one or more of these exceptions. In those instances, the duty is imposed by statute and not the common law.

Duty by Relationship

A duty to assist another can be created by the existence of a personal relationship. The most common examples are parent to child and spouse to spouse. In such personal relationships, a level of dependence exists that gives rise to criminal liability for failure to assist the party who is in danger. There is no bright-line rule for determining if a duty is owed. The more that one party becomes dependent upon another party or the parties become dependent upon one another, the more likely that a duty to assist is created.

Generally, any time a joint enterprise is undertaken by two or more parties, it can be assumed that a duty to assist one another during that enterprise is created. For example, if two people decide to go river rafting, they must rescue one another during that rafting trip, provided that that the rescuer is not endangered by attempting the rescue.

In the parent-child relationship, a parent can be guilty of manslaughter if the child dies as a result of the parent's failure to seek medical attention for the child when he or she is sick, or for failing to pull the child out of a pool when the child is drowning. The same would be true of a spouse. If a wife permitted her husband to die when she could have saved his life by summoning medical attention, she could be criminally liable. In addition, it has been held that employers owe a duty to assist their employees. For example, the master of a ship must attempt to rescue a seaman who has fallen overboard.[21]

Duty by Contract

A duty to act can be created in a third way, by contract. For example, physicians are hired to care for the health of their patients. If a doctor watches as a patient slowly dies, doing nothing to save the patient's life when there were measures that could have been taken, the doctor is liable for homicide. The same is true of a lifeguard. The lifeguard is hired to save those who are drowning, and if a lifeguard sits and watches a swimmer drown when the swimmer could have been saved, the lifeguard is liable for homicide.

Remember, the general rule is that people owe no duty to rescue others. So, if an expert swimmer happens to be on the beach when another person is drowning, the expert swimmer can watch the person drown without risking criminal liability.

Assumption of Duty

Even though the general rule is that people do not have a duty to rescue strangers, it is possible, either expressly or by one's actions, to make an *assumption of duty*. The assumption is express if it is stated orally or in writing. Assumption is different from duty premised on contract, in that assumptions are gratuitous. If Sidney is at a pool and agrees to care for another's child, then Sidney has assumed the duty expressly. If the child falls into the pool, and Sidney takes no action to save the child, Sidney is liable for murder if the child drowns.

It is possible through one's actions to assume the duty to rescue someone. Assume that Sidney is now at a lake. One person, David, is swimming, and three other people are relaxing on the beach. David begins to scream for help. Sidney jumps up and dives into the water to rescue David. Halfway out to David, he changes his mind and returns to shore. By the time he returns to shore, it is too late for someone else to make the swim to David, and David dies. In this case, Sidney assumed the duty of the rescue by beginning the rescue attempt. However, whether Sidney is liable for murder depends on what condition the drowning person was left in after Sidney changed his mind. If Sidney's actions caused the other three people on the beach to fail to attempt a rescue, then Sidney's actions left David in a worse condition than he would have been in had Sidney not begun the rescue. However, if Sidney's actions did not prevent anyone else from attempting a rescue, then Sidney's action did not put David in a worse situation, and Sidney is not liable for murder, even if the other person fails in the rescue attempt.

Finally, note that we can easily change this last example into an express assumption. All that has to be added is a statement by Sidney to the others on the beach that he will swim out and rescue David. Such a statement, if it caused others to forgo a rescue attempt, is an express assumption of duty.

Creating Danger

Any time a person creates the circumstance that endangers a stranger, a duty to save the stranger is created. This is true whether the danger was caused intentionally or negligently. So, if an arsonist sets fire to a house that is believed to be empty and is discovered not to be, the arsonist must attempt to save anyone inside. If not, the arsonist is also a murderer. The same would be true of a negligently caused fire. If an electrician begins a fire in a home and does nothing to warn the inhabitants, the electrician is also liable for murder.

Causation

Some acts are criminal even though the prohibited result does not occur. For example, it is a crime to lie when testifying in court (the crime of perjury). Assume that the purpose of the lie is to deceive the jury and change the outcome of the case. Even if no juror, or anyone else for that matter, believes the lie, and the purpose is not achieved, it is a crime. Causation is not an issue in such crimes.

For crimes that do require a particular result, the act must be the "cause" of the result. In criminal law, two forms of causation exist: factual and legal. If either of these "causes" is missing, then a defense as to the intent of the crime exists. Even if so, the actor may be convicted of a lower, non-intent crime.

An act is the *cause in fact* of the result if the result would not have occurred unless the act occurred. This is known as the *sine qua non* test, which means that "but for" the conduct the harm would not have resulted.

Legal cause must also be proved. Legal causation focuses on the degree of similarity between the defendant's intended result and the actual result. It also examines the similarity between the intended manner used to bring about a result and the actual manner that caused the result. Generally, the greater the similarity between the purpose and the result, and the manner intended and the manner that actually caused the result, the more likely that the defendant is the legal cause. Legal cause is also commonly referred to as **proximate cause**. *Proximate* means nearly, next to, or close. In the context of criminal causation, it refers to the relationship between the act and the result. The result must be a consequence of the act, not a coincidence. A happening is

---

BALLENTINE'S

legal cause   1. The proximate cause of an injury. 2. Probable cause. 3. Cause that the law deems sufficient.

proximate cause   As an element of liability in a tort case, that cause which, unbroken by any intervening cause, produced the injury, and without which the result would not have occurred; the primary cause; the efficient cause. Note that the proximate cause of an injury is not necessarily the final cause or the act or omission nearest in time to the injury.

proximately caused by an act if a reasonable person would have foreseen and expected the result. This is called **foreseeability**.

Most problems raised in this area involve legal causation, not factual causation. This is because, to prove factual causation, it must be shown that the defendant took an act which set into motion the events that led to the prohibited result. The question that should be asked is, had the defendant not taken the act or acts in question, would the result have happened? If the answer is no, then the defendant is the factual cause. Determining legal causation is more troublesome, however.

Let us examine a few examples. Hank shoots Mark intending to kill him. Mark dies from the gunshot wound. Hank is the factual cause of the murder because it was his conduct that caused Mark to die. To state it another way, "but for" Hank's act Mark would not have died. Hank is also the legal cause of Mark's death because the resulting death is identical to Hank's intention.

Now assume that Hank intended only to injure Mark, not to kill him. Accordingly, he shot Mark in the arm. Mark then contacted a hospital, which dispatched an ambulance. The paramedics who arrived to assist Mark negligently administered a dangerous medication, which caused his death. Hank continues to be the factual cause of Mark's death, because if he had not injured Mark the medical attention that ended Mark's life would not have been necessary. However, Hank is not the legal cause of Mark's death. This is because the result greatly differs from Hank's intent. There is not enough similarity between Hank's purpose when he shot Mark (to cause an injury) and the resulting harm (Mark's death).

Note that it is common for legal cause to be lacking when an **intervening cause** exists, as it does in this example. An *intervening cause* is a happening that occurs after the initial act and changes the outcome stemming from that act. Intervening causes act to block the connection between an act and the result, because the intervening cause changes what would have been the result if the result had flowed freely from the act. Intervening causes can negate or lower criminal liability for the particular result. However, lower crimes may continue to be punishable. In the preceding example, the intervening cause is the negligent medical care of the paramedics. Hank's intent was not to cause Mark's death, and, as such, he was not the legal cause of Mark's death. Of course, Hank may also have a mens rea defense.

BALLENTINE'S

foreseeable   That which may be anticipated or known in advance; that which a person should have known.

intervening cause   A cause that intrudes between the negligence of the defendant and the injury suffered by the plaintiff, breaking the connection between the original wrongful act or omission and the injury, and itself becoming the proximate cause of the injury.

Assume that Hank shot Mark intending to kill him, but because Hank is a poor shot he only injured Mark. As before, the paramedics who treat Mark negligently administer the wrong medication and cause his death. Again, Hank is the factual cause of Mark's death. Whether he is the legal cause is debatable. Even though the intended result occurred, it occurred in a manner entirely unintended. If the manner in which the result occurs differs significantly from the manner that was intended, the defendant may not be liable. This appears consistent with common notions of fairness—why should Hank be liable for murder when at least part of the blame belongs to the paramedics? Courts are split on this issue, and some would find that Hank is liable for intent murder, whereas others would hold Hank liable for a lower murder.

If a victim suffers the intended injury while attempting to avoid the injury, the defendant is liable for the crime, even though the manner is entirely different than intended. So if Mark is struck and killed by a bus while running from Hank, who intends to stab Mark to death, Hank is considered both the legal and factual cause of Mark's death. There is a limit to this theory; that is, there must be some nexus between the unintended manner and the act. If a reasonable person would not have expected the result to occur, the defendant is not liable. So, if Mark was not killed by a passing bus, but rather by a hit on the head by a piano accidentally dropped by movers, Hank is not the legal cause of his death. This is true even though Mark would not have happened to be under the piano if he were not running from Hank.

In the rare instance where two events happen at the same time (simultaneously), and both could be the legal cause of the outcome, then both are treated as the legal cause. This is true even if only one event was the actual cause. For example, if two people shoot a victim at the same moment, then both are liable for murder. However, it is possible that only one actually caused the death. If it is not possible to determine which bullet was the actual cause of death, then both people are liable. If it can be determined which bullet was responsible for killing the victim, then the other party is relieved of responsibility for murder (although not attempted murder).

Even though the preceding examples dealt with purposeful crimes, remember that the principle applies to all crimes that require a particular result. The result need not be one that comes about purposefully or intentionally. Crimes of recklessness and negligence may require a specific result to be criminal. Reckless homicide requires that the behavior that is reckless actually cause a death.

The Model Penal Code also requires that the conduct in question be the actual result or cause of the result. Also, under the Model Penal Code, if a particular result is necessary to prove a crime, then the "element is not established unless the actual result is a probable consequence of the actor's conduct." Further, the Code states that the crime is not proven if the actual result is different from the defendant's purpose, unless:

1. The resulting harm is the same, however it occurred to the wrong person or thing (transferred intent).

2. The actual harm is not as great or serious as intended.

3. The actual harm involves the same kind of injury or harm as intended and is not *too remote or accidental* in its occurrence to have a bearing on the actor's liability.

These apply to all levels of culpability under the Code—that is, purposeful, knowing, reckless, and negligent—and must be adjusted accordingly. So, if the crime is one of recklessness or negligence, then the Code's criteria should be viewed in light of risks and probable results and not purpose.[22]

The phrase "too remote or accidental" is the Code's proximate cause requirement. It is the same as discussed earlier, except that the drafters of the Code chose not to use the phrase "proximate cause." In *People v. Warner-Lambert Co.*, a company and some of its officers were indicted for manslaughter and negligent homicide. The charges stemmed from an industrial accident at one of Warner-Lambert's plants. The high court of New York dismissed the indictments, finding that the defendants were not the proximate cause of the plant employees' deaths because the explosion that caused their deaths was not foreseeable.

PEOPLE

v.

WARNER-LAMBERT CO.

51 N.Y.2d 295, 414 N.E.2d 660 (1980),

cert. denied, 450 U.S. 1031 (1981)

On the day on which the explosion occurred, Freshen-Up gum, which is retailed in the shape of a square tablet with a jelly-like center, was being produced at the Warner-Lambert plant by a process in which filled ropes of the gum were passed through a bed of magnesium stearate (MS), a dry, dustlike lubricant which was applied by hand, then into a die-cut punch (a Uniplast machine) which was sprayed with a cooling agent (liquid nitrogen), where the gum was formed into the square tablets. Both the MS (normally an inert, organic compound) and the liquid nitrogen were employed to prevent the chicle from adhering to the sizing and cutting machinery, the tendency to adhere being less if a dry lubricant was used and the punch was kept at a low temperature. The process produced a dispersal of MS dust in the air and an accumulation of it at the base of the Uniplast machine and on overhead pipes; some also remained ambient in the atmosphere in the surrounding area.

Both MS and liquid nitrogen are considered safe and are widely used in the industry. In bulk, MS will only burn or smoulder if ignited; however, like many substances, if suspended in the air in sufficient concentration the dust poses a substantial risk of explosion if ignited. ... Liquid nitrogen is highly volatile, is easily ignited and, if ignited, will explode. Among possible causes of such ignition of either liquid oxygen or ambient MS are electrical or mechanical sparks.

* * *

There was proof that an inspection of the plant by Warner-Lambert's insurance carrier in February, 1976, had resulted in advice to the insured that the dust condition in the Freshen-Up gum production area presented an explosion hazard and that the MS concentration was above the [low point where explosion could occur], together with recommendations for installation of a dust exhaust system and modification of electrical equipment to meet standards for dust areas. Although a variety of proposals for altering the dust condition were considered by the individual defendants in consultations and communications with each other and some alterations in the MS application were made, both ambient and settled MS dust were still present on November 21, 1976.

* * *

The issue before us, however, is whether defendants could be held criminally liable for what actually occurred, on theories of reckless or negligent conduct, based on the evidence submitted to this Grand Jury, viewed in the light most favorable to the People. The focus of our attention must be on the issue of culpability, taking into account the conduct of the defendants and the factors of foreseeability and of causation, all of which in combination constitute the ultimate amalgam on which criminal liability may or may not be predicated.

First, we look at the evidence as to the actual event or chain of events which triggered the explosion—evidence which may only be characterized as hypothetical and speculative. ... The prosecution hypothesizes that under what it describes as "the most plausible of theories" the initial detonation was attributable to mechanical sparking. ...

Another explanation for the initial explosion was offered by an expert called by the prosecution who hypothesized that liquid oxygen ... dripped onto settled MS dust at the base of the Uniplast, became trapped there and then, when subjected to the impact caused by a moving metal part, reacted violently, causing ignition of already dispersed MS.

Viewed most favorably to the People, the proof with respect to the actual cause of the explosion is speculative only, and as to at least one of the major hypotheses—that involving oxygen liquefaction—there was no evidence that the process was foreseeable or known to any of the defendants. In sum, there was no proof sufficient to support a finding that defendants foresaw or should have foreseen the physical cause of the explosion. This being so there was not legally sufficient evidence to establish the offenses charged or any lesser included offense.

The "Year and a Day Rule"

At common law, a person could not be charged with murder if the victim did not die within one year and one day after the act took place. The rule was one of causation. It was developed to prevent a conviction for murder at a time in history when medical science was not precise enough to determine the actual cause of a person's death. If a person lived for more than a year and a day after being injured by a defendant's acts and then died, it was assumed that medical science could not pinpoint the exact cause of death and that to hold the defendant liable would be unjust. It is questionable, in light of the advances in medicine, whether the rule should continue to exist;[23] it has been abolished in many states.

SIDEBAR   AVOIDING PROSECUTION As David Lebron Cross sits in a Cobb County, Georgia, jail, he has developed a great appreciation for common law. And well he should, because it may be England's creation of the "year-and-a-day rule" that will keep him from going to trial for murder.

Cross was charged with child abuse in August 1987, after he allegedly shook his four-month-old daughter, Sala, so hard she incurred brain damage and became comatose. Doctors determined that the baby would not recover and recommended she be taken off life support. Cross, however, fought attempts by his wife, Linda Lawson Cross, to let Sala die.

Finally, in December 1988, Fulton County Superior Court Judge Don Langham ruled that keeping Sala alive by artificial means was "cruel and inhumane." The infant was taken off life support and died within a few weeks, seventeen months after she was first hospitalized.

Cross was indicted for homicide. Prosecutor Fonda Clay said Cross admitted shaking the baby, but said he did it because Sala was choking on her bottle. Prosecutors claim, though, that Cross had abused the child before, breaking one of her legs and two ribs just two weeks before the alleged shaking.

But on August 2, Cobb County Superior Court Judge Watson White granted a defense motion to throw out the murder indictment because the infant's death occurred more than a year and a day after the alleged incident.

"After reviewing the law, I don't see anywhere in any cases or statutes where the year-and-a-day rule has been revoked," White said. "Therefore, it must still be in effect."

Child-abuse prosecutor Bruce Hornbuckle, who is handling the case, plans an appeal directly to the Georgia Supreme Court.

"The year-and-a-day rule is archaic and out of date with today's medical technology," he said. "In the year 1200, when a guy died two years after getting hit in the head with a brick, this was probably a good law."

Now, he said, the law "opens the door for murderers to use advances in medical technology to ... beat the murder rap."

Cross's attorney said there was no intentional plan to keep Sala alive long enough to invoke the year-and-a-day rule. "Is the rule open to abuse? Yes," Cohen said. "Is it still the law in Georgia? Yes. Should David Cross be charged with murder? No."

Hornbuckle plans to argue on appeal that when the Georgia legislature rewrote the criminal code in 1968 and did not include the year-and-a-day rule, it in effect voided it.

According to briefs filed by Hornbuckle, courts in Michigan, New Jersey, Ohio, Oklahoma, Pennsylvania, and Rhode Island have abolished the rule, while only Maryland and Missouri have upheld it.

Of the thirteen states that had enacted the rule by statute, only four retained it as of 1986. New York and Oregon courts held that the rule was abrogated when the legislature failed to include it in comprehensive criminal code revisions. Also, California and Washington have revised their rules to prohibit murder charges when the victim's death occurs *three years* and a day after the assault.

"Authorities across Georgia have frequently chosen not to try cases because of the year-and-a-day rule," said Joseph Chambers, executive director of the Prosecuting Attorneys Council in Georgia.

"The common-law rule was never designed to allow child abusers to avoid a murder conviction through advances in medical technology, and every state legislature should consider revising it. But on the other hand, it's also unfair for defendants to have such serious charges hanging over their heads all their lives. At some point there has to be an end to when you hold a person responsible for an act that occurred years earlier."

In a similar case in Warren County, Pennsyvania, near Pittsburgh, Tracey Crane is expected to stand trial this winter for the murder of her daughter, Leslie. Crane and her husband, David, had opposed the removal of life-support systems that were keeping their daughter alive.

Excerpted from the October 1990 issue of the ABA Journal, the *Lawyer's Magazine*, published by the American Bar Association.

Concurrence

In this chapter you have learned that there are two primary components of crimes, the mental and the physical. Although a showing of mens rea is not required for every crime, there must be a showing of some act or omission for all crimes.

For crimes that have both a mental and a physical element, an additional requirement of concurrence must be proved. *Concurrence* is the joining of mens rea and the act. The mens rea must be the reason that the act was taken. Stated another way, the mental state must occur first and set into motion the act. For example, Doug hates Andy and desires to see him dead. Because of this feeling, Doug waits for Andy to leave the house one night and runs him down with a car. In such a case, Doug's mens rea set into motion the act that caused Andy's death. Now imagine that Doug accidentally kills Andy in an auto accident. After the accident Doug exclaims his happiness over Andy's demise. In this case, the mens rea occurred after the act. It was not the catalyst for the act that killed Andy, and, as such, there was no concurrence.

The mere fact that the mental state happens before the act does not mean that there is concurrence. There must be a connection between the intent and the act; the mens rea must set the act into motion. So if Doug forms the desire to kill Andy today, but takes no action to further the desire, he cannot be charged with murder a year later when he accidentally shoots Andy while hunting.

As stated by the Court of Appeals of Indiana:

> Unless statutorily stated otherwise, it is black letter law that in order to constitute a crime "criminal intent" ... must unite with an overt act, and they must concur in point of time. There must be a criminal act or omission as well as criminal intent. A felonious intent unconnected with an unlawful act constitutes no crime. ... A person can only be punished for an offense he has committed and never for an offense he may commit in the future. A crime cannot be predicated upon future acts or upon contingencies or the taking effect of some future event.[24]

Review Questions

1. In criminal law, causation is broken down into two forms. Name and briefly describe each.

2. Can a person be prosecuted for failing to save a stranger from danger? Why or why not?

3. What is concurrence?

4. What is an omission?

5. The Model Penal Code recognizes four types of mens rea. Name and briefly describe each.

6. What is vicarious liability?

7. What is a rebuttable presumption? An irrebuttable presumption?

8. Can corporations and other associations be guilty of crimes?

9. Distinguish mens rea from motive.

Review Problems

1–6. Many prisoners in the state and federal correctional systems are held at minimum-security "farms." Only inmates considered not to be dangerous are housed at these facilities because of the minimal security. In fact, in many cases it is possible for inmates to simply walk off. Of course, most do not leave the premises, because to do so results in an increased sentence (either due to a conviction for escape or a decrease in "good time") and a likelihood that the sentence will be spent in prison rather than the more desirable farm. Despite this, prisoners of these facilities do escape. What follows are several different sets of facts involving a ficticious inmate, Spike Vincelli. Read each and discuss the defenses, if any, that Spike may have against a charge of escape. Discuss each in light of the following two statutes:

Statute I:
   It shall be unlawful for any person committed to any correctional facility to escape from that facility. Escape is defined as passing beyond the borders of a facility with an intent to never return or being lawfully beyond the borders of the facility and not returning when required to do so with an intent to never return. Violation of this statute constitutes a felony.

Statute II:
   It shall be unlawful for any person committed to any correctional facility to leave the premises of the facility. Leaving is defined as passing over the boundary lines of the facility. Violation of this statute constitutes a misdemeanor.

1. On June 21, Spike Vincelli received a telephone call from a hospital informing him that his mother had been involved in a serious accident. That evening Spike left to see his mother, intending to return in the morning.

2. On June 21, Spike Vincelli had his first epileptic seizure. The seizure caused Spike to fall outside the boundary line surrounding the facility.

3. On June 21, Spike Vincelli decided that he was bored with living on the farm. That night he walked off the premises and fled for a friend's house 300 miles away, intending never to return.

4. On June 21, Spike Vincelli became involved in a fight with Ben Ichabod. In a fit of rage, Ben picked Spike up and threw him over the fence surrounding the farm. Spike was caught outside the fence by a guard before he had an opportunity to return.

5. In early April, Spike Vincelli decided that he was going to escape. He developed a plan that called for him to leave in July and meet his brother, who was passing through the area. As part of the plan, Ben Ichabod, a fellow inmate, was enlisted to pick Spike up off the ground and throw him over the fence that surrounded the facility. However, Ben, who is not very bright, threw Spike over the fence on June 21.

6. On June 21, Spike Vincelli became involved in a fight with Ben Ichabod. Ben, in a fit of rage, picked Spike up and threw him over the fence surrounding the facility. While outside the fence Spike became overcome with a sense of freedom and ran from the facility.

7. Fred failed to show up for a date he had made with Penni. Penni, who was angered by Fred's actions, decided to vent her anger by cutting the tires of Fred's automobile. However, Penni did not know what make of automobile Fred drove and mistakenly cut the tires of a car owned by Fred's neighbor, Stacey. Penni is now charged with the "purposeful destruction of personal property." Penni claims that her act was not purposeful because she did not intend to cut the tires of Stacey's car. Discuss this defense.

8. William, an experienced canoeist, was hired by a Boy Scout troop to supervise a canoe trip. While on the trip two boys fell out of their canoe and began to drown. William watched as the boys drowned. Is William criminally liable for the deaths?

9. Sherri, who was near bankruptcy, decided to burn her house down and make an insurance claim for the loss. Sherri started the fire, which spread to a neighbor's house located twenty feet from Sherri's home. Unknown to Sherri, her neighbor was storing massive quantities of dynamite in the home. The fire at the neighbor's house spread to the room where the explosives were being stored, and the resulting explosion caused such vibrations that a construction worker one block away fell off a ladder and subsequently died from the fall. Sherri is charged with arson and murder. She has pled guilty to arson, but maintains that she is not liable for the death of the worker. Is she correct?

10. The following statute was enacted by State Legislature:

> It shall be unlawful for any person to be a pedophile. Pedophilia is defined as a condition where a person over the age of seventeen years possesses a sexual desire for a person under the age of eight years.

While attending a group therapy session, Jane admitted that she had sexual interest in boys under eight years of age. A member of the group contacted the local police and reported Jane's statement. Jane was subsequently arrested and charged with violating the quoted statute. Discuss her defenses, if any.

11. Ashley, Amy, and Karen are roommates in college. They occupy a four-bedroom apartment, and all share in the bills and household duties. One weekend a friend of Karen's, Janice, came to visit. Janice arrived on Thursday and was scheduled to stay until Monday. She stayed in the extra bedroom. On Thursday evening Ashley discovered, while she was watching Janice unpack, that Janice had a significant amount of cocaine in one suitcase. Later that night, Ashley discussed this matter with Karen, who stated, "I'm sure she does—why does it matter to you?" Ashley immediately confronted Janice and told her that she would have to remove the cocaine from the premises or Ashley would call the police. Janice picked up the suitcase, carried it to her car, and placed it in the trunk. The next morning, when Karen learned what Ashley had done, she encouraged Janice to bring the suitcase back into the apartment.

    On Sunday morning the police arrived with a warrant to search the apartment. The search uncovered the suitcase in the extra bedroom. Later, at the police station, the suitcase was opened and the drugs were discovered. All four women were charged with possession. Do Amy, Ashley, or Karen have a defense? The jurisdiction where they live applies the Model Penal Code.

12. In some nations, vicarious criminal liability is much broader than in the United States. For example, parents may be vicariously liable for the criminal acts of their children until the children reach adulthood. Should such laws be adopted in the United States? Explain your answer.

Notes

[1] J. Goldstein, et al., *Criminal Law: Theory and Process* (New York: Free Press, 1974).

[2] 21 AM. JUR. 2d *Criminal Law* 129 (1981).

[3] *See United States v. Birkenstock,* 823 F.2d 1026 (7th Cir. 1987); *United States v. Pompanio,* 429 U.S. 10 (1976).

[4] LaFave & Scott, *Criminal Law* (Hornbook Series, St. Paul: West, 1986), at 217.

[5] LaFave & Scott at 34.

[6] *See Lambert v. California,* 355 U.S. 225 (1957), in which the United States Supreme Court found that a strict liability statute was violative of the due process clause of the United States Constitution.

[7] LaFave & Scott at 244–45.

[8] *See United States v. Dotterweich,* 320 U.S. 277 (1943).

[9] Model Penal Code § 2.07 deals with liability of corporations and unincorporated associations.

[10] Model Penal Code § 2.02, General Requirements of Culpability.

[11] Kaplan & Weisberg, *Criminal Law* (Boston: Little, Brown, 1986).

[12] Model Penal Code § 2.02(2)(c).

[13] The Model Penal Code actually recognizes three "objective elements" that may have differing culpability levels. Those are circumstance, result, and

conduct. Also, the Code provides, at § 2.02(4), that one mental state shall apply to an entire offense, unless a contrary intent is plain.

[14] Model Penal Code § 2.01.

[15] *Id.*

[16] From N. Morris, "Somnambulistic Homicide: Ghosts, Spiders, and North Koreans," 5 *Res Judicata* 29 (1951).

[17] A. Loewy, *Criminal Law,* 2d ed. (Nutshell Series, St. Paul: West, 1987).

[18] LaFave & Scott, at 200.

[19] Model Penal Code § 2.01(4).

[20] Vermont and Rhode Island impose a duty to rescue. *See* Vt. Stat. Ann. tit. 12, § 519; R.I. Gen. Laws § 11-56-1.

[21] *United States v. Knowles,* 26 F. Cas. 800 (N.D. Cal. 1864).

[22] Model Penal Code § 2.03.

[23] Loewy at 55.

[24] *Gebhard v. State,* 484 N.E.2d 45, 48 (Ind. Ct. App. 1985).

CHAPTER 4

CRIMES AGAINST THE PERSON

CHAPTER OUTLINE

Studying Crimes

In the next three chapters you will learn about many crimes. It would be impossible to include a discussion of all crimes. Each city and state has its own unique laws. What follows is a discussion of the major crimes recognized, in some form, in most jurisdictions. The crimes have been categorized as crimes against the person, crimes against property, and crimes against the public. Although it is common to make these distinctions, do not become involved with understanding why these classifications have been made, as they are used only for organizational purposes. In a sense, all crimes are offenses against the public. That is why the public prosecutes crimes, and private individuals may not. Also, any offense "against property" is actually injuring a person, not the property. A stolen television set does not long to be returned to its rightful owner. However, the rightful owner does feel wronged and desires the return of the stolen item. In a sense the classifications are often accurate in that they describe the focus of the criminal conduct. The focus of a thief's act is property; hence, a crime against property. The focus of a rapist's attack is a human; hence, a crime against a person.

All of the following crimes have been broken into parts. Each part of a crime is an **element** of that crime. At trial, every element of a crime must be proven beyond a reasonable doubt by the prosecution. If any element is not proven beyond a reasonable doubt, the accused must be found not guilty. The rule requires that each element be proved individually. That is, if a crime consists of six elements, and a jury is convinced that five have been proven, but cannot say that the sixth has been proven beyond a reasonable doubt, then there must be a not-guilty verdict. This is true even if the jury was solidly convinced that all the other elements were true and generally believed that the defendant committed the crime. Later you will learn more about the "beyond a reasonable doubt" standard.

Finally, you may notice that, often, if one crime has been proven, all the elements of a related lesser crime can also be proved. For example, if a defendant is convicted of murdering someone with a hammer, he has also committed a battery of the victim. In such circumstances, the lesser offense merges into the greater offense. This is the **merger** doctrine. Under this doctrine, both crimes may be charged, but if the defendant is convicted of the more serious crime the lesser is absorbed by the greater, and the defendant is not punished for both. If acquitted of the greater charge, the defendant may be convicted of the lesser.

BALLENTINE'S
---

element   A component or essential part of something.

merger of offenses   The doctrine that when a lesser offense is a component of a more serious offense, prosecution can be only for the greater offense.

Source: Uniform Crime Reports, U.S. Department of Justice, Federal Bureau of Investigation, 1995.

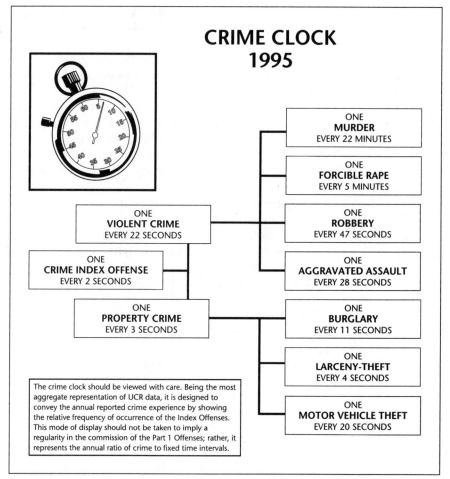

CRIME CLOCK 1995

ONE
MURDER
EVERY 22 MINUTES

ONE
FORCIBLE RAPE
EVERY 5 MINUTES

ONE
VIOLENT CRIME
EVERY 22 SECONDS

ONE
ROBBERY
EVERY 47 SECONDS

ONE
CRIME INDEX OFFENSE
EVERY 2 SECONDS

ONE
AGGRAVATED ASSAULT
EVERY 28 SECONDS

ONE
PROPERTY CRIME
EVERY 3 SECONDS

ONE
BURGLARY
EVERY 11 SECONDS

ONE
LARCENY-THEFT
EVERY 4 SECONDS

ONE
MOTOR VEHICLE THEFT
EVERY 20 SECONDS

The crime clock should be viewed with care. Being the most aggregate representation of UCR data, it is designed to convey the annual reported crime experience by showing the relative frequency of occurrence of the Index Offenses. This mode of display should not be taken to imply a regularity in the commission of the Part 1 Offenses; rather, it represents the annual ratio of crime to fixed time intervals.

Homicide

Homicide is the killing of one human being by another. Not all homicides are crimes. It is possible to cause another person's death accidentally, that is, accompanied by no mens rea, which gives rise to criminal liability.

Criminal homicide occurs when a person takes another's life in a manner proscribed by law. The law proscribes more than intentional killings. Under the Model Penal Code, purposeful, knowing, negligent, and reckless homicides may be punished.

The mens rea part of homicide is important. The determination of what mens rea was possessed by the defendant (actually, what mens rea can be proven by the prosecution) will usually determine what crime may be punished. At common law, various forms of murder were developed. This is where we begin.

Homicide and the Common Law

Initially, at common law, all murders were punished equally: the murderer was executed.[1] Over time, judges realized that the rule was harsh, and the belief that not all homicides should be punished equally developed. As a result, homicides were divided into murder and manslaughter. Manslaughter was punished by incarceration, not death.

Murder, at common law, was defined as: (1) The unlawful killing of a (2) human being with (3) malice aforethought. It was the requirement of malice aforethought that distinguished murder from manslaughter. Although malice aforethought was defined differently among the states, the following types of homicide became recognized as murder under the common law:

1. When the defendant intended to cause the death of the victim.
2. When the defendant intended to cause serious bodily harm, and death resulted.
3. When the defendant created an unreasonably high risk of death that caused the victim's death, regardless of the defendant's mens rea. This was known as "depraved-heart murder."
4. When the doctrine of felony-murder was applicable.

All criminal homicides that did not constitute murder were treated as manslaughter. Today, nearly every jurisdiction further divides murder into degrees, and most divide manslaughter into voluntary and involuntary. Few jurisdictions rely on the common-law definition of malice aforethought. However, many states continue to recognize felony-murder.

The Felony-Murder Doctrine

At common law, one who caused an unintended death during the commission (or attempted commission) of any felony was guilty of murder. This became known as **felony-murder.** Under the early common law all felonies were punished by death. Generally, most of the crimes that were felonies under the common law posed a threat to human life. This threat was one justification for the harshness of the rule. However, as

---
BALLENTINE'S

felony murder rule The rule that a death which occurs by accident or chance during the course of the commission of a felony is first-degree murder. The felony murder rule, which is a common law doctrine, has been modified by statute in most states.

the common law developed, many new crimes were created, many of which did not involve serious threat to human life. For this reason the felony-murder doctrine was very harsh, as it applied to all felonies regardless of their relative dangerousness to human life. In time, courts began to limit the application of the rule to specified felonies; specifically, those perceived as posing the largest threat to human life. It was common to apply the rule to rape, mayhem, arson, kidnapping, and robbery.

For example, Andy and Gene decide to rob the First National Bank. They agreed to use whatever amount of violence is necessary to carry out the robbery. During the robbery a bank teller summoned the police by use of a silent alarm. As Andy and Gene were leaving the bank, the police shouted to them, ordering their surrender. Andy then fired a shot from his gun and fatally wounded a police officer. Using the felony-murder rule, both Gene and Andy are criminally liable for the death of the police officer, even though Gene did not fire the weapon or conspire with Andy to kill the officer.

The felony-murder rule acts to impute the required mens rea to the defendant and to create a form of vicarious liability between co-felons. The rule imputes mens rea because it applies in situations of unintended death; however, murder in the first degree is a specific-intent crime. The rationale is that one who engages in inherently dangerous crimes should be aware of the high risk to human life created by the crime. Vicarious liability is also imposed in some states; that is, all the individuals involved in the perpetration of the crime may be criminally liable for the resulting death.

Today, most states have felony-murder statutes. Generally, the following must be shown to establish a felony-murder:

1. The defendant must have been engaged in the commission, or attempted commission, of a named felony, and
2. during the commission, or attempted commission, of that felony a death occurred, and
3. there is a causal connection between the crime and the death.

In most jurisdictions the legislature has specified the crimes that must be committed, or attempted, for the rule to apply. A few jurisdictions have limited the application of the rule to crimes that were felonies at common law, and others have limited the rule to felonies that involve a threat to human life.

To satisfy the second requirement, it must be determined when the commission of the crime began and when it concluded. This appears to be an easy task, and is in most cases, but there are instances when it is not clear. Suppose that a robber knew that a large sum of money was being transferred between a bank and an armored car at a particular time and intended to steal the money during that transfer. Also assume that the traffic was heavier than anticipated by the robber on the day of the planned robbery and, in an effort to arrive at the bank on time, the robber ran a stop sign. While passing through the intersection, the robber struck another vehicle, killing the driver. Was this death during the commission, or attempted commission, of the robbery? What if a police officer were to chase an individual from the scene of a felony and get shot fifteen minutes and one mile away from the scene of the crime? Is this during the commission, or attempted commission, of the felony? It is likely that no felony-murder would be found in the first example, because the death was too far removed from actual commission of the crime. The result would be different if the robber struck and killed the motorist while fleeing from the police immediately after commission of the holdup. This answers the second question. Courts have generally held that deaths that occur during the flight of a felon are "during the commission of the felony." However, the chase must be immediate, and the rule does not apply if there is a gap between the time the crime occurred, or was attempted, and the time the chase begins.

Requirement number three can be a troublesome requirement. In many ways this requirement is similar to the causation requirement discussed in Chapter 3 regarding actus reus. That is, the commission, or attempted commission, of the felony must be the legal cause (proximate cause) of the death. The death must be a "consequence, not coincidence" of the act; the resulting death must have been a foreseeable consequence of the act. So, if a patron of a store suffers a heart attack during a robbery, which was precipitated by the crime, the robbers are guilty of felony-murder if the patron dies. However, if a patron who is unaware of an ongoing robbery suffers a heart attack and dies, the robbers are not liable for the death. The mere fact that the death and the crime occurred simultaneously does not mean that the robbers were the legal cause of the death.

In some states, the act that causes the death of the victim need not be taken by one of the perpetrators of the crime. For example, if Gene and Andy become involved in a shootout with the police after they rob the First National Bank, and the police accidentally shoot an innocent bystander, then Gene and Andy are guilty of felony-murder. This is because they began the series of events which led to the death of the bystander. However, if a police officer (or another) kills one of many felons who are jointly involved in the commission of the crime, it is generally held that the other felons are not guilty of felony murder.[2]

Although the felony-murder rule does impose vicarious liability between co-felons, this aspect is limited. If a defendant can prove that he did not take the act which caused the death; did not authorize, plan, or encourage the act of his co-felon; and had no reason to believe that his cohort would commit the act, he has a defense to felony-murder in some jurisdictions. Note that the rules concerning parties (principals and accomplices) to crimes may create liability independent of the felony-murder rule. (See Chapter 7 for a discussion of parties to crimes.)

Finally, note that in most jurisdictions that continue to recognize felony-murder, the murder is treated as first-degree murder for the purpose of sentencing. Other statutes provide that felony-murders that occur during named felonies are to be treated as first-degree murder and that murders during "all other felonies" are to be treated as second-degree murder. Even if the statute that creates this "all other felony" category does not expressly state that the felony must involve a danger to human life, it is common for courts to impose the requirement.

In the *Losey* case, a defendant appealed his conviction of involuntary manslaughter and aggravated burglary. The Ohio Court of Appeals applied a statute which read, "No person shall cause the death of another as a proximate result of the offender's committing or attempting to commit a felony." The statute named the crime involuntary manslaughter. The case is interesting from a causation perspective. Read the case and decide for yourself if the defendant should be punished for the death that occurred.

STATE
v.
LOSEY
23 Ohio App. 3d 93, 491 N.E.2d 379 (1985)

Defendant testified that he approached a house located at 616 Whitehorne Avenue shortly after 11:00 P.M. on November 25, 1983; that he knocked at the front door and, upon receiving no response, forced open the door and proceeded to attempt to remove a bicycle. His friend, who had been waiting outside, yelled that a car was slowly approaching. The defendant then placed the bicycle beside the front door and departed, leaving the front door open behind him. James Harper, the owner of 616 Whitehorne Avenue, testified that he heard a noise at approximately 1:00 A.M. Shortly thereafter, his mother, with whom he resided, appeared at his bedroom door inquiring about the noise. They proceeded together to the living room, whereupon they discovered the open front door and the bicycle standing near the door. James Harper stated that he told his mother to go back to her bedroom while he went to

check the rest of the house. After so checking, he returned to the living room and was calling the police when his mother appeared in the hallway looking very upset and then collapsed. He called an emergency squad, which attempted to revive Mrs. Harper for almost an hour when the squadmen pronounced her dead. Prior to the burglary, Mrs. Harper had returned from bingo at approximately 10:00 P.M. that evening and had gone to bed. Based on these facts, the trial court found defendant guilty of aggravated burglary and involuntary manslaughter.

* * *

The doctor's testimony established that defendant's conduct was a cause of Mrs. Harper's death in the sense that it set in motion events which culminated in her death. However, it still must be determined whether defendant was legally responsible for her death—whether the death was the proximate result of his conduct. It is not necessary that the accused be in a position to foresee the precise consequence of his conduct; only that the consequence be foreseeable in the sense that what actually transpired was natural and logical in that it was within the scope of the risk created by his conduct. ...

By the same token, in this case, the causal relationship between defendant's criminal conduct and Mrs. Harper's death was not too improbable, remote, or speculative to form a basis for criminal responsibility. Although the defendant did not engage in loud or violent conduct calculated to frighten or shock, his presence was nevertheless detected by Mrs. Harper .... [Conviction affirmed.]

Misdemeanor Manslaughter

Similar to the felony-murder rule, one may be guilty of misdemeanor manslaughter if a death results from the commission of a misdemeanor, not a felony. Conviction of misdemeanor manslaughter results in liability for manslaughter, often involuntary manslaughter, and not murder.

Just as the felony-murder doctrine has been limited in recent years, so has the crime of misdemeanor manslaughter. This is due in large part to the significant increase in the creation of nonviolent crimes by legislatures and administrative bodies. Many states require that the misdemeanor be *malum in se,* and crimes that are *malum prohibitum* cannot be a basis for misdemeanor manslaughter. Requiring that the misdemeanor have a mens rea element is another limitation; that is, strict liability crimes may not be the basis for misdemeanor manslaughter. There is a trend to reject the misdemeanor manslaughter rule (as there is with the felony-murder rule) and require that one of the four types of culpability recognized by the Model Penal Code (purposeful, knowing, negligent, or reckless) be present before imposing liability.

Statutory Approaches to Homicide

Although the common law recognized only one form of murder, most states now divide murder into degrees; most often into first and second degrees. **First-degree murder** is the highest form of murder and is punished more severely than second-degree murder. **Second-degree murder** is a higher crime than manslaughter.

BALLENTINE'S
---

first-degree murder   Murder committed deliberately with malice aforethought, that is, with premeditation.

second-degree murder   A murder that does not fall into the category of first-degree murder; a murder committed with intent to kill, but without premeditation or deliberation.

SIDEBAR SERIAL AND MASS MURDERERS IN THE UNITED STATES Few crimes generate as much attention as those committed by serial killers and mass murderers.

Serial killers are individuals who kill over long periods of time. Serial killers tend to follow patterns, such as stalking of victims with similar physical characteristics. Ritual is a common pattern of the serial killer, as is sexual motivation.

It is estimated that there are as many as 50 to 100 serial killers in the United States at any given time. The span of killing by most serial killers is longer than four years. The number of serial murders appears to be increasing. Between 1975 and 1988, the number of victims rose from 29 to 42 yearly. In total, between 1975 and 1988, serial killers accounted for as many as 2,161 murders. Most serial killers have been men.

Unlike serial murderers, mass murderers do not act cryptically. A mass murderer randomly kills many people within a short period of time, often minutes. The murders usually occur in a public place, and it is common for the murderer to commit suicide at the close of the killing. Between 1949 and 1990, mass murderers were responsible for at least 150 deaths. Mass murderers are also usually men.

Sources: Eric Hickey, *Serial Murderers and Their Victims* (Brooks/Cole Publishing 1991); "Serial-Murder Aftershocks," *Newsweek,* Aug. 12, 1991; "Silence of the Wolves," *Newsweek,* Feb. 3, 1992.

First- and Second-Degree Murder

For a murder to be of the first degree, the highest crime, it must be shown that the homicide was willful, deliberate, and premeditated. Generally, first-degree murder applies whenever the murderer has as a goal the death of the victim. *Willful,* as used in first-degree murder, is a specific-intent concept. To be willful, the defendant must have specifically intended to cause the death.

Deliberate is usually defined as a cool mind, not acting out of an immediate passion, fear, or rage. The term *premeditated* means to think beforehand. Similar to deliberate, it eliminates impulsive acts from the grasp of first-degree murder. It is commonly said that there must be a gap in time between the decision to kill and the actual act. Of course, the length of the gap is the critical issue. Most courts hold that the gap in time must be "appreciable." Again, this term describes little. The fact is that courts differ greatly in how they define *appreciable.* There are many reported cases where a lapse of only seconds was sufficient.[3] Some courts have held that all that need be shown is that the defendant had adequate time to form the intention before taking the act; the length of time is not determinative of the question.[4]

In *State v. Snowden,* the defendant appealed his conviction of first-degree murder, claiming that he lacked premeditation, and, as such, he should have been convicted of second-degree murder, not first.

Decisions such as this obscure the difference between first- and second-degree murder. Do you agree with the Idaho Court that there can be premeditation even if there is "no appreciable space of time between

```
                              CIRCUIT COURT
   STATE OF WISCONSIN         CRIMINAL DIVISION        MILWAUKEE COUNTY
   - - - - - - - - - - - - - - - - - - - - - - - - - - - - - - - - - -
   STATE OF WISCONSIN, Plaintiff                    INFORMATION

            vs.                              CRIME(S):
                                             See Charging Section Below
   Jeffrey L. Dahmer    05/21/60             STATUTE(S) VIOLATED
   924 N. 25th St.                           See Charging Section Below
   Milwaukee, WI                             COMPLAINING WITNESS:
                                             Donald Domagalski
                    Defendant,               CASE NUMBER:
                                             F-912542
   - - - - - - - - - - - - - - - - - - - - - - - - - - - - - - - - - -
```

I, E. MICHAEL MC CANN, DISTRICT ATTORNEY FOR MILWAUKEE COUNTY, WISCONSIN, HEREBY INFORM THE COURT THAT THE ABOVE NAMED DEFENDANT IN THE COUNTY OF MILWAUKEE, STATE OF WISCONSIN,

COUNT 01: FIRST DEGREE MURDER

COUNT 12: FIRST DEGREE INTENTIONAL HOMICIDE

on or about June 30, 1991, at 924 North 25th Street, City and County of Milwaukee, did cause the death of another human being, Matt Turner a/k/a Donald Montrell, with intent to kill that person contrary to Wisconsin Statutes section 940.01(1).

Upon conviction of each count of First Degree Intentional Homicide and each count of First Degree Murder, Class A Felonies, the penalty is life imprisonment.

DATED

                                        E. MICHAEL MC CANN
                                        DISTRICT ATTORNEY

_____9/10/91_____   *E. Michael McCann*
                                 District Attorney

                                        Jeffrey L. Dahmer
                                            9.10.91

Jeffrey L. Dahmer 9.10.91
x The statement on page
1 is accurate as it applies   (3)
to this pg
        Jeffrey L. Dahmer
               9.10.91

Part of criminal information in Dahmer serial murder case (only count 12 is shown; the other counts were similar).

the intention to kill and the act of killing?" Note that the facts of this case did not require mention of the prior case where it was held that "no appreciable" time has to be shown. The fact that the autopsy evidenced that the murder occurred after the victim suffered torture would justify a murder conviction under the statute.

STATE
v.
SNOWDEN
79 Idaho 266, 313 P.2d 706 (1957)

Defendant Snowden had been playing pool and drinking in a Boise pool room early in the evening. With a companion, one Carrier, he visited a club near Boise, then went to nearby Garden City. There the two men visited a number of bars, and defendant had several drinks. Their last stop was the HiHo Club.

Witnesses related that while defendant was in the HiHo Club he met and talked to Cora Lucyle Dean. The defendant himself said he hadn't been acquainted with Mrs. Dean prior to that time, but he had "seen her in a couple of the joints up town." He danced with Mrs. Dean while at the HiHo Club. Upon departing from the tavern, the two left together.

In statements to police officers, that were admitted in evidence, defendant Snowden said after they left the club Mrs. Dean wanted him to find a cab and take her back to Boise, and he refused because he didn't feel he should pay her fare. After some words, he related:

> She got mad at me so I got pretty hot and I don't know whether I back handed her there or not. And, we got calmed down and decided to walk across to the gas station and call a cab.

They crossed the street, and began arguing again. Defendant said: "She swung and at the same time she kneed me again. I blew my top."

Defendant said he pushed the woman over beside a pickup truck which was standing near a business building. There he pulled his knife—a pocket knife with a two-inch blade—and cut her throat.

The body, which was found the next morning, was viciously and sadistically cut and mutilated.

An autopsy surgeon testified the voice box had been cut, and that this would have prevented the victim from making any intelligible cry. There were other wounds inflicted while she was still alive—one in her neck, one in her abdomen, two in the face, and two on the back of the neck. The second neck wound severed the spinal cord and caused her death. There were other wounds all over the body, and her clothing had been cut away. The nipple of her right breast was missing. There was no evidence of sexual attack on the victim; however, some of the lacerations were around the breasts and vagina of the deceased. ...

> [M]urder is defined by statute as follows:
> All murder which is perpetrated by means of poison, or lying in wait, torture, or by any other kind of willful, deliberate and premeditated killing, or which is committed in the perpetration of, or attempt to perpetrate arson, rape, robbery, burglary, kidnapping, or mayhem, is murder in the first degree. All other murders are of the second degree.

The defendant admitted taking the life of the deceased.

The principal argument of the defendant pertaining to [the charge of premeditated murder] is that the defendant did not have sufficient time to develop a desire to take the life of the deceased, but rather his action was instantaneous and a normal reaction to the physical injury which she dealt him. ...

> There need be no appreciable space of time between the intention to kill and the act of killing. They may be as instantaneous as successive thoughts of the mind. It is only necessary that the act of killing be preceded by a concurrence of will, deliberation, and premeditation on the part of the slayer, and, if such is the case, the killing is murder in the first degree.

In the present case, the trial court had no other alternative than to find the defendant guilty of willful, deliberate, and premeditated killing with malice aforethought in view of the defen-dant's acts in deliberately opening up a pocket knife, next cutting the victim's throat, and then hacking and cutting until he had killed Cora Lucyle Dean ... .

Note that the statute mentioned in *Snowden* to describe first-degree murder is used by many jurisdictions. Those murders that result from poisoning, follow torture, or are traditional felony-murders are often designated first-degree murder. Second-degree murder is commonly given the negative definition "all murders that are not of the first degree are of the second." Second-degree murders differ from first in that the defendant lacked the specific intent to kill or lacked the premeditation and deliberation element of first-degree murder.

SIDEBAR   HOMICIDE IN THE UNITED STATES   There is one murder in the United States every twenty-two minutes. A total of 24,526 people were murdered or the subject of a nonnegligent manslaughter in 1993. This was 9.5 of every 100,000 persons in the United States. Most people are murdered with guns, primarily handguns. Knives, poisons, fists, and other weapons are also used to commit homicides. Murder con-stituted 0.2 percent of all crimes in 1992.

Source: Uniform Crime Reports, U.S. Department of Justice, Federal Bureau of Investigation, 1993 & 1994.

Intent to Do Serious Bodily Harm and the Deadly Weapon Doctrine

One method of reducing a murder from the first degree to the sec-ond is by proving that the defendant did not intend to kill, but only in-tended to cause the victim serious bodily harm. Note that if the defendant intended less than serious bodily harm the crime is either manslaughter or a form of reckless or negligent homicide.

This is an area where inferences are important. Juries (or judges, if the court is acting as the finder of fact) are permitted to view the facts surrounding the murder and determine what the defendant's state of mind was at the time the act occurred. A jury may conclude from the facts that the defendant did intend to cause the death of the victim and con-vict of first-degree murder. If a jury concludes that the defendant did not in-tend to cause the death of the victim, but that the defendant did intend to cause serious bodily injury, then the crime is second-degree murder.

A related inference used in murder cases is the *deadly weapon doctrine.* This is a rule that permits juries to infer that a defendant intended to kill his or her victim if a **deadly weapon** was used in the killing. Being an inference, this conclusion does not have to be drawn; this is a decision for the factfinder. If a jury were to conclude that a defendant's use of a deadly weapon indicated that murder was intended, then a first-degree murder conviction would be warranted. So, if Gwen intended only to injure Fred by shooting him, but Fred died as a result of the wound, then a jury could convict Gwen of first-degree murder. Of course, the jury could reject the inference if they believed that Gwen did not intend to kill Fred, and in that case either second-degree murder (if her intent was to inflict serious bodily injury) or manslaughter would be appropriate.

Any device or item may be a deadly weapon if, from the manner used, it is calculated or likely to produce death or serious bodily injury.[5] The Model Penal Code defines a deadly weapon as "any firearm, or other weapon, device, instrument, material, or substance, whether animate or inanimate, which in the manner it is used or is intended to be used is known to be capable of producing death or serious bodily injury."[6] Under these definitions, some items that are not normally considered deadly may be deadly weapons if their use is calculated to cause serious bodily injury or death. The opposite is also true; some items that are normally considered deadly may not be, if used in a manner that does not pose a threat of serious harm or death. Hence, a bowling ball may be transformed from a recreational device into a deadly weapon when it is used to crush a person's skull. A gun, probably the most obvious example of a deadly device, when used for its designed purpose, may not be deemed deadly if used to hit someone over the head. A person's hands and feet are not normally deadly weapons. However, if it can be shown that the victim was significantly smaller than the defendant or that the defendant was especially expert in the use of his or her hands to cause injury, then they may constitute deadly weapons.

In the *Labelle* case, the inference created by the deadly weapon doctrine was used to affirm a trial court conviction of attempted murder.

AIDS and Murder

Acquired immunodeficiency syndrome (AIDS) and other contagious diseases raise interesting criminal law situations. First, the transmission of a disease can be criminal. For example, passing AIDS to another, if intentional, is either attempted murder, if the disease is not passed to the victim, or murder, if the disease is successfully passed to the victim.

BALLENTINE'S

deadly weapon   A weapon that is likely to cause death or serious bodily injury when used in the manner in which it was designed to be used.

LABELLE
v.
STATE
550 N.E.2d 752 (Ind. 1990)

Appellant waived his right to a jury trial and was tried to the court and found guilty of attempted murder ... and carrying a handgun without a license ... .

The evidence produced at trial which tended to support the determination of guilt shows that members of the Outlaws motorcycle gang, who refer to themselves as "brothers," sometimes frequent the Beehive Tavern in Indianapolis. On February 2, 1987, appellant was a patron of the Beehive. He asked Oliphant, the bartender and co-owner of the bar, whether the Outlaws had come into the bar before, and Oliphant informed him that they had. Appellant remained at the Beehive until closing time and returned the next night. By 11:00 P.M., at least three employees and several patrons were in the bar. Three members of the Outlaws, including the victim, Allen Mayes, were there shooting pool. Sometime after 11:00, appellant threw a beer can at the stage, whereupon Oliphant asked him to leave, and appellant spat in his face. Oliphant testified, "[appellant said] that we're going to a funeral[,] to get my brothers together because we were going to a funeral. ... [Appellant] told me I wasn't worth killing but a few of them—a few people in here were. And he proceeded to walk out the door." Oliphant stated that the three Outlaws were standing by the bar about ten feet from the door as he followed appellant out and that they were in roughly the same place when he came back in. Two or three minutes later, a shot rang out and Mayes was struck in the neck by a bullet and fell to the floor.

Fifteen to twenty minutes after the shooting, appellant was found under a truck which was parked across the street from the Beehive. A crowd which included the victim's two compan-ions stood outside the bar and watched as appellant was being placed under arrest, and one of the Beehive's managers testified that appellant shouted at the two men, "Scumbags, you tell your brothers the angels are on their way[.] I got your brother."

The door to the bar has a diamond-shaped window, which is taped to leave unobstructed only a two- or three-inch peephole. Looking into the bar from the outside, the peephole is approximately five feet, seven inches off the ground. Police found a bullet hole in the taped area to the right of the peephole. ... [the police] searched the underneath side of the truck and found a .38 caliber revolver on the transmission brace, above the approximate spot appellant's head had been when he was under the truck. ... [The medical expert] testified that, based on test results, it was his opinion that the bullet in Mayes's neck was from a .38 caliber weapon. ...

Appellant also claims that there was insufficient evidence of intent to kill to support a conviction for attempted murder. ... This court held there [in a previous case] that intent may be inferred from the use of a deadly weapon in a manner likely to cause injury or death and upheld the conviction. This Court has repeatedly upheld convictions for murder and attempted murder where the State sought to carry its burden of proof on the issue of intent by producing evidence that the defendant fired a gun in a crowd or at a group of people.

Appellant conceded in his testimony that he did fire a shot at the Beehive, but maintained that he was trying to hit a light over the door to the bar. He testified that he could not see into the bar because of the tape on the window and his distance from the door and that he had no intention of shooting any person, but intended only to aggravate Oliphant. ...

State of mind can be established by the circumstances surrounding an incident. Appellant questioned the bartender the night before the shooting as to whether the Outlaws frequented the Beehive. ... The eye-level location of the peephole and the proximity of the bullet hole to it would support an inference that the shot was fired into this inhabited barroom in a manner calculated to strike anyone standing at the bar in the upper body or head. This constitutes utilization of a deadly weapon in a manner likely to cause injury or death. There was sufficient evidence to support the trial court's verdict.

The judgment of the trial court is affirmed.

Second, the unintentional but criminally negligent or reckless passing of such a disease may be criminal under negligent manslaughter statutes. Sharing a needle with another, knowing that it has been used by an HIV-infected individual, falls into this category, as does the passing of the disease by a prostitute who knows of her infection to a client.

Third, due to the nature of the disease, it is often not discovered until long after it is contracted, and death may not occur for many years. This poses problems in jurisdictions that continue to follow the year-and-a-day rule or other similar rules.

Fourth, in some situations, defendants have claimed that, because of the low probability of infecting another person, it is a factual impossibility to commit murder using AIDS. *See United States v. Moore, 669 F. Supp. 289 (D. Minn. 1987), aff'd,* 846 F.2d 1163 (8th Cir. 1988), in which a defendant asserted that his conviction for attempted murder (the defendant, who was infected with AIDS, spat on and caused his blood to spray into a victim's mouth and eyes) should be set aside because his acts did not amount to a "substantial step" toward the commission of murder. His conviction was affirmed.

Fifth, AIDS may be characterized as a deadly weapon, and therefore, a charge of assault may be elevated to assault with a deadly weapon. Similarly, attacks leading to death may be treated as murder under the deadly weapon doctrine.

In most states, preexisting laws (e.g., murder, attempted murder, and intentional transmission of venereal disease) are relied upon to prosecute AIDS-related crimes. However, a few states have enacted statutes specifically directed at the intentional or negligent transmission of AIDS.

SIDEBAR   CRIME IN THE UNITED STATES: GUNS AND VIOLENCE Guns play a prominent role in violence in the United States. Sixty percent of all murders in the United States are committed with guns, and 80 percent of those were committed with a handgun. In a recent year, 12,000 people were killed with guns, and guns were used to injure another 70,000 people. Guns cost this nation multiple billions of dollars yearly, in medical care expenses, premature death, and long-term disability costs.

The victims of gun attacks tend to be young and black. In recent years, more than 80 percent of murder victims aged 15 to 19 were killed with guns. The firearm murder rate was 105.3 per 100,000 black males aged 15 to 19 and only 9.7 for white males of the same ages. A victim of an assault or robbery is more likely to die if the perpetrator possesses a gun.

Most guns used in murders are not lawfully acquired. The majority are either stolen or borrowed.

Source: Firearms and Violence (National Institute of Justice, Feb. 1994).

Manslaughter

At common law, murder was an unlawful killing with malice afore-thought. **Manslaughter** was an unlawful killing without malice aforethought. Just as was the case with murder, the common law did not divide manslaughter into degrees. Whenever the states began codifying homicides, it was common for manslaughter to be divided into degrees, commonly referred to as voluntary and involuntary, although a few jurisdictions used first- and second-degree language. Today, many jurisdictions continue to recognize two forms of manslaughter.

The important fact is that manslaughter is a lesser crime than murder, and, accordingly, is punished less severely. It is a lesser crime because some fact or facts exist that make the defendant less culpable than a murderer in the eyes of the law. The most common fact that mitigates a defendant's culpability is the absence of a state of mind that society has decided should be punished as murder. Even though society has decided that, because of such extenuating circumstances, a defendant should not be punished as a murderer, it has also decided that some punishment should be inflicted.

Provocation

Provocation of the defendant by the victim can reduce a homicide from murder to manslaughter. In jurisdictions that grade manslaughter,

---

BALLENTINE'S

manslaughter   The killing of a human being, without premeditation or malice and without legal excuse or justification. Voluntary manslaughter occurs when a homicide is intentional but the result of sudden passion or great provocation. Involuntary manslaughter is an unintentional killing in the course of doing an unlawful act not amounting to a felony or while doing a lawful act in a reckless manner. There are various degrees of manslaughter, which are not consistent from jurisdiction to jurisdiction.

provocation   Words or conduct that incite anger or passion or that cloud judgment and the ability to reason.

a provoked killing is treated as the higher manslaughter, whether that be called first-degree or voluntary.

The theory of provocation, also known as "heat of passion manslaughter," is that a defendant was operating under such an anger or passion that it was impossible for the defendant to have formed the desire to kill, which is required for both first- and second-degree murder. The defense of provocation applies to instances in which people act without thinking; the impulsive act being the result of the victim's behavior.

Again, an objective test is used when examining the defense of provocation. To prove provocation, it must be shown that the provoking act was so severe that a reasonable person may have also killed. It does not require that a reasonable person would have killed; only that a reasonable person would have been so affected by the act that homicide was possible. A few states have enumerated the acts that may act to negate intent to kill (and reduce the homicide to manslaughter) in their manslaughter statutes. Any act not included may not be used by a defendant to reduce a murder charge.

Catching one's spouse in the act of adultery is an example of an act that is considered adequate provocation to reduce any resulting homicide to manslaughter. This rule applies only to marriages and not to other romantic relationships. Generally, serious assaults (batteries) may constitute adequate provocation.

If two people are engaged in "mutual combat," then any resulting death may be reduced from murder to voluntary manslaughter. The key to this defense is mutuality. If it can be shown that the victim did not voluntarily engage in the fight, then the defense of mutual combat is not applicable, and the defendant is responsible for murder.

It is widely held that words and gestures are never adequate provocation. This is true regardless of how vile or vicious a statement or gesture is to the defendant. However, some recent cases have distinguished between statements that are informational and those that are not. In such situations, if a statement provides information of an act, and that act would be sufficient provocation, if witnessed, then the statement may also be provocation.

In the *Schnopps* case, the trial judge refused to instruct the jury on the alternative of manslaughter, as opposed to murder. The trial judge followed the rule that statements are never adequate provocation. The appellate court reversed the judge, holding that the statements made by the defendant's wife directly before he killed her may have been adequate provocation for a jury to find voluntary manslaughter and not murder.

Usually, when claiming adultery as provocation, one must have actually caught his or her spouse in the act. Also, the general rule is that words are not adequate provocation. What did the court do in the *Schnopps* case? It appears that the court attempted to sidestep those rules, in a manner that would permit the benefit of the defense without changing the rules. It did this by holding that in adulterous situations, an admission of adultery to one's spouse, when uttered for the first time, is as shocking as finding one's spouse engaged in the act.

Finally, the defense will not be available if there was a sufficient "cooling-off" period. That is, if the time between the provocation and the homicide was long enough for a defendant to regain self-control, then the homicide will be treated as murder and not manslaughter.

COMMONWEALTH
v.
SCHNOPPS
383 Mass. 178, 417 N.E.2d 1213 (1981)

Schnopps testified that his wife had left him three weeks prior to the slaying. He claims that he first became aware of the problems in his fourteen-year marriage at a point about six months before the slaying. According to the defendant, on that occasion he took his wife to a club to dance, and she spent the evening dancing with a co-worker. On arriving home, the defendant and his wife argued over her conduct. She told him that she no longer loved him and that she wanted a divorce. Schnopps became very upset. He admitted that he took out his shotgun during the course of this argument, but he denied that he intended to use it. ... [The defendant and his wife continued to have marital problems for the next few months.]

On the day of the killing, Schnopps had asked his wife to come to their home and talk over their marital difficulties. Schnopps told his wife that he wanted his children at home, and that he wanted the family to remain intact. Schnopps cried during the conversation and begged his wife to let the children live with him and to keep their family

together. His wife replied, "No, I am going to court, you are going to give me all the furniture, you are going to get the Hell out of here, and you won't have nothing." Then, pointing to her crotch, she said, "You will never touch this again, because I have got something bigger and better for it."

On hearing those words, Schnopps claims that his mind went blank, and that he went "berserk." He went to a cabinet and got out a pistol he had bought the day before, and he shot his wife and himself. ... [Schnopps lived and his wife died.]

Schnopps argues that "[t]he existence of sufficient provocation is not foreclosed absolutely because a defendant learns of a fact from oral statements rather than from personal observation," and that a sudden admission of adultery is equivalent to a discovery of the act itself, and is sufficient evidence of provocation.

Schnopps asserts that his wife's statements constituted a "peculiarly immediate and intense offense to a spouse's sensitivities." He concedes that the words at issue are indicative of past as well as present adultery. Schnopps claims, however, that his wife's admission of adultery was made for the first time on the day of the killing. ...

Reversed and remanded for new trial on the manslaughter issue.

Imperfect Self-Defense and Defense of Others

If Gwen harms Sue while defending herself from Sue's attack, Gwen is said to have acted in self-defense. Self-defense, when valid, normally works to negate criminal liability entirely. So, if Gwen kills Sue to avoid serious bodily harm or death, she has committed an excused homicide.

What happens if Gwen was incorrect in her belief that her life was endangered by Sue? This is known as an imperfect self-defense and does not negate culpability entirely. It may, however, reduce liability. Thus, Gwen may be liable only for voluntary manslaughter and not murder. For Gwen to be successful in her claim, she must prove that she had a good faith belief that her life was in danger and that the killing appeared to be necessary to protect herself.

A person may also have an imperfect self-defense when an excessive amount of force is used as protection. So, if Gwen was correct in her belief that she needed to use force for her protection, but used excessive force, she receives the benefit of reduced liability. Again, there must be a reasonable, although incorrect, belief that the amount of force used was necessary.

The concept of self-defense is extended to the defense of others. In such situations, one may be privileged to harm another to prevent that person from injuring or killing someone else. Just as with an imperfect self-defense, if one has a mistaken, but reasonable, belief that another is in danger, and kills as a result of that belief, then he or she is responsible for voluntary manslaughter rather than murder. Also, if one uses deadly force when a lesser amount of force would have been sufficient to stay the attack, liability is limited to manslaughter, provided the belief that deadly force was necessary was reasonable under the circumstances.

Involuntary Manslaughter

The lowest form of criminal homicide in most jurisdictions is involuntary manslaughter, sometimes named second-degree manslaughter. In most instances involuntary manslaughter is a form of negligent or reckless manslaughter.

You have already learned the misdemeanor manslaughter rule. In jurisdictions that recognize the rule, the person who commits the misdemeanor that results in an unintended death is responsible for the lowest form of criminal homicide.

Involuntary manslaughter also refers to negligent homicide, vehicular homicide, and similar statutes that punish for unintended, accidental deaths. The classic vehicular homicide is when a motorist runs a red light, strikes another car, and causes the death of the driver or passenger of that automobile. Some states, such as Illinois, make vehicular homicide a separate crime from involuntary manslaughter and impose a lesser punishment for vehicular homicide.[7]

Be aware that many states now have specific statutes dealing with deaths caused by intoxicated drivers. Often the punishment is greater if the death is the result of a drunk or otherwise impaired driver.

The term *negligent* has a different meaning in criminal law than in civil law. In tort law, any act that causes another harm that a reasonable person would not have taken leads to liability. In criminal law, more must be shown. The risk taken by the defendant must be high and pose a threat of death or serious bodily injury to the victim. In addition, some jurisdictions require that the defendant be aware of the risk before liability can be imposed. Of course, knowledge can be inferred from the defendant's actions. Some jurisdictions do not require knowledge of the risk (scienter).

The Model Penal Code Approach to Homicide

The Model Penal Code states that "A person is guilty of criminal homicide if he purposely, knowingly, recklessly, or negligently causes the death of another human being."[8] The Code then classifies all criminal homicides as murder, manslaughter, or negligent homicide. This is done by taking the four mens rea (purposeful, knowing, reckless, and negligent) and setting them into one of the classifications. There is some overlap; for example, under some conditions a reckless homicide is murder, and under other conditions it is manslaughter. Let us look at the specifics of the Code.

As you would guess, all purposeful and knowing homicides are murder under the Model Penal Code. Additionally, a reckless homicide is murder when committed "under circumstances manifesting extreme indifference to the value of human life." The Code then incorporates a "felony-murder" type rule, by stating that recklessness and indifference to human life are presumed if the accused was engaged in the commission or attempted commission of robbery, rape, arson, burglary, kidnapping, or felonious escape. So, if an accused is involved in one of those crimes, and a death results, then he may be charged with murder under the Code. Note that the Code only creates a presumption of recklessness and indifference, which may be overcome at trial. Murder is the highest form of homicide, and the Code declares it to be a felony of the first degree.

Manslaughters are felonies of the second degree under the Code. All reckless homicides, except those previously described, are manslaughters. Just as was true at common law, the Code contains a provision that reduces heat-of-passion murders to manslaughter. Specifically, the Code states that a homicide, which would normally be murder, is manslaughter when it is "committed under the influence of extreme mental or emotional disturbance for which there is reasonable explanation or excuse. The reasonableness of such explanation or excuse shall be determined from the viewpoint of a person in the actor's situation under the circumstances he believes them to be."

Last, negligent homicides are entitled just that and are felonies of the third degree.

Life, Death, and Homicide

The actus reus of murder and manslaughter is the taking of a human life. Determining when life begins and ends can be a problem in criminal law, especially when dealing with fetuses.

At common law, it was not a crime to destroy a fetus, unless it was "born alive." To be born alive, the fetus must leave its mother's body and exhibit some ability to live independently. Some courts required that the umbilical cord be cut and that the fetus show its independence thereafter before it was considered a human life. Breathing and crying are both proof of the viability of the child.

Today, many states have enacted feticide statutes that focus on the viability of the fetus. Once it can be shown that the fetus is viable, that is, could live independently if it were born, then anyone who causes its death has committed feticide. Of course, this does not apply to abortion. Since the United States Supreme Court decision in *Roe v. Wade*, 410 U.S. 113 (1973), a woman possesses a limited right to abort a fetus she carries. Thus, states may not prohibit abortions that are protected under that decision. The primary purpose of feticide statutes is to punish individuals who kill fetuses without the mother's approval, as occurred in the *Keeler* case (see Chapter 2).

At the other end of the spectrum is death. Medical advances have made the determination of when death occurs more complex than it was only years ago. For a long period of time, a person was considered dead when there was no heartbeat and no breathing. Today, artificial means can be used to sustain both heart action and respiration. That being so, should one be free of criminal homicide in cases where the victim is being kept "alive" by artificial means and there is no reasonable hope of recovery? Should a physician be charged with murder for "pulling the plug" on a patient who has irreversible brain damage and is in a coma? Using the respiration and heart function test, it would be criminal homicide to end such a treatment. However, many states now use brain death, rather than respiration and heartbeat, to determine when life has ended. In states that employ a brain death definition, it must be shown that there is a total cessation of brain function before legal death exists. The importance of defining death is illustrated by the *Fierro* case.

Suicide

Successful suicide was a crime under the common law of England. The property owned by the one who committed suicide was forfeited to (taken by) the Crown. In early American common law attempted suicide was a crime, usually punished as a misdemeanor. Today suicide is not treated as a crime. However, it is possible to restrain and examine

STATE
v.
David FIERRO
124 Ariz. 182, 603 P.2d 74 (1979)

The facts necessary for a resolution of this matter on appeal are as follows. Between 8 and 9 o'clock on the evening of 18 August 1977, Victor Corella was given a ride by Ray Montez and his wife Sandra as they were attempting to locate some marijuana. In the vicinity of 12th Street and Pima, Ray Montez heard his name called from another car. He stopped his car, walked over to the other car and saw that the passenger who had called his name was the defendant Fierro. Defendant told Ray Montez that his brother in the "M," or "Mexican Mafia," had instructed the defendant to kill Corella. Ray Montez told defendant to do it outside the car because he and his wife "did not want to see anything."

Montez returned to his car. Defendant followed and began talking with Corella. Corella got out of the car. Montez started to drive away when defendant began shooting Corella. Corella was shot once in the chest and four times in the head. ... Corella was maintained on support systems for the next three days while follow-up studies were completed which confirmed the occurrence of brain death. The supportive measures were terminated and he was pronounced dead on 22 August 1977. ...

CAUSE OF DEATH

At the trial, Dr. Hugh McGill, a surgical resident at the Maricopa County Hospital, testified that:

> After surgery he was taken to the intensive-care unit. He was evaluated by a neurosurgeon who felt there was nothing we could do for his brain, he had brain death. He remained somewhat stable over the next two or three days. We had follow-up studies that confirmed our impression of brain death and because of that supportive measures were terminated and he was pronounced dead, I believe, on the 22nd. ...

Defendant initially argues that the termination of support systems by attendant doctors three days after Corella suffered "brain death" was the cause of Corella's death [and as such, he could not be responsible for Corella's death]. ...

In the instant case, the body of the victim was breathing, though not spontaneously, and blood was pulsating through his body before the life support mechanisms were withdrawn. Because there was an absence of cardiac and circulatory arrest, under the common-law rule he would not have been legally dead. Under the Harvard Medical School test and Proposal of the National Conference of Commissioners on Uniform State Laws he was, in fact, dead before the life supports were withdrawn as he had become "brain" or "neurologically" dead prior to that time. We believe that while the common-law definition of death is still sufficient to establish death, the [brain death test] is also a valid test for death in Arizona.

individuals who have attempted to commit suicide under civil psychiatric commitment laws.

It continues to be criminal to encourage or aid another to commit suicide. In most situations such a commission is treated as murder. Assisting suicide may be treated as murder, or, as in Michigan, it may be a separate crime that is punished less severely.

The most well-known suicide cases involve Dr. Jack Kevorkian of Michigan. Dr. Kevorkian, a physician, assisted twenty terminally ill persons in committing suicide between 1990 and 1994.

Dr. Kevorkian's license to practice medicine was suspended in 1991 for his behavior, and criminal charges have been filed against him on several occasions. The first three cases were dismissed because the statute under which he was charged was held unconstitutional.

The Michigan legislature enacted a new law in February 1993 that provides for as much as four years imprisonment and a $2,000 fine for providing the physical means by which another attempts or commits suicide or participates in a physical act by which another attempts or commits suicide. The person charged must have had knowledge that the other person intended to commit suicide.[9]

At the time of this writing, Dr. Kevorkian had been charged under the new law and the issue is now before the Michigan Court of Appeals.[10] At one time, while in jail, Dr. Kevorkian staged a hunger strike to protest the law and his prosecution. During one period of his release, he was ordered to wear an electronic leg tether to ensure that he would not assist in any suicides while his case was pending. Dr. Kevorkian contends that the right to commit, and assist in the commission of a, suicide is protected by due process. This is yet to be resolved.

Corpus Delicti

Corpus delicti is a Latin phrase that translates as "the body of a crime." Prosecutors have the burden of proving the corpus delicti of crimes at trial. Every crime has a corpus delicti. It refers to the substance of the crime. For example, in murder cases the corpus delicti is the death of a victim and the act that caused the death. In arson, the corpus delicti is a burned structure and the cause of the fire.

A confession of an accused is never enough to prove corpus delicti. There must be either direct proof or evidence supporting a confession.

In murder cases the corpus delicti can usually be proved by an examination of the victim's corpse. After an autopsy a physician will usually be prepared to testify that the alleged act either did, or could have, caused the death. In some instances, the body of a victim cannot be located. Such "no body" cases make the job of the prosecution harder. Even so, if evidence establishes that the person is dead, such as blood stains and discovered personal effects, then murder may be proven. Of course, the prosecution must also show that the defendant caused the death. So, if a defendant confesses to a murder, or makes other incriminating statements, and no other evidence is found, no corpus delicti exists, and the defendant cannot be convicted. However, if blood matching the victim's is discovered where the defendant stated the murder occurred, then a murder conviction can be sustained.

———————————————————— BALLENTINE'S ————————————————————

corpus delicti   Means "the body of the crime"; the fact that a crime has actually been committed.

SIDEBAR CRIME IN THE UNITED STATES: VIOLENT CRIME Violent crime is at one of its highest levels in United States history. Only during two other periods (1931–1934 and 1979–1981) has violent crime been as high as during the 1990s.

 The murder rate (per capita figures) is twice as high in the United States as in Spain, which has the second highest crime rate of industrialized nations. It is four times as high as the Canadian murder rate, eight times as high as England's, and as much as ten times as high as Japan's.

 Regrettably, most violence falls on ethnic minorities; the lifetime risk of murder for a black male is 42 per 1,000 people and 18 per 1,000 among Native American males. It is only 6 per 1,000 for white males and 3 per 1,000 for white females.

 Violent crime is much higher in urban areas than rural, and the larger a city becomes, the greater its crime rate. More than 2,000 violent crimes are committed for every 100,000 people in cities with populations greater than one million. This is triple the nation's rate as a whole.

Sources: Understanding and Preventing Crime (National Institute of Justice, Feb. 1994); Erika Fairchild, *Comparative Criminal Justice Systems* (Wadsworth Publishing 1993).

Assault and Battery

Assault and **battery** are two different crimes, although they commonly occur together. As with homicide, all states have made assaults and batteries criminal by statute.

A *battery* is an intentional touching of another that is either offensive or harmful. The mens rea element varies among the states; however, most now provide for both intentional and negligent battery. Of course, negligence in criminal law involves a greater risk than in civil law. To be negligent in criminal law, there must be a disregard of a high risk of injury to another; in tort law, one need only show a disregard of an ordinary risk. The Model Penal Code provides for purposeful, knowing, and reckless batteries. In addition, if one uses a deadly weapon, negligence may give rise to a battery charge. Otherwise, negligence may not provide the basis for a battery conviction.

The actus reus of battery is a touching. An individual need not touch someone with his or her actual person to commit a battery. Objects that

-----BALLENTINE'S-----

assault An act of force or threat of force intended to inflict harm upon a person or to put the person in fear that such harm is imminent; an attempt to commit a battery. The perpetrator must have, or appear to have, the present ability to carry out the act.

battery The unconsented-to touching or striking of one person by another, or by an object put in motion by him, with the intention of doing harm or giving offense. Battery is both a crime and a tort.

are held are considered extensions of the body. If Sherry strikes Doug with an iron, she has battered him regardless of the fact that her person never came into contact with his. Likewise, items thrown at another are extensions of the person who took the act of propelling them into the air. If Doug were to injure Sherry with a knife he threw at her, then he has battered her.

A touching must be either offensive or harmful to be a battery. Of course, any resulting physical injury is proof of harm. The problem arises when one touches another in a manner found offensive to the person being touched, but there is no apparent physical injury. For example, a man who touches a woman's breast without her consent has committed a battery because the touching is offensive. If a person touches another in an angry manner, a battery has been committed, even though the touching was not intended to injure the party and in fact does no harm.

There are two breeds of assault. First, when a person puts another in fear or apprehension of an imminent battery, an assault has been committed. For example, if Gary attempts to strike Terry, but Terry evades the swing by ducking, Gary has committed an assault. The rule does not require that the victim actually experience fear; apprehension of an impending battery is sufficient. Apprehension is simply an expectation of an unwanted event. Also, the threat must be imminent to rise to the level of an assault. A threat that one will be battered in the future is not sufficient. So, if Terry told Gary that he was "going to kick the shit out of him in one hour," there is no assault.

Because an apprehension by the victim is required, there is no assault under this theory if the victim was not aware of the assault. For example, if X swings his arm at Y intending to scare Y, but Y has her back turned and does not see X's behavior, then there is no assault. This is not true of batteries. If X strikes Y, a battery has been committed, regardless of whether Y saw the punch coming.

The second type of assault is an attempted battery. This definition remedies the problem just discussed. Any unsuccessful battery is an assault, regardless of the victim's knowledge of the act. Of course, it must be determined that the act in question would have been a battery if it had been completed.

To prove battery it must be shown that a contact was made. This is not necessary to prove an assault. However, it is possible to have both an assault and a battery. If John sees Henry swing the baseball bat that strikes John, there has been an assault and battery. However, due to the doctrine of merger the defendant will only be punished for the higher crime of battery.

Aggravated Assault and Battery

Under special circumstances, an assault or battery can be classified as aggravated. If aggravated, a higher penalty is imposed. The process of defining such crimes as more serious than simple assaults and batteries varies. Statutes may call such crimes aggravated assault or battery; or may refer to specific crimes under a special name, such as assault with intent to kill; or may simply use the facts at the sentencing stage to enhance (increase) the sentence; or may refer to such as a higher assault, such as felony assault rather than misdemeanor assault. In any event, the following facts commonly aggravate an assault or battery.

The assault is aggravated if the assault or battery is committed while the actor is engaged in the commission of another crime. So, if a man batters a woman while possessing the specific intent to rape her, he has committed an aggravated battery. This is true regardless of whether the rape was completed. If a defendant is stopped before he has committed the rape, but after he has assaulted or battered the victim, there has been an aggravated battery. Hence the crime may be titled "assault with an intent to commit rape" or "assault with intent to murder."

It is also common to make assault and battery committed on persons of some special status more serious. Law enforcement officers or other public officials often fall into this category. Of course, the crime must relate to the performance or status of the officer to be aggravated. For example, if an off-duty police officer is struck by an angry neighbor over a boundary dispute, the battery is not aggravated. Examples of other protected classes of individuals are minors and the mentally disabled.

The extent of injury to the victim may also lead to an increased charge. Usually a battery may be aggravated if the harm rises to the level of "serious bodily injury." Some states specifically state that certain injuries aggravate the crime of battery, such as the loss of an eye. Mayhem, a related crime, is discussed next.

SIDEBAR CRIME IN THE UNITED STATES In 1992, there were 1,126,974 aggravated assaults in the United States; that is, 442 aggravated assaults per 100,000 people. This crime accounted for 7.8 percent of all crimes in the United States in 1992.

Source: Uniform Crime Reports, U.S. Department of Justice, Federal Bureau of Investigation, 1993.

Mayhem

Mayhem, originally a common-law crime, is the crime of intentionally dismembering or disfiguring a person. The crime has an interesting origin. In England, all men were to be available to fight for the king. It was a serious crime to injure a man in such a manner as to make him unable to fight. Early punishments for mayhem were incarceration, death, and the imposition of the same injury that had been inflicted on the victim. Originally, only dismemberment that could prevent a man from fighting for the king was punished as mayhem. As such, cutting off a man's leg or arm was punishable, whereas cutting off an ear was not. Of course, causing a disfigurement was not mayhem.

Today, both disfigurement and dismemberment fall under mayhem statutes. Many jurisdictions specifically state what injuries must be sustained for a charge of mayhem. Causing another to lose an eye, ear, or limb are examples, as is castration.

Some states no longer have mayhem statutes, but have chosen to treat such crimes as aggravated batteries.

Sex Crimes

This section deals with crimes that involve sex. Keep in mind that crimes such as assault and battery may be sexually motivated. For example, if a man touches a woman's breast, he has committed a battery (provided that the touching was unwelcome).

The phrase "sex crimes" actually encompasses a variety of sexually motivated crimes. Rape, sodomy, incest, and sexually motivated batteries and murders are included. Obscenity, prostitution, abortion, distribution of child pornography, and public nudity are examples of other sex-related offenses.

Although certain offenses are universally prohibited, other offenses vary among the states. For example, rape is criminal in all states, but prostitution is not.

BALLENTINE'S

mayhem   A form of aggravated assault, the crime of maliciously disabling or disfiguring a person.

Rape

At common law, the elements of **rape** were (1) Sexual intercourse with (2) a woman, not the man's wife (3) committed without the victim's consent and by using force. Many problems were encountered with this definition. First, the common-law definition required that the rapist be a man. Hence, women and male minors could not be convicted of rape. Also, the *marital rape exception* provided that men could not be convicted of raping their wives. Similarly, a man could not be charged with battering his wife if the battery was inflicted in an effort to force sex. This exception was founded upon the theory that when women married they consented to sex with their husbands upon demand. Additionally, many courts wrote that to permit a woman to charge her husband with such a crime would lead to destruction of the family unit. Finally, the last requirement, with force and without consent, led many courts to require victims to resist the attack to the utmost and to continue to resist during the rape.

States have changed the common-law definition of rape to remedy these problems. First, most states have worded their statutes to permit minors and women to be charged with rape. While there are few cases of women actually raping men, or other women, there are several cases where women have been convicted as principals to the crime.[11] The Model Penal Code is gender-neutral as to all sex crimes except rape.[12]

The marital rape exception has been abolished in most states. A few states have retained the rule in modified form, such as Ohio, which provides immunity to a husband except when he is separated from his wife.[13]

Finally, the last requirement has changed significantly. A person need not resist to the extent required under the common law. What is required now is proof that the victim did resist. However, a victim need not risk life or serious bodily injury in an attempt to prevent the rape. So if a woman simply tells a man on a date "I don't want to," there has been inadequate resistance. The result would be different if the man produced a gun and told the woman he would kill her if she resisted.

―――――――――――――――――BALLENTINE'S―――――――――――――――――

rape   Sexual intercourse with a woman by force or by putting her in fear or in circumstances in which she is unable to control her conduct or to resist ... .
Under the common law definition of the crime, only a female can be raped and only a male can perpetrate the crime. In recent years, however, courts in several states have held that the rape statutes of their jurisdictions are gender-neutral and apply equally to perpetrators of either sex.

So, the elements of rape, under new statutes, are: (1) Sexual intercourse (2) with another against that person's will or without that person's consent and (3) by the use of force or under such a threat of force that a reasonable person would have believed that resistance would have resulted in serious bodily harm or death.

Note that one element has not changed, namely, the definition of sexual intercourse. Generally, the contact must be penis-vagina; anal sex, fellatio, and other acts are usually punished under sodomy statutes. The requirement is the same today as it was under the common law. The "slightest penetration" of the woman's vulva is sufficient. The man need not ejaculate.

Some states grade rape according to the extent of injuries that the victim received and whether the victim knew the rapist. The Model Penal Code punishes rape as a felony in the second degree, unless serious bodily injury occurs or the victim was not a social companion of the rapist, in which case the rape is of the first degree.

CRIME IN THE UNITED STATES   In 1993 there were 104,806 reported forcible rapes in the United States. This number includes attempted rapes and assaults with intent to rape; however, non-forcible rapes, such as statutory rape, are not included. Rapes constituted 0.8 percent of all crimes in the United States in 1992. The actual number of rapes is likely much higher, as rape is believed to be one of the most under-reported crimes.

Source: Uniform Crime Reports, U.S. Department of Justice, Federal Bureau of Investigation, 1994.

Nonforcible Rape

Under some circumstances, one may commit a rape even though the other party consented to the sexual contact. So-called **statutory rape** is such a crime. The actus reus of statutory rape is sexual intercourse with someone under a specified age, commonly sixteen. The purpose of the law is to protect those the law presumes are too young to make a mature decision concerning sex. Hence, consent is not relevant. So, a rape has occurred when a girl under sixteen consents to sexual intercourse with a male aged eighteen or older.

In most states, statutory rape is a strict liability crime. The act of having sex with someone below the specified age is proof alone of guilt. No showing of mens rea is required. A few states impose a knowledge requirement. In those states, if the accused can convince the jury that there was reason to believe that the other party was "of age," then the

---
BALLENTINE'S
---

statutory rape   Sexual intercourse with a female under the age of consent, with or without her consent.

accused is acquitted. For example, if a fifteen-year-old girl tells a boy that she is seventeen, she indeed looks seventeen, and she shows the boy a falsified identification bearing that age, he would have a defense to statutory rape.

In many states, only females are protected by statutory rape laws. If a boy of fifteen years has sex with a girl of seventeen years, the law will not punish her as they would the boy if the ages were turned around. It has been alleged that such treatment is violative of the Equal Protection Clause of the United States Constitution. The United States Supreme Court has rejected that claim by reasoning that one of the goals of such statutes is the prevention of teenage pregnancy. Because females can be impregnated, states have a legitimate interest in prosecuting males who have sex with females who are under the age of consent.[14] Using this analysis a state may prosecute males only, as females cannot impregnate young men or women. However, many acts by adult females (or adult males to young males) may be prosecuted under another law, such as child molestation or criminal deviate conduct.

Similar to statutory rape, having sex with those who are incapable of consenting due to mental or emotional disability is also rape.

Sodomy

Sodomy is defined by *Webster's New World Dictionary* (3d ed., 1988) as "any sexual intercourse held to be abnormal, esp. bestiality or anal intercourse between two male persons." Many statutes now include sodomy in "criminal deviate conduct" statutes. Sodomy is prohibited in most states, and in most jurisdictions fellatio, cunnilingus, bestiality, homosexual activity, anal sex, and sometimes masturbation are included. There is substantial disagreement concerning whether such acts should be prohibited between consenting adults. Those who support sodomy laws usually do so for religious reasons. Those who oppose such laws contend that two adults should be permitted to engage in any sexual conduct they desire, provided that no one is injured. In any event, one practical problem exists; enforcement of sodomy laws is nearly impossible. Determining what sexual acts people engage in privately is not an easy task. Additionally, law enforcement appears to have no incentive to enforce such laws when there appears to be no resulting injury, and there is substantial noncompliance with many sodomy laws, such as fellatio and cunnilingus.

---BALLENTINE'S---

sodomy A term whose definition varies from state to state, but which, at its broadest, criminalizes sexual relations between persons of the same sex, sexual contact per anus or per os between unmarried persons, and sexual intercourse with animals. Sodomy is also referred to as "the crime against nature" or *buggery*.

Those who oppose enforcement of sodomy laws between consenting adults do not oppose punishment of those who force acts of sodomy on others. At common law, a man had to have penile-vulva contact to commit rape. If a man forced oral or anal sex on a woman, he committed sodomy. Sodomy was also punished severely. Many states continue to prohibit sodomy, even in marriage. Some prosecutors are using sodomy laws to punish homosexuals for their sexual activity, and the United States Supreme Court has upheld such applications of sodomy laws.[15]

Rape Shield Laws

So-called **shield laws** were enacted in the 1970s and 1980s in an effort to protect rape victims from harassment by defense attorneys at trial. Before such laws existed, defense attorneys often would use evidence of a victim's prior sexual conduct to infer that the victim had consented to the act. It is thought that the humiliation of the rape itself, matched with this treatment at trial, accounted for the nonreporting of many rapes.

In an effort to protect victims from unwarranted abuse at trial, rape shield laws were enacted. Evidence of prior sexual conduct, except with the defendant, is not permitted at trial. Also, evidence of a victim's reputation in the community is inadmissible.

Incest

Sex between family members is *incest,* is a crime. Generally, law enforcement is concerned with abuse of children, although it is also a crime for two consenting adult family members to engage in sex. Often, when an adult family member is involved with a child, other statutes, such as child molestation laws, will also apply.

The actus reus of incest is intercourse, or other sexual conduct, between family members. Normally, incest laws parallel marriage laws for a definition of *family.* That is, if two people are permitted to marry under state law, then they are also permitted to engage in sex, regardless of marriage. It is common for states to prohibit marriage of individuals of first cousin affinity and closer.

If the incestuous party is a parent, courts often attempt to seek family counseling and therapy rather than incarceration. However, in extreme situations criminal penalties can be severe, and civil remedies allow removal of the child from the home, as well as termination of parental rights.

-------------------------------BALLENTINE'S-------------------------------

shield laws   Statutes that, in cases involving forcible sex crimes, prohibit the prosecution from introducing the victim's sexual history (especially alleged promiscuity or immorality) into evidence.

Sex Offenses Against Children

Most states have a number of statutes specifically aimed at protecting children from sexual abuse and exploitation. Indiana has five statutes that directly pertain to sexual activity with children. Those statutes are:

INDIANA CODE § 35-42-4-3 Child Molesting

(a) A person who, with a child under twelve (12) years of age, performs or submits to sexual intercourse or deviate sexual conduct commits child molesting, a Class B felony. However, the offense is a Class A felony if it is committed by using or threatening the use of deadly force, or while armed with a deadly weapon, or if it results in serious bodily injury.

(b) A person who, with a child under twelve (12) years of age, performs or submits to any fondling or touching, of either the child or the older person, with intent to arouse or to satisfy the sexual desire of either the child or the older person, commits child molesting, a Class C felony. However, the offense is a Class A felony if it is committed by using or threatening the use of deadly force, or while armed with a deadly weapon.

(c) A person sixteen (16) years of age or older who, with a child of twelve (12) years of age or older but under sixteen (16) years of age, performs or submits to sexual intercourse or deviate sexual conduct commits child molesting, a Class C felony. However, the offense is a Class A felony if it is committed by using or threatening the use of deadly force, or while armed with a deadly weapon.

(d) A person sixteen (16) years of age, or older who, with a child twelve (12) years of age or older but under sixteen (16) years of age, performs or submits to any fondling or touching, of either the child or the older person, with intent to arouse or to satisfy the sexual desires of either the child or the older person, commits child molesting, a Class D felony. However, the offense is a Class B felony if it is committed by using or threatening the use of deadly force, or while armed with a deadly weapon.

(e) It is a defense that the accused person reasonably believed that the child was sixteen (16) years of age or older at the time of the conduct.

(f) It is a defense that the child is or has ever been married.

INDIANA CODE § 35-42-4-4 Child Exploitation

(b) Any person who knowingly or intentionally:

    (1) manages, produces, sponsors, presents, exhibits, photographs, films, or videotapes any performance or incident that includes sexual conduct by a child under sixteen (16) years of age; or

    (2) disseminates, exhibits to another person, offers to disseminate or exhibit to another person, or sends or brings into Indiana for dissemination or

exhibition matter that depicts or describes sexual conduct by a child under sixteen (16) years of age; commits child exploitation. ...

(c) A person who knowingly or intentionally possesses:

    (1) a picture;

    (2) a drawing;

    (3) a photograph;

    (4) a negative image;

    (5) undeveloped film;

    (6) a motion picture;

    (7) a videotape; or

    (8) any pictorial representation;

that depicts sexual conduct by a child who is, or appears to be, less than sixteen (16) years of age and that lacks serious literary, artistic, political or scientific value commits possession of child pornography. ...

INDIANA CODE § 35-42-4-5 Vicarious Sexual Gratification

(a) A person eighteen (18) years of age or older who knowingly or intentionally directs, aids, induces, or causes a child under the age of sixteen (16) to touch or fondle himself or another child under the age of sixteen (16) with intent to arouse or satisfy the sexual desires of a child or the older person commits vicarious sexual gratification. ...

(b) A person eighteen (18) years of age or older who knowingly or intentionally directs, aids, induces, or causes a child under the age of sixteen (16) to:

    (1) engage in sexual intercourse with another child under sixteen (16) years of age;

    (2) engage in sexual conduct with an animal other than a human being; or

    (3) engage in deviate sexual conduct with another person ... commits vicarious sexual gratification. ...

INDIANA CODE § 35-42-4-6 Child Solicitation

A person eighteen (18) years of age or older who knowingly or intentionally solicits a child under twelve (12) years of age to engage in:

(1) sexual intercourse;

(2) deviate sexual conduct; or

(3) any fondling or touching intended to arouse or satisfy the sexual desires of either the child or the older person; commits child solicitation. ...

INDIANA CODE § 35-42-4-7 Child Seduction

(e) If a person who is:

(1) at least eighteen (18) years of age; and
(2) the guardian, adoptive parent, adoptive grandparent, custodian ... of a child at least sixteen (16) years of age but less than eighteen (18) years of age; engages in sexual intercourse or deviate sexual conduct with the child, the person commits child seduction. ...

Note that statutory rape falls under the child molestation statute in Indiana. Also, the defense of a good faith and reasonable belief that a child is of statutory age is recognized by statute.

The number of people charged with committing sex crimes against children is increasing. Many of those charged are nonbiological guardians. This has led to statutes such as Ind. Code § 35-42-4-7, "Child seduction," which was added to Indiana's sex offenses statutes in 1987.

Kidnapping and False Imprisonment

Kidnapping

Kidnapping was a misdemeanor at common law, although it was regarded as a very serious crime, often resulting in life imprisonment. Felonies were often punished by death at the early common law. Today kidnapping is a felony and carries a harsh penalty in most states. Additionally, if the kidnapping takes the victim across state lines, the crime is a violation of the Federal Kidnapping Act.[16] The federal government, usually the Federal Bureau of Investigation, may become involved in any kidnapping twenty-four hours after the victim has been seized, by virtue of the Federal Kidnapping Act, which creates a presumption that the victim has been transported across state lines after that period of time.[17]

The elements of kidnapping are (1) The unlawful (2) taking and confinement and (3) asportation of (4) another person (5) by use of force, threat, fraud, or deception.

The taking of the victim must be unlawful. Thus, arrests made by police officers while engaged in their lawful duties are not kidnappings. Neither is it kidnapping for a guardian to take a ward from one place to another, so long as the action is lawful. However, when an officer, or other, acts completely without legal authority, he or she may not be shielded from liability.

There must be a taking and confinement. Confinement is broadly construed. If Pat puts a gun to Craig's back and orders him to walk a half

---
BALLENTINE'S

kidnapping The crime of taking and detaining a person against his or her will by force, intimidation, or fraud.

mile to Pat's home, there has been a confinement. Generally, there must be a restriction of the victim's freedom to take alternative action.

This taking and confinement must occur as a result of threat, force, fraud, or deception. Of course, Pat's gun in the example is ample threat to satisfy this requirement. Deception may also be used to gain control over the victim. For example, if Jon convinces his estranged wife to enter a house under the pretense of discussing their marital difficulties and then locks the door, he has fraudulently gained control over her.

Finally, there must be an asportation of the victim. *Asportation* means movement. The issue of the amount of movement necessary to meet this requirement is the most controversial question concerning kidnapping as a crime. The Model Penal Code and most states now hold that if the kidnapping is incidental to the commission of another crime, there is insufficient asportation; some courts speak in terms of a movement of a "substantial distance."[18] To be incidental, a kidnapping must simply be a product of an intent to commit another crime. If a bank robber orders a teller to move from her window to the safe to fill a bag with money, four of the elements of kidnapping are present; however, the third element, asportation, has not been established because the movement was only incidental to the robbery. The result may be different if the teller was ordered to move to the safe for the purpose of raping her. The issue of substantial distance was raised in *Commonwealth v. Hughes*. In that case the court focused on whether the movement substantially increased the risk of harm to victim.

COMMONWEALTH
v.
HUGHES
399 A.2d 694 (Pa. Super. Ct. 1979)

[The appellant approached the victim, Ms. Helfrich, who was seated on a park bench.] Appellant asked Ms. Helfrich if she wanted to go for a ride or smoke some marijuana with him. When Ms. Helfrich refused, appellant left. Minutes later, the appellant returned, placed a sharp kitchen knife to her throat, and stated, "I think you are going for a ride." Appellant forced Ms. Helfrich to walk to his car one and one-half blocks away and threatened to kill her if she resisted. Once in the car, he drove around the Media area in a reckless manner for approximately two miles and stopped his car in an abandoned lot surrounded by trees. He then forced Ms. Helfrich into the wooded area where he raped her. ...

"A person is guilty of kidnapping if he unlawfully removes another a substantial distance, under the circumstances, from the place where he is found or if he unlawfully confines another for a substantial period in a place of isolation." ...

The framers of the Model Penal Code were aware of the experience of other jurisdictions when they drafted the model kidnapping statute. They recognized that "[w]hen an especially outrageous crime is committed there will be a public clamor for the extreme penalty and it is asking too much of public officials and juries to resist such pressures." ... To combat the undesirable situation of charging kidnapping to obtain a higher permissible sentence, the framers of the Model Penal Code drafted the kidnapping statute restrictively. ... The drafters made explicit their "purpose to preclude kidnapping convictions based on trivial changes of location having no bearing on the evil at hand."

Drawing from the experience of other jurisdictions, the comments to the Model Code, and the fact that the Pennsylvania statute is similar to the Model Penal Code statute of kidnapping, it is clear to us that the legislature intended to exclude from kidnapping the incidental movement of a victim during the commission of a crime which does not substantially increase the risk of harm to the victim.

Turning to the case at hand, we find that the movement of the victim was not a trivial incident to the other crime charged. Although the victim was removed only a distance of two miles, the wooded area to which she was brought was in an isolated area, seemingly beyond the aid of her friends and police. Under the circumstances, two miles is a substantial enough distance to place the victim in a completely different environmental setting removed from the security of familiar surroundings. (In addition, the movement itself seriously endangered the victim as she was subject to a knife poised at her throat and to the reckless driving of appellant. At one point, appellant drove onto a one-way street in the wrong direction.) ... Accordingly, the conviction is sustained.

Many statutes specifically state that if the acts of asportation and confinement occur in furtherance of named crimes, then there is a kidnapping. Such statutes commonly include kidnapping for ransom, political reasons, rape, and murder. It is also common to upgrade kidnappings for these reasons. One type of kidnapping that is usually graded low is the taking of a child by a parent in violation of a court order.

Parental Kidnapping

With a dissolution of marriage comes the separation of property owned by the couple, as well as a custody order if the couple has children. Often, costly and bitter custody disputes are also the result of divorce. In recent years "childnapping," or kidnapping of one's own child in violation of a custody order, has received much public attention.

Due to the rise in the number of such acts, new statutes specifically aimed at parental kidnapping have been adopted. The federal government entered this arena in 1980 by enacting the Parental Kidnapping Prevention Act.[19] Although this statute does not concern itself with criminal sanctions for childnapping, it does require that all states respect child custody orders of other states. That is, a person cannot escape a court order concerning custody of the child by kidnapping the child and fleeing to another jurisdiction. Interestingly, the federal government has left the actual punishment of parental kidnapping to the states. The federal kidnapping act specifically excludes such acts from its reach. Thus, kidnapping by a parent must be punished in a state court. This may occur in the state from which the child is taken or in any state where the parent takes the child.

Kidnapping of one's own child is normally punished less severely than other kidnappings. This is sensible because many "childnappings" do not create a risk to the child's welfare; rather, they are the result of an overzealous, loving parent. Obviously, the crime should be punished because of the harm to the custodial parent, but the crime does not have the same evil motive a kidnapping with an intent to rape or murder does.

False Imprisonment

The crime of **false imprisonment** is similar to kidnapping, and in fact all kidnappings involve a false imprisonment. The opposite is not true. Not all false imprisonments are kidnappings. A false imprisonment occurs when (1) one person (2) interferes (3) with another's liberty (4) by use of threat or force (5) without authority. The primary distinction between the two crimes is the absence of asportation as an element of false imprisonment.

Today, some states have one statute that encompasses both false imprisonment and kidnapping. Such statutes are drafted so that the crime is graded, often elevating the crime if the motive is ransom, rape, serious bodily injury, or murder.

Stalking

In recent years, **stalking** has been the subject of considerable media, public, and legislative attention. Public awareness of stalking increased when prominent public figures who were the victims of stalkers, including politicians, actors, and law enforcement officials, began to speak out.

Stalking posed unique problems to law enforcement officials, prosecutors, and judges. Before 1990, no state had a law specifically aimed at combatting stalking. Therefore, preexisting criminal laws, such as assault, battery, and threats, as well as the use of restraining orders, were relied upon in dealing with stalkers. But these laws proved ineffective. Often there is no assault, battery, or provable threat until the victim has been injured or murdered. Even when one of these crimes could be proven, sentences were short. Restraining orders also proved to give victims little protection.

BALLENTINE'S
---

false imprisonment   The unlawful restraint by one person of the physical liberty of another.

stalking   The crime of willfully, maliciously, and repeatedly following or harassing another and making threats intended to put the person in imminent fear of death or serious bodily injury.

In response to the growing public interest in stalking, California enacted the nation's first stalking law in 1990. By 1993, another forty-six states enacted similar laws.[20]

Stalking laws vary in their elements, but most include a list of acts that satisfy the actus reus of the crime. These include following, harassing, threatening, lying in wait, or conducting surveillance of another person. Usually, one act does not amount to stalking; rather, there must be a pattern or scheme of acts. The first statutes had as a mens rea element a specific intent to cause emotional distress, or to invoke fear of bodily injury or death. However, this has proven ineffective, as stalkers, who are often suffering from emotional or mental illness, often do not have a specific intent to cause fear or harm, even though either or both of these are likely to result. Many states, such as Washington, have remedied this by lowering the mens rea to actual or constructive knowledge. So long as the stalker should have known that the victim would suffer distress or fear, the mens rea satisfies this breed of stalking law. Through these laws, the police may intercede before violence occurs.

Even before stalking laws, many states criminalized harassment. Personal harassment, telephone harassment, and other specific forms of harassment are commonly included in these laws. However, as mentioned earlier, these statutes were not effective in stopping stalkers, primarily because of the short sentences violators usually received.

Civil Rights and Hate Crimes

The federal and state governments have enacted laws criminalizing acts that encroach upon an individual's civil liberties. It is a crime against the United States for two or more persons to conspire to injure, oppress, threaten, or intimidate a person for exercising a federally secured right.[21]

In addition, any person acting pursuant to state law or authority (under color of law) who deprives a person of a federally secured right due to alienage, race, or color is guilty of a federal civil rights crime.[22] Because of the "color of law" requirement, defendants are usually state or local officials. It was under this statute that the police officers who beat Rodney King in Los Angeles were tried and convicted in federal court. In addition to criminal remedies, victims may seek civil remedies under a separate civil rights statute.[23] States have similar civil rights laws.

So-called "hate crimes" laws have become popular in recent years. By 1993, forty-nine states had enacted hate crimes statutes.[24] Although commonly referred to as hate crimes, most of these statutes do not actually declare an act criminal; rather, they are sentence enhancements for crimes in which the motive was the victim's race, ethnicity, religion, or other factor.

Florida's hate crime law reads as follows:

Evidencing prejudice while committing offense; enhanced penalties

———————————— ▥ ————————————

(1) The penalty for any felony or misdemeanor shall be reclassified as provided in this subsection if the commission of such felony or misdemeanor evidences prejudice based on the race, color, ancestry, ethnicity, religion, sexual orientation, or national origin of the victim:

   (a) A misdemeanor of the second degree shall be punishable as if it were a misdemeanor of the first degree.

   (b) A misdemeanor of the first degree shall be punishable as if it were a felony of the third degree.

   (c) A felony.of the third degree shall be punishable as if it were a felony of the second degree.

   (d) A felony of the second degree shall be punishable as it were a felony of the first degree.
   [The statute then provides for civil remedies to victims in subsection 2.]

(3) It shall be an essential element of this section that the record reflect that the defendant perceived, knew, or had reasonable grounds to know or perceive that the victim was within the class delineated herein.[25]

———————————————————————

Hate crimes laws have been attacked on First Amendment grounds as violating a person's right to expression. Clearly, a statute that makes a person's beliefs, and the expression of those beliefs, criminal is unconstitutional. But the Supreme Court has upheld statutes that enhance sentences when otherwise prohibited acts are taken because of a prejudicial motive. For example, a state cannot make it illegal to hate a particular ethnic group. Further, with few exceptions (e.g., fighting words), the state may not regulate a person's First Amendment right to express hatred of a particular group. But if the person's beliefs motivate a criminal act, such as a trespass or battery, then the sentence for that crime may be enhanced.

Review Questions

1. What is the primary distinction between first- and second-degree murder?

2. What is felony-murder?

3. What is the difference between an assault and a battery?

4. What is the marital rape exception?

5. John caught his wife having sex with another man. In a fit of rage, he killed his wife. What crime has been committed?

6. What is meant by the phrase "imperfect self-defense"?

7. What is the primary distinction between false imprisonment and kidnapping?

8. Under the common law, if a person cut another's limb off, what crime was committed?

9. Give an example of a nonforcible rape.

10. What was the common-law definition of murder?

Review Problems

1. State Statute reads: "Any act of 1. sexual intercourse 2. with another person 3. against that person's will and 4. by use of force or under such a threat of force that resistance would result in serious bodily injury or death, is rape." Explain how this statutory definition of rape differs from the common-law definition.

2. On May 5, Mark and Sam, who had been neighbors for three years, argued over Sam's construction of a ditch, which diverted water onto Mark's property. Mark told Sam to stop construction of the ditch or he "would pay with his life." The following day, Mark and Sam met again in Sam's garage. Within minutes Mark became very angry and cut Sam's leg with an axe he found in Sam's garage. After cutting Sam he panicked and ran home. Sam attempted to reach a telephone to call for help, but the cut proved fatal.

   Mark has been charged with first-degree murder. He claims that he had no intent to kill Sam; rather, he only intended to hit him on the leg with the dull, flat side of the axe in an effort to scare Sam. Discuss the facts and explain what crimes could be proved and why.

3. On July 1, 1990, Jeff shot Megan during a bank robbery. Megan remained on life-support systems until September 4, 1991. At that time the systems were disconnected and she ceased breathing. On June 15, 1991, her physician declared her brain dead. It was not until September 4, 1991, that her family decided to stop the life-support system. Jeff is charged with murder. Discuss any defenses he may have.

4. Penelope and Brenda had been enemies for years. One evening Penelope discovered that Brenda had attempted on many occasions to "pick up" Penelope's boyfriend. Penelope told a friend that she was "going to fix Brenda once and for all—that she was going to mess her face up bad." That evening Penelope waited for Brenda outside of her home and attacked her with a knife. Penelope slashed her in the face four times and cut off one ear. Brenda reported the event to the police, who have turned it over to the county prosecutor's office. As the office legal assistant, you have been assigned the task of determining what crime can be charged.

5. State Statute reads: "It shall be a felony for any person to purposefully, knowingly, or recklessly cause the death of another person by the use of poison or other toxins." Eddie Farmer spread a toxic insecticide on his

crops, which eventually mixed with rainwater and made its way into his neighbor's well. The insecticide was new, but recommended by other farmers who had used it successfully. His neighbor's seven-year-old son, Mikie, died from the poisons in the water. Eddie has been charged with violating the state statute. Is he liable?

6. One evening after a play Tracy was approached by a woman who pointed a pistol at her and ordered her to "give me all your money and jewelry." Tracy removed her jewels and handed them over, but told the robber that her money was in her purse, which was in the trunk of her car. The robber asked her where her car was parked, and Tracy pointed to a car thirty feet away. Tracy was then ordered to go to the automobile, remove the purse, and give it to the robber. She complied, and the woman ran off. The thief was eventually captured and tried for aggravated robbery and kidnapping. She was convicted of both and has appealed the kidnapping conviction. What do you think her argument would be to reverse the kidnapping conviction?

7. Do you believe that prostitution and solicitation of prostitution are victimless crimes? If so, does the threat of AIDS and other communicable diseases change your decision?

8. Make your best argument in support of legalizing (decriminalizing) prostitution.

9. Consider your life experiences. Have you ever committed a technical stalking (such as repeatedly seeking the affection of an uninterested person)?

Notes

1 A. Loewy, *Criminal Law,* 2d ed. (Nutshell Series, St. Paul: West, 1987).

2 *See Commonwealth v. Redline,* 391 Pa. 486, 137 A.2d 472 (1958).

3 *See* LaFave & Scott, *Criminal Law* § 7.7 (Hornbook Series, St. Paul: West, 1986).

4 *State v. Corn,* 278 S.E.2d 221 (N.C. 1981).

5 *Labelle v. State,* 550 N.E.2d 752 (Ind. 1990); *see also* LaFave & Scott at § 7.2(b).

6 Model Penal Code § 210.0(4).

7 *See* Ill. Rev. Stat. ch. 38, para. 9-3.

8 The Model Penal Code addresses homicide at § 210.0 *et seq.*

9 Mich. Comp. Laws Ann. § 752.1027.

10 "U.S. Judge Strikes Down Charges Against Suicide Doctor," *Reuters,* Jan. 27, 1994.SA

11 *See* 65 Am. Jur. 2d *Rape* 28 (1976).

12 Model Penal Code § 213.

13 Ohio Rev. Code § 2907.

14 *Michael M. v. Superior Court,* 450 U.S. 464 (1981).

[15] *See Bowers v. Hardwick,* 478 U.S. 186 (1986).

[16] 18 U.S.C. § 1201.

[17] 18 U.S.C. § 1201(b).

[18] Model Penal Code § 212.1.

[19] 28 U.S.C. § 1738A.

[20] Karen Brooks, "The New Stalking Laws: Are They Adequate to End Violence?," 14 *Hamline J. Pub. L. & Pol'y* 259 (1993).

[21] 18 U.S.C. § 241.

[22] 18 U.S.C. § 242.

[23] 42 U.S.C. § 1983.

[24] *People v. Superior Court,* 15 Cal. App. 4th 1593, 1599 (1993).

[25] Fla. Stat. Ann. § 775.085.

CHAPTER 5

CRIMES AGAINST PROPERTY AND HABITATION

CHAPTER OUTLINE   Arson

Burglary

Theft Crimes

Arson

Arson is a crime against property. In addition, it is a crime against habitation. Crimes against habitation developed because of the importance of peoples' homes. In England and the United States, the concept that a "man's home is his castle" is one with great influence. A home is not merely property, but a refuge from the rest of the world. As such, special common-law crimes developed that sought to protect this important sanctuary. Arson and burglary are such crimes.

At common law, arson was defined very narrowly. It was the (1) malicious (2) burning of a (3) dwelling house of (4) another. This definition was so narrowly construed that an owner could burn her own property with an intent to defraud her insurer and not be guilty of arson, because she did not burn the dwelling of another.[1] In addition, the structure burned had to be a *dwelling*, which was defined as a structure inhabited by people. This definition did include outhouses and the area directly around the home (*curtilage*), so long as the area was used frequently by people. However, the burning of businesses and other structures was not arson.

To be a burning, the dwelling must actually sustain some damage, although slight damage was sufficient. If the structure is simply charred by the fire, there is a burning. However, if the structure is only smoke-damaged or discolored by the heat of a fire, which never touched the building, there is no arson. Finally, causing a dwelling to explode is not arson, unless some of the dwelling is left standing after the explosion and is then burned by a fire caused by the explosion.

At common law, malice was the mens rea of arson. As was true of murder at common law, *malice* meant evil intent. However, an intentional or extremely reckless burning would suffice.

Today, the definition of arson has been broadened by statute in most, if not all, states. It is now common to prosecute an owner of property for burning his own building, if the purpose was to defraud an insurer or to cause another injury. Be aware that the fraud may constitute a separate offense: defrauding an insurance carrier. Also, the structure burned need not be a dwelling under most statutes, though most statutes aggravate the crime if a dwelling is burned. Although the common law did not recognize explosions as a burning, the Model Penal Code and most statutes do.[2]

The mens rea for arson under the Model Penal Code is purposeful and reckless. If a person starts a fire or causes an explosion with the purpose of destroying the building or defrauding an insurer, a felony of

---
BALLENTINE'S

arson The willful and malicious burning of a building. In some jurisdictions, arson includes the deliberate burning of any structure.

the second degree has been committed. It is a felony of the third degree to purposely start a fire or cause an explosion and thereby recklessly endanger person or structure.[3] Note that under the Model Penal Code the fire need not touch the structure, as was required by the common law. Setting the fire is enough to satisfy the burning requirement.

Arson is often graded. The burning of dwellings is usually the highest form of the crime. The burning of uninhabited structures is usually the next highest form of arson, and arson of personal property, if treated as arson, is the lowest.

Burglary

The (1) breaking and entering (2) of another's dwelling (3) at night (4) for the purpose of committing a felony once inside, was **burglary** at common law. A burglary, or entry of a dwelling, may be for the purpose of theft, rape, murder, or another felony. For that reason, burglary is a crime against habitation, as well as against property and person.

The first element, the actus reus, a breaking, can be satisfied by either an actual break-in or by a constructive breaking. If one enters a dwelling by simply passing through an open door or window (a trespass), there is no breaking. Generally, there has to be some act on the part of the defendant to change the condition of the house so as to gain entry. For example, opening an unlocked door or window is a breaking, while passing through an open door or window is not a breaking. Of course, picking a lock and breaking a window or door are breakings.

A burglar may also gain entry by a constructive breaking. A constructive breaking occurs when one uses fraud or force to gain entry. So, if a burglar poses as a telephone repairworker to gain entry, then the

--------BALLENTINE'S--------

burglary   At common law, the offense of breaking and entering a dwelling at night with the intent to commit a felony ... . The crime of burglary has been broadened by statute to include entering buildings other than dwellings, with or without a breaking, and regardless of the time of day or night.

breaking element has been satisfied. The same is true if the owner consents to the burglar's entry under threat or the use of force.

Once the breaking occurs, there must be an entry of the home. The burglar does not need to fully enter the structure; an entry occurs if any part of the burglar's body enters the house. So, the individual who breaks a window and reaches in to grab an item has entered the house.

Modern statutes have eliminated the breaking requirement, although most still require some form of "unlawful entry." Because trespasses, frauds, and breakings are unlawful, they satisfy modern statutory requirements.

The second element required that the breaking and entry be of another person's dwelling. As with arson, at common law the structure had to be a dwelling. The person who lives in the dwelling does not have to be the owner, only an occupant. As such, rental property is included. Interestingly, at least one court has held that churches are dwellings, regardless of whether a person actually resides in the church, premised on the theory that churches are God's dwellings.[4] The dwelling had to belong to another person, so one could not burglarize his or her own property. No jurisdiction continues to require that the structure be a dwelling. Most statutes now refer to all buildings or other structures.[5] However, if the structure burglarized is a dwelling, most states punish the crime more severely than if it was another type of building.

The third requirement was that the burglary occur at night. Although this is no longer an element of burglary, many states do aggravate the crime if it happened at night.

The fourth element is that the person entering must have as a purpose the commission of a felony once inside. This is the mens rea of the crime. If the person's intent is only to commit a misdemeanor, there is no burglary. If Jay's intent is to murder Mark, there is a burglary. It is not a burglary if Jay's intent is to punch Mark in the nose.

Of course, many breaking and enterings with an intent to commit a burglary are not completed. A burglar may be caught by surprise by someone who was not known to be inside and flee from the property. It also happens that burglars are caught in the act by occupants who return to the building. In any event, what is important is that the intended felony need not be completed. All that need be proven is that the accused entered with an intent to commit a felony. As is always true, proving a person's subjective mental state is nearly impossible. Thus, juries are permitted to infer intent from the actions of the defendant. A jury did just that in the *Lockett* case.

Some statutes now provide that intent to commit any crime is sufficient, whether misdemeanor or felony. However, many continue to require an intent to commit either a felony or any theft.

In summary, most jurisdictions have changed burglary in such a way that the following elements are common: (1) an unlawful entry

(2) of any structure or building (3) for the purpose of committing a felony or stealing from the premises (4) once inside.

As mentioned, burglary may be graded and higher penalties imposed if the act occurred at night; involved a dwelling, or was perpetrated at a dwelling that was actually inhabited at the time of the crime; or was committed by a burglar with a weapon.

State of ILLINOIS
v.
Gerry LOCKETT
196 Ill. App. 3d 981, 554 N.E.2d 566 (1990)

Gerry Lockett was charged with residential burglary, convicted after a jury trial, and sentenced to 8 years imprisonment. ...

At about 3:00 A.M. on November 27, 1987, Allan Cannon entered his apartment, which he shared with his sister. Cannon noticed a broken window in his sister's bedroom. He then saw a man, whom he did not know, standing about six feet away from him in the apartment hallway. The only light came from the bathroom off the hallway. The man said to Cannon, "I know your sister." Cannon fled the apartment to call the police from the nearby El station. Outside his apartment, Cannon saw the man running down an alley. Cannon described the man to police as a dark black man with curly hair, about 5′5″ weighing about 200 pounds.

Cannon returned to his apartment and noticed that his bicycle had been placed on his bed, and that his sister's baby clothes, which had been packed in bags, had been thrown all over. Although the apartment was in a general state of disarray, which Cannon admitted was not uncommon, nothing had been taken. ...

Lockett also argues, without merit, that the evidence could not support an inference of his intent to commit a theft. But when Cannon entered his apartment, he found a broken window and later noticed a rock and broken glass on the floor, indicating that the window had been broken from outside. Cannon also discovered contents of the apartment had been rearranged and thrown about. Even assuming that Lockett was, as he said, an acquaintance of Cannon's sister, and that the Cannons, as defense counsel implied, were less than diligent housekeepers, Lockett's presence, without permission, in the dark, empty apartment, at 3 A.M., supported the jury's inference of intent to commit a theft.

Theft Crimes

Introduction to Theft Crimes

There are many types of theft. It is theft to take a pack of gum from a grocery store and not pay for it; for a lawyer to take a client's trust fund and spend it on personal items; for a bank officer to use a computer to make a paper transfer of funds from a patron's account to the officer's with an intent to later withdraw the money and abscond; and to hold a gun on a person and demand that property and money be surrendered. However, they are all fundamentally different crimes.

Some thefts are more violative of the person, such as robbery, and others are more violative of a trust relationship, such as an attorney absconding with a client's money. The crimes also differ in the methods by which they are committed. A robbery involves an unlawful taking. Embezzlement, however, involves a lawful taking with a subsequent unlawful conversion.

Larceny was the first theft crime. It was created by judges as part of the common law. The elements of larceny were very narrow and did not cover most thefts. Larceny began as one crime, but developed into many different crimes. This was not a fluid, orderly development, for two reasons. First, when larceny was first created, well over 600 years ago, the purpose of making larceny criminal was more to prevent breaches of the peace (fights over possession of property) than to protect ownership of property. Larceny did not prohibit fraudulent takings of another's property. The theory was that an embezzlement or other theft by trick was less likely to result in an altercation (breach of the peace) between the owner and the thief, because the owner would not be aware of the theft until after it was completed. Using this theory, many courts were reluctant to expand the scope of larceny. Second, at early common law, larceny was punishable by death. For this reason, some judges were reluctant to expand its reach.[6]

Eventually, two other theft crimes were created, embezzlement and false pretenses. Despite the creation of these crimes, many theft acts continued to go unpunished because they fell into the cracks that separated the elements of the three common-law theft crimes. Some courts attempted to remedy this problem by broadening the definitions of the three crimes. However, computers, electronic banking, and other technological advances have led to new methods of stealing money and property, posing problems not anticipated by the judges who created the common-law theft crimes. Some states have changed their definitions of larceny, false pretenses, and embezzlement be more contemporary. Other states have simply abandoned the common-law crimes and have enacted consolidated theft statutes. The common-law theft crimes, modern consolidated theft statutes, and the Model Penal Code approach to theft are discussed here.

SIDEBAR

CRIME IN THE UNITED STATES

The United States Department of Justice includes shoplifting, pocket-picking, purse-snatching, thefts from automobiles, thefts of motor vehicles, and all other thefts of personal property, which occur without the use of force, as larceny for the purpose of the Uniform Crime Reporting Program. That program shows that there were nearly 8 million reported larcenies in the United States in 1993. That is one larceny every four seconds. Larceny accounted for 55 percent of all crimes in 1992.

Source: Uniform Crime Reports, United States Department of Justice, Federal Bureau of Investigation, *1993 & 1994.*

Larceny

At common law the elements of **larceny** were: (1) the trespassory taking (2) and carrying away (*asportation*) (3) of personal property (4) of another (5) with an intent to permanently deprive the owner of possession. The actus reus of larceny was the taking and carrying away of personal property of another. The mens rea was the intent to permanently deprive the owner of possession.

To have had a common-law larceny, there must have been a "taking" of property. A taking alone would not have sufficed; the taking must have been unlawful or trespassory. That is, the property must be taken by the defendant without the owner's consent. This element is only concerned with the method that the defendant used in acquiring possession. For example, if Mandy takes Sean's wallet from his hand, she has committed a taking. However, if Sean were to give Mandy his wallet with the understanding that she is to return it at a specified time, there is no unlawful taking when she does not return it; she lawfully acquired possession of the wallet. Taking property from another without that person's consent was a trespass under the common law, but failing to return property was not.

In an effort to protect employers (masters) from theft by their employees (servants), the theory of *constructive possession* was created. This theory held that when an employee received actual possession of the employer's property as part of the job, the employer maintained "constructive possession" while the employee had custody of the property. If this theory had not been developed, employees would have been free to steal property entrusted to them, as larceny required a trespassory taking. Of course, if an employee took property that was not under his or her care, there was a trespassory taking.

Interestingly, the theory of constructive possession was never extended to other relationships. This led to the creation of a new crime, embezzlement.

Once the taking has been effected, the defendant must carry away the property. This carrying away is called *asportation*. Generally, any asportation, even slight movement, will satisfy this requirement. The term *asportation* is deceiving, as not all property has to be "carried away" to satisfy this requirement. Riding a horse away will satisfy the requirement, as will driving another's automobile. Most states have done away with the asportation requirement by statute.

Third, the item stolen must be personal property. Land and items attached to land (e.g., houses) are considered real property. Theft of such property was not larceny. All other property is personal property.

BALLENTINE'S

larceny   The crime of taking personal property, without consent, with the intent to convert it to the use of someone other than the owner or to deprive the owner of it permanently. Larceny does not involve the use of force or the threat of force.

Objects that are movable property are personal property. In the early years of larceny, there was a further requirement that the item stolen be tangible personal property. Tangible personal property includes most items, such as automobiles, books, electronic equipment, and the like. Documents, such as stocks, bonds, and promissory notes, which represent ownership of something, are considered intangible property. It was not larceny to steal intangible personal property. Under modern statutes, most states have broadened theft to include all types of property.

The fourth element is that the personal property taken and carried away must be owned by another. One cannot steal from oneself. However, the rule has been extended to prohibit prosecution of a partner for taking partnership assets and joint tenants from taking each other's things; also, because husband and wife were one person under the common law, it was not possible for spouses to steal from one another.

Finally, the mens rea element: It is required that the defendant intend to permanently deprive the owner of possession of the property. In short, to be a thief one must have an intent to steal. If Jack takes Eddie's lawnmower, intending to return the mower when he has completed his mowing, he has not committed larceny, as he did not possess an intent to permanently deprive Eddie of his possession of the mower. Also, the accused must intend to deprive an owner (or possessor) of property to be guilty of larceny. If an accused had a good faith belief that he had lawful right to the property, the requisite mens rea did not exist, and there was no larceny.

Although proving "an intent to permanently deprive the owner of possession" is the common method of proving the mens rea of larceny, it is not the only method. Courts have held that if the property is held so long that it causes the owner to lose a significant portion of its value, a larceny has occurred. Some cases have held that if the property is taken with an intent to subject the property to substantial risk, there is a larceny. Of course, the intent must exist at the time of taking. To illustrate this last method, imagine a thief who steals a plane intending to use the plane in a daredevil show. In such a case the thief is subjecting the property to a substantial risk, and even though the intent was to return the plane when the show was over, there is a larceny.

Embezzlement

The definition of larceny left a large gap that permitted people in some circumstances to steal from others. That gap was caused by requiring a trespassory taking of the property. For various reasons, people entrust money and property to others. The intent is not to transfer ownership (title), only possession. A depositor of a bank gives possession of money to the bank; a client may give an attorney money to hold in a trust account; a stockbroker may keep an account with a client-investor's money in it. In all of these situations the money is taken lawfully; there is no trespassory taking. So, what happens if the person entrusted with the money *converts* (steals) it after taking lawful possession? At the early common law, it was not a crime. However, the thief could have been sued for recovery of the stolen money.

This theory was carried to an extreme in a case in which a bank teller converted money handed to him by a depositor to himself, by placing the money in his own pocket. It was held that there was no larceny, because the teller acquired the money lawfully. The court also determined that there was no larceny under the theory of constructive possession, because the employer (bank) never had possession of the money. If the teller had put the money in the drawer and then taken it, the bank would have had constructive possession, and he would have committed larceny. The result was that the teller was guilty of no crime.[7] Unsatisfied with this situation, the English Parliament created a new crime: **embezzlement.**

The elements of embezzlement are (1) conversion (2) of personal property (3) of another (4) by one who has acquired lawful possession (5) with an intent to defraud the owner.

To prove embezzlement, the prosecution must first show that an act of **conversion** occurred. Conversion is the unauthorized control over property with an intent to permanently deprive the owner of its possession or which substantially interferes with the rights of the owner.

As was the case with larceny, only tangible personal property was included. Today, nearly all forms of personal property may be embezzled. Also, the property had to belong to another. One could not embezzle one's own property.

The element that distinguished embezzlement from larceny was the taking requirement. Whereas larceny required a trespassory taking, embezzlement required lawful acquisition. Accountants, lawyers, bailees, executors of estates, and trustees are examples of those who can commit embezzlement.

To satisfy the mens rea requirement of embezzlement, it must be shown that the defendant possessed an "intent to defraud." Mere negligent conversion of another's property is not embezzlement. Because the mens rea requirement is so high, bona fide claims of mistake of fact and law are valid defenses. If an accountant makes an accounting error and converts a client's money, there is no embezzlement. This is a mistake of fact. If a friend you loaned money to keeps the money with

---
————————————— BALLENTINE'S —————————————

embezzlement   The fraudulent conversion of property, including but not limited to money, with which a person ... has been entrusted.

conversion   Control over another person's personal property which is wrongfully exercised; control applied in a manner that violates that person's title to or rights in the property. Conversion is both a tort and a crime.

the mistaken belief that he is allowed to in order to offset damage you caused to his property last year (when the law requires that he sue you for the damage), there is no embezzlement. This is a mistake of law and negates the intent required, as does a mistake of fact.

Embezzlement is prohibited in all states. Some states have retained the name *embezzlement*; others have named it theft and included it in a consolidated theft statute. Embezzlement, which occurs in interstate commerce, federally insured banks, and lending institutions, or involves officers and agents of the federal government, is also made criminal by the statutes of the United States.[8] 18 U.S.C. § 641 is the embezzlement of public monies, property, and records statute. Violation of that provision, if the property embezzled has a value of $100 or greater, results in a fine of up to $10,000 and ten years in prison. The remainder of that statute deals with embezzlement of nonpublic property that occurs in interstate commerce or by federal officials. The penalties vary for each provision.

False Pretenses

At common law, it was not larcenous to use lies (false representations) to gain ownership of property. For example, if Brogan were to sell Sean a ring containing glass, while representing to Sean that the ring contained a diamond, it was not larceny under the early common law, even though Brogan knew that the ring contained glass. The early judges believed strongly in the the concept of *caveat emptor*, which translates as "let the buyer beware."

As it had done with embezzlement, Parliament decided to make such acts criminal. It did so by creating the crime of **false pretenses**. The elements of false pretenses are (1) a false representation of (2) a material present or past fact (3) made with knowledge that the fact is false (4) and with an intent to defraud the victim (5) thereby causing the victim to pass title to property to the actor.

To prove the first element, it must be shown that the actor made a false representation. This representation may be made orally or by writing, or may be implied by one's actions. The law does not require that people disclose all relevant information during a business transaction —*caveat emptor* still exists in that regard. The law does, however, require that any affirmative statements (or implications from actions) be true. So, if a buyer fails to ask if property has a lien against it, there is no false

---

BALLENTINE'S

false pretenses   The crime of obtaining the money or property of another by fraudulent misrepresentation. The essential elements of the offense are an intentional false statement concerning a material fact, in reliance on which title or possession is surrendered.

pretense if the seller does not inform the buyer of such. The opposite is true if the buyer inquires about existing liens and encumbrances and is told there are none.

The false representation must be important to the transaction. If the statement is important, the law says that it is *material*. Generally, a representation is material if it would have had an impact on the victim's decision making had the victim known the truth at the time the transaction took place. For example, if Connie represents to Pam that the lighter in a used car she is selling works, when it does not, she has not committed false pretenses. However, if she states to Pam that the automobile recently had its engine replaced, that would be material and she would be liable for false pretenses if she knew that the statement was untrue.

The fact conveyed by the actor must not only be material, but it must also concern a present fact or past fact. In this context, *present* refers to the time of the transaction. Statements of expected facts, promises, predictions, and expectations cannot be the basis of false pretenses. So, if Aaron buys an automobile from Kathy and promises to pay her in six months, it is no crime if he fails to pay because he loses his source of income during that period. To permit breaches of such promises to be criminal would be the same as having a debtor's prison, which is not recognized in the United States. The same is not true if Aaron made the promise but had no intent of paying the debt. Some states treat this as false pretenses under the theory that his state of mind at the time of the sale was fraudulent. Some states do not treat his action as criminal and place the burden on Kathy to seek her own remedy in a civil cause of action. It is also necessary that the representation be one of fact. Accordingly, opinions are not included. Of course, the line between fact and opinion is often unclear.

It must also be proved that the defendant knew the statement was false. An unintentional misrepresentation is not sufficient to establish this element in most jurisdictions, although most jurisdictions will find knowledge if the lower mens rea standard, recklessness, is proved.

The defendant must have the additional mens rea of "intent to defraud." As with other theft crimes, if one has a bona fide belief that the property belongs to him or her, there is a defense. In addition to intending to defraud the victim, it must also be shown that the victim was defrauded. Hence, if the victim was aware of the falsity of the statement and entered into the bargain anyway, there has been no crime.

Finally, the misrepresentation must be the cause of the victim passing title to property to the defendant. *Title* is ownership. Transferring possession to the defendant is not adequate. However, causing one to transfer possession of property by use of fraud was a type of larceny, known as *larceny by trick*. Just as with larceny and embezzlement, only tangible personal property was included within the grasp of the prohibition at early common law. Today, false pretenses usually includes all property that is subject to the protection of larceny—in most instances, this includes all personal property.

Fraudulent Checks

Related to the crime of false pretenses is the crime of acquiring property or money by writing a check (draft) from an account that has insufficient funds to cover the draft. The act appears to fall into the category of false pretenses. Some theorize that a check is a promise of future payment, and, accordingly, the check does not meet the "representation of present or past fact" requirement of false pretenses. Courts have rejected that theory and held that at the time one drafts a check, a representation is made that there are adequate funds in the account to pay the amount drafted.

Today, most states have bad-check statutes. Conviction of these laws, for the most part, results in a less serious punishment than conviction on false pretenses.[9] Three common material elements are found in bad-check statutes. First, the mens rea may be proven by showing either an intent to defraud the payee or knowledge that there were insufficient funds in the account. Second, the check must be taken in exchange for something of value; third, there must have been insufficient funds in the account.

Mail Fraud

Another crime related to false pretenses is mail fraud.[10] Mail fraud is a crime against the United States, because the mail system is run by a federal agency. Using the United States mail system with an intent to defraud another of money or property is mail fraud. The intended victim need not be defrauded; the act of sending such mails with the intent to defraud is itself criminal.

Mail fraud has become increasingly important in recent years, because it often is the foundation of a RICO count.

Racketeer Influenced and Corrupt Organizations Act

Another federal statute that deals with fraud is the **Racketeer Influenced and Corrupt Organizations Act,** commonly known as RICO.[11] The United States Congress enacted RICO in the early 1970s in an attempt to curb organized crime.

─────────────────────BALLENTINE'S─────────────────────

Racketeer Influenced and Corrupt Organizations Act   A federal statute, commonly referred to as RICO, which criminalizes racketeering that affects interstate commerce or persons or businesses engaged in interstate commerce.

Judicial interpretation of RICO has led to much controversy in recent years. Some people contend that the effect of court opinions has been to extend the prohibition of RICO beyond Congress's original intent. Today, all businesses, not just traditional organized crime, are subject to RICO.

To establish a RICO violation, the United States must prove that the (1) defendant received money or income (2) from a pattern of racketeering activity and (3) invested that money in an enterprise (business), (4) which is in interstate commerce or affects interstate commerce.

The second element is the key to proving a RICO violation. The term *pattern* means two or more acts, referred to as the predicate acts. Those acts must fall into the definition of a "racketeering activity." The statute provides a list of state and federal crimes that are considered to be racketeering. Murder, kidnapping, extortion, and drug sales and transportation are examples of the state crimes included in the list. Mail fraud, wire fraud, white slave traffic, securities fraud, and bribery are a few examples of the federal crimes included. Mail fraud is often the basis of a RICO violation, because the mails are often used by such enterprises.

For example, the Supreme Court announced, in a 1994 decision, that RICO could apply to a coalition of antiabortion groups that were alleged to have conspired, through a pattern of racketeering, to shut down abortion clinics.[12] In that case, extortion, including alleged threats of assault, was used to satisfy this element.

Violation of RICO can result in serious criminal penalties. In addition, victims of such activity may sue civilly and receive treble damages, costs, and attorney fees. RICO also provides for **forfeiture** of property in criminal proceedings. *Forfeiture* is the taking of property and money of a defendant by the government. Many crimes have forfeiture provisions. A forfeiture is not the same as a fine. Both forfeitures and fines are levied as punishment, but the focus of a fine is generally to hurt a defendant's pocketbook. Forfeitures are specifically aimed at getting the property or money connected to the crime for which the individual was convicted. So, in a RICO situation, a convicted party could stand to lose the enterprise itself, as well as all profits from that activity.

The *H.J.* case is a civil case. However, many aspects of civil RICO are identical to criminal RICO. One such aspect is the pattern requirement. Whether the case is civil or criminal, a pattern of racketeering must be proven. The United States Supreme Court addressed the pattern question because the various appellate courts of the United States were divided on how to define that phrase. This case is also a good illustration of how "legitimate businesses" are subject to RICO.

BALLENTINE'S

forfeiture A deprivation of money, property, or rights, without compensation, as a consequence of a default or the commission of a crime; civil forfeiture.

H.J. INC.
v.
NORTHWESTERN BELL TELEPHONE CO.
492 U.S. 229 (1989)

Petitioners, customers of respondent Northwestern Bell Telephone Co., filed this putative class action in 1986 in the District Court for the District of Minnesota. Petitioners alleged violations of 18 U.S.C. §§ 1962(a), (b), (c), and (d) by Northwestern Bell and other respondents—some of the telephone company's officers and employees, various members of the Minnesota Public Utilities Commission (MPUC), and other unnamed individuals and corporations—and sought an injunction and treble damages under RICO's civil liability provisions, §§ 1964(a) and (c).

The MPUC is the state body responsible for determining the rates that Northwestern Bell may charge. Petitioners' 5-count complaint alleged that between 1980 and 1986 Northwestern Bell sought to influence members of the MPUC in the performance of their duties—and in fact caused them to approve rates for the company in excess of a fair and reasonable amount—by making cash payments to commissioners, negotiating with them regarding future employment, and paying for meals, for tickets to sporting events and the like, and for airline tickets.

* * *

Our guides in the endeavor must be the text of the statute and its legislative history. We find no support in those sources for the proposition, espoused by the Court of Appeals for the Eighth Circuit in this case, that predicate acts of racketeering may form a pattern; only then they are part of separate illegal schemes. Nor can we agree with those courts that have suggested that a pattern is established merely by proving two predicate acts ... .

The legislative history, which we discussed in [another case] shows that Congress indeed had a fairly flexible concept of a pattern in mind. A pattern is not formed by "sporadic activity," and a person cannot "be subjected to the sanctions of [RICO] simply by committing two widely separated and isolated criminal offenses. ... Instead, "[t]he term 'pattern' itself requires the showing of a relationship" between the predicates and of "the threat of continuing activity. ..." It is this factor of *continuity plus relationship* which combines to produce a pattern. RICO's legislative history reveals Congress's intent that to prove a pattern of racketeering activity a plaintiff or prosecutor must show that the racketeering predicates are related, *and* that they amount to or pose a threat of continued criminal activity.

Forgery

Another crime related to fraud is **forgery**. *Forgery* is the (1) making of (2) false documents (or the alteration of existing documents making them false) (3) and passing the document (4) to another (5) with an intent to defraud.

The purpose of forgery statutes is both to prevent fraud and to preserve the value of written instruments. This is important because if forgery were to become common, people would no longer trust commercial

---
BALLENTINE'S

forgery   The false making, material alteration, or uttering, with intent to defraud or injure, of any writing that, if genuine, might appear to be legally effective or the basis for legal liability.

documents, such as checks and contracts. The effect that would have on commerce is obvious.

The actus reus of forgery is the making of the document. That involves the actual writing and drafting of the document, as well as passing the document (*uttering*) to a potential victim. The mens rea of forgery is knowledge of the falsity of the document and an intent to defraud.

In many jurisdictions, forgery and uttering are separate crimes. In those states one must only make the false instrument and possess an intent to defraud. The defendant need not present the document (utter) to the victim. That act, when accompanied with an intent to defraud, is the crime of *uttering*.

Receiving Stolen Property

Not only is it a crime to steal another's property, but it is also a crime to receive property that one knows is stolen, if the intent is to keep that property. In essence, one who buys or receives as a gift property that is known to be stolen is an accessory (after the fact) to the theft. Although the law applies to anyone who violates its prohibitions, the primary focus of law enforcement is *fences*, people who purchase stolen property with the intent of reselling the property for a profit. They act as the retailers of stolen property, with the thieves acting as suppliers.

The elements of **receiving stolen property** are (1) receiving property (2) that has been stolen (3) with knowledge of its stolen character (4) with an intent to deprive the owner of the property.

Receipt of the property may be shown either by showing actual possession or constructive possession of the property. Constructive possession occurs any time the defendant has control over the property, even though the defendant does not have actual possession. For example, if one makes arrangements for stolen property to be delivered to one's home, there is receipt once the property is in the house, even if the defendant was not present when the property was delivered. Receiving includes not only purchases of stolen property, but also other transfers, such as gifts.

The property in question must have been stolen. In this context, stolen property includes that property acquired from larcenies, robberies, embezzlement, extortion, false pretenses, and similar crimes.

BALLENTINE'S

receiving stolen property   Receiving property with the knowledge that it is stolen property, and with fraudulent intent. Although receiving stolen property is a crime separate and distinct from the crime of stealing the property, if the theft was recent there is a rebuttable presumption that the theft was committed by the person in possession of the property.

The final two elements deal with the mens rea of the crime of receiving stolen property. It is necessary that the defendant knew of the property's stolen character at the time of acquiring the property. Actual knowledge that the property was stolen is required. However, if it can be proven that the defendant had a subjective belief that the goods were stolen, but lacked absolute proof of that fact, the crime has still been committed. The fact that a reasonable person would have known that the property was stolen is not enough to convict for receiving stolen property. If one receives property under a bona fide belief that he or she has claim to the property, he or she is not guilty of receiving stolen property, even though that belief was unfounded.

The last element requires that the receiver of the property intend to deprive the owner of the property. Of course, if a defendant intends to keep the property for himself or herself, then this requirement is met. The language of the crime is broader, however, and includes any intent to deprive the owner of the use, ownership, or possession of the property. Thus, if one receives the property intending to destroy it or to give it as a gift, this element has been satisfied.

Not only do the states prohibit receiving stolen property, but the federal government also makes it a crime to receive stolen property that has traveled in interstate commerce or to receive stolen property while on lands controlled by the United States.[13]

Robbery

The material elements of **robbery** are (1) a trespassory taking (2) and carrying away (asportation) (3) of personal property (4) from another's person or presence (5) using either force or threat (6) with an intent to steal the property.

Robbery is actually a type of assault mixed with a type of larceny. Because of the immediate danger created by the crime of robbery, it is punished more severely than either larceny or simple assault. Robbery was a crime under the common law and is a statutory crime in all states today.

The elements of trespassory taking, asportation, intent to steal, and that the property belong to another, are the same as for larceny. However, robbery also requires that the property be taken from the victim's person or presence. So property taken from another's hands, off another's body, or from another's clothing is taken from the person. Property that is taken from another's presence, but not from the person, also qualifies. For example, if a bank robber orders a teller to stand back

---

BALLENTINE'S

robbery   The felonious taking of money or any thing of value from the person of another or from his or her presence, against his or her will, by force or by putting him or her in fear.

while the thief empties the cash drawer, there has been a robbery. The states differ in their definitions of "from another's presence," but it is generally held that property is in a victim's presence any time the victim is in control of the property. This is true in the bank robbery example, as the teller was exercising control over the cash drawer at the time of the robbery.

It is also necessary that the crime be committed with the use of force or threat. This element is the feature that most distinguishes robbery from larceny. As far as force is concerned, if any force is used beyond what is necessary to simply take the property, there is robbery. For example, it is larceny, not robbery, if a pickpocket steals a wallet free of the owner's knowledge. Only the force necessary to take the wallet was used. It is robbery, however, if the victim catches the pickpocket, and an altercation ensues over possession of the wallet. The same result is true when dealing with purse snatchers. If the snatcher makes a clean grab and gets away without an altercation, it is larceny from the person. If the victim grabs the bag and fights to keep it, then it is robbery. A threat of force may also satisfy this requirement. So, if the robber states to the victim, "Give me your wallet or I'll blow your head off," there is a robbery, even though there was no physical contact.

In most jurisdictions, the threatened harm must be immediate; threats of future harm are not adequate. It is also possible that the threat will be to someone else, such as a family member. The thief who holds a man's wife and threatens to harm her if the man does not give up his money is not free from the charge of robbery because the person giving up the money is not the one threatened.

The mens rea of robbery is the specific intent to take the property and deprive the owner of it. As with the other theft crimes, a good faith, but incorrect, claim of right to the property is a defense. In *Richardson v. United States*, 403 F.2d 574 (D.C. Cir. 1968), a defendant's claim of right to money was a gambling debt. The trial court did not permit the illegal debt to be used as a defense, but the appellate court reversed. It stated in its opinion that:

> The government's position seems to be that no instruction on a claim of right is necessary unless the defendant had a legally enforceable right to the property he took. But specific intent depends upon a state of mind, not upon a legal fact. If the jury finds that the defendant believed himself entitled to the money, it cannot properly find that he had the requisite specific intent for robbery.

Not only is robbery a crime pursuant to state law, but the United States has also prohibited certain robberies. Robbery of a federally insured bank is an example.[14]

Robbery is usually, if not always, graded. Robbery is graded higher if it results in serious injury to the victim or is committed using a deadly weapon.

SIDEBAR   CRIME IN THE UNITED STATES   Robbery is defined as the "taking or attempting to take anything of value from the care, custody, or control of a person or persons by force or threat of force or violence and/or by putting the victim in fear. During 1993, there were a total of 659,757 reported robberies under this definition. There is one reported robbery every 47 seconds in the United States. Robberies constituted 4.7 percent of all crimes in the United States in 1992.

Source: Uniform Crime Reports, U.S. Department of Justice, Federal Bureau of Investigation, *1993 & 1994.*

Extortion

Extortion is more commonly known as *blackmail*. Extortion is similar to robbery because both involve stealing money under threat. However, the threat in a robbery must be of immediate harm. Extortion involves a threat of future harm. At common law, extortion applied only against public officers. Today, extortion is much broader. The elements of extortion are (1) the taking or acquisition of property (2) of another (3) using a threat (4) with an intent to steal the property. In a few jurisdictions, the extortionist must actually receive the property, whereas others require only that the threat be made.

A threat of future physical harm will do, as will threats to injure another's reputation, business, financial status, or family relationship. As was the case with robbery, the threat may be directed at one person and the demand for property made on another. For example, if a thief states to John, "Give me $100,000 or I will kill your wife," he is an extortionist, even though he has not threatened John.

The threatened conduct itself need not be illegal to be extortion. For example, if Stacey tells Lisa that she is going to inform the authorities of Lisa's involvement in illegal drug trade unless Lisa pays her $10,000, she is an extortionist, even though informing the police of the activity is not only legal, but encouraged by society.

The federal government has made it a crime for federal officers to extort the public, to be involved in an extortion that interferes with interstate commerce, and to extort another by threatening to expose a violation of federal law.

The *Dioguardi* case deals with extortion in the labor relations area. In most situations it is proper for unions and employees to threaten to picket an employer. In this case the threats were not part of usual labor-management relations; they were made with the purpose of extorting corporate money. Accordingly, the threats were found to be extortion, not protected labor activity.

──────────────BALLENTINE'S──────────────

extortion   The criminal offense of obtaining money or other thing of value by duress, force, threat of force, fear, or color of office.

PEOPLE
v.
DIOGUARDI
8 N.Y.2d 260, 203 N.Y.S.2d 870 (1960)

The Appellate Division has reversed defendants' convictions for extortion and conspiracy to commit extortion, dismissed the indictment, and discharged them from custody. In addition to the conspiracy count, the indictment charged defendants with extorting $4,700 from the officers of two corporations. Said corporations were non-union, conducted a wholesale stationery and office supply business in Manhattan, did an annual business of several million dollars, and their stock was wholly owned by a family named Kerin. Anthony Kerin, Sr., president and "boss" of the Kerin companies, made all the important corporate decisions. The other two corporate officers were his son Kerin, Jr., and one Jack Shumann.

Defendant McNamara, the alleged "front man" in the extortive scheme, was an official of Teamster's Local 295 and 808, as well as a member of the Teamster's Joint Council. Defendant Dioguardi, the immediate beneficiary of the payments and the alleged power behind the scene, was sole officer of Equitable Research Associates, Inc.—a *publishing house,* according to its certificate of incorporation, a *public relations concern,* according to its bank account and the Yellow Pages of the telephone directory, a *labor statistics concern,* according to its office secretary and sole employee, and a *firm of labor consultants,* according to its business card. ...

[During late 1955 and early 1956 various unions were attempting to unionize Kerin's business. The two primary unions involved in this attempt were both locals of the Teamsters. Eventually, one union began picketing the business while the other was on the premises handing out literature.]

The appearance of the picket line—which truck drivers from two companies refused to cross—thoroughly alarmed the Kerin officers, since they were in an "extremely competitive business," and a cessation of incoming or outgoing truck deliveries for as short a period as two weeks would effectively force them out of business.

* * *

McNamara assured Kerin, Sr., that his troubles could be ended, and *would be,* if he did three things: (1) "joined up" with McNamara's local 295, (2) paid $3,500 to Equitable to defray the "out-of-pocket" expenses incurred by the various unions that had sought to organize the companies, and (3) retained Equitable as labor consultant at $100 per month for each company for the period of the collective bargaining contract. ... McNamara repeatedly assured Kerin, Sr., that the picketing would stop immediately and the companies would be guaranteed labor peace if his program were accepted.

Kerin, Sr., stated that he was not adverse to having his employees organized by local 295, if it was a good honest union, and that he could "accept the idea of a hundred dollars a month as a retainer fee for labor counsel and advise." He protested against the proposed payment of $3,500, however, as an "extraordinary charge" that sounded "like a hold-up," to which McNamara replied: "It may seem that way to you, Mr. Kerin, but that is the amount of money that these unions that have sought to organize you ... have expended, and *if we are going to avoid further trouble and further difficulties, it is my suggestion that you pay that to the Equitable Associates."*

* * *

Upon the proof in this record, a jury could properly conclude that defendants were guilty of extortion—cleverly conceived and subtly executed, but extortion nonetheless. The essence of the crime is obtaining property by a wrongful use of fear, induced by a threat to do an unlawful injury. It is well-settled law in this State that fear of economic loss or harm satisfies the ingredient of fear necessary to the crime.

Consolidated Theft Statutes

The distinctions among the three common-law crimes of theft, larceny, embezzlement, and false pretenses, are often hard to draw. This fact, matched with the belief that there is no substantive difference between stealing by fraud or by quick use of the hands, has led many jurisdictions to do away with the common-law crimes of larceny, false pretenses, and embezzlement, and replace them with a single crime named theft. Exactly what crimes are included in such statutes differs, but larceny, false pretenses, and embezzlement are always included. Many jurisdictions also add one or more of the following: fraudulent checks; receiving stolen property; and extortion.

These statutes often use the language of the common law in defining theft. For example, Florida's statute reads:

> A person is guilty of theft if he knowingly obtains or uses, or endeavors to obtain or to use, the property of another with intent to, either temporarily or permanently: (a) Deprive the other person of a right to the property or a benefit therefrom or Appropriate the property to his own use or to the use of any person not entitled thereto.[15]

This statute includes the three common-law theft crimes. The primary change of consolidated theft statutes is that prosecutors no longer need to charge which specific crime has occurred. At trial, if the jury decides that a defendant has committed a larceny and not an embezzlement, they can convict. At common law, if the defendant was charged with embezzlement, not larceny, the jury would be forced to acquit if they determined that the defendant committed larceny rather than embezzlement.

Robbery is usually not included in consolidated theft statutes because of its significant threat of harm. Consolidation usually includes only misappropriations of property that do not pose serious risks to life.

Of course, those crimes that are included in consolidation statutes are not always punished equally. Grading of such offenses based on the amount of property appropriated, the nature of the theft, and the type of property stolen is common.

The Model Penal Code Consolidation

The Model Penal Code contains a comprehensive consolidation of theft offenses.[16] Provided that a defendant is not prejudiced by doing so, the specification of one theft crime by the prosecution does not prohibit a conviction for another. So if the defendant is specifically charged with larceny, he or she may be convicted of false pretenses or embezzlement by a jury.

The Code recognizes the following forms of theft:

1. Theft by taking (includes common-law larceny and embezzlement).
2. Theft by deception (includes common-law false pretenses).
3. Theft by extortion.
4. Theft of property known to be mislaid, misdelivered, or lost, and no reasonable attempt to find the rightful owner is made.
5. Receiving stolen property.
6. Theft of professional services by deception or threat.
7. Conversion of entrusted funds.
8. Unauthorized use of another's automobile.

The Code declares that thefts are felonies of the third degree if the amount stolen exceeds $500 or if the property stolen is a firearm, automobile, airplane, motorcycle, motorboat, or other vehicle, and, in cases of receiving stolen property, if the receiver of the property is a fence, then it is a felony of the third degree regardless of the value of the property. The Code makes all unauthorized uses of automobiles misdemeanors.

Because the crime of robbery involves a danger to people, it is treated as a separate crime.[17] If during the commission of a theft the defendant inflicts serious bodily injury upon another, threatens serious bodily injury, or threatens to commit a felony of the first or second degree, there is a robbery. It is a felony of the second degree unless the defendant attempts to kill or cause serious bodily injury, in which case it is a felony of the first degree.

Forgery is also treated as a separate offense.[18] Forgery is treated as a felony of the second degree if money, securities, postage stamps, stock, or other documents issued by the government are involved. It is a felony of the third degree if the forged document affects legal relationships, such as wills and contracts. All other forgeries are misdemeanors.

Destruction of Property

Every year a significant amount of financial loss is the result of destruction of property. Arson accounts for much of this total, but not all. Most, if not all, states have statutes making the destruction of another's property criminal. These laws may be part of the statute covering arson or may be a separate section of the criminal code.

Destruction of property, commonly called **criminal mischief**, is normally a specific-intent crime and includes all types of destruction

---
BALLENTINE'S

malicious (criminal) mischief   The willful destruction of the property of another. It is a tort and, in most jurisdictions, a crime as well.

that affect the value or dignity of the property. For example, defacing the tombstone of a Jew by painting a swastika on it would be criminal mischief, even though the paint can be removed and the tombstone is left physically unharmed.

Mischief is often graded so that offenses against public property, which result in damage in excess of a stated dollar amount, or which involve a danger to human life, are penalized more heavily than others. The most serious mischiefs are usually low-grade felonies, and the remainder misdemeanors. For example, the Kentucky mischief statutes read:

Ky. Rev. Stat. § 512.020

(1) A person is guilty of criminal mischief in the first degree when, having no right to do so or any reasonable ground to believe that he has such right, he intentionally or wantonly defaces, destroys, or damages any property causing pecuniary loss of $1,000 or more.

(2) Criminal mischief in the first degree is a Class D felony.

Ky. Rev. Stat. § 512.030

(1) A person is guilty of criminal mischief in the second degree when, having no right to do so or any reasonable ground to believe that he has such a right, he intentionally or wantonly defaces, destroys, or damages any property causing pecuniary loss of $500 or more.

(2) Criminal mischief in the second degree is a Class A misdemeanor.

Ky. Rev. Stat. § 512.040

(1) A person is guilty of criminal mischief in the third degree when:

(a) Having no right to do so or any reasonable ground to believe that he has such right, he intentionally or wantonly defaces, destroys or damages any property; or

(b) He tampers with property so as knowingly to endanger the person or property of another.

(2) Criminal mischief in the third degree is a Class B misdemeanor.

At common law, hairline distinctions existed among the three crimes against property: larceny, embezzlement, and false pretenses. Today, statutes in most states have consolidated theft crimes so that the focus is now on whether a theft occurred, not whether the correct crime has been charged. These consolidation statutes include larceny, false pretenses, and embezzlement. Although it varies, often such statutes will also include receiving stolen property, various forms of fraud, and extortion. Robbery and forgery are treated as separate crimes.

Arson and burglary are separate crimes because they involve more than a threat to property. At common law, only residences were protected by arson and burglary laws. Because of the sanctity that our culture attaches to dwellings and because of the danger to human life created by arson and burglary, these crimes received special attention. Today, arson and burglary have been broadened to include more than just dwellings.

In addition to criminal remedies for these crimes, victims often have civil remedies available. As previously discussed, the victim is responsible for filing and proving such a civil case. However, a prior admission of guilt (or conviction) may prevent the defendant from relitigating his or her innocence in a civil trial.

Computer Crimes

Computer-related crimes cost U.S. businesses $3.5 billion yearly, and that figure does not include unreported crimes.[19] Moreover, the number of computer-related crimes is rapidly growing.

Computer crimes take two general forms. First, computers can be the target of a crime. Theft of hardware and software is an example. Destruction and vandalism of computers is another crime where the computer is itself the target of an unlawful act. Viruses are also used to destroy computer programs.

A second form of computer crime involves using a computer as a tool in the commission of a crime. Violating privileges by improperly obtaining confidential information, threat and harassment through cyberspace, and the illegal distribution of pornography fall into this category. Computers can also be used to steal. Obtaining illegal entry into a bank's computer records from a personal computer in order to steal money is an example, as is using another person's personal identification number and bank card to access an automatic teller machine.

Many computer-related crimes are punishable without special computer crimes laws. Existing penal laws such as theft, larceny, and criminal mischief may include computer activity. For example, stealing funds from a bank through a computer can usually be prosecuted under existing theft laws if a special computer theft statute has not been enacted. Similarly, criminal mischief statutes could be used to prosecute the intentional destruction of computer programs by viruses.

In addition to existing laws, the federal government and several states have enacted special legislation to deal with computers and crimes. The Federal Counterfeit Access Device and Computer Fraud and

Abuse Act became law in 1984 and was amended in 1986 by the Computer Fraud and Abuse Act. That law prohibits:

1. A knowing, unauthorized access to information contained in a federal interest computer.
2. An intentional, unauthorized access to financial information held by a financial institution or credit agency.
3. An intentional, unauthorized access of a computer of the United States that would affect the government's operation of the computer.
4. Thefts of property by use of computer as a result of a knowing and intentional scheme to defraud.
5. Knowingly altering, damaging, or destroying information within a federal interest computer or preventing the authorized use of such a computer.
6. Knowingly trafficking in any password without authorization if the trafficking affects interstate commerce or is used by or for the United States government.

Some of these crimes are misdemeanors and others are felonies. The private sector expends considerable resources in the prevention and detection of computer crimes. Law enforcement agencies have been forced to hire investigators and consultants with computer expertise to effectively investigate claims and educate the public in preventing computer crimes. As computer use and dependence increase, so will computer crimes.

On the other side, computer technology has advanced law enforcement in some respects. The **National Crime Information Center** (NCIC) is used by law enforcement agencies nationwide in the reporting and detection of wanted persons. Computers are used to organize and manage case files. Graphics programs are used to recreate crimes and to project a fugitive's appearance after donning a disguise or after having aged. These are but a few of the uses computers play in law enforcement.

Review Questions

1. What is "constructive breaking," when referring to the crime of burglary?

2. Define larceny.

BALLENTINE'S

National Crime Information Center (NCIC)   [A] computerized network used by police departments across the country to determine if there are outstanding warrants on a suspect or an arrestee, to locate missing persons, and to trace stolen vehicles, guns, and the like.

3. What is criminal mischief?

4. Embezzlement is often punished more severely than simple larceny. Why?

5. What does the acronym RICO represent? What are the basic elements of RICO?

6. What are "fences"? At common law, what crime do fences commit?

7. How is destruction of a building by explosion treated by the Model Penal Code? At common law?

8. Brogan runs by a woman on the street and grabs her purse as he passes her. The purse is easily pulled from her arm, and Brogan's intent is to keep the contents. What crime has been committed?

9. Brogan runs by a woman on the street and grabs her purse as he passes her. The woman catches the strap and fights to keep the purse; however, the strap breaks, and Brogan is successful. He keeps the contents of the purse. What crime has been committed?

10. What is the difference between forgery and uttering?

Review Problems

1. Arson is quite different today than it was at common law. What are the major differences?

2. Burglary is quite different today than it was at common law. What are the major differences?

3. Doug and Sherri are an elderly couple who are retired and residing in Florida. Both have suffered substantial physical deterioration, including vision loss and poor memory. Ned, who had coveted their 1962 Corvette for years, told the couple that they should trust him with their financial affairs, including giving him title to their vehicle. He told the two that he would drive them to the places they needed to go, but that state law required that his name appear on the title of the car, as he would be the sole driver. Doug and Sherri complied with his request, believing that his statement concerning Florida law was correct.

   Subsequently, the couple created a trust account and named Ned as trustee. The purpose of the account was to provide Ned with a general fund from which he was to pay the household bills. Ned withdrew all the money and placed it into his personal account. When this occurred, the couple contacted Ned, who claimed to know nothing of the account. Sherri contacted the local prosecutor, who conducted an investigation. Through that investigation, it was discovered that Ned held title to the Corvette.

You work for the prosecutor. Your assignment is to determine what crimes have been committed, if any. Your state has no theft statute, but recognizes common-law theft crimes.

4. Gary and Paige were friends until they discovered that they shared an interest in Tracy. After Paige won her affection, Gary became enraged and took a key and ran it down the side of Paige's car. He then poured gasoline over the car and set it on fire. Gary has been arrested. What crimes should be charged?

5. Kevin was walking down the sidewalk that passed in front of Sean's home. As he passed Sean's house, he looked in a front window and noticed a carton of soft drinks sitting in the kitchen. As he was thirsty, Kevin broke the front window and crawled into Sean's house. Once inside, he poured himself a glass of cola and sat down at the dining room table. While seated at the table, he picked up a ring with a value in excess of $1,000, and put it into his pocket. When he finished his drink, he placed the empty glass in the sink and left. He later sold the ring and bought a stereo with the proceeds. What crimes have been committed, using common-law theft crimes?

6. Brogan has an affair with Janice, who is married. After Janice ends the affair, Brogan threatens to tell Janice's husband about their sexual involvement unless Janice pays Brogan $5,000. Janice complies. What crime has been committed?

7. Penni is working the night shift at a local convenience store when Craig and Guido come in. Craig states to Penni, "Give us all the money in the register and we will not hurt you. Give us any trouble and we will knock the #?!@ out of you!" Penni complied. What crime has been committed? What if they had been brandishing weapons?

8. Discuss what crimes you think should be included in consolidated theft statutes and why. Explain why particular crimes should be left out of such a statute.

Notes

1 5 Am. Jur. 2d *Arson* 2 (1962).

2 Model Penal Code § 220.1.

3 Model Penal Code § 220.1(1) and (2).

4 *People v. Richards,* 108 N.Y. 137, 15 N.E. 371 (1988).

5 LaFave & Scott, *Criminal Law* 797 (Hornbook Series, St. Paul: West, 1986).

6 A. Loewy, *Criminal Law,* 2d ed. (Nutshell Series, St. Paul, West, 1987).

7 *Bazeley's Case,* 2 East P.C. 571 (Cr. Cas. Res. 1799); *see* LaFave & Scott, *Criminal Law* § 8.1 (Hornbook Series, St. Paul: West, 1986).

8 18 U.S.C. § 641 *et seq.*

[9] LaFave & Scott, *Criminal Law* § 8.9 (Hornbook Series, St. Paul: West, 1986).

[10] 18 U.S.C. § 1341.

[11] 18 U.S.C. § 1961 *et seq.*

[12] *N.O.W. v. Scheidler,* 114 S. Ct. 798 (1994).

[13] 18 U.S.C. § 2311 *et seq.*

[14] 18 U.S.C. § 2113.

[15] Fla. Stat. Ann. § 812.012 *et seq.*

[16] Model Penal Code § 223 *et seq.* deals with theft offenses.

[17] *Id.* § 222.1.

[18] *Id.* § 224.1.

[19] "Trespassers Will Be Prosecuted: Computer Crime in the 1990's," 12 *Computer L.J.* 61, 62 (1993).

CHAPTER 6

CRIMES AGAINST THE PUBLIC

Defining a "Crime Against the Public"

Chapters 4 and 5 were concerned with crimes that victimize individuals or entities, such as corporations and other business organizations. This chapter examines crimes that do not have individual victims. These are crimes involving the public welfare, social order, and society's morals.

Religion has played a strong role in determining what acts, which do not harm anyone, should be illegal. Of course, religious groups do not dictate such policy—this would violate the First Amendment's prohibition of mixing church and state. Religion does, however, influence the moral values of the members of a society. In the United States this influence is predominately Christian. This is the reason that some acts which directly harm no one are prohibited.

Some critics call for an end to "victimless crimes." In spite of this, many victimless crimes exist and are likely to continue to be prohibited. However, in a democracy such as the United States, it is important to examine such crimes carefully to avoid an unwarranted infringement of civil liberties. The more a law is premised upon a moral judgment, the greater the scrutiny should be.

Some of the crimes discussed here bear directly upon the administration of government and justice and less upon moral determinations. For example, contempt of court is a crime against the public, and the premise of its prohibition is the theory that if society punishes offenders, others will comply with court orders, and the administration of justice will be enhanced. Prostitution is an example of a crime that is prohibited more for moral reasons than any other.

The crimes included in this chapter have been divided into four subsections: crimes against public morality; crimes against the public order; crimes against the administration of government; and crimes against the environment.

Crimes Against Public Morality

Prostitution and Solicitation

Often said to be the oldest profession, **prostitution** is prohibited in every state except Nevada, where each county is given the authority to determine whether to make it criminal.

───────────────── BALLENTINE'S ─────────────────

prostitution   Engaging in sexual intercourse or other sexual activity for pay. A man as well as a woman may be a prostitute.

Prostitution is defined as (1) providing (2) sexual services (3) in exchange for compensation. In a few states, only intercourse is included in the definition of sexual services. In most states, however, sexual services include sodomy, fellatio, cunnilingus, and the touching of another's genitals. The Model Penal Code includes homosexual and other deviate sexual conduct in its definition of sexual activity.[1]

The service must be provided in exchange for compensation. The person who is sexually promiscuous, but unpaid, goes unpunished. Compensation normally means money, but it can come in any form. Thus, the prostitute who accepts legal services from a lawyer in exchange for sexual services has received compensation. Where prostitution is illegal, it is common for prostitutes to use businesses, such as massage parlors and escort services, as a front.

Solicitation is a related crime. Any person who engages in selling sex, buying sex, or attempting to buy sex is guilty of solicitation. Note that a prostitute may be guilty of both solicitation and prostitution, if the prostitute makes the first contact with the buyer. There need not be the actual sale of sex for solicitation—only an attempt to sell sexual services. The clients of prostitutes, when prosecuted, are charged with solicitation.

The Model Penal Code states that "A person commits a violation if he hires a prostitute to engage in sexual activity with him, or if he enters or remains in a house of prostitution for the purpose of engaging in sexual activity."[2]

Those who promote prostitution (*pimps*) are usually punished more severely than prostitutes and customers. The Model Penal Code makes knowingly promoting prostitution a felony of the third degree if a child under sixteen years of age is prostituted; the defendant's wife, child, or other ward is prostituted; the defendant forces or encourages another to engage in prostitution; or the defendant owns, controls, or manages a house of prostitution. In all other cases promotion is a misdemeanor.

Nearly all sex-for-hire cases fall under state jurisdiction. However, the federal government may be involved in prosecution when a prostitute is transported in interstate commerce, or any other person is transported in interstate commerce for an immoral purpose.[3]

Deviate Sexual Conduct

Rape and related crimes were discussed in Chapter 4. That chapter focused on sexual behavior that results in harm to a victim. This discussion is different, as there is usually no victim other than society as a whole. Deviate sexual conduct has many definitions, but most states include fellatio, cunnilingus, anal sex, and all homosexual activity within the grasp of their deviate sexual statutes. Therefore, consenting adults, married or not, may be prosecuted for participating in such sexual activity.

The foundation of the prohibition of sodomy and related acts is morality. Many religions, including Christianity, believe that all sex other than vaginal intercourse between a man and woman is deviate. The reality is that many, if not most, people engage in sex that falls into the definition of deviate sex. For this reason, it is argued that such acts are normal and should not be prohibited. Others argue that it does not matter if the behavior is normal or deviate—that sex between two consenting adults is private and involves no victims and, as such, is of no concern of the government. However, such laws continue to exist. Further, they have survived constitutional challenges in most instances.

Despite continued prohibition of sodomy, and related acts, in many states, the laws are seldom enforced. One reason is that law enforcement officials have shown a reluctance to enforce such laws, often because crimes perceived as more serious are time-demanding and leave little manpower and resources to enforce victimless crimes. In addition, there simply is the problem of discovering violations. Most sexual conduct occurs privately, and thus the police rarely discover violations independently. Of course, those who participate in prohibited sexual conduct are not likely to report their sex partners' acts to law enforcement.

BOWERS
v.
HARDWICK
478 U.S. 186 (1986)

MAJORITY OPINION BY JUSTICE WHITE:

In August 1982, respondent was charged with violating the Georgia statute criminalizing sodomy by committing that act with another adult male in the bedroom of respondent's home. After a preliminary hearing, the District Attorney decided not to present the matter to the grand jury unless further evidence developed.

Respondent then brought suit in the Federal District Court, challenging the constitutionality of the statute insofar as it criminalized sodomy. He asserted that he was a practicing homosexual, that the Georgia sodomy statute, as administered by the defendants, placed him in imminent danger of arrest, and that the statute for several reasons violates the Federal Constitution. ...

This case does not require a judgment on whether laws against sodomy between consenting adults in general, or between homosexuals in particular, are wise or desirable. It raises no question about the right or propriety of state legislative decisions to repeal their laws that criminalize homosexual sodomy, or of state court decisions invalidating those laws on state constitutional grounds. The issue presented is whether the Federal Constitution confers a fundamental right upon homosexuals to engage in sodomy and hence invalidates the laws of the many States that still make such conduct illegal. ...

Respondent, however, asserts that the result should be different where the homosexual conduct occurs in the privacy of the home. He relies on *Stanley v. Georgia*, 394 U.S. 557 (1969), where the Court held that the First Amendment prevents convicting for possessing and reading obscene material in the privacy of his home: "If the First Amendment means anything, it means that a State has no business telling a man, sitting alone at his house, what books he may read or what films he may watch."

Stanley did protect conduct that would not have been protected outside the home, and it partially prevented the enforcement of state obscenity laws; but the decision was firmly grounded in the First Amendment. The right pressed upon us here has no similar support in the text of the Constitution, and it does not qualify for recognition under the prevailing principles for construing the Fourteenth Amendment. ...

[The vote of the Court was 5–4. Justice White wrote the majority opinion. Chief Justice Burger and Justices Powell, O'Connor, and Rehnquist joined in that opinion. Burger and Powell also filed concurring opinions. Justice Stevens filed a dissenting opinion, which Justices Brennan and Marshall joined. Justice Blackmum also filed a dissent in which Justices Marshall, Brennan, and Stevens joined.]

DISSENTING OPINION BY JUSTICE BLACKMUN:

This case is no more about a "fundamental right to engage in homosexual sodomy," than *Stanley v. Georgia* was about a fundamental right to watch obscene movies. ... Rather, this case is about "the most comprehensive of rights and the most valued by civilized men," namely, "the right to be left alone." ...

Like Justice Holmes, I believe that "[i]t is revolting to have no better reason for a rule of law than that so it was laid down in the time of Henry IV. It is still more revolting if the grounds upon which it was laid down have vanished long since, and the rule simply persists from blind imitation of the past." I believe we must analyze respondent's claim in light of the values that underlie the constitutional right to privacy. If that right means anything, it means that, before Georgia can prosecute its citizens for making choices about the most intimate aspects of their lives, it must do more than assert that the choice they have made is an "abominable crime not fit to be named among Christians." ...

"Our cases long have recognized that the Constitution embodies a promise that a certain private sphere of individual liberty will be kept largely beyond the reach of government"... . In construing the right to privacy, the Court has proceeded along two somewhat distinct, albeit complementary, lines. First, it has recognized a privacy interest with reference to certain decisions that are properly for the individual to make. ... Second, it has recognized a privacy interest with reference to certain places without regard for the particular activities in which the individuals who occupy them are engaged. ...

Only the most willful blindness could obscure the fact that sexual intimacy is a "sensitive, key relationship of human existence, central to family life, community welfare, and the development of human personality." The fact that individuals define themselves in a significant way through their intimate sexual relationships with others suggests, in a Nation as diverse as ours, that there may be many "right" ways of conducting those relationships, and that much of the richness of a relationship will come from the freedom an individual has to choose the form and nature of these intensely personal bonds. ...

The behavior for which Hardwick faces prosecution occurred in his own home, a place to which the Fourth Amendment attaches special significance. ... Just as the right to privacy is more than the mere aggregation of a number of entitlements to engage in specific behavior, so too, protecting the physical integrity of the home is more than merely a means of protecting specific activities that often take place there. ...

I can only hope ... the Court soon will reconsider its analysis and conclude that depriving individuals of the right to choose for themselves how to conduct their intimate relationships poses a far greater threat to the values most deeply rooted in our Nation's history than tolerance of nonconformity could ever do. Because I think the Court today betrays those values, I dissent.

Indecent Exposure and Lewdness

Indecent exposure, or the exposure of one's "private parts" in public, was a common-law misdemeanor. Today, the crime is usually criminalized by state statute or local ordinance.

Most indecent exposure laws require (1) an intentional exposure (2) of one's private parts (3) in a public place. In some jurisdictions, it is required that the exposure be done in an "offensive manner."

In 1991, the United States Supreme Court examined a public nudity statute in the context of nude barroom dancing. In *Barnes v. Glen Theater, Inc.,* 501 U.S. 560 (1991), the Court upheld an Indiana statute that required dancers to wear pasties and g-strings. Although the court found that nude dancing was expressive conduct, it determined that states may require the dancers to cover their genitals. The court did say that erotic performances were protected by the First Amendment, provided the dancers wear a scant amount of clothing. The Court upheld the law because it determined that the state's objective was not to regulate expression, but to regulate for order and morality. Further, the Court held that the interference with expression was minimal.

The Model Penal Code prohibits public indecency. The Code goes further with a provision proscribing all lewd acts that the defendant knows are likely to be observed by others who would be "affronted or alarmed" by the acts.[4]

Obscenity

Congress shall make no law respecting the establishment of religion, or prohibiting the free exercise thereof; *or abridging the freedom of speech,* or of the press; or the right of the people peaceably to assemble, and to petition the Government for a redress of grievances.

This is the First Amendment to the United States Constitution. Most, if not all, states have a similar provision in their constitutions. The italicized portion represents the only protection of speech in the Constitution. Because it is brief and broad, it is dependent upon a great amount of interpretation to give it meaning. Also, because of its brevity and broadness, courts often interpret it differently. Even the Supreme Court has changed its interpretation of the clause, in particular areas, on several occasions. Freedom of speech encompasses far more than will be examined in this chapter. What will be discussed here is the extent of governmental power to regulate conduct that it deems to be indecent. Specifically, this section addresses sexually explicit materials, including films, books, and erotic dancing.

It is well-established that the term *speech,* as used in the First Amendment, means more than spoken utterances. It includes all forms of expression.

Both the federal and state governments regulate conduct, speech, books, movies, and other forms of expression that are believed to be "obscene." State governments are the most involved with regulating obscenity, due to general police power (the power to regulate for the health, welfare, and safety of citizens). However, the federal government is also involved; for example, it has criminalized sending obscene materials through the mail.[5]

Not all indecencies may be criminalized. Simply because something strikes one person as indecent does not mean that it should be prohibited. People have differing values, and to allow governments to prohibit all conduct (or other things) that is found offensive by some member of society would be to allow our government to criminalize all aspects of life. In addition, people perceive things differently. For example, in 1990 the Cincinnati Arts Center was charged with obscenity for displaying photographs taken by a respected artist, Robert Mapplethorpe. Included in the photos were depictions of nude children. The prosecutor contended that the pictures were obscene. A jury did not agree. The Arts Center and its director were acquitted, and many of the jurors commented that the testimony of art experts convinced them that the pictures had serious artistic value and were not obscene.[6]

It is important that the First Amendment be flexible and tolerant of new ideas and methods of expression. Simply because the majority of citizens would not see value in a form of expression does not mean it has no value. If the opposite were true, then expression aimed at particular minority groups could be censored. This is not to say that there is no limit on the freedom of expression. When considering sexually oriented expression, that line is drawn when the expression becomes obscene.[7]

Obscenity has proven to be an elusive concept for the Supreme Court. Through a series of decisions, from 1957 to the present, the Court has attempted to define *obscenity*. The famous quotation from Justice Potter Stewart ("I shall not today attempt further to define [obscenity]; and perhaps I could never succeed in intelligibly doing so. But I know it when I see it."—*Jacobellis v. Ohio*, 378 U.S. 184 [1964]) is a testament to the difficulty in defining such a concept. It also reflects what many people believe, that they may not be able to define obscenity, but they recognize it when they see it.

In *Roth v. United States*, 354 U.S. 476 (1957), it was held that obscenity is not protected by the First Amendment because it lacks redeeming social importance. The Court then established a test for determining whether something was obscene, and, as such, not protected by the First Amendment. That test was "whether to the average person, applying contemporary community standards, the dominant theme of the material taken as a whole appeals to prurient interest." In addition, the material had to be "utterly without redeeming social value." Simply because "literature is dismally unpleasant, uncouth, and tawdry is not enough to make it "obscene."[8]

In 1973 the Supreme Court reexamined the *Roth* obscenity test in *Miller v. California*, 413 U.S. 15 (1973). In *Miller* the Court rejected the requirement that the material be "utterly without redeeming social value," and lowered the standard to lacking "serious literary, artistic, political, or scientific value." The test under *Miller* has three parts:

1. The average person, applying contemporary community standards, would find that the work, taken as a whole, appeals to the prurient interest and

2. the work must depict or describe, in a patently offensive manner, sexual conduct specifically defined by the applicable state law, and

3. the work, when taken as a whole, must lack serious literary, artistic, political, or scientific value.

The *Miller* test makes it easier for states to regulate sexual materials. An "average person" has been equated with a reasonable person, as used in tort law.[9] The material must appeal to "prurient interest." Materials that have a tendency to excite a lustful, "shameful or morbid interest in nudity, sex or excretion" meet the prurient interest element.[10] Material that provokes normal, healthy, sexual desires is not obscene because it does not appeal to prurient interest.[11]

The Court gave examples in *Miller* of "patently offensive" materials that included depictions or descriptions of "ultimate sex acts, normal or perverted, actual or simulated ... of masturbation, excretory functions, and lewd exhibition of the genitals."

One area where the states have substantially more power to regulate obscenity is when minors are involved. The Court has held that all child pornography is unprotected because of the special protection necessary to protect children from exploitation.[12] Similarly, governments may prohibit the distribution and sale of erotic materials to minors, even if such materials are not obscene.[13] Also, in *Osborne v. Ohio*, 494 U.S. 103 (1990), the Supreme Court held that a person may be convicted for possession of child pornography in the home. This is an exception to the general rule that a person may possess obscene material in the home.

As mentioned in *Miller*, governments may control the time, place, and manner of expression. Accordingly, certain restrictions may be valid that deal with expression in certain places, such as establishments that sell alcohol. (Chapter 8 addresses constitutional defenses to criminal accusations and discusses other time, place, and manner issues.)

One place where the power of the government to regulate sexually explicit materials is lessened is in homes. In many respects, the law reflects the attitude that a "man's home is his castle," and deserves special protection. Thus, the United States Supreme Court struck down the conviction of a man for possession of obscene materials in his home.[14] However, as previously mentioned, a person is not privileged to possess child pornography in the home.

The Model Penal Code makes it a misdemeanor to knowingly or recklessly do any of the following:[15]

1. Sell, deliver, or provide (or offer to do one of the three) any obscene writing, picture, record, or other obscene representation.
2. Present or perform in an obscene play, dance, or other perform-ance.
3. Publish or exhibit obscene materials.
4. Possess obscene materials for commercial purposes.
5. Sell or otherwise commercially distribute materials represented as obscene.

The Code presumes that anyone who distributes obscene materials in the course of business has done so knowingly or recklessly.

Material is considered obscene under the Code if "considered as a whole, its predominant appeal is to prurient interest, that is, a shameful or morbid interest, in nudity, sex, or excretion, and if in addition it goes substantially beyond customary limits of candor in describing or representing such matter." Note that the Code's definition is similar to the Supreme Court's definition. The Code does add the requirement that the material go beyond "customary limits of candor." The Code makes it an affirmative defense that the obscene material was possessed for governmental, scientific, educational, or other justified causes. It also is not a crime for a person to give such materials to personal asso-ciates in noncommercial situations. The Code focuses on punishing commercial dissemination of obscene material.

Obscenity is a complex area of law. Many different criminal prohi-bitions exist throughout the states and federal government that focus on the sale, distribution, and possession of sexually oriented materials, performance of erotic dance, and public nudity. So long as minors are not involved, the activity is protected unless it is obscene. To determine whether pornography is obscene (hardcore), one must apply the three-part *Miller* test. The states are free to regulate if children are involved, either as participants in the erotic materials (or performance) or as buy-ers of erotic materials, even if the material is not obscene.

Because of the plethora of cases in this area, it is strongly recom-mended that thorough research be conducted. There is a good chance that precedent with similar facts may be found. Beware, however, that this is an issue that often leaves courts split. Be sure that the opinions you find reflect the law of your jurisdiction.

Crimes Against the Public Order

Introduction

Crimes against the public order are crimes that involve **breaches of the peace**. The phrase *breaches of the peace* refers to all crimes that involve disturbing the tranquility or order of society. Making breaches of the peace criminal has its roots in early English common law. In England, breaches of the peace by individuals were criminal, as were breaches by groups.

Three groups of breaches were recognized; all were punished as misdemeanors. If three or more people met with an intention of causing a disturbance, they committed the common-law offense of unlawful assembly. If the group took some action in an attempt to breach the peace, they were guilty of rout; if they were successful, the crime was riot.

Today, all jurisdictions prohibit breaches of the peace in some form by statute. The names of statutory crimes include disorderly conduct, unlawful assembly, riot, inciting violence, unlawful threat, and vagrancy.

Riot and Unlawful Assembly

Most states now have legislation that prohibits groups of people from meeting with the purpose of committing an unlawful act or committing a lawful act in an unlawful manner. This crime may be named unlawful assembly or riot. A group, or "assembly," is a specified minimum number of people, often three or five. Some jurisdictions continue to recognize the distinctions between unlawful assembly, rout, and riot.

The Model Penal Code recognizes two related crimes: riot and failure to disperse. Both crimes require an assembly of two or more persons who are behaving disorderly. If the purpose of the assembly is to commit a crime (felony or misdemeanor), to coerce public officials to act or not act, or if a deadly weapon is used, then the crime is riot.[16]

Failure to disperse occurs when a law enforcement officer, or other official, orders the members of a group of three or more to disperse, and someone refuses. The disorderly conduct that the assembly is engaged in must be "likely to cause substantial harm or serious inconvenience, annoyance, or alarm," before an officer may order the group to disperse. This provision is included because the freedoms to associate and assemble are protected by the First Amendment to the United States

---

BALLENTINE'S

breach of the peace   Conduct that violates the public order or disturbs the public tranquility.

Constitution, and such activity may be regulated only when it poses a threat to person, property, or society.

Most jurisdictions punish these crimes as misdemeanors. However, they may be elevated to felony if committed with a dangerous weapon, if someone is injured as a result of the activity, or if law enforcement officers are obstructed from performing their duties. The Model Penal Code makes rioting a felony of the third degree and failure to disperse a misdemeanor.

Disturbing the Peace

As mentioned, individuals may also commit crimes against the public order. Disturbing the peace is such a crime. This crime is also known as disorderly conduct, threat, excessive noise, and affray. In essence, any time the public order or tranquility is unreasonably interrupted by an individual, disturbance of the peace has occurred. States may have one law that encompasses all such acts or separate statutes for each.

Disturbances may occur in hundreds of forms. One may disturb the peace by making loud noises in a residential area at midnight, by attempting to cause fights with others, or by encouraging others to engage in similar conduct. Statutes often also prohibit indecent language and gestures.

These statutes are often broadly worded and are vague. As such, they are often attacked as being unconstitutional. The defenses of overbreadth and vagueness are discussed in Chapter 8 on defenses and are not covered here. One defense that will be examined is the First Amendment right to free speech and its relationship to offensive words and gestures.

As you have learned, the First Amendment protects all forms of expression. This protection prohibits government from making expression criminal. However, exceptions to the First Amendment have been created. Words that have a likelihood of causing a riot are such an exception. That is, even though the words are expression, they may be punished. The reason is obvious: riots lead to property damage, personal injuries, and sometimes death. As such, the interest of the government to control such behavior outweighs the First Amendment interest.

The **fighting words** doctrine is another exception. The Supreme Court has defined *fighting words* as those that inflict injury, tend to incite an immediate breach of the peace, or by their nature will cause a violent reaction by a person who hears them.[17] Laws that regulate speech

---
BALLENTINE'S

fighting words Words which tend to incite a breach of the peace; a category of speech that the Supreme Court has declared is not protected by the First Amendment guaranty of freedom of speech.

that is allowed to be regulated, such as fighting words, must be drafted narrowly; that is, only the conduct intended must be prohibited. If a law is drawn which has the effect of making fighting words and legitimate speech illegal, it is unconstitutional and void.

The defendant in the *Witucki* case was convicted of disorderly conduct. The court found that his speech was unprotected because he used fighting words.

CITY OF LITTLE FALLS
v.
Edwin George WITUCKI
295 N.W.2d 243 (Minn. 1980)

On December 11, 1978, a Morrison County Court jury found defendant guilty of disorderly conduct in violation of Little Falls, Minnesota, Ordinances. ...

At approximately 11:00 P.M. on September 19, 1978, defendant Edwin George Witucki and a few of his friends entered the West Side Bar in Little Falls, Minnesota. Just outside the building defendant found a cat which he carried into the building and placed on the bar. Pursuant to defendant's request, one bartender served the cat some beef jerky and a shotglass of cream and served defendant a drink.

About five minutes later, the other bartender, Paula Erwin, told defendant to take the cat outside. He refused. She told him he was cut off from being served until the cat was removed. He responded, "I let you slip once too many times, I'm not going to let you slip again." Erwin, for the third time, told defendant to remove the cat. He responded by saying, "Hey, Butch, I don't have to take any of your crap." She then turned to return to the other end of the bar, and Witucki called her a "black-haired witch," a "cocksucker," and a "son-of-a-bitch."

When asked at trial about her reaction to the words, Erwin testified, "I didn't care for them very well. It scared me. There was nothing I could do about it. There were no guys around so I thought the best thing for me to do, because I was really mad at the time, was just to walk away from

him." She also testified that calling the police or any sort of violent action on her part would not be wise or safe because he might wait for her outside after hours and because he was much larger than she and there were no men around to help her.

* * *

The question is, did defendant's words in the circumstances in which they were uttered constitute "those personally abusive epithets which, when addressed to the ordinary citizen, are as a matter of common knowledge, inherently likely to provoke violent reaction." ...

In *In re S.L.J.* the appellant was a fourteen-year-old girl who yelled "fuck you pigs" at two police officers. ... The court noted that although "no ordered society would condone the vulgar language" and although "her words were intended to, and did, arouse resentment in the officers, the constitution requires more before a person can be convicted for mere speech." The court held that where the words were spoken in retreat by a small teenage girl who was between fifteen and thirty feet from the two police officers sitting in their squad car, "there was no reasonable likelihood that [the words] would tend to incite an immediate breach of the peace or to provoke violent reaction by an ordinary, reasonable person.

In *Cohen v. California*, 403 U.S. 15, 91 S.Ct. 1780, 29 L. Ed. 2d 284 (1971), the defendant wore a jacket on which the words "Fuck the Draft" were plainly visible. The words were not directed against the person of any possibly offended person; they were directed against the draft.

The instant case is readily distinguishable from both *In re S.L.J.* and *Cohen v. California.* Unlike the defendant's language in *Cohen,* Witucki's language was directed at and was intended to be about a person, namely Erwin. The abusive language hurled by defendant at Erwin could readily be found by a jury to be inherently likely to incite violence. Defendant was not, as in *Cohen,* merely expressing a controversial political opinion in a vulgar way; he was directly insulting and intimidating an innocent person.

* * *

The fact that the words used by appellant are vulgar, offensive, and insulting, and that their use is condemned by an overwhelming majority of citizens does not make them punishable under the criminal statutes of this state unless they fall outside the protection afforded to speech by the First Amendment.

* * *

Defendant's speech in this case is not a "trifling and annoying instance of individual distasteful abuse of a privilege." He addressed such abusive, vulgar, insulting and obscene language toward the bartender that his language was properly found to be within the fighting words category of unprotected speech. ... [Conviction affirmed.]

Incitement/Advocacy of Unlawful Conduct

Whenever one person, acting independently, encourages another to commit an unlawful act or intends to cause a riot, the crimes of incitement of lawful behavior or incitement of riot may be charged. Unlike riot, which requires a group, one person may commit this crime. Unlike disturbing the peace, it may be committed in a peaceful manner.

However, because the First Amendment applies, such statutes must be narrowly drawn. In fact, only speech which creates a **clear and present danger** may be controlled. The United States Supreme Court has said that "incitement of imminent lawless action" may be regulated.[18] Anything less may not be regulated. Hence, merely advocating unlawful conduct in the abstract is protected. Advocating future unlawful conduct is also protected, as it poses no imminent threat.

Threats

Finally, in the speech arena, threats are addressed. Threat statutes may make threatening individuals, groups, or even property criminal. Threats to harm people are similar to assaults. However, threat is broader, as it often protects property and the people at large. The purpose of threat statutes is to preserve public order, and the purpose of assault statutes is to protect individuals.

BALLENTINE'S

clear and present danger The test of whether speech is capable of creating such a substantial danger to the security of the country that it is not protected under the First Amendment.

For example, if a defendant were to call in a bomb threat to a public office, there would be no assault, but there is a threat. A person may be guilty of threat by making the prohibited statements, even if untrue. So, if a defendant makes a bomb threat, but has placed no bomb in the building, a crime has been committed. Threats are misdemeanors in most jurisdictions and are punished less severely than assaults. In the *Thomas* case, the defendant was convicted under the Kentucky threat statute.

THOMAS
v.
Commonwealth of KENTUCKY
574 S.W.2d 903 (Ky. Ct. App. 1978)

The case for the Commonwealth was based solely on the testimony of Gladys Thomas. Mrs. Thomas on direct examination stated that on the Friday before she went to swear out the warrant that she was in her front yard cutting weeds with a butcher knife when appellant came out of the house, hit her across the back with his hand, laughed and ran into a barber shop next door. Appellant then came back laughing and hit her across the back with a belt and then ran into a liquor store about three doors down from the house. Appellant continued to aggravate Mrs. Thomas until she asked him to go and get her a coke. Mrs. Thomas then testified thusly:

> So, we went about an hour, an hour and a half after my mom left and he came in and said, "I told you to get ready to go," and I said, "I'm not going," and he grabbed me by the hair of the head and threw me against the refrigerator and said, "you are going to I will kill you and prove self-defense. This is one time everything is on my side. So, just get dressed and let's go somewhere and show everybody what a happy family we are."

Next, Mrs. Thomas gave testimony concerning the circumstances surrounding the threat which is the basis for the charge against appellant:

> So, on Wednesday, he came in and he said, "I will come home. I'm coming home." I said, "you can't. You absolutely cannot. I went and applied for welfare," and he said, "I have to tell the man,

Mr. Clark, that I'm here or I'll be in trouble." One thing led to another and he jumped in the middle of the floor and said, "you and Brenda have got me against the wall. You're going to get me in trouble. I will cut both your heads off before I go back." Those are almost the exact words. And I looked around and the little girl was standing right in the screen door.

On cross examination, Mrs. Thomas testified that this threat was made in the late afternoon and that on the next morning, on July 15, 1976, she sent and got a warrant.

[The applicable Kentucky statute] provides thusly:

> A person is guilty of terroristic threatening when:
> (a) He threatens to commit any crime likely to result in death or serious bodily injury to another person or likely to result in substantial property damage to another person; or
> (b) He intentionally makes false statements for the purpose of causing evacuation of a building, place of assembly, or facility of public transportation.
> (c) Terroristic threatening is a Class A misdemeanor.

This court believes that [this statute] is not unconstitutionally vague and overbroad since the conduct proscribed, "threaten[ing] to commit a crime likely to result in death or serious physical injury" is not protected under either the Kentucky or United States Constitutions. Further, the language of the statute is sufficiently explicit to put the average citizen on notice as to the nature of the conduct so proscribed.

This court is aware of the recent decision in *U.S. v. Sturgill*, 563 F.2d 307 (6th Cir. 1977), which invalidated [another Kentucky statute] on the basis that it was unconstitutionally overbroad. [The invalidated statute] provides: "A person is guilty of harassment when with intent to harass, annoy or alarm another person he: (b) In a public place, makes an offensively coarse utterance, gesture, or display, or addresses abusive language to any person present."

In *Sturgill*, the court held that in order for a statute, which punishes spoken words only, to withstand an attack on its constitutionality, it must be first authoritatively interpreted by the state courts as not interfering with speech protected by the First Amendment.

This case can be distinguished from *Sturgill*, in that the language so proscribed under [the terroristic

threatening statute] is clearly without constitutional protection under the First Amendment. ...

Certainly, [the terroristic threat statute] does not apply in the case of idle talk or jesting. The defendant's intent to commit the crime of "terroristic threatening" can be plainly inferred from the defendant's own words and the circumstances surrounding them. All the statute requires is that the defendant threaten "to commit any crime likely to result in death or serious physical injury to another person or likely to result in substantial property damage to another person."

[Conviction] Affirmed.

Vagrancy and Panhandling

Vagrancy, as a criminal law issue, has received considerable attention. Most states and municipalities have statutes that forbid vagrancy. At common law, a *vagrant* was one who wandered from place to place with no means of support, except the charity of others. At one time, in early English law, vagrancy applied to disorderly persons, rogues (a dishonest wanderer), and vagabonds (a homeless person with no means of support).

Beginning in the 1880s, it was common in the United States for statutes to prohibit a wide range of behavior as vagrancy. These statutes were drafted broadly to allow law enforcement officers considerable discretion in their enforcement. This discretion was used to control the "undesirables" of society. Many statutes made the status of being homeless, a gambler, and a drug addict a crime.

Today, states may not make personal status, such as drug addiction or alcoholism, a crime. The United States Supreme Court has held that doing so violates the Eighth Amendment's prohibition of cruel and unusual punishment.[19] However, until 1972, people found undesirable by the police could be arrested under broadly worded vagrancy statutes for "wandering," or walking around a city, because this was an act, not a status. This ended in 1972 when the United States Supreme Court handed down *Papachristou v. City of Jacksonville.*, 405 U.S. 156 (1972). The Court announced in that case that vagrancy statutes that prohibit walking around, frequenting liquor stores, being supported by one's wife, and similar behavior, to be "too precarious for a rule of law" and violative of the Due Process and Cruel and Unusual Clauses of the Constitution.

The result of *Papachristou* has been more narrowly drawn vagrancy statutes. Today such laws focus on more particularized behavior, and in many instances a mens rea element has been added. This prevents simple acts, such as walking at night, from being criminal. For example, a vagrancy law may prohibit "loitering or standing around with an intent to gamble," or "loitering or standing in a transportation facility [e.g., bus station] with the intent of soliciting charity."

In recent years panhandling (begging) has increasingly become a problem for most cities. Panhandlers often choose to congregate in and near public transportation egresses and ingresses, because of the large number of people who use such facilities. Because panhandlers are sometimes aggressive and intimidating to patrons of such facilities, some jurisdictions have chosen to prohibit begging at public transportation sites.

As the number of homeless persons grows in the United States, so will the problems associated with vagrancy and panhandling. Examine statutes and ordinances that prohibit such activities with an awareness that they must be drawn carefully to avoid a First Amendment speech problem. Also be aware that other constitutional provisions may be implicated, such as the First Amendment's freedom of association and the Due Process and Equal Protection Clauses of the Fifth and Fourteenth Amendments.

Drug and Alcohol Crimes

Introduction

Crimes that involve the use or sale of narcotics and alcohol may be classified in many ways. In one sense, such activity offends many people in society and appears to be an offense against the public morality. Whenever a pimp uses a young woman's drug addiction to induce her to become involved in prostitution, it appears to be a crime against an individual.

Drug and alcohol crimes are included in this section because of their impact on the order of society. Alcohol-related driving accidents are the cause of many fatalities. Drug addiction often is the cause of other crimes, such as theft, assaults, and prostitution. Police report that a number of domestic problems are caused by alcohol and drugs and that much of the violence directed toward law-enforcement officers is drug-related. Large cities, such as Detroit and Washington, D.C., have experienced a virtual drug boom, which has led to increased assaults, batteries, and drug-related homicides. Many addicts, desperate for a "fix," steal for drug money.

Drug and alcohol use are also expensive. Corporate America has recently awakened to the expenses associated with employee drug use. Employees who use drugs have a high absenteeism and low productivity.

Decreased performance caused by drug use can be costly, in both human and dollar terms. This is true especially in positions that require great concentration or pose risks to others, such as that of commercial pilots. In addition to business expenses, the high cost of rehabilitation can disable a family financially, and the price of drug-abuse detection and prosecution is high.

Alcohol Crimes

Let it not be mistaken, alcohol is a drug. However, the law treats alcohol differently than it does other drugs. Alcohol may be legally possessed, consumed, and sold, subject only to a few restrictions. Narcotics, on the other hand, are significantly restricted. Their sale, possession, and consumption are limited to specific instances, such as for medical use. The federal government, as well as every state, has statutes that spell out what drugs are regulated.

There are many alcohol-related crimes. Public drunkenness laws make it criminal for a person to be intoxicated in a public place. This crime is a minor misdemeanor and rarely prosecuted, as many law enforcement agencies have a policy of allowing such persons to "sleep it off" and then releasing them.

All states have a minimum age requirement for the sale or consumption of alcohol. Those below the minimum age are minors. Any minor who purchases or consumes alcohol is violating the law. Additionally, any adult who knowingly provides alcohol to a minor is also guilty of a crime, commonly known as contributing to the delinquency of a minor.

Merchants holding liquor licenses may be subject to criminal penalties for not complying with liquor laws, such as selling alcohol on holidays, Sundays, or election day, as well as for selling alcohol to minors. A merchant who violates liquor laws may also suffer the civil penalty of revocation of liquor license.

Alcohol and automobiles have proven to be a deadly and expensive combination. All states have laws that criminalize driving while under the influence of alcohol or drugs. Driving while under the influence of alcohol or drugs, driving while intoxicated, and driving with an unlawful blood-alcohol level are the names of these crimes.

These statutes are generally of two genres. One type of law generally prohibits the operation of a motor vehicle while under the influence of any drug, including alcohol. To prove this charge, the quantity of the drug or alcohol in the defendant's system is not at issue; the defendant's ability to operate the vehicle safely is. In such cases, field sobriety tests are often required of the suspect. These are tests that the suspect usually performs at the location where the police made the stop. Coordination, spatial relations, and other driving-related skills are tested by field sobriety tests.

The second type of law prohibits driving a motor vehicle any time a person's blood-alcohol level is above a stated amount. The states vary in the quantity required, although 10 percent (.10) is common. The effect of these laws is that an irrebuttable presumption is created. The law presumes that anyone with the stated blood-alcohol level or above cannot safely operate a motor vehicle. Under such statutes, evidence that a person can safely operate a motor vehicle with a blood-alcohol level greater than the maximum allowed is not permitted.

In recent years drunk driving has received considerable public and legislative attention. The result has been stricter laws and greater punishment for offenders. The once-common police practice of driving drunk drivers home is virtually nonexistent today.

First offenses are usually misdemeanors. Second or third offenses are felonies. In many jurisdictions, there has been a move toward alcohol treatment rather than incarceration. This often involves house arrest, alcohol treatment, and defensive driving education. Also, while in these programs, convicted persons are commonly required to submit to periodic blood or urine screening.

For first-time offenders, these programs have many advantages over prison. First, the focus is on curing the alcohol problem. If successful, the possibility of repetition is eliminated. Second, convicted persons are often permitted to continue to work and maintain family relationships. Finally, the cost of administration of alcohol programs is lower than the cost of incarceration. The value of such programs for repeat offenders is questionable, and in many jurisdictions jail time is required as early as a second conviction.

Drug Crimes

Unlike alcohol, possession of other drugs is a crime. Every state and the federal government have enacted some variation of the Uniform Controlled Substance Act, a model act (similar to the Model Penal Code) drafted by the Commissioners on Uniform Laws. These statutes establish schedules of drugs that categorize drugs based on their danger, potential for abuse, and medical benefits. These factors then determine a drug's allowed usage. For example, one schedule exists for drugs that may not be used under any condition, and another schedule permits use for medical and research purposes only. There are three basic drug crimes: possession, sales/distribution, and use.

SIDEBAR   CRIME IN THE UNITED STATES Drug use is common to those arrested in the United States. Of the females arrested in America in 1992, 65 percent tested positive for the presence of an illegal drug. The rate for men was 62 percent. Arrestees charged with possession and sales of drugs had the greatest incidence of positive tests. Overall, more than 50 percent of all persons charged, excluding sex and traffic offenses, tested positive for drugs.

Cocaine was the most prevalent drug for both males and females who tested positive, followed by marijuana and opiates.

Source: Drug Use Forecasting Annual Report (1992), National Institute of Justice, *1993.*

Possession of prohibited drugs is a crime. Of course, actual possession is sufficient actus reus, but some jurisdictions also make constructive possession criminal. Constructive possession permits conviction of those people who exercise dominion and control over property where the illegal drug is located, even though the person has no "actual physical possession" of the prohibited narcotic. However, the Model Penal Code[20] and most jurisdictions require knowledge that the drug was present before culpability is imposed. As such, if a guest stays in Robert's home, Robert is not criminally liable for any drugs the guest has stowed away, unless Robert is aware of their presence. Once Robert becomes aware, he must see that the drugs are removed within a reasonable time or risk a possession charge.

First-time conviction of possession, if the quantity is small, is a misdemeanor and normally results in probation. In many states, if a person pleads guilty, submits to a term of probation, and successfully completes the probation, then no adjudication of guilt is entered; so, no record of conviction exists. Probation terms usually include drug counseling, periodic drug testing, and no other arrests during the period. This type of procedure is known as *deferred sentencing* or *suspended imposition of sentence.* See Chapter 11 for a discussion of sentencing.

The sale or distribution of prohibited drugs is the second primary drug offense. Generally, it is punished more severely than possession. Not only are sales prohibited, but any "delivery" or "distribution" of drugs is also illegal. "Possession with an intent to deliver or sell" is similar to simple possession, except a mens rea of intending to sell must be proven. Possession with an intent to sell or deliver is punished more severely than possession, often punished equally with actual sale or delivery.

The quantity of the drug involved affects the level of punishment for both possession and sale/distribution offenses. Other factors, such as selling to minors, may aggravate the sentence.

Unauthorized use of a controlled substance is also a crime. The user must be knowing. So, if a person takes a pill containing a controlled substance that someone gives him or her, who represented it to be an aspirin, there is no crime. Of course, the taking must be voluntary. If a person is forced down and injected with an illegal drug, he or she has committed no crime.

Recall from the earlier discussion of actus reus that addiction to controlled substances may not be made criminal. The United States

Supreme Court has held that criminalizing a person's status as an addict is cruel and unusual punishment, as prohibited by the Eighth Amendment to the United States Constitution.[21] It is permitted, however, to punish a person for the act of taking a controlled substance.

RICO and CCE

You have already learned that the Racketeer Influenced and Corrupt Organizations Act (RICO) was enacted to fight organized crime in all its forms. Another federal statute, Continuing Criminal Enterprise (CCE),[22] was enacted specifically to combat drug trafficking. The statute is aimed at prosecuting the people at the top of the drug dealing and smuggling pyramid, and, accordingly, it has become known as the "Drug Kingpin statute."

A person engages in a criminal enterprise if (1) he is an administrator, organizer, or other leader (2) of a group of five or more people (3) who are involved in series of drug violations. A *series* of violations means three or more drug convictions.[23]

Conviction of CCE results in stern punishment. A general violation receives twenty years to life in prison. Second convictions carry thirty years to life. If a person is determined to be a "principal leader," the amount of drugs involved was enormous, or the enterprise made $10 million or more in one year from drugs, then life imprisonment is mandatory. Fines may also be imposed. Also, the statute provides for imprisonment or death when murder results from the enterprise.[24]

Finally, the Comprehensive Forfeiture Act of 1984[25] applies to both RICO and CCE violations. This statute permits the government to seize property and money that is used in the commission of the crimes and that is a product of the crimes. So, if a drug dealer uses a boat to smuggle drugs, the boat can be seized, even though it may have been purchased with "honest" money. Any items acquired with drug money may be seized, as can bank accounts and trusts.

SIDEBAR   RICO AND CCE IN ACTION   RICO and CCE are two potent tools that federal law enforcement officials have to combat businesses with a criminal mission (criminal enterprises). The penalties for violating these laws are higher than for other laws directed at the same criminal behavior.

Regardless of the publicity and attention RICO and related statutes have received, they are not commonly used by federal prosecutors. For example, in 1990, only 996 RICO and 128 CCE prosecutions were filed in the United States, although 17,135 people were prosecuted for drug trafficking under other laws. In total, only 2 percent of all criminals in the federal system are convicted of racketeering or CCE crimes.

The most common predicate offenses upon which racketeering charges are based are gambling, drugs, and threats. RICO and CCE cases consume more time and effort than other crimes. On average, CCE cases take twice as long to complete as cases for other offenses and RICO cases take 50 percent longer.

Defendants are less likely to plead guilty in RICO and CCE cases, are just about as likely to be convicted, and are usually punished more severely than defendants convicted under similar laws. Most people prosecuted under these laws are white males.

Source: Prosecuting Criminal Enterprises (Bureau of Justice Statistics 1993).

Crimes Against the Administration of Government

Perjury

Perjury was a crime at common law and continues to be prohibited by statute in all states.

The basic elements of perjury are: (1) The making of a (2) false statement (3) with knowledge that it is false (4) while under oath. To gain a conviction, the prosecution has the tough burden of proving the mens rea: that the person who made the statement knew that it was false. As with other crimes, juries are permitted to infer a defendant's knowledge from surrounding facts.

In addition, the statement must be made while under oath. Be aware that this includes far more than testifying in court. Most laws cover all statements made before one authorized to administer oaths. Therefore, perjury laws apply to people who sign affidavits before notary publics, appear as witnesses before a court reporter (e.g., for deposition) or a grand jury, and before all others who have the authority to administer oaths. For those individuals who have a religious objection to "swearing," the law permits an affirmation. This is simply an acknowledgment by the witness that the testimony he or she renders is truthful. The law treats an affirmation in the same manner as it does an oath.

Some jurisdictions require that the false statement be "material," or important to the matter. This prevents prosecutions for trivial matters. Some jurisdictions have defined *materiality* as any matter that may affect the outcome of a case. If a statement is not material, even if untrue, then a perjury conviction is not permitted.

———————————————BALLENTINE'S———————————————

perjury   Giving false testimony in a judicial proceeding or an administrative proceeding; lying under oath as to a material fact; swearing to the truth of anything one knows or believes to be false. Perjury is a crime. A person who makes a false affirmation is equally a perjurer.

A related crime is **subornation of perjury**. This occurs when one convinces or procures another to commit perjury. One who commits subornation is treated as a perjurer for the purpose of sentencing.

In addition to being a crime in every state, the United States has also made perjury criminal by statute. 18 U.S.C. § 1621 reads:

> Whoever (1) having taken an oath before a competent tribunal, officer, or person, in any case in which a law of the United States authorizes an oath to be administered, that he will testify, declare, depose, or certify truly ... is true, willfully and contrary to such oath states or subscribes any material matter which he does not believe to be true. ...

Of course, truth is a complete defense to a charge of perjury. What is truthful is not always easy to determine, and in most questionable cases prosecutors choose not to pursue the matter. This is in large part due to the mens rea element.

Bribery

As is true of perjury, **bribery** was a crime at English common law. Actually, bribery was initially a violation of biblical law, because it was wrong to attempt to influence judges, who were considered to be God's earthly representatives. Eventually, the crime was recognized by the courts of England.

Today, bribery is a statutory crime in the states and in the United States. The essential elements of the crime are (1) soliciting or accepting (2) anything of value (3) with the purpose of (4) violating a duty or trust. Two primary forms of bribery are that of a public official and commercial bribery.

As mentioned, bribery began as a prohibition of influencing a judge. The crime was eventually extended to include bribery of all public officials and public servants. Statutes make it bribery to be the one accepting or giving the "thing of value." Hence, if a corporate official gives a public official money in exchange for awarding a contract to the company, both the corporate officer and the public official have committed bribery.

Most bribery statutes declare that unsuccessful offers are bribes. Thus, if the public official rejects the offer of the corporate officer, there is still a bribery violation. The offer need not be of money in exchange for a favor; anything of value is sufficient. Automobiles, tickets

---

BALLENTINE'S

subornation of perjury The crime of persuading or inducing another person to commit the crime of perjury.

bribery The crime of giving something of value with the intention of influencing the action of a public official.

to a St. Louis Cardinals game, and a promise of sexual favors all satisfy this requirement.

The offer must be made to a *public official* or *servant*. Both terms are defined broadly. Further, the offeror must be seeking to influence the official in a matter over which the official has authority. Most courts have held that whether the officer actually had the authority to carry out the requested act is not dispositive; the issue is whether the offeror believes that the official possesses the authority. Awarding of government contracts, setting favorable tax assessments, and overlooking civil and criminal violations are examples of corrupt acts.

The offer alone makes the offeror guilty of bribery. For the public official to be convicted, there must be an acceptance. This usually means that the official does the requested act; however, it is widely held that an acceptance is all that is necessary to support a conviction.

Bribery has been extended beyond the public affairs realm to commercial life. Whenever a person who is engaged in business activities breaches a duty or trust owed to someone (or something, such as a business organization) in exchange for something of value, bribery has been committed.

The Model Penal Code declares that commercial bribery is a misdemeanor. The Code applies to people in specific positions, such as lawyers, accountants, trustees, and officers of corporations.[26] Anyone who makes an offer to someone in one of these positions to violate the trust or duty created by the position is guilty of bribery. Of course, any person holding such a position who accepts such an offer is also guilty of bribery. The Code specifically states that any person who holds himself or herself out to the public to be in the business of appraising the value of services or commodities is guilty of bribery if he or she accepts a benefit to influence the decision or appraisal. Knowing that one is violating the trust is the mens rea under the Code.

If a seller for the Widgcom Company were to offer the purchasing agent of Retailers, Inc., money in exchange for receiving the contract to supply Retailers with Widgets for the next year, commercial bribery has occurred. A corporate officer who accepts free personal air travel in exchange for buying all corporate airline tickets from the same airline has committed bribery.

Finally, note that there are statutes that prohibit "throwing" athletic contests for pay. That is, any player, coach, owner, or official who accepts a benefit to cause one participant to win or lose commits bribery. These laws often apply to both professional and amateur sports.

Tax Crimes

We have all heard the quip, "In life, only two things are certain, death and taxes." Tax revenues are the lifeblood of government. In the

United States, people are taxed at the federal level, state level, and local level (county, municipal, and school district taxes). These taxes come in many forms, including income tax, gift and estate tax, sales tax, and excise taxes. Tax laws apply to individuals, estates, and business entities.

All taxing authorities have statutes that impose both civil and criminal penalties for violation of tax laws. Common violations of tax laws are tax evasion, failing to file a required tax return, filing a fraudulent return, and unlawful disclosure of tax information. These are not the only crimes related to taxes, however, as shown by the applicable federal statutes, which embody sixteen tax-related crimes.[27]

Tax evasion involves paying less tax than required or under-reporting one's income with the intent of paying less tax. The federal statute covering tax evasion reads:

26 U.S.C. § 7201 Attempt to evade or defeat tax

||||

Any person who willfully attempts in any manner to evade or defeat any tax imposed by this title or the payment thereof shall, in addition to other penalties provided by law, be guilty of a felony and, upon conviction thereof, shall be fined not more than $100,000 ($500,000 in the case of a corporation), or imprisoned not more than 5 years, or both, together with the costs of prosecution.

Tax fraud, a crime closely related to evasion, involves using fraud or false statements to avoid a tax obligation. This may occur in many ways, including falsifying statements that are provided to a revenue agency, such as fraudulent receipts used for deductions. Filing false tax returns is also a form of tax fraud.

Failure to file a required tax return is also criminal. The relevant federal statute reads:

26 U.S.C. § 7203 Willful failure to file return, supply information, or pay tax

||||

Any person required under this title to pay any estimated tax or tax, or required by this title or by regulations made under authority thereof to make a return, keep any records, or supply any information, who willfully fails to pay such estimated tax or tax, make such return, keep such records, or supply such information ... [shall] be guilty of a misdemeanor and, upon conviction thereof, shall be fined not more than $25,000 ($100,000 in the case of a corporation), or imprisoned not more than 1 year, or both, together with the costs of prosecution.

BALLENTINE'S

tax evasion   Willfully avoiding payment of taxes legally due ... .

tax fraud   The crime of tax evasion. Tax evasion which is intentional but not willful is civil fraud.

Note that § 7203 applies to anyone who is required to file a tax return, pay a tax, or supply information. Therefore, this provision can be the basis of a prosecution of an employer who pays her employees in cash and makes no report to the Internal Revenue Service. Likewise, although some entities are not taxed, such as partnerships, they are required to file informational returns, and failure to do so violates this provision.

Tax evasion, filing fraudulent tax returns, and the unauthorized disclosure of information are crimes of commission. That is, an affirmative act is required to commit these crimes.

Failing to file a required return, or other information, is an act of omission. Proving such crimes requires not proof of an illegal act, but that a required act was not taken. The quoted statutes require willful violations. Negligence in preparing a tax return or in filing the return is not criminal. However, such errors may lead to civil penalties.

The willfulness requirement was considered by the Supreme Court in *Cheek v. United States*.

CHEEK
v.
UNITED STATES
498 U.S. 192 (1991)

Willfulness, as construed by our prior decisions in criminal tax cases, requires the Government to prove that the law imposed a duty on the defendant, that the defendant knew of this duty, and that he voluntarily and intentionally violated this duty. We deal first with the case where the issue is whether the defendant knew of the duty purportedly imposed by the provision of the statute or regulation he is accused of violating, a case in which there is no claim that the provision at issue is invalid. In such a case, if the Government proves actual knowledge of the pertinent legal duty, the prosecution, without more, has satisfied the knowledge component of the willfulness requirement. But carrying this burden requires negating a defendant's claim of ignorance of the law or a claim that because of a misunderstanding of the law, he had a good-faith belief that he was not violating any of the provisions of the tax laws. This is so because one cannot be aware that the law imposes a duty upon him and yet be ignorant of it, misunderstand the law, or believe that the duty does not exist. In the end, the issue is whether, based on all the evidence, the Government has proved that the defendant was aware of the duty at issue, which cannot be true if the jury credits a good-faith misunderstanding and belief submission, whether or not the claimed belief or misunderstanding is objectively reasonable.

In this case, if Cheek asserted that he truly believed that the Internal Revenue Code did not purport to treat wages as income, and the jury believed him, the Government would not have carried its burden to prove willfulness, however unreasonable a court might deem such a belief. ...

We thus disagree with the Court of Appeals' requirement that a claimed good-faith belief must be objectively reasonable if it is to be considered as possibly negating the Government's evidence purporting to show a defendant's awareness of the legal duty at issue. Knowledge and belief are characteristically questions for the fact-finder.

Tax laws require the disclosure of all income and profits. This includes income from illegal sources. Gamblers are required to report their winnings, prostitutes their income, and drug dealers the profits derived from their sales. Failure to report income from illegal acts is the same as failure to report legally earned income. Because requiring people to report income from illegal activities raises a self-incrimination problem, tax laws require that all information obtained be kept confidential. Tax officials are not permitted to disclose such information to law enforcement authorities, and to do so is *unlawful disclosure*. The privilege against self-incrimination is discussed more thoroughly in Chapter 8.

In the *Moon* case, the tax evasion and fraud conviction of Reverend Sun Myung Moon, father of the "Moonies," was upheld by the Second Circuit Court of Appeals.

UNITED STATES
v.
Sun Myung MOON
718 F.2d 1210 (2d Cir. 1983)

Defendants argue that the evidence presented was insufficient to find them guilty beyond a reasonable doubt on the substantive tax offenses charged in Counts Two through Six. To find defendants guilty of fraud in the filing of Moon's income tax returns, the jury had to find that statements contained in the returns which were verified as true were in fact false, and that these false statements were willfully made. ...

Under the government's theory of the case, Moon failed to report interest income earned on the Chase Manhattan Bank accounts that he purportedly owned and income recognized as a result of distribution of Tong Il stock to him at no cost. Appellants' principal contentions at trial were that the Chase accounts and Tong Il stock belonged to the Church, that Moon merely held these assets as the nominee, agent, and/or trustee of the Church, and that therefore he was not taxable on either the Chase interest or Tong Il stock distribution.

In concluding that the jury properly found the Chase accounts and Tong Il stock to be Moon's personal property, we start first with the fact that the Chase accounts and Tong Il securities were maintained in Moon's name and controlled by him. Second, some funds clearly destined for Church entities were put in existing Church bank accounts which were owned and controlled by Church operations. Third, from his handling of the Chase accounts and Tong Il stock Moon seemingly regarded them as his own, not belonging to the Church. Fourth, high-ranking members of the Church were told that the Chase funds belonged to "Father," not to the Church. ...

We turn to the evidence that Moon willfully filed income tax returns for the 1973–75 tax years knowing that these returns contained false information. ... Willfulness in tax fraud cases has become equated with bad faith, want of justification, or knowledge that the taxpayer should have reported more income than he did. ...

The evidence presented on this issue, although circumstantial, was sufficient to sustain the jury's verdict. The salient points follow. Moon signed his 1974 and 1975 returns, acknowledging that he had read them and that they were accurate, and he signed an RSC–12 form giving similar assurances as to his 1973 return; Moon and Kamiyama both knew of Moon's interest income at Chase and income from the distribution of Tong Il stock; Moon actively supervised all of his personal financial matters and never signed anything until he understood it. ... [Conviction affirmed.]

Obstruction of Justice

Obstruction of justice refers to any number of unlawful acts. As a general proposition, any act that interferes with the performance of a public official's duties obstructs justice. However, the crime is most commonly associated with law enforcement and judicial officials.

The types of acts that fall under such statutes include tampering with witnesses or jurors, interfering with police officers, destroying evidence needed for a court proceeding, and intentionally giving false information to a prosecutor in an effort to hinder a prosecutorial effort. However, obstruction statutes are drafted broadly, thereby permitting creative prosecutions. For example, it is common for women who are physically abused by their husbands to contact the police during a violent episode and demand the husband's arrest, usually in an effort to get the man out of the house. Once the husband is arrested, many women lose interest in prosecuting and often refuse to testify against their husbands in court. In such a case, a prosecutor could charge the wife with obstruction of justice because of her refusal to testify.

Resisting arrest is a similar crime. At common law, one could resist an unlawful arrest. Although a few jurisdictions have retained this rule, this is not presently the law in most jurisdictions. Most states have followed the Model Penal Code approach, which prohibits even moderate resistance to any arrest.[28] It is a wise rule, considering the remedies that are available if a police officer makes an unlawful arrest. If the arrest is unlawful, but in good faith, the arrestee will be released either at the police station or after the first judicial hearing. If the arrest was unlawful and made maliciously, the arrestee not only will be released, but also has a civil cause of action for false imprisonment and violation of civil rights.

Contempt

Failure to comply with a court order is contemptuous, as is taking any act with the purpose of undermining a court's authority or intending to interfere with its administration and process. Although statutes provide for contempt, it is widely accepted that the contempt power is inherent.

Contempt is broken down into direct and indirect criminal contempt and direct and indirect civil contempt. *Direct contempt* refers to acts that occur in the presence of the judge. Although usually in the courtroom, the judges' chambers and office area are included. *Indirect*

―――――――――BALLENTINE'S―――――――――

contempt An act of disrespect toward a court or legislative body; deliberate disobedience of a court order.

contempt refers to actions taken outside the presence of a court, but which are violative of a court order.

Criminal contempt is levied to punish a person for violating a court order. Civil contempt, in contrast, does not have punishment as its purpose. It is intended to coerce a person into complying with a court order. For example, if Mary refuses to testify at a trial despite an order to testify, the judge may order her confined until she complies. Once she testifies, she is free. It is often said that civil contemnors hold the keys to their jail cells, whereas criminal contemnors do not. In theory, one who has been held in civil contempt can be punished for criminal contempt after complying with the court order. In practice this seldom occurs, presumably because judges and prosecutors feel that the civil punishment imposed is adequate.

The contempt power is significant. Indirect criminal contemnors are entitled to all the protections of other criminal defendants, such as a right to a trial, assistance of counsel, and proof beyond a reasonable doubt. Direct criminal contemnors have no such rights, as the act took place in the presence of a judge. However, any sentence imposed may be appealed and reviewed for fairness.

Civil contemnors have few rights. They do not possess the rights of those accused of crimes, because civil contempt is not considered a criminal action. In most instances they enjoy no right to appeal. A civil contemnor holds his or her own key; he or she must comply with the court's order. Of course, if an appellate court determines that the underlying order is unlawful, the civil contemnor is released. However, they may be charged with criminal contempt for failure to comply with the order before it was held unlawful by an appellate court. The fact that a court order may be nullified at some future date does not justify noncompliance. Court orders must be obeyed to assure the orderly administration of justice.

TWO CASES OF CONTEMPT   Contempt of court orders are common in domestic law cases. One case, which received considerable media attention, involved Dr. Elizabeth Morgan, who refused to obey a court order to disclose the location of her child, Heather, claiming that her ex-husband had molested the child. The judge ordered that she disclose the location of the child so her ex-husband could exercise his court-ordered visitation rights. She refused, and the judge ordered that she be incarcerated until she disclosed the child's whereabouts. Dr. Morgan spent a total of 759 days in jail and was released only after an act of Congress limited the amount of time a civil contemnor could spend in jail to one year.

A case from Houston, Texas, teaches that the contempt power of judges is powerful. Houston attorney John O'Quinn was found in criminal contempt by a federal district judge for sleeping in a jury room. The basis for the contempt citation was an order from the judge that O'Quinn (and others) "stay out of the facilities up here on this floor unless you get prior permission." The Fifth Circuit Court of Appeals reversed the conviction, finding that the judge's order was too vague. However, this is a good example of the breadth of the contempt power; had the judge's order been more specific, it would have been upheld.

Source: "A Hard Case of Contempt," *Time,* Sept. 18, 1989; "A Mother's 759 Days of Defiance," *U.S. News & World Report,* Oct. 9, 1989.

Legislatures also have the power to cite for contempt. Legislatures, usually through committees, conduct hearings and other proceedings when considering bills and amendments to statutes. The contempt power serves the same function for legislatures that it does for courts. It furthers the orderly performance of legislative duties. Refusal to testify before a legislative body (usually a committee), to produce documents or other items, and disrupting a proceeding are examples of legislative contempt. Persons charged with legislative contempt possess the same rights as defendants charged with other crimes. In most instances, legislative bodies refer contempt cases to prosecutors, rather than adjudicating such cases themselves.

Crimes Against the Environment

With the modernization of the United States has come a threat to the environment. The air and water that people depend upon for sustenance have become polluted. Many species of flora and fauna have been lost and many more are threatened.

Modernization threatens the environment in several ways. By "developing" land, habitats are lost. Also, the use of dangerous chemicals and toxins has become commonplace. In many industries, toxic byproducts of manufacturing are common. Toxic wastes and substances pose use, transportation, and disposal problems. The release of dangerous substances into the air or into water endangers the health and safety of the public. It is estimated that air pollution kills 14,000 people annually and that 100,000 workers die annually from exposure to toxins.[29] The increased population aggravates the problem. Greater numbers of people place greater stress on natural systems. Resources are depleted faster and nature's cleansing process becomes strained and less effective.

Today, there is a large body of environmental law that, to some extent, addresses these problems. The federal government's policy is to create and maintain conditions in which man and nature can exist in productive harmony. Both the federal and state governments play a role in regulation of the environment, although the federal government has the larger part currently. The federal government's role in regulating the environment dates back to at least 1899, when Congress enacted a statute making it a crime to discharge pollutants into navigable waters.

Several federal administrative agencies are charged with overseeing the enforcement and administration of environmental laws, including the Environmental Protection Agency, the Coast Guard, the Department of the Interior, the Occupational Health and Safety Commission, and the Department of Justice. Federal law provides for administrative, civil, and criminal sanctions on environmental law violators.

There are two classes of environmental laws. One class of laws is intended to further the public health and safety. The Clean Air Act, the Clean Water Act, and similar statutes are examples of this type of environmental regulation. A second class of laws is intended to protect the environment itself, for its aesthetic, recreational, and other value. The Endangered Species Act is an example of a conservation law. Of course, many laws serve both objectives.

Until recently, environmental offenses were not usually treated as criminal; rather, they were viewed as civil or administrative infractions. The federal government relied almost exclusively on administrative and civil processes to enforce environmental laws. Fines were the most common penalty sought by the government against offenders.

The belief that environmental violations are serious and should be prosecuted as criminal offenses is a recent development. For example, one of the most notorious environmental cases was Love Canal, where it was discovered in 1978 that the improper disposal of toxins was causing death and illness to local residents. An entire community was forced to relocate to escape the danger—yet not one person was prosecuted in the Love Canal case.

The fear of another Love Canal, or an accident like the one involving Union Carbide in Bhopal, India, where 2,000 people were killed and 200,000 people were injured, and the dangers posed by other environmental wrongs led Congress to strengthen environmental laws. The measures included added criminal sanctions. Relying on civil remedies alone had proved ineffective. Individuals were not being held accountable and corporations found it more cost-effective to violate the law and pay any fines than to comply with the law.

Therefore, although most violations continue to be handled through civil and administrative proceedings, the number of environmental criminal cases is increasing. Of the 500 largest corporations in the United States, one-fourth have been convicted of an environmental crime or have been subject to civil penalties for violating environmental laws.[30] Within the Department of Justice is a special division charged with prosecuting environmental law crimes.

Unlike at common law, today business entities, such as corporations, may be charged with crimes. Fines and dissolution of a corporation are examples of the penalties that may be imposed. Charging corporations for environmental violations is common. Of course, individuals may also be charged with violating environmental laws and corporate employees may be charged for actions taken on behalf of a corporation. It is not a defense for an employee to claim that he or she was following a supervisor's directive, nor may it be a defense for the supervisor to claim that he or she is innocent because he or she delegated performance of the act to an employee.

Some environmental crimes are strict liability. Others, and of course those that can be punished with jail time, require some mens rea, usually a knowing violation.

Several federal environmental laws contain criminal sanctions. The most significant of these laws are the Clean Water Act; the Clean Air Act; the Comprehensive Environmental Response, Compensation, and Liability Act; the Resource Conservation and Recovery Act; the Occupational Safety and Health Act; the Toxic Substances Control Act; the Federal Insecticide, Fungicide, and Rodenticide Act; the Emergency Planning and Community Right-to-Know Act; and the Endangered Species Act. The first eight statutes are examples of regulation for the public health, and the final statute is a conservation law. All these laws provide for administrative and civil remedies and procedures, in addition to criminal sanctions.

Clean Water Act

The Clean Water Act (CWA)[31] regulates the discharge of pollutants into the nation's navigable waters. The CWA establishes a scheme of permits and reporting. The contamination of water with a pollutant, without a permit or exceeding the limits of a permit, is criminal under the Clean Water Act.

Both negligent and knowing acts are criminalized and may be punished with fines and imprisonment. A knowing act is punished more severely than a negligent act. Offenders who have acted negligently may be sentenced to one year in prison, whereas knowing offenders may be sentenced to three years in prison.[32] Fines may also be imposed for both, in addition to any civil remedies.

Also, the CWA contains a "knowing endangerment" provision. If a person violates the CWA with knowledge that the violation "places another person in imminent danger of death or serious bodily injury," the offender may be sentenced to up to fifteen years in prison, and significant fines may be imposed.

Finally, false reporting under the Act is criminal and may be punished by up to two years in prison, in addition to a fine.

Clean Air Act

The goal of the Clean Air Act (CAA) is to preserve air quality. It does this by regulating emissions of dangerous substances into the air.

Similar to the CWA in its criminal aspects, the CAA criminalized negligent and knowing violations of its mandates, punishing the latter more severely.[33] Further, it contains knowing endangerment and false reporting provisions.

Comprehensive Environmental Response, Compensation and Liability Act

The Comprehensive Environmental Response, Compensation and Liability Act (CERCLA) is commonly known as *Superfund*. The purpose of CERCLA is to identify and clean up existing hazardous waste sites.

Any person who knowingly falsifies or destroys any required record or who fails to report a spill of hazardous materials may be punished with fines and imprisonment.[34]

Resource Conservation and Recovery Act

The Resource Conservation and Recovery Act (RCRA) is similar to CERCLA in that they regulate the same subject matter: hazardous materials. However, CERCLA is an after-the-fact regulation intended to clean up existing sites, whereas RCRA is intended to regulate the day-to-day use, storage, transportation, handling, and disposal of hazardous materials.

There are no negligent violations under RCRA; rather, the mens rea for conviction of its prohibitions is knowledge. For example, the knowing transportation of hazardous waste to an unlicensed facility; the knowing treatment, storage, or disposal of hazardous waste without a permit; and the knowing violation of a permit are criminal and may be punished with both imprisonment and fines. As with the CWA and the CAA, knowingly endangering another enhances the punishment for a violation of RCRA.[35]

Occupational Safety and Health Act

The Occupational Safety and Health Act (OSHA) regulates the work environment of the American worker. The objective of the law is to create safe working conditions. There is a plethora of regulations enforcing this mandate.

Any employer who causes the death of an employee as a result of noncompliance with OSHA may be prosecuted and sentenced to imprisonment and a fine. Of course, the employer may also be liable under other criminal laws, such as negligent manslaughter.

Additionally, OSHA requires employers to notify their employees of potential exposure to dangerous chemicals and to provide information and resources to protect the employees. Failure to notify employees of this risk is a criminal omission under OSHA. False reporting is also a crime under this statute.

Toxic Substances Control Act

The Toxic Substances Control Act (TSCA) is the most comprehensive federal law concerning dangerous substances. The Environmental Protection Agency (EPA) is delegated considerable authority under the TSCA to regulate the sale, manufacture, development, processing, distribution, and disposal of toxic substances. Under the TSCA, the EPA is empowered to ban, or otherwise control, the production and distribution of chemicals. Asbestos and radon are examples of chemicals that the EPA has heavily regulated under the TSCA.

Any person who knowingly or willfully violates the TSCA concerning the manufacture, testing, or distribution of a chemical may be punished with both a fine and imprisonment. Also, false reporting, failing to maintain records, and failing to submit records as required by law are criminal acts under the TSCA.[36]

Federal Insecticide, Fungicide, and Rodenticide Act

Chemicals that are lethal to pests may also be lethal or at least harmful to humans. In addition to being inhaled, pesticides find their way into human drinking water and food.

The Federal Insecticide, Fungicide, and Rodenticide Act (FIFRA) delegates to the EPA the task of regulating the manufacture, sale, distribution, and use of these chemicals. Some chemicals are forbidden; there are limits on the use of others. There are labelling and reporting requirements.

Knowing violations of any of FIFRA's requirements are criminal and may be punished with fines and imprisonment.[37]

Emergency Planning and Community Right-to-Know Act

Bhopal, India; Chernobyl; and closer to home, Three Mile Island—all three are reminders that accidents happen, or that the actions of one person, such as a terrorist, can cause a tragedy of enormous proportion. In both the Chernobyl and Bhopal incidents, there was no planning or preparation for an accident.

The purpose of the Emergency Planning and Community Right-to-Know Act is to better prepare the community in which a facility is sited for disaster and to inform the community about emissions of hazardous substances by the facility. The Act requires facilities that use or produce chemicals to report both accidental and routine releases of substances into the air or water. Further, facilities are required to provide local officials (e.g., hospitals) with information about the chemicals used.

Knowing or willful failure to give notice of a release may be punished by both imprisonment and a fine.

Endangered Species Act

The Endangered Species Act (ESA)[38] and the Marine Mammal Protection Act represent a different form of environmental law from those discussed so far. The purpose of these laws is not to protect the public health; rather, the intent is to preserve the integrity of the environment itself.

The ESA establishes a program of conservation of threatened and endangered species of plants and animals and the habitats where they are found. The law is co-administered by the Departments of Interior, Commerce, Agriculture, and Justice.

The ESA prohibits the sale, taking, possession, importation, and exportation of endangered species and the products of those species. Violations of the law are punishable by both fines and imprisonment.

Marine Mammal Protection Act

Similar to the ESA, the Marine Mammal Protection Act (MMPA)[39] is intended to protect and conserve marine mammals. The taking of such creatures without a permit by a U.S. flag vessel while on the high seas is a crime. The taking, possession, and trade of animals protected under the law is prohibited within the United States unless a permit has been obtained. Fines and imprisonment may be imposed on violators.

These are but a few of the federal environmental laws. Also, many states have similar laws. In some instances, the states have been delegated the authority to enforce federal law. Environmental laws affect every person, not just businesses that use or trade in hazardous materials.

Because of overpopulation, high-density urbanization, industrialization, resource exploitation, and technological advances, every person has a duty to be environmentally aware, and the laws of the nation impose environmental obligations on the individual. The proper disposal of trash, car batteries, and motor oil, and the regulation of hunting and fishing, are examples of environmental laws that affect the daily lives of members of the public.

Review Questions

1. Andy approaches Roberta, who is standing on a street corner, and offers her $50 for sex. Roberta, an undercover vice officer, arrests Andy. What crime should he be charged with?

2. Is there a constitutional right to engage in homosexual conduct between mature, consenting adults?

3. When may a state regulate material that is thought to be sexually repulsive? What constitutional provision hinders governments from regulating such expression?

4. What are fighting words? Are they protected by the First Amendment?

5. Is proof that a driver's blood-alcohol level exceeded the statutory maximum the only way to prove that a driver was under the influence? Is it a valid defense for a driver-defendant to claim that she could drive safely, even though her blood-alcohol level exceeded the amount allowed by statute?

6. What are the elements of Continuing Criminal Enterprise, and who is the statute aimed at?

7. What are the basic elements of bribery? The Model Penal Code recognizes two types of bribery. Name the two.

8. Distinguish criminal contempt from civil contempt. Do the same for direct contempt and indirect contempt.

9. Is this statement true? "Perjury is a law that applies only to judicial proceedings." Explain your answer.

10. What are the elements of indecent exposure?

Review Problems

1. Are the following statutes constitutional? Explain, if not.

STATUTE ONE: LOITERING

Any person who loiters in a place in an unusual manner for longer than fifteen minutes and reasonably causes a person to be concerned for their safety must identify himself to police when requested. Any person who refuses to identify himself under these circumstances or takes flight when approached by a police officer is guilty of loitering.

STATUTE TWO: LOITERING

Any person who continually loiters in public parks without apparent employment or who lives off the handouts of others is guilty of loitering.

2. State law prohibits "hardcore pornography." Among the many prohibitions of the law is a provision making it a felony to possess or sell materials that are known to depict bestiality (sex between a human and an animal). Sam, a local adult bookstore owner, sold a magazine to

Herb entitled "Wild on the Farm." The magazine was sealed, and its contents were not visible. The magazine was delivered to Sam in error, part of a large shipment of magazines and books.

During a raid on Sam's establishment the local police discovered the sales ticket reflecting Herb's purchase, his name, and his address. The police then obtained a search warrant for Herb's home and found the magazine during their search. Sam and Herb have both been charged with violating the state's obscenity law. Should they be convicted? Explain your answer.

3. Do you believe that acts that harm no one, but that most members of society find immoral, should be criminalized? Explain your position.

4. How has bribery been changed since it has become a statutory crime?

5–7. Classify each of the following as direct or indirect contempt and civil or criminal contempt.

5. During a personal injury trial, Noah told the judge to "kiss my ass" and then threw an apple, striking the judge in the head.

6. During a union dispute, a judge ordered striking employees back to work. They refused to comply with the order and the judge ordered that each employee pay $50 per day until he or she returned to work.

7. Jon received a court order to tear down a fence he had constructed. The order was served by a sheriff. Immediately after the sheriff handed the order to him, Jon screamed, "Forget that idiot judge, I'm not tearing down the fence!" Jon never removed the fence, and the judge had him arrested, and ordered him to remain in jail until he agreed to comply with the order.

8. Consider and discuss this statement: Possession and use of drugs or alcohol should not be a crime. The only dangers presented from these substances arise when a person works, drives, or conducts some activity that requires the full use of the senses, while under their influence. Criminal statutes should be narrow and proscribe only the harm sought to be prevented. No harm is created by use in controlled environments, such as in the home. Accordingly, statutes should only proscribe engaging in certain undertakings while under the influence of alcohol or drugs.

Notes

1 Model Penal Code § 251.2(1).

2 Model Penal Code § 251.2(5).

3 18 U.S.C. § 2421.

4 Model Penal Code § 251.1.

5 18 U.S.C. § 1461.

6 Anderson, "Mapplethorpe Photos on Trial," *A.B.A. J.* 28 (Dec. 1990).

7 There are other limits on First Amendment freedoms. Some of these are discussed in Chapter 8, in the constitutional defenses section.

8 *Manual Enterprises, Inc. v. Day,* 370 U.S. 478 (1962) (opinion by Justice Harlan).

9 50 Am. Jur. 2d *Lewdness, Indecency, etc.* 7 (1970).

10 *See Roth v. United States,* 354 U.S. 476, 487, n.20 (1957).

11 *United States v. Guglielmi,* 819 F.2d 451 (4th Cir. 1987).

12 *See New York v. Ferber,* 458 U.S. 747 (1982).

13 *See Capitol News Co. v. Metropolitan Government,* 562 S.W.2d 430 (Tenn. 1978).

14 *Stanley v. Georgia,* 394 U.S. 557 (1969).

15 Model Penal Code § 251.4.

16 Model Penal Code § 250.1.

17 *Champlinsky v. New Hampshire,* 315 U.S. 568 (1942).

18 *Brandenburg v. Ohio,* 395 U.S. 444 (1969).

19 See Chapter 3 on personal status as an act.

20 Model Penal Code § 2.01(4).

21 *Robinson v. California,* 370 U.S. 660 (1962).

22 21 U.S.C. § 848.

23 *United States v. Brantley,* 733 F.2d 1429 (11th Cir. 1984).

24 21 U.S.C. § 848(e).

25 21 U.S.C. § 853(a).

26 Model Penal Code § 224.8.

27 26 U.S.C. § 7201 *et seq.*

28 Model Penal Code § 3.04(2)(a)(i).

29 Michael Norton, *Federal Environmental Criminal Law Enforcement in the 1990's* 1 (ALI-ABA, C868, 1993).

30 *Id.*

31 33 U.S.C. § 1319(a).

32 33 U.S.C. § 1319(c).

33 42 U.S.C. § 7413.

34 42 U.S.C. § 9603.

35 42 U.S.C. § 6928.

36 15 U.S.C. §§ 2614–2615.

37 7 U.S.C. § 136i–1(d).

38 16 U.S.C. §§ 1531–1543.

39 16 U.S.C. §§ 1361–1384, 1401–1407.

CHAPTER 7

PARTIES AND INCHOATE OFFENSES

Parties to Crimes

Not all crimes are committed by only one person. Not all planned crimes are completed. This chapter examines the two issues of group criminal responsibility and uncompleted crimes. Those who participate in a crime are referred to as *parties*. Uncompleted crimes are referred to as *inchoate crimes*.

At common law, there were four parties to crimes: principals in the first degree; principals in the second degree; accessories before the fact; and accessories after the fact.

A **principal** in the first degree is the participant who actually committed the proscribed act. For example, three people (A, B, and C) agree to rob a grocery store. A enters the store and points a gun at a checker and demands that money be placed in a bag. A is a principal in the first degree.

A principal in the second degree is a party who aids, counsels, assists, or encourages the principal in the first degree during commission of the crime. A party must be present during a crime to be a principal in the second degree. However, constructive presence is sufficient. Whenever a party is physically absent from the location of the crime, but aids from a distance, that party is a principal in the second degree. So, if B, from our hypothetical case, waits in the getaway car outside the store, B is a principal in the second degree. First-degree and second-degree principals are punished equally. Principals in the second degree are also referred to as *accomplices,* as are accessories before the fact.

Anyone who aids, counsels, encourages, or assists in the preparation of a crime, but is not physically present during the crime, is an **accessory** before the fact. If C, an expert in bank security, assisted in planning the robbery, then C is an accessory before the fact. The primary distinction between a principal in the second degree and an accessory before the fact is the lack of presence during the crime of an accessory before the fact.

At common law, accessories could not be convicted until the principals were convicted. In addition, procedural rules made it more difficult to convict accessories than principals. These rules are no longer the law. Statutes group principals in the first and second degree together with accessories before the fact and punish all equally.

The mens rea of an accomplice (before and during a crime) is usually intentional (specific) in common-law terms, or knowing or purposeful

---

BALLENTINE'S

principal   A principal in the first degree is a person who commits a crime, either in person or through an innocent agent; a principal in the second degree is a person who is present at the commission of a crime, giving aid and encouragement to the chief perpetrator.

accessory   A person who is involved with the commission of a crime but who is not present at the time it is committed.

Parties to a
Burglary

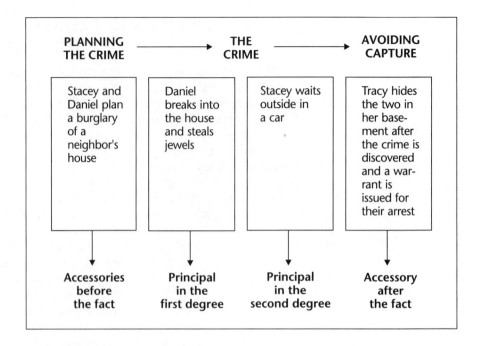

in Model Penal Code language. Negligent and reckless acts do not make a person a principal in the second degree or an accessory.

Accessories after the fact continue to be treated differently. A person is an accessory after the fact if: (1) aid, comfort, or shelter is provided to a criminal (2) with the purpose of assisting the criminal in avoiding arrest or prosecution (3) after the crime is committed (4) and the accessory was not present during commission of the crime. D is an accessory after the fact, if A and B flee to D's house and D hides A and B from the police. It is possible to be an accessory both before and after the fact. Hence, if C were to hide A and B from the police, C would be both an accessory before and after the fact. Accessories after the fact are not punished as severely as the other three classifications of parties.

The mental state required to prove that a person was an accessory after the fact is twofold: first, it must be shown that the defendant was aware of the person's criminal status (scienter) and second, that the defendant intended to hinder attempts to arrest or prosecute the criminal.

Inchoate Crimes

Not all planned crimes are completed. Because of the danger posed by substantial planning, accompanied by an intent to carry out a plan, some uncompleted crimes may be punished.

By punishing inchoate acts, the deterrent purpose of the criminal justice system is furthered. If the rule were otherwise, law enforcement officials would have no incentive to intervene in a criminal enterprise before it is completed. By punishing attempt, conspiracy, and solicitation, an officer may prevent a planned criminal act from occurring without risking losing a criminal conviction.

Attempt

The reasons planned crimes are not always successful are numerous. In some instances, law enforcement intervention prevents completion of a crime. If a police officer stops Penny from shooting Tom moments before she commits the act, should she be free from criminal liability because she was not successful? The law answers that question in the negative, calling such uncompleted crimes *attempt*.

Attempt was not a crime at early common law; however, attempt cases do appear later in English common law. The first cases began to appear in the late 1700s and early 1800s.[1] Many of the early cases have been traced to an English court that is no longer in existence, the Star Chamber. Today, attempt is recognized in the United States by all states.

The purpose of attempt laws is to deter people from planning to commit crimes; to punish those who intended to commit a crime, but were unsuccessful; and to encourage law enforcement officers to prevent unlawful activity. The last may appear obvious; however, if it were not for making attempts illegal, police would have an incentive to permit illegal acts, so as to be able to punish the wrongdoer.

There are essentially three elements to all attempts. One, the defendant must intend to commit a crime. Two, the defendant must take some act in furtherance of that intent. Three, the crime is not completed.

First, the mens rea element: The defendant must intend to take some act that amounts to a crime; in common-law language, specific intent, and under the Model Penal Code, knowingly or purposefully. Some statutes specifically identify what crime must be intended, whereas others simply refer to an intent to commit any felony. In any event, the accused must intend to commit some specific crime, such as murder, rape, or theft.

The second element, the actus reus of attempt, can be problematic. The problem revolves around this question: how close to completion of the intended crime must a defendant come to be guilty of attempt? It is well established that thoughts alone do not establish a crime; mere preparation without anything further does not amount to the crime of

---

————BALLENTINE'S————

attempt   An act done with the intent to commit a crime, which would have resulted in the crime being committed except that something happened to prevent it. The line between an attempt and mere preparations is often difficult to draw; it is a matter of degree.

attempt. The failing student who sits at home and contemplates how to "do in" his criminal law instructor commits no crime. It is not until the student goes further that he can be liable for attempt.

Various tests are used to determine if an act is close enough to completion to permit an attempt conviction. The four commonly used tests are proximity, res ipsa loquitur, probable desistance, and the Model Penal Code's "substantial steps" test.

The *proximity test* examines what acts have been taken and what acts are left to be taken to complete the crime. Justice Holmes said that there "must be a dangerous proximity to success."[2]

The *res ipsa loquitur test* (also called the *unequivocality test*) looks at crimes individually and finds an act, a certain point in time, which indicates that the defendant has "no other purpose than the commission of that specific crime."[3] For example, most courts have held that once a defendant hires another to commit a crime, attempt has been committed. The step of hiring the person who will complete the crime crosses the line between mere preparation and illegal act.

The third test, *probable desistance*, focuses on the likelihood that the defendant would have followed through with the crime had the opportunity existed. The foundation of the theory is that all people may plan illegal acts at some time in life, but that there is a point where most stop. Any person who passes this line of demarcation has exhibited that the crime would have been completed, had the situation permitted. Critics have attacked this test, claiming that the determination of such a line, if it exists, is arbitrary.

The Model Penal Code uses a *"substantial step"* to completion test.[4] That is, one is guilty of attempt if substantial steps have been taken toward commission of a crime. The Code specifically states that the conduct in question must "strongly corroborate" the actor's criminal purpose. The Code goes further and lists acts that may constitute attempts, provided that they "strongly corroborate" an intent to commit a crime. That list includes:

1. Lying in wait or searching for the intended victim.

2. Enticing or seeking to entice the intended victim to go to the place where the crime will be committed.

3. Investigating the location where the crime is to be committed.

4. Unlawfully entering a structure where the crime is to be committed.

5. Possession of materials necessary to complete the crime, provided that the tools are specially designed for the commission of the crime.

6. Possession, collection, or fabrication of materials to be used in the crime, near the scene of the crime, when the materials serve no lawful purpose.

7. Soliciting someone to commit a crime.

Keep in mind that different results are possible if these tests are applied to the same facts. In the *Murray* case, the line between preparation and attempt is examined. Do you agree with the court?

PEOPLE
v.
MURRAY
15 Cal. 160 (1859)

The evidence in this case entirely fails to sustain the charge against the defendant of an attempt to contract an incestuous marriage with his niece. It only discloses declarations of his determination to contract the marriage, his elopement with the niece for that avowed purpose, and his request to one of the witnesses to go for a magistrate to perform the ceremony. It shows very clearly the intention of the defendant, but something more than mere intention is necessary to constitute the offense charged. Between preparation for the attempt and the attempt itself, there is a wide difference. The preparation consists of devising or arranging the means or measures necessary for the commission of the offense;

the attempt is the direct movement toward the commission after the preparation is made. To illustrate: a party may purchase and load a gun, with the declared intention to shoot his neighbor; but until some movement is made to use the weapon upon the person of his intended victim, there is only preparation and not attempt. For the preparation, he may be held to keep the peace; but he is not chargeable with any attempt to kill. So in the present case, the declarations, and elopement, and request for a magistrate, were preparatory to the marriage; but until the officer was engaged, and the parties stood before him, ready to take the vows appropriate to the contract of marriage, it cannot be said, in strictness, that the attempt was made. The attempt contemplated by the statute must be manifested by acts that would end in the consummation of the particular offence, but for the intervention of circumstances independent of the will of the party. [Conviction reversed.]

Regardless of which test is applied, if a defendant has a change of heart and does not complete the crime, even after crossing the line, then abandonment may be a valid defense.

Of course, the abandonment must be voluntary. Generally, any reason which causes a defendant to desist, other than the defendant's independent decision not to complete the crime, falls outside the defense. A criminal who chooses to not rob a store because a police officer arrives at the scene moments before the planned act was to occur is not entitled to the defense of abandonment.

Two other defenses which arise in the context of attempt are legal and factual impossibility. **Legal impossibility** refers to the situation when a defendant believes that his or her acts are illegal when they are not.

—————————————————— BALLENTINE'S ——————————————————

legal impossibility A person who is unable to commit a crime because of legal impossibility cannot be convicted of a crime he or she intends or attempts. By contrast, a person who is unable to complete a criminal act because of factual impossibility may nonetheless be criminally responsible.

If a defendant takes an act believing it illegal, when it is actually lawful, he or she is not liable. The law of attempt does not punish one for attempting to do a lawful thing, even if the person had an evil mind.

Factual impossibility refers to situations when people attempt to commit a crime, but it is impossible to do so. For example, John breaks into his friend's school locker to steal property, but discovers that the locker is empty. Distraught by the situation, John decides to relax by smoking marijuana. Unknown to John, the cigarette contains no marijuana or other illegal drug. John has made two factual errors. In both instances John could be convicted because factual impossibility is not a defense. This rule is justified by the fact that the defendant possessed the required mens rea and took all the acts necessary to commit the offense. The only reason the crime was not fully completed was because of an extraneous fact unknown to the defendant.

In the *Haines* case, a defendant appealed his conviction for attempted murder. He alleged that because of factual improbability, he did not take a "substantial step" toward completing a murder.

STATE
v.
HAINES
545 N.E.2d 834 (Ind. Ct. App. 1989)

On August 6, 1987, Lafayette, Indiana, police officers John R. Dennis (Dennis) and Brad Hayworth drove to Haines' apartment in response to a radio call of a possible suicide. Haines was unconscious when they arrived and was lying face down in a pool of blood. Dennis attempted to revive Haines and noticed that Haines' wrists were slashed and bleeding. When Haines heard the paramedics arriving, he stood up, ran toward Dennis, and screamed that he should be left to die because he had AIDS. Dennis told Haines they were there to help him, but he continued yelling and stated he wanted to [infect Dennis with the disease.] Haines told Dennis that he would "use his wounds" and began jerking his arms at Dennis, causing blood to spray into Dennis' mouth and eyes. Throughout the incident, as the officers attempted to subdue him, Haines repeatedly yelled that he had AIDS, that he could not deal with it, and that he was going to make Dennis deal with it.

Haines also struggled with emergency medical technicians Dan Garvey (Garvey) and Diane Robinson, threatening to infect them with AIDS, and began spitting at them. When Dennis grabbed Haines, Haines scratched, bit, and spit at him. At one point, Haines grabbed a blood-soaked wig and struck Dennis in the face with it. This caused blood again to splatter onto Dennis' eyes, mouth, and skin. When Dennis finally handcuffed Haines, Dennis was covered with blood. He also had scrapes and scratches on his arms and a cut on his finger that was bleeding.

When Haines arrived at the hospital, he was still kicking, screaming, throwing blood, and spitting at Dennis, Garvey, and another paramedic ... . Haines again announced that he had AIDS and that he was going to show everyone else what it was like to have the disease and die. At one point Haines bit Garvey on the upper arm, breaking the skin. ...

Haines was charged with three counts of attempted murder. At trial, medical experts testified that the virus could be transmitted through blood, tears, and saliva. They also observed that policemen, firemen, and other emergency personnel are generally at risk when they are exposed to body products. One medical expert observed that Dennis was definitely exposed to the HIV virus and others acknowledged that exposure of infected blood to the eyes and the mouth is dangerous, and that it is easier for the virus to enter the bloodstream if there is a cut in the skin.

Following a trial by jury, Haines was convicted of three counts of attempted murder on January 14, 1988. On February 18, 1988, Haines moved for judgment on the evidence as to the three counts of attempted murder, which the trial court granted. The trial court did enter judgment of conviction on three counts of battery as a class D felony. Haines was orderecl to serve a two-year sentence on each count to run consecutively.

The only issue before us is whether the trial court erred in granting Haines' motion for judgment on the evidence and vacating the three counts of attempted murder.

PARTIES' CONTENTIONS

The State maintains that the trial court erred in granting Haines' motion for judgment on the evidence because the trial judge misconstrued tbe requirements of proof necessary to constitute a substantial step in accordance with the law of attempt. Haines responds that his conduct did not constitute a substantial step toward murder as charged, because all evidence relating to the AIDS virus was introduced by the defense which led only to an inference in favor of Haines.

CONCLUSION

The trial court erred in granting Haines' motion for judgment on the evidence.

This appeal presents a novel question in Indiana.

* * *

Contrary to Haines' contention that the evidence did not support a reasonable inference that his conduct amounted to a substantial step toward murder, the record reflects otherwise. At trial, it was definitely established that Haines carried the AIDS virus, was aware of the infection, believed it to be fatal, and intended to inflict others witb the disease by spitting, biting, scratching, and throwing blood. ... His biological warfare with those attempting to help him is akin to a sinking ship firing on its rescuers.

Haines misconstrues the logic and effect of our attempt statute ... .

"It is no defense that, because of a misapprehension of the circumstances, it would have been impossible for the accused person to commit the crime attempt." ... [O]ur supreme court observed:

> It is clear that section (b) of our statute rejects the defense of impossibility. It is not necessary that there be a present ability to complete the crime, nor is it necessary that the crime be factually possible. When the defendant has done all that he believes necessary to cause the particular result, regardless of what is actually possible under existing circumstances, he has committed an attempt. ...

In accordance with [the statute], the State was not required to prove that Haines' conduct could actually have killed. It was only necessary for the State to show that Haines did all that he believed necessary to bring about an intended result, regardless of what was actually possible. ... Haines repeatedly announced that he had AIDS and desired to infect and kill others. At the hospital, Haines was expressly told by doctors that biting, spitting, and throwing blood was endangering others.

While [the statute] rejects the defense of impossibility, some jurisdictions provide for the dismissal of a charge or reduction in sentence on the basis of "inherent impossibility" if the defendant's conduct was so inherently unlikely to result or culminate in the commission of a crime. ...

While we have found no Indiana case directly on point, the evidence presented at trial renders any defense of inherent impossibility inapplicable in this case. ...

In addition to Haines' belief that he could infect others, there was testimony by physicians that the virus may be transmitted through the exchange of bodily fluids. ...

From the evidence in the record before us we can only conclude that Haines had knowledge of his disease and that he unrelentingly and unequivocally sought to kill the persons helping him by infecting them with AIDS, and that he took a substantial step towards killing them by his conduct, believing that he could do so, all of which was more than a mere tenuous, theoretical, or speculative "chance" of transmitting the disease. From all of the evidence before the jury, it could have concluded beyond a reasonable doubt that Haines took a substantial step toward the commission of murder.

Thus, the trial court improperly granted Haines' motion for judgment on the evidence ... . The trial court's judgment is reversed with instructions to reinstate the jury's verdict and resentence Haines accordingly.

The Indiana Court of Appeals rejected factual impossibility (leaving open the issue of inherent factual impossibility) as a defense and rejected the factual assertion that AIDS cannot be transmitting through spitting and throwing blood on a person. Further, the court found that the acts of spitting and throwing blood on a person by a person with AIDS are substantial steps toward the commission of murder, thereby supporting an attempted murder conviction.

Conspiracy

Conspiracy is (1) an agreement (2) between two or more persons (3) to commit an unlawful act or a lawful act in an unlawful manner. The agreement is the actus reus of the crime, and the intent to commit an unlawful act or a lawful act in an unlawful manner is the mens rea.

In some jurisdictions, the agreement alone satisfies the actus reus. In others, some act must be taken in furtherance of the objective of the agreement. Although at least one jurisdiction requires the conspirators to take "substantial steps" to be liable for conspiracy, most require less; often proof of an "overt act" will sustain a conviction. Hence, although mere preparation is not sufficient to impose liability for attempt, it is sufficient in many jurisdictions to prove conspiracy.

At least two people must join in the agreement. One limitation on this rule is the **concert of action rule** (**Wharton's Rule**). Under this rule, two people cannot be charged with conspiracy when the underlying offense itself requires two people. For example, gambling is a crime that requires the acts of at least two people. Wharton's Rule prohibits convictions of both gambling and conspiracy. Adultery and incest are other examples. This is not true of murder, as murder can be committed

---
BALLENTINE'S

conspiracy   An agreement between two or more persons to engage in a criminal act or to accomplish a legal objective by criminal or unlawful means.

concert of action rule   The rule that if one of the elements of a crime is such that it can only be committed by two persons acting together, such mutual action cannot also be a conspiracy. This principle is also referred to as the *Wharton Rule*.

by one person. Wharton's Rule is limited, however, to two people. So if three people agree to gamble, a conviction of gambling and conspiracy to commit gambling is permitted.

The mens rea of conspiracy has two aspects. First, conspirators must have an intent to enter into an agreement. Second, conspirators must possess a specific intent to commit some unlawful objective. That objective must be to commit an unlawful act or a lawful act in an unlawful manner. The language of conspiracy speaks of doing unlawful acts, not necessarily criminal. This is important because some acts, when taken by an individual, may lead to civil, but not criminal, liability. However, when the same acts are taken by a group, the law of conspiracy makes them criminal. This is common in the area of fraud.

The mens rea requirement of conspiracy is strict. Contrary to the general rule, mistake of law and fact are often accepted defenses. It is a defense for a party to have been under the mistaken belief that the group's actions and objectives were legal. This is because the conspiracy must be corrupt; the parties must have had an evil purpose for their union.

What if a party withdraws from the conspiracy while it is ongoing? As a general rule, withdrawal is not a defense, because the crime was complete when the parties entered into the agreement. However, if the jurisdiction requires an agreement plus an overt act or substantial steps, and the withdrawal is made before those acts occur, there is no criminal liability on behalf of the withdrawn party. To determine when withdrawal occurred, courts look to the defendant's actions. Withdrawal is effective at the time his or her acts would have conveyed to a reasonable person, standing in a co-conspirator's shoes, that he or she was abandoning the conspiracy. Additionally, the withdrawal must occur within a time that permits the other parties to abandon the objective. A last-second withdrawal, when it is too late to stop the wheels from turning, is not a defense. The Model Penal Code recognizes voluntary withdrawal as an affirmative defense.[5]

A few procedural issues are unique to conspiracy. As a whole, these rules favor prosecution. First, conspiracy is considered a crime, independent of any crime that is the objective of the conspiracy. If Amy and Ashley conspire to murder Elsa, they have committed two offenses: murder and conspiracy to murder. It is not a violation of the Fifth Amendment's double jeopardy prohibition to punish both crimes (cumulative punishment). Conspiracy to commit a crime and the commission of that crime do not merge into one. This is why conspiracy can be inchoate; it can be charged in cases where the objective is not met. If Amy and Ashley are not successful in their murderous plot, they are still liable for conspiracy to murder. One exception to the general rule of cumulative punishments is Wharton's Rule, discussed earlier.

Prosecutors must show an agreement between two or more parties to prove conspiracy. This creates some difficulties at trial. One difficulty concerns whether alleged co-conspirators should be tried together or separately. Because the United States Supreme Court has approved trial of all parties either at the location where the agreement was entered into or at any location where an act in furtherance of the conspiracy occurred, defendants are usually tried together.[6] It is possible for a defendant to be tried in a location where he or she has never been, and some argue that this is unconstitutional. In addition, critics argue that trying defendants together creates an increased likelihood of conviction because a form of "guilt by association" occurs in juror's minds.

Another procedural irregularity is the **co-conspirator hearsay rule**. **Hearsay** is an out-of-court statement. Although hearsay evidence is normally inadmissible at trial, the co-conspirator exception permits the statements of one party that are made out of court to be admitted. The rule is limited to statements made during planning and commission of the conspiracy; statements made after it is completed are inadmissible.

Because two people (or more) are required to have a conspiracy, if only two people are charged, and one is acquitted, then the other cannot be punished. For example, Edgar and Robert are charged and tried together for conspiring to rob a bank. If the jury acquits one, the other must also be acquitted. At least two people must be convicted. So, if a group of people are charged, and the jury acquits all but two, the convictions stand.

Finally, be aware that many statutes deal with conspiracies, even though they are not named so. You have already examined two federal conspiracy statutes, the Racketeer Influenced and Corrupt Organizations Act and Continuing Criminal Enterprise. In recent years there has been a rise in the number of conspiracy filings. This is largely the result of RICO and related statutes and because of the procedural advantages that prosecutors have, as discussed earlier.

Solicitation

You have already encountered **solicitation** in the discussion of prostitution. But solicitation is much broader than attempting to engage someone in prostitution. Solicitation is the (1) encouraging, requesting, or commanding (2) of another (3) to commit a crime.

───────────────────────────BALLENTINE'S───────────────────────────

coconspirator's rule   The rule of evidence that statements made by a person involved in a conspiracy may be used as evidence of the guilt of all the conspirators.

hearsay   The testimony of a witness as to a statement made to him or her outside of court, or made to someone else who told him or her what was said, that is offered in court to prove the truth of the matter contained in the statement.

solicitation   The crime of encouraging or inciting a person to commit a crime.

Solicitation is a specific-intent crime: the person must intend to convince another to commit an offense. Although the crime may be prostitution, it can be any crime in most jurisdictions. A few states limit the pool to felonies. The actus reus of the crime is the solicitation.

The crime is different from attempt, because the solicitation itself is a crime, and no act to further the crime need be taken. Of course, if Gwen asks Tracy to kill Jeff, and the deed is completed, then Gwen is an accessory before the fact of murder, as well as a solicitor.

Review Questions

1. Distinguish a principal in the first degree from a principal in the second degree. Which is punished more severely?

2. A person who helps principals prepare to commit a crime, but is not present during the commission, is called what?

3. Has Jan committed attempted murder if she decides to kill her sister and mentally works out the details of when, how, and where?

4. What are the elements of conspiracy?

5. What is hearsay? What is the co-conspirator hearsay rule?

6. What is meant by the phrase "inchoate crimes"?

7. What is the difference between solicitation and attempt?

Review Problems

1-3. Use the following facts to answer questions one through three.

Abel and Baker were inmates sharing a cell in state prison. During their stay they planned a convenience store robbery for after their release. They decided which store to rob, when they would rob it, and what method they would use. Having frequented the store on many occasions, Abel knew that the store had a safe and that the employees did not have access to its contents. Neither Abel or Baker had any experience with breaking into safes and decided to seek help.

Accordingly, they sought out "Nitro," a fellow inmate who was a known explosives expert. They requested his assistance and promised to pay him one-third of the total recovery. He agreed. However, he would only be able to teach the two how to gain entry to the safe, because he was not scheduled for release until after the day they had planned for the robbery. He added that he owned a house in the area and that it would be available for them to use as a "hide-out until the heat was off."

The two were released as planned and drove to the town where the store was located. As instructed by Nitro, the two went to a store and purchased the materials necessary to construct an explosive, which was to be used to gain entry to the safe. That evening Abel and Baker went to the store with their homemade explosive. They left the car they were traveling in and went to the rear of the store to gain entry through a back door. However, as they entered the alley behind the store, they encountered a police officer. The officer, suspicious of them, examined their bag and discovered the bomb. Abel and Baker escaped from the officer and stayed in Nitro's house for three days before being discovered and arrested.

1. What crimes has Abel committed?

2. What crimes has Baker committed?

3. What crimes has Nitro committed?

4. John and Tyrone have a fight in a bar. Tyrone returns home, climbs into bed, and suffers a fatal heart attack. John, still angry from the earlier fight, climbs through a window into Tyrone's room and shoots Tyrone twice in the head. Has John committed a murder? Attempted murder? Explain your answer.

Notes

1 *See Rex v. Scofield,* Cald. 397 (1784) and *Rex v. Higgins,* 2 East 5 (1801).

2 *Hyde v. United States,* 225 U.S. 347 (1912).

3 Turner, "Attempts to Commit Crimes," 5 *Cambridge L.J.* 230, 236 (1934).

4 Model Penal Code § 5.01.

5 Model Penal Code § 5.03.

6 *Hyde v. United States,* 225 U.S. 347 (1912).

CHAPTER 8

FACTUAL AND STATUTORY DEFENSES

"Defense" Defined

Criminal defendants usually claim that they are innocent of the charges against them. A defendant's reason for asserting that he is innocent is called a *defense.* Defenses can be factual: "I didn't do it!" They can also be legal: "I did it, but the case was filed after the statute of limitation had run." Many defenses have been developed under the common law; however, many others have been created by legislation. Finally, some defenses find their origin in the constitutions of the states and federal government. Some defenses are complete (perfect); that is, if successful, the defendant goes free. Other defenses are partial; the defendant avoids liability on one charge, but may be convicted of a lesser offense.

This chapter examines several factual and statutory defenses. Chapter 9 discusses constitutional defenses.

Affirmative Defenses

There is a special class of defenses known as **affirmative defenses.** Affirmative defenses go beyond a simple denial; they raise special or new issues, which, if proven, can result in an acquittal or lesser liability. Defenses that raise the question of a defendant's mental state to commit a crime (e.g., insanity and intoxication), whether justification or excuse existed to commit the crime (e.g., self-defense), and alibi fall into the affirmative defenses class.

As a general rule, criminal defendants may sit passively during trial, as the prosecution bears the burden of proving the government's allegations. In all instances, **burden of proof** refers to two burdens, the burden of production and the burden of persuasion. Because it is not practical to require prosecutors to prove that every defendant was sane, was not intoxicated, or did not have justification to use force, the burdens for affirmative defenses are different than for other defenses. First, defendants have the duty of raising all affirmative defenses. At trial this

---
BALLENTINE'S
---

affirmative defense   A defense that amounts to more than simply a denial of the allegations in the plaintiff's complaint. It sets up new matter which, if proven, could result in a judgment against the plaintiff even if all the allegations of the complaint are true.

burden of proof   The duty of establishing the truth of a matter; the duty of proving a fact that is in dispute. In most instances the burden of proof, like the burden of going forward, shifts from one side to the other during the course of a trial as the case progresses and evidence is introduced by each side.

means that defendants must produce some evidence to support the defense. This is known as the **burden of production**. Defendants do not have to convince the factfinder that the defense is valid. They are only required to bring forth enough evidence to establish the defense.

After defendants have met the burden of production, the **burden of persuasion** then must be met. There is a split among the states; some require the defendant to carry this burden, whereas others require it of the prosecution. If the defendant has the burden, then he or she must convince the factfinder that the defense is true. Defendants must prove this by a preponderance of evidence. In jurisdictions that require prosecutors to disprove an affirmative defense, there is again a split as to the standard of proof required. Some require proof by a preponderance and others require proof beyond a reasonable doubt.

Some of the defenses covered in this chapter are affirmative defenses. It is necessary to research local law to determine which procedure is followed in a particular jurisdiction and what defenses are considered affirmative defenses.

Insanity

Few aspects of criminal law have received as much public attention as the insanity defense. The defense has also been the subject of considerable scholastic research and discussion. Some critics charge that the defense should not be available. Others criticize not the availability of such a defense, but the particular tests employed to determine sanity. Despite its critics, insanity is recognized by nearly all jurisdictions as a defense. At least three states—Montana, Utah, and Idaho—have abolished the insanity defense. In 1994, the U.S. Supreme Court denied certiorari in a case challenging such a law as violative of due process.

In reality, insanity is a mens rea defense. If a defendant was insane at the time of the crime, it is unlikely that the requisite mens rea existed. It is generally held that one who is insane is incapable of forming a rational purpose or intent. In fact, in most jurisdictions defendants may put on evidence to establish that insanity prevented the requisite

---
BALLENTINE'S

burden of going forward (production) The duty of a party, with respect to certain issues being tried, to produce evidence sufficient to justify a verdict before the other party is obligated to produce evidence to the contrary. ... [A]lso referred to as the *burden of evidence*, the *burden of proceeding*, and the *burden of producing evidence*. The burden of going forward may shift back and forth between the parties during the course of a trial.

burden of persuasion The ultimate burden of proof; the responsibility of convincing the jury, or, in a nonjury trial, the judge, of the truth.

mens rea from being formed. This is the defense of **diminished capacity**. It is a direct attack on the mens rea element of the crime, separate from the defense of insanity. If successful, the result could be conviction of a lesser, general-intent crime. However, a few states have made defendants choose between the insanity defense and the assertion of lack of mens rea due to insanity.

The theory underlying the defense of insanity is that no purpose of criminal law is served by subjecting insane persons to the criminal justice system. Because they have no control over their behavior, they cannot be deterred from similar future behavior. Similarly, no general deterrence will occur, as others suffering from a mental or physical disease of the mind cannot alter their behavior. The one purpose that may be served, incapacitation, is inappropriate if the defendant no longer suffers from a mental disease, or if the disease is now controlled. If the defendant continues to be dangerous, there is no need to use the criminal justice system to remove him or her from society, because this can be accomplished using civil commitment.

Something that must be remembered is that criminal law has its own definition of insanity. Other areas of law (e.g., civil commitment) use different tests, as do other professions (e.g., psychiatry). Each jurisdiction is free to use whatever test it wishes to determine insanity. Three tests are used to determine sanity in the criminal law context: M'Naghten; irresistible impulse; and the Model Penal Code. A fourth test, the Durham, is no longer used in any jurisdiction, but is mentioned because of its historical significance.

SIDEBAR   TWINKIES, WITCHCRAFT, PMS, and MORE   A number of interesting insanity-related defenses have been raised by defendants. Although some are in the nature of full insanity defenses, most are asserted as diminished-capacity defenses.

One of the most famous is the so-called "Twinkie defense," raised by a defendant in California who was charged with murdering a mayor and another official. He claimed that his large consumption of white sugar, primarily through snack foods, caused him to have a diminished capacity. The defense was successful in reducing the crime from murder to manslaughter. He was sentenced to a short prison term and committed suicide after his release. The California legislature responded to the decision by barring diminished-capacity defenses in future cases.

In addition to the Twinkie defense, all of the following have been pleaded by defendants in support of either an insanity or diminished-capacity defense: premenstrual syndrome, involuntary subliminal television intoxication, brainwashing syndrome, and posttraumatic stress disorder. One defendant even asserted a witchcraft defense, claiming that witchcraft made him do it.

BALLENTINE'S
---

diminished capacity   The rule that a criminal defendant, although not sufficiently mentally impaired to be entitled to a defense of insanity, may have been so reduced in mental capacity ... that he or she was incapable of forming the mental state necessary, in law, for the commission of certain crimes.

Many states have followed California's lead and eliminated the diminished-capacity defense. Others require defendants to choose between asserting insanity or diminished capacity.

M'Naghten

In 1843 Daniel M'Naghten was tried for killing the British prime minister's secretary. M'Naghten was laboring under the paranoid delusion that the prime minister was planning to kill him, and he killed the minister's secretary, believing him to be the prime minister. The jury found M'Naghten not guilty by reason of insanity.[1] The decision created controversy, and the House of Lords asked the justice of the Queens Bench to state what the standards for acquittal on the grounds of insanity were.[2] Those standards were attached to the decision and set forth the following standard, known as the **M'Naghten** test.

1. At the time that the act was committed
2. the defendant was suffering from a defect of reason, from a disease of the mind, which caused
3. the defendant to not know
    a. the nature and quality of the act taken or
    b. that the act was wrong.

This test has become known as the M'Naghten, or the right-wrong test. It is the test used by most jurisdictions today. First, the defendant must have suffered from a disease of the mind at the time the act occurred. *Disease of the mind* is not clearly defined, but it appears that any condition that causes one of the two events from the third part of the test is sufficient. That is, any disease of the mind that causes a defendant to not know the quality of an act or that an act is wrong is sufficient. In at least one case extremely low intelligence was found adequate.[3]

The phrase "the defendant must not know the nature and quality of the act" simply means that the defendant did not understand the consequences of his or her physical act. The drafters of the Model Penal Code gave the following illustration: a man who squeezes his wife's

---

BALLENTINE'S

M'Naghten rule A test employed in a number of jurisdictions for determining whether a criminal defendant had the capacity to form criminal intent at the time he or she committed the crime of which he or she is accused. Specifically, the M'Naghten rule is that an accused is not criminally responsible if he or she was laboring under such a defect of reason from disease of the mind that he or she either did not know the nature of his or her act or, if he or she did, that he or she did not know it was wrong. The M'Naghten rule is also referred to as the *right and wrong test*.

neck, believing it to be a lemon, does not know the nature and quality of his actions.[4]

What is meant by "wrong," as used in the M'Naghten test? Courts have defined it two ways. One asks whether the defendant knew that the act was legally wrong, and the other asks whether the defendant knew that the act was morally wrong.

Irresistible Impulse

Under the M'Naghten test, a defendant who knew that his or her actions were wrong, but could not control his or her behavior because of a disease of the mind, is not insane. This has led a few jurisdictions, which follow M'Naghten, to supplement the rule. These states continue to follow the basic rule, but add that a defendant is not guilty by reason of insanity if a disease of the mind caused the defendant to be unable to control his or her behavior. This is true even if the defendant understood the nature and quality of the act or knew that the behavior was wrong. This is known as **irresistible impulse**.

Irresistible impulse-type tests actually predate M'Naghten and can be found in American cases as far back as 1863.[5] Of course, the largest problem with implementing the irresistible impulse test is distinguishing acts that can be resisted from those that cannot.

Durham

In 1871 the New Hampshire Supreme Court rejected the M'Naghten test and held that a defendant was not guilty because of insanity if the crime was the "product of mental disease." No other jurisdictions followed New Hampshire's lead until 1954, when the District of Columbia Court of Appeals handed down *Durham v. United States*, 214 F.2d 862 (D.C. Cir. 1954). Generally, the **Durham test** requires an acquittal if the defendant would not have committed the crime if he or she had not been suffering from a mental disease or mental defect.

BALLENTINE'S
---

irresistible impulse   An impulse to commit an act that one is powerless to control. "Irresistible impulse" is the test used in some jurisdictions to determine insanity for purposes of a criminal defense. This test asks: Although the defendant is able to understand the nature and consequences of his or her act, and to understand that it is wrong, is he or she unable because of mental disease to resist the impulse to do it?

Durham rule   A test for establishing insanity for the purpose of a defense to criminal prosecution, in some jurisdictions. Under this test, a defendant's criminal responsibility is determined on the basis of whether his or her unlawful act was the result or "product" of "mental disease or mental defect."

Durham was overturned in 1972 by the District of Columbia Court of Appeals in favor of a modified version of the Model Penal Code test.[6] Today, Durham is not used by any jurisdiction.

The Model Penal Code Test

The Model Penal Code contains a definition of insanity similar to, but broader than, the M'Naghten and irresistible impulse tests. This test is also referred to as the *substantial capacity test*. The relevant section of the Code reads:[7]

> A person is not responsible for criminal conduct if at the time of such conduct as a result of mental disease or defect he lacks substantial capacity either to appreciate the criminality [wrongfulness] of his conduct or to conform his conduct to the requirements of law.

The Code is similar to M'Naghten in that it requires that mental disease or defect impair a defendant's ability to appreciate the wrongfulness of his or her act. The final line, "conform his conduct to the requirements of law," incorporates the irresistible impulse concept.

The Code's approach differs from the M'Naghten and irresistible impulse test in two important regards. First, the Code requires only substantial impairment, whereas M'Naghten requires total impairment of the ability to know the nature or wrongfulness of the act. Second, the Code uses the term "appreciate," rather than "know." The drafters of the Code clearly intended more than knowledge, and, as such, evidence concerning the defendant's personality and emotional state are relevant.

The Model Penal Code test has been adopted by a few jurisdictions. The federal courts used the test until Congress enacted a statute that established a test similar to the M'Naghten test.[8] That statute places the burden of proving insanity, by clear and convincing evidence, on the defendant.

Procedures of the Insanity Defense

Insanity is an affirmative defense. In the federal system and in many states, defendants must provide notice to the court and government that insanity will be used as a defense at trial. These statutes usually require that the notice be filed a certain number of days prior to trial. This notice provides the prosecution with an opportunity to prepare to rebut the defense prior to trial.

In most instances, lay testimony is not adequate to prove insanity; psychiatric examination of defendants is necessary. The judge presiding over the case will appoint a psychiatrist, who will conduct the exam and make the findings available to the judge. Often defendants wish to have a psychiatrist of their own choosing perform an examination. This is not a problem if the defendant can afford to pay for the service. In the case of indigent defendants who desire an independent mental examination, statutes often provide reimbursement from the government for independent mental examinations up to a stated maximum. In the federal system, trial courts may approve up to $1,000 in defense-related services. Defendants who seek reimbursement for greater expenses must receive approval from the chief judge of the circuit.[9]

As with all affirmative defenses, the defendant bears the burden of production at trial. Generally, the defendant must present enough evidence to create some doubt of sanity. The states are split on the issue of persuasion. Some require that the prosecution disprove the insanity claim, usually beyond a reasonable doubt. In other jurisdictions the defendant bears the burden of persuasion, usually by preponderance of the evidence. One exception is federal law, which requires the defendant to prove insanity by the higher standard—clear and convincing evidence.[10]

Disposition of the Criminally Insane

Contrary to popular belief, those adjudged insane by a criminal proceeding are not immediately and automatically released. In most jurisdictions, after a defendant has been determined "not guilty by reason of insanity," the court (the jury in a few states) must then make a determination of whether the person continues to be dangerous. If so, commitment is to be ordered. If the defendant is determined not to be dangerous, then release follows. A few jurisdictions have followed the Model Penal Code approach,[11] which requires automatic commitment following a finding of not guilty by reason of insanity. This is the rule in the federal system.[12]

In theory, those committed have a right to be treated for their mental disease. In fact, because of lack of funds, security concerns, and overcrowding problems in facilities, adequate treatment is often not provided.

Once a committed person has been successfully treated and is no longer a danger, release is granted. The determination of dangerousness is left to the judge, not hospital administrators or mental health professionals—an often-criticized practice. Patients, doctors, government officials, and even the judge can begin the process of release. Some states provide for periodic reviews of the patient's status in order to determine the propriety of release. The relevant federal statute reads, in part:[13]

> When the director of the facility in which an acquitted person is hospitalized ... determines that the person has recovered from his mental disease or defect to such an extent that his release, or his conditional release under a prescribed regimen of medical, psychiatric, or

Insanity and
Criminal Procedure

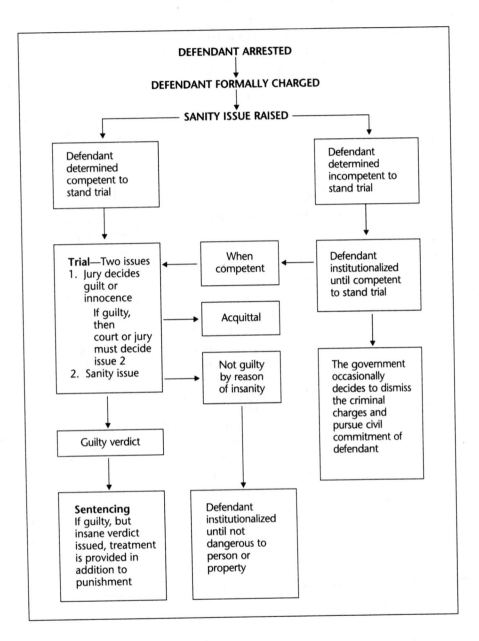

psychological care or treatment, would no longer create a substantial risk of bodily injury to another person or serious damage to property of another, he shall promptly file a certificate to that effect with the clerk of the court that ordered the commitment ... The court shall order a discharge of the acquitted person or, on the motion of the attorney for the government or on its own motion, shall hold a hearing [to determine if the patient is dangerous].

At that hearing, the defendant has the burden of proving by clear and convincing evidence that a risk to people or property is not created by release.

Finally, some states have a "guilty, but mentally ill" verdict. Juries may return such a verdict when the defendant's illness does not rise to the level of negating culpability, but when treatment should be provided in addition to incarceration.

Insanity at the Time of Trial

The United States Supreme Court has held that a defendant who is insane at the time of trial may not be tried.[14] The Court found that the Due Process Clauses of the Fifth and Fourteenth Amendments require that a defendant be able to assist in his or her defense and understand the proceeding against him or her.

The test for determining insanity in this context is different from that discussed earlier. Insanity exists when a defendant lacks the capacity to understand the proceedings or assist in his or her defense. This simply means that defendants must be rational, possess the ability to testify coherently, and be able to meaningfully discuss their cases with their lawyers.

If defendants are unable to stand trial because they are insane, they are usually committed until they are competent. Many statutes have mandatory commitment of defendants determined incompetent to stand trial. However, indefinite confinement is unconstitutional, based solely upon a finding of incompetence to stand trial. Generally, the Supreme Court has held that a lengthy (eighteen months or longer) detention (awaiting competence to stand trial) is tantamount to punishment and violative of the Due Process Clause.[15] In such cases, there must be a separate finding of dangerousness to continue to hold such persons.

A mistrial is to be declared in the event that a defendant becomes incompetent during a trial, and defendants who are sane at trial but become insane before sentencing should be sentenced to a psychiatric facility.

Last, the Supreme Court has held that a person who has become insane after being sentenced to death may not be executed until his or her sanity is regained.[16] The constitutional basis of the Court's decision was the Eighth Amendment's prohibition of cruel and unusual punishment. Justice Marshall has stated that "It is no less abhorrent today than it has been for centuries to exact in penance the life of one whose mental illness prevents him from comprehending the reasons for the penalty or its implications."[17]

Duress and Necessity

Consider these facts: Terry Teller is ordered by bank robber, who is brandishing a gun, to place the money in her drawer in a bag and to give it to bank robber or "she will be planted six feet under." Has Terry committed theft? Although the elements of theft may be satisfied, she has the defense of **duress**. To prove duress, one must show (1) that one was threatened (2) and that the threat caused a reasonable belief (3) that the only way of avoiding serious personal injury or death to oneself or others (4) was to commit the crime. Duress was recognized at common law and continues to be a statutory defense today.

First, it must be shown that a threat was made. Second, the threat must create a reasonable fear of immediate serious bodily harm or death. This fear must be reasonable; that is, even if the person making the threat had no intention of following through, the defense is still valid if a reasonable person would have thought the threat was real. Hence, even if bank robber never intended to kill Terry, she has the defense of duress. Terry need not be the one threatened for her to be able to claim duress. So if bank robber threatened to kill a customer unless Terry complied, Terry could claim duress. The fear must not only be reasonable, but it must also be of serious bodily injury or death. If bank robber exclaims, "Put the money in the bag or I'll smack you across the face," the threatened danger is not sufficient to support the defense of duress. In addition, the threat of harm must be imminent or immediate. Threats of future harms are not adequate duress.

One limitation that is recognized nearly everywhere is that murder is not justified by duress. This rule is criticized, rightfully so, because it does not account for those situations where taking one life may save many more.

It is no defense to a crime to claim that one was only carrying out the orders of a superior, such as an employer or military superior. This issue was addressed in *United States v. Calley.*

The court mentioned that the order's illegality was "apparent upon even cursory evaluation by a man of ordinary sense and understanding." What if an order appears to be legal and the person who follows it has a reasonable belief of its legality? In such cases, the defense of duress does apply.[18]

BALLENTINE'S

duress Coercion applied for the purpose of compelling a person to do, or to refrain from doing, some act. ... Duress may be a defense ... to a criminal prosecution if the defendant committed the crime out of a well-grounded fear of death or serious bodily harm.

UNITED STATES
v.
CALLEY
46 C.M.R. 1131 (1975)

[D]uring midmorning on 16 March 1968 a large number of unresisting Vietnamese were placed in a ditch on the eastern side of My Lai and summarily executed by American soldiers.

[PFC] Meadlo gave the most graphic and damning evidence. He had wandered back into the village alone after the trial incident. Eventually, he met his fire team leader, Specialist Four Grzesik. They took seven or eight Vietnamese to what he labeled a "ravine," where Lieutenants Calley, Sledge, and Dursi and a few other Americans were located with what he estimated as seventy-five to a hundred Vietnamese. Meadlo remembered also that Lieutenant Calley told him, "We got another job to do, Meadlo," and that the appellant started shoving people into the ravine and shooting them. Meadlo, in contrast to Dursi, followed the directions of his leader and himself fired into the people at the bottom of the "ravine." Meadlo then drifted away from the area but he doesn't remember where.

Specialist Four Grzesik found PFC Meadlo, crying and distraught, sitting on a small dike on the eastern edge of the village. He and Meadlo moved through the village, and came to the ditch, in which Grzesik thought were thirty-five dead bodies. Lieutenant Calley walked past and ordered Grzesik to take his fire team back into the village and help the following platoon in their search. He also remembered that Calley asked him to "finish them off," but he refused.

Specialist Four Turner saw Lieutenant Calley for the first time that day as Turner walked out of the village near the ditch. Meadlo and a few other soldiers were also present. Turner passed within fifteen feet of the area, looked into the ditch and saw a pile of approximately twenty bodies covered with blood. He saw Lieutenant Calley and Meadlo firing from a distance of five feet into another group of people who were kneeling and squatting in the ditch. ...

Of the several bases for his argument that he committed no murder at My Lai because he was void of mens rea, appellant emphasized most of all that he acted in obedience to orders. ...

An order of the type appellant says he received is illegal. Its illegality is apparent upon even cursory evaluation by a man of ordinary sense and understanding. ...

We find no impediment to the findings that appellant acted with murderous mens rea, including premeditation.

Necessity is similar to duress. However, whereas duress is created by human pressures, necessity comes about by natural forces. When a person is confronted with two choices, both causing harm, he or she is to choose the lesser harm. If he or she does, he or she may have the defense of necessity to the act taken. For example, a person may be justified in breaking into someone's cabin to avoid freezing to death. Or a captain of a ship may be justified in a trespassory use of another's dock, if setting ashore is necessary to save the ship and its passengers.

──────────── BALLENTINE'S ────────────

necessity   That which is compelled by natural forces and cannot be resisted. Necessity is a defense in a criminal prosecution if the defendant committed the crime to prevent a more serious harm from occurring.

Necessity is a broad and amorphous concept. As a general proposition, it applies any time a person is confronted with the task of choosing between two or more evils. The harm avoided need not be bodily injury; it can also be harm to property. Of course, choosing property over life is never justified. Finally, if an alternative existed that involved less harm than the chosen act, the defense is invalid.

Duress and necessity are complete defenses. When valid, they result in acquittal of all related charges.

Use-of-Force Defenses

In some situations, the law permits actors to use physical force against others. Self-defense, defense of others, defense of property, and use of force to make arrests fall into this area. Self-defense, defense of others, and defense of property, when successful, are complete defenses. Imperfect self-defense (including defense of another) does not lead to acquittal; however, it does reduce murder to manslaughter.

Self-Defense

To prove **self-defense**, it must be shown that the actor (1) was confronted with an unprovoked, (2) immediate threat of bodily harm, (3) that force was necessary to avoid the harm, (4) and that the amount of force used was reasonable.

One who initiates an attack on another cannot claim self defense, as a general proposition. There are two exceptions to this rule. First, if an attacker is met with excessive force in return, then he or she may defend himself or herself. For example, Mike attacks Norm with his fists, and in defense Norm uses a deadly weapon. In such a circumstance, Mike may also use deadly force to protect himself. Second, if an attacker withdraws from the attack and is pursued by the intended victim, then he or she may claim self-defense. Suppose Randy attacks Sue with an intent to sexually assault her. After he grabs her, she displays a gun, and he runs. If Sue follows after him, intending to cause him harm, then he would be privileged to use force to defend himself.

BALLENTINE'S
---

self-defense The use of force to protect oneself from death or imminent bodily harm at the hands of an aggressor. A person may use only that amount of force reasonably necessary to protect himself or herself against the peril with which he or she is threatened; thus, deadly force may be used in self-defense only against an aggressor who ... uses deadly force.

The threat of harm must be immediate in most jurisdictions. Threat of future harm does not justify using force against another. To satisfy this requirement, the harm must be one that will occur unless force is used, and no other means of avoiding the harm exists. However, this principle is occasionally stretched. For example, some jurisdictions have permitted a jury to be instructed on the **battered woman syndrome** defense. Under this defense a woman who is constantly abused by her husband may be justified in using force at a time when there is not strictly "immediate danger." The theory is that women in such circumstances have two choices: either wait for their husbands to kill them or strike first in a form of offensive self-defense. Critics of this defense contend that because other remedies are available, such as leaving the husband and obtaining a court order restraining him from bothering her, there is no immediate danger.

Finally, the force used to defend oneself must be reasonable. It would be unreasonable to knife a person who is attempting to slap one's hand. Deadly force may be used to defend against an attack that threatens serious bodily injury or death. Deadly force may not be used to defend against other attacks.

All jurisdictions require that a person retreat from an attack, if possible, before using deadly force. This is known as the **retreat** doctrine. There are many exceptions to the doctrine. Retreat is not required whenever it poses a danger to the party, nor is retreat expected from one's home (the "castle" doctrine). Police officers are not required to retreat when performing their lawful duties. The Model Penal Code has a retreat provision that recognizes these exceptions:

> The use of deadly force is not justifiable ... [if] the actor knows that he can avoid the necessity of using such force without complete safety by retreating or by surrendering possession of a thing to a person asserting a claim of right thereto or by complying with a demand that he abstain from any action which he has no duty to take, except that (1) the actor is not obliged to retreat from his dwelling or place of work, unless he was the initial aggressor ... . [19]

The Code provides that public officials need not retreat during the performance of their duties. There is no duty to retreat rather than using nondeadly force.

BALLENTINE'S

battered woman syndrome   A psychological condition in which a woman commits physical violence against her husband or mate as a result of the continued physical or mental abuse to which he has subjected her. The courts are split with respect to the admissibility of expert testimony ... to prove the psychological effects of continued abuse.

retreat to the wall   A term referring to the doctrine, in effect in some jurisdictions, that before a person is entitled to use deadly force in self-defense he or she must attempt to withdraw from the encounter by giving as much ground as possible.

Also, notice that the Code requires not only retreat, but that "thing[s]" be surrendered and one comply with another's demands before deadly force is used. Of course, one can later use civil law to recover unlawfully taken items or to recover for complying with a demand that caused damage. The aggressor will be liable both civilly and criminally for such unlawful demands.

Defense of Others

It is also a justified use of force to defend another. The rules are similar to that of self-defense: there must be a threat of immediate danger to the other person; the perception of threat must be reasonable; the amount of force used must be reasonable; and deadly force may be used only to repel a deadly attack.

At common law, one was only privileged to defend those with whom a special relationship existed, such as parent and child. Today, most jurisdictions permit any person to use force to protect another.

What happens when a person uses force to defend another who is *not* privileged to use force? For example, Perry is an undercover police officer attempting to arrest Norm, who is resisting. Randa observes what is happening and comes to Norm's defense, believing that Norm was being unlawfully attacked. There is a split of authority concerning this problem. Some jurisdictions limit the authority of the defender to use force to the privilege held by the person being attacked. Because Norm was not privileged to use force against the police officer, Randa is guilty of assault. Other states, however, use an objective test. Under such a test, if a reasonable person standing in Randa's shoes would have believed that force was justified, then he or she would be acquitted.

Defense of Property and Habitation

At common law and by legislative enactment today, one may use force to defend property. As with defending oneself, only reasonable force may be used. Because property is not as valuable as life, deadly force may not be used to protect property. Thus, one must allow another to take or destroy property before killing to defend it. No force is reasonable if other methods of protecting the property were available. So, if one has ample time to seek assistance from the police or the courts, force would be unreasonable. In contrast, if an enemy appears at one's house and begins to destroy a car in the driveway, force would be permitted to protect the vehicle. The actor must have a reasonable belief that his or her property is in danger of trespass or destruction and that the force used was necessary to defend the property.

The basic rules concerning defense of property also apply to defense of habitation: one must have a reasonable belief that the property is threatened; only reasonable force may be used to protect the property; and other nonviolent remedies must be utilized before resorting to force. However, one difference between dwellings and other property is that deadly force may be used, under some circumstances, to protect one's home.

In early common law, the security of the home was as important as life itself. Therefore, people were permitted to use deadly force against any forcible intruder after warning the person not to enter. Today the rule has been narrowed, and statutes now commonly require that the occupant must believe that the intruder intends to commit a felony once inside before deadly force may be used.

The Model Penal Code allows the use of deadly force if either (1) the intruder is attempting to take the dwelling (with no legal claim to do so) or (2) the intruder is there to commit a crime (arson, burglary, theft) and has threatened deadly force or poses a substantial risk to those inside.[20]

This provision of the Code incorporates a self-defense concept. Remember, the rules of self-defense apply in the home also. So, any time a person's life (or another's) is threatened, deadly force may be used.

Some people choose to protect their property with manmade devices, such as electric fences and spring guns. Others have used natural protection, such as dogs and snakes. Whichever is used, the rules are the same. If the device employs nondeadly force, it is likely to be lawful. An electric fence that does not have sufficient electric current to kill is a justified use of force.

However, the result is often different when one uses deadly force. There are two perspectives on the use of deadly traps to protect property. One permits the use of deadly force so long as the person who set the trap would have been permitted to use such force himself or herself, if he or she had been present. So, if a murderer gains entry to a house and is killed by a spring gun, the occupant is not criminally liable because he or she would have been privileged to use deadly force against the murderer. The second perspective, adopted by the drafters of the Model Penal Code, rejects the use of deadly traps in all instances.[21] This position is sound, as deadly traps do not discriminate between the dangerous and the non-dangerous. The occupant who sets such a trap is simply lucky if the intruder is a criminal and not a firefighter responding to a blaze in the home.

Imperfect Self-Defense

The so-called "imperfect self-defense" is actually a mens rea defense. It applies to situations when a person cannot make a successful self-defense (or defense of another) claim, but because he or she lacked malice aforethought (or purpose), the crime should not be murder, but manslaughter. The defense applies only to homicides and is not recognized everywhere.

As stated, a person must have a reasonable belief that he or another is in danger of serious bodily injury or death before deadly force may be used. What if a person possesses a good faith, but unreasonable belief? Self-defense is unavailable, but because there is no malicious intent, purpose, or malice aforethought (depending on the jurisdiction's definition of murder), the crime is reduced to manslaughter. The defense is available in a second situation: whenever a person who initiates an attack using nondeadly force later justifiably uses deadly force to defend herself.

Arrests

Sometimes it is necessary for law enforcement officers to use force to execute their duties and to defend themselves. When a police officer uses force in defense of another's attack, the rules of self-defense that you have already learned apply. In addition, because the use of force is an integral part of law enforcement, it is often justified. However, a person making an arrest does not have an unlimited right to use force against an arrestee. This section examines a person's right to resist an unlawful arrest, the so-called "citizen's arrest," and arrests by law enforcement officers.

Resisting Unlawful Arrests

In some states, people may use force to resist an unlawful arrest. The amount of force is usually limited to nondeadly, although some jurisdictions permit one to use deadly force. Of course, if a person uses force against a lawful arrest, he or she is fully liable for whatever crime results (assault, battery, or murder), as well as for resisting a lawful arrest.

The rule permitting force to resist a lawful arrest evolved during a time when arrestees were detained for long periods before appearing before a court, jail conditions were extremely poor, and no civil remedies existed for unlawful arrests. In light of these harsh facts, public policy was best served by permitting people to resist unlawful arrests.

Today, many jurisdictions have adopted an approach closer to the Model Penal Code's, which prohibits any resistance to an arrest by a law enforcement officer. This is the sensible approach, as the reasons for permitting resistance no longer exist: arrestees must be promptly brought before judges and released if there is no probable cause. When available, bail is set immediately. Also, federal law now permits civil suits against law enforcement officers for violation of a person's civil rights. Prohibiting resistance advances two important public policy objectives: first, it fosters obedience to police and, second, it reduces violence.

Arrests by Law Enforcement Officers

A law enforcement officer is privileged to use reasonable force to apprehend criminals and to prevent those incarcerated from escaping. At common law, police could use all but deadly force to arrest misdemeanants and deadly force to arrest felons. This latter rule was justified by the fact that all felons were put to death at early common law.

In 1974 a Memphis, Tennessee, police officer shot and killed a fifteen-year-old male who was fleeing a burglary. The boy had stolen forty dollars. The family of the deceased boy sued the police department in federal court for violating his constitutional rights. The case ended up before the United States Supreme Court.

In *Tennessee v. Garner,* 471 U.S. 1 (1985), the Court held that the use of deadly force by a police officer is a "seizure" under the Fourth Amendment. Accordingly, the test used to determine whether the use of deadly force is proper is the Fourth Amendment's test: reasonability. The Court then held that the use of deadly force is reasonable only when the person fleeing is a dangerous felon. The Court did not state what standard must be applied in cases of nondeadly force.

In 1989 the Court handed down *Graham v. Connor,* in which the standard was set for all preconviction arrests. In that opinion, the Court held that all seizures are to be evaluated under the Fourth Amendment reasonableness standard.

GRAHAM
v.
CONNOR
490 U.S. 386 (1989)

This case requires us to decide what constitutional standard governs a free citizen's claim that law-enforcement officials used excessive force in the course of making an arrest, investigatory stop, or other "seizure" of his person. We hold that such claims are properly analyzed under the Fourth Amendment's "objective reasonableness" standard. ...

On November 12, 1984, Graham, a diabetic, felt the onset of an insulin reaction. He asked a friend, William Berry, to drive him to a nearby convenience store so he could purchase some orange juice to counteract the reaction. Berry agreed, but when Graham entered the store, he saw a number of people ahead of him in the checkout line. Concerned about the delay, he hurried out of the store and asked Berry to drive him to a friend's house instead.

Respondent Connor, an officer of the Charlotte, North Carolina, Police Department, saw Graham hastily enter and leave the store. The officer became suspicious that something was amiss and followed Berry's car. About one-half mile from the store, he made an investigatory stop. Although Berry told Connor that Graham was simply suffering from a "sugar reaction," the officer ordered Berry and Graham to wait while he found out what, if anything, had happened at the convenience store. When Officer Connor returned to his patrol car to call for backup assistance, Graham got out of the car, ran around it twice, and finally sat down on the curb, where he passed out briefly.

In the ensuing confusion, a number of other Charlotte police officers arrived on the scene in response to Officer Connor's request for backup. One of the officers rolled Graham over on the sidewalk and cuffed his hands tightly behind his back, ignoring Berry's pleas to get him some sugar. Another officer said: "I've seen a lot of people with sugar diabetes that never acted like this. Ain't nothing wrong with the M.F. but drunk. Lock the S.B. up." Several officers then lifted Graham up from behind, carried him over to Berry's car, and placed him face down on the hood. Regaining consciousness, Graham asked the officers to check in his wallet for a diabetic decal that he carried. In response, one of the officers told him to "shut up" and shoved his face down against the hood of the car. Four officers grabbed Graham and threw him head-first into the police car. A friend of Graham's brought some orange juice to the car, but the officers refused to let him have it. Finally, Officer Connor received a report that Graham had done nothing wrong at the convenience store, and the officers drove him home and released him.

At some point during the encounter with the police, Graham sustained a broken foot, cuts on his wrists, a bruised forehead, and an injured shoulder; he also claims to have developed a loud ringing in his right ear that continues to this day. ... [The Court then discussed previous cases which held that a due process standard should be applied in all cases of excessive force. To be successful using the due process standard, a plaintiff had to prove the actions of the police were "sadistic and malicious."]

We reject this notion that all excessive force claims brought under § 1983 [a federal statute permitting cases against government officials to be brought in federal court] are governed by a single generic standard. As we have said many times, § 1983 "is not itself a source of substantive rights," but merely provides "a method for vindication of federal rights elsewhere conferred. ... In addressing an excessive force claim brought under § 1983, analysis begins by identifying the specific constitutional right allegedly infringed by the challeged application of force. ... In most instances, that will be either the Fourth Amendment's prohibition against unreasonable seizures of the person, or the Eighth Amendment's ban on cruel and unusual punishments, which are the two primary sources of constitutional protection against physically abusive governmental conduct. ...

Today we make explicit what is implicit in *Garner's* analysis, and hold that *all* claims that law-enforcement officers have used excessive force—deadly or not—in the course of an arrest, investigatory stop, or other "seizure" of a free citizen should be analyzed under the Fourth Amendment and its "reasonableness" standard. ...

The "reasonableness" of a particular use of force must be judged from the perspective of a reasonable officer on the scene, rather than with the 20/20 vision of hindsight. ... The calculus of reasonableness must embody allowance for the fact that police officers are often forced to make split-second judgments—in circumstances that are tense, uncertain, and rapidly evolving—about the amount of force that is necessary in a particular situation.

As in other Fourth Amendment contexts, however, the "reasonableness" inquiry in an excessive force case is an objective one: the question is whether the officer's actions are "objectively reasonable" in light of the facts and circumstances confronting them, without regard to their underlying intent or motivation.

Exactly how *Tennessee v. Garner* is affected by *Graham* remains to be seen. There are two theories. First, some contend that *Graham* emasculates *Tennessee v. Garner* by overruling the dangerousness standard. That is, in cases where deadly force is used, it need not be shown that the person posed a danger to the police or another—it only has to be proved that the use of the force was reasonable. The second theory, similar to the first, contends that all claims of excessive force are to be judged under the reasonableness standard, but that *Tennessee v. Garner* sets a threshold: that the use of deadly force on a nondangerous fleeing suspect is *per se* unreasonable. Under the first theory, a jury would be permitted to determine whether the use of deadly force on a nondangerous fleeing felon was reasonable. Using the second theory, if a jury decided that the victim of deadly force did not pose a danger, they would not be permitted to return a finding that the officer's actions were reasonable.

Finally, note that police officers are often put into positions where they must defend themselves, such as during an arrest. The same rules discussed earlier concerning self-defense apply in these situations, with one exception: police officers are not required to retreat. Thus, if a police officer is involved in an arrest that involves escalating violence, it is possible that the police officer may have to use deadly force to defend against the criminal's attack.

Arrests by Citizens

At common law, a private citizen was privileged to arrest those who committed a felony or misdemeanor (which amounted to a breach of the peace) in his presence. Some jurisdictions have retained this rule and others have changed it by statute.

In jurisdictions that have changed the rule, it is common to permit so-called *citizens' arrests* any time probable cause exists to believe that the person has committed a felony. In most jurisdictions a citizen may not arrest a misdemeanant unless the person making the arrest witnessed the crime. Even in such cases, only certain misdemeanors may lead to such an arrest.

The reason for these rules is to provide citizens who make such arrests with immunity from civil and criminal prosecution. However, the citizen must be privileged to make the arrest and, even when privileged, a reasonable amount of force must be used.

In some jurisdictions, a private person making an arrest may use deadly force only when the person is in fact a felon. The jurisdictions employing this rule are split: some permit the use of deadly force by private citizens to arrest for any felony and others only for specific felonies (e.g., murder and rape). These jurisdictions are similar in one important regard. The person against whom the deadly force is used must have *in fact* committed the crime. A reasonable, but incorrect, belief that the person has committed a crime is not a defense. So, if Pat kills Sam while attempting to arrest Sam for a crime he did not commit, Pat is liable for manslaughter, even though she had a reasonable belief that he committed the crime. Some states have followed the Model Penal Code approach, which prohibits the use of deadly force by private persons in all circumstances.[22]

The results are different if a private person is assisting a law enforcement officer. In fact, many states have statutes that require citizens to assist police officers upon order. In such cases, the private party is privileged to use whatever force is reasonable. In addition, a private person responding to a police officer's order to assist in an arrest is privileged, even if the police officer was exceeding his or her authority and had no cause to make the arrest. In such instances, the police officer may be liable for both his or her own actions and the actions of the private party summoned. Of course, there are limits to the rule. For example, a private person who obeys a police officer's order to strike an already apprehended and subdued criminal would not be privileged.

Infancy

At common law, it was a complete defense to a charge that the accused was a child under the age of seven at the time the crime was committed. It was irrebuttably presumed that children under seven were incapable of forming the requisite mens rea to commit a crime. A rebuttable presumption of incapacity existed for those between seven and fourteen years of age. The presumption could be overcome for those between seven and fourteen if the prosecution could prove that the defendant understood that the criminal act was wrong.

Few minors are charged with crimes today. This is the result of the advent of the juvenile court systems in the United States. Currently each state has a juvenile court system that deals with juvenile delinquency and neglected children.

Statutes vary, but it is common for juvenile courts to be given exclusive jurisdiction over criminal behavior of juveniles. However, some states give concurrent jurisdiction to criminal courts and juvenile courts. If concurrent, the juvenile court usually must waive jurisdiction before the criminal court can hear the case. Determining who is a juvenile also differs, with some jurisdictions utilizing a method similar to the common law (irrebuttable and rebuttable presumptions) and others simply setting an age cutoff, such as fourteen or sixteen.

The purpose of the juvenile justice system differs from that of the criminal justice system. Whereas criminal law has punishment as one of its major purposes, the purpose of the juvenile system is not to punish, but to reform the delinquent child.

Intoxication

In this context, *intoxication* refers to all situations in which a person's mental or physical abilities are impaired by drugs or alcohol. It is generally said that voluntary intoxication is a defense if it has the effect of negating the required mens rea. In common-law language, this means that if intoxication prevents a defendant from being able to form a specific intent, then the crime is reduced to a similar general-intent crime. For the crime of murder, intoxication is a defense if it prevents the defendant from forming the premeditation, deliberation, or purposeful element. In such cases the charge is reduced from first-degree to second-degree murder. Not all states recognize voluntary intoxication as a defense.

In the rare case of involuntary intoxication, the defendant is relieved of liability entirely. To be successful with such a claim, the defendant is required to show that the intoxication had the same effect as insanity. In jurisdictions using the M'Naghten test for insanity, a defendant is required to prove that the intoxication prevented him or her from knowing right from wrong.

Mistake

People may be mistaken in two ways. First, one may believe that some act is legal when it is not. This is a mistake of law. Second, a person may not understand all the facts of a given situation. This is a mistake of fact. As a general proposition, mistake of fact is a defense, and mistake of law is not. However, many exceptions to each rule have been developed. A few of these exceptions are noted here.

Mistake of fact is a defense whenever it negates the mens rea aspect of a crime. For example, an intent to steal another's property is an element of theft. If an attorney picks up a briefcase believing it to be his when it is actually someone else's, it is not theft. The mistake negates the intent to steal. To be valid, mistakes must be made honestly and in good faith.

Although honest mistakes of fact usually constitute a defense, there are exceptions. One exception is obvious: strict liability crimes, as there is no requirement of mens rea to negate.

In some instances, an honest but unreasonable mistake of fact may not eliminate culpability entirely; however, it may reduce the crime. The imperfect self-defense previously discussed falls into this category.

We have all heard, if not quipped, "Ignorance of the law is no excuse." As a general rule, this statement is true. There are two situations in which a person can make a mistake of law. The first occurs when an individual is unaware that his or her actions are prohibited by statute: "I didn't know it was against the law not to file a tax return!" The second occurs when a person takes an act, under the color of a legal right and in good faith, only to find out later that the act was illegal. For example, a landlord may have a reasonable, but mistaken, belief that she has a right to take possessions from a tenant's house to satisfy a delinquent rent debt.

For the most part, unawareness that an act is illegal is not a defense. The law presumes that everyone knows what is legal and what is not. Mistakes that fall into the second group act to negate mens rea and are more likely to be successful. The landlord in the example would not be guilty of larceny because of the mistake. Another example of such a defense is when a person has a reasonable, but mistaken, belief that he or she has the authority to take a person into custody. Therefore, officers who arrest people in good faith, but without probable cause, are not guilty of kidnapping or criminal confinement.

Another exception to the rule that mistake of law is no defense exists when a person relies on statutes, judicial opinions, or certain administrative decisions that later turn out to be wrong. The rule is sound for two reasons. First, as a matter of public policy it is not wise to prosecute people for acting in conformity with the law. The result would be individual interpretation of all laws and disregard for those statutes, regulations, or judicial decisions believed incorrect. Second, as a matter of due process, it appears that no notice has been provided that compliance with the law will be punished.

Finally, one defense that is not accepted is reliance on the advice of counsel. If a lawyer advises a client that a particular act is legal when it is not, the client will be liable for the crime if the act is taken.

Entrapment

To what extent should police officers be permitted to encourage someone to commit a crime? This question underlies the defense of **entrapment**. Entrapment occurs when law enforcement officers encourage another to commit a crime with the intent of arresting and prosecuting that person for the commission of that crime.

Perjury traps are another form of entrapment. Perjury traps are committed by prosecutors whenever they inquire of a witness as to matters that are tangential or peripheral to an investigation in order to catch the witness in perjury.[23]

BALLENTINE'S

entrapment   Inducing a person to commit a crime he or she is otherwise not inclined to commit, in order to bring a criminal prosecution against him or her. Such conduct by law enforcement authorities is an affirmative defense to a prosecution for the crime into which the defendant was entrapped.

Entrapment is a defense of recent development, although all states and the federal government recognize some form of the defense today. There is no constitutional basis for the entrapment defense, so each jurisdiction is free to structure the defense in any manner. Of course, a state may also do away with the defense, although none have done so. This is a sound policy decision, as most people would agree that there must be some limit on police conduct. However, where the line should be drawn is debated. Currently two tests are used to determine whether a defendant was entrapped: the subjective and objective tests.

The test used in the federal system and most widely used by the states is the subjective test. The test attempts to distinguish between those who are predisposed to commit crime from those who are not. The test is subjective; the defendant's mental state at the time of the encouragement is imperative. A defendant is predisposed if he or she is ready to commit the crime and is only awaiting the opportunity. The Supreme Court has said that the subjective test is designed to draw a line between the "unwary innocent and the unwary criminal."[24]

Under the subjective approach, evidence of the defendant's criminal record may be relevant to show predisposition. For example, recent drug convictions may evidence a predisposition to enter into future drug purchases or sales.

The second method of determining whether a person was entrapped is objective. The Model Penal Code[25] adopts this approach, as do a minority of states. The objective approach does not focus on the particular defendant's predisposition, but asks whether the police conduct creates a "substantial risk that an offense will be committed by persons other than those who are ready to commit it."[26]

The defendant's actual state of mind is not relevant to this inquiry, and, accordingly, evidence of a defendant's criminal history is irrelevant. Under this approach, a defendant may be acquitted even though he or she was predisposed to commit the crime. Suppose a police officer offers a prostitute $150,000 for sex. The prostitute would have agreed had the officer offered $50. Using the subjective approach, the prostitute would be convicted because she was predisposed to engage in prostitution. However, in jurisdictions using the objective test, she may have been entrapped, as women who do not normally sell sex might be encouraged to do so for $150,000.

In many states entrapment may not be used to defend against crimes involving violence to people, such as battery and murder. The Model Penal Code also takes this view.

Alibi and Consent

Alibi and consent are two factual defenses. An **alibi** is a claim by a defendant that he or she was not present at the scene of the crime at the time it was committed. Whenever a defendant asserts an alibi, he or she is simply refuting the government's factual claims. Alibi is an affirmative defense and defendants are usually required to give the government notice of the alibi claim prior to trial. Alibi notice laws have been approved by the Supreme Court.[27] Of course, the government must prove the elements of the crime (e.g., presence at the crime) beyond a reasonable doubt. This means that the defendant bears no burden in an alibi defense.

Victim **consent** is a defense to some crimes, such as rape or larceny. That is, if a person consents to sex or to give you his property, there is no crime. Consent is, however, not a defense to many crimes, such as statutory rape, incest, child molestation, battery, and murder.

Statutes of Limitation

Many crimes must be prosecuted within a specified time after being committed. A **statute of limitation** sets the time limit. If prosecution is initiated after the applicable statute has expired, the defendant is entitled to a dismissal.

Statutes vary in length, and serious crimes, such as murder, have no limitation. Generally, the higher the crime, the longer the statute. Statutes begin running when the crime occurs; however, statutes may be tolled in some situations. *Tolling* refers to stopping the clock. The time during which a defendant is a fugitive is commonly tolled. For example, assume that the limitation on felony assault is six years. The assault

---
BALLENTINE'S

alibi The defense that the accused was elsewhere at the time the crime was committed.

consent Agreement; approval; acquiescence; being of one mind. ... As a defense to a prosecution for rape, consent is an exercise of one's intelligence in making a choice between resistance and uncoerced assent, based upon knowledge of the significance of the act and of the moral issues involved.

statutes of limitations Federal and state statutes prescribing the maximum period of time during which various types of civil actions and criminal prosecutions can be brought after the occurrence of the injury or the offense.

was committed on June 1, 1991. Normally, prosecution would have to be started by June 1, 1997. However, if the defendant was fugitive from June 1, 1991 to June 1, 1993, then the statute would be tolled, and the new date of limitation would be June 1, 1998.

At common law there were no limitations. Statutes of limitation are legislative creations. There is no constitutional basis for limiting the time in which to prosecute someone for criminal behavior. This being so, legislatures are free to alter or abolish statutes of limitation. If there is no limitation fixed, prosecution may occur any time after the crime.

Sometimes a prosecution for a serious crime may begin after the statute on a lesser included crime has expired. For example, battery is a lesser included crime of aggravated battery. Assume that aggravated battery has a six-year statute and battery three. In most jurisdictions, a prosecutor may not circumvent the three-year statute by charging aggravated battery and including the lesser battery offense in the information or indictment. After the time has run out on the lesser offense, but not on the more serious offense, the defendant is either convicted of the greater offense or acquitted, but can no longer be convicted on the lesser offense. However, at least one jurisdiction does not follow this rule.[28]

Review Questions

1. What are affirmative defenses? How do affirmative defenses differ from other defenses?

2. What are the elements of the M'Naghten test for insanity? Irresistible impulse? Model Penal Code?

3. What must be proven to support a claim of self-defense?

4. What is the retreat doctrine?

5. What is imperfect self-defense? When is it applicable?

6. When may a law enforcement officer use deadly force to stop a fleeing suspect?

7. What is entrapment? What are the two tests used to determine if a defendant was entrapped?

8. May an insane defendant be tried? If not, what standard is used to determine whether the defendant is insane?

9. What is a statute of limitations?

10. Distinguish legal from factual impossibility and state whether a person is criminally culpable in both circumstances.

Review Problems

1. Should law enforcement be permitted to encourage children to engage in criminal activity with the purpose of arresting and prosecuting the child? Should law enforcement be permitted to use family and friend relationships to induce another to engage in criminal activity with the purpose of arresting and prosecuting the family member or friend? How about preying on another's drug or alcohol addiction?

2. Ira stabbed his good friend, inflicting a fatal wound. At trial, a psychiatrist testified that Ira could not control his behavior, as he has a brain tumor that causes him to act violently. The doctor also testified that the condition did not impair Ira's ability to know what he was doing or that it was wrong. Assume that the jury believes the psychiatrist's explanation. Would Ira be convicted in a jurisdiction which uses the M'Naghten test? The irresistible impulse test? The Model Penal Code?

3. Jane was attacked by an unknown man. She was able to free herself and ran to a nearby house, with the man chasing close behind. She screamed and knocked at the door of the house. The occupants of the house opened the door and she requested refuge. The occupant refused, but Jane forced her way into the house. To gain entry, Jane had to strike the occupant. Once inside, she used the telephone to contact the police, who responded within minutes. At the insistence of the occupants of the house, Jane has been charged with trespass and battery. Does she have a defense?

4. Gary and Gene were both drinking at a bar. Gary became angered after Gene asked Gary's wife to dance. Gary walked up to Gene and struck him in the face. Gene fell to the floor, and as he was returning to his feet Gary hit him again. In response, Gene took a knife out of his pocket and attacked Gary with it. Gary then shot Gene with a gun he had hidden in his coat. The injury proved fatal. What crime has Gary committed?

Notes

1 *M'Naghten's Case,* 8 Eng. Rep. 718 (H.L. 1843).

2 LaFave & Scott, *Criminal Law* § 4.2A(a) (Hornbook Series, St. Paul: West, 1986).

3 *State v. Johnson,* 290 N.W. 159 (Wis. 1940).

4 Model Penal Code, Tent. Draft 4, at 156.

5 LaFave & Scott at § 4.2(d).

6 *United States v. Brawner,* 471 F.2d 969 (D.C. Cir. 1972).

7 Model Penal Code § 4.01(1).

8 18 U.S.C. § 17.

9 18 U.S.C. § 3006A(e)(3).

10 18 U.S.C. § 17.

11 Model Penal Code § 4.08.

12 18 U.S.C. § 4243(a).

13 18 U.S.C. § 4243(f).

14 *Dusky v. United States,* 362 U.S. 402 (1960).

15 *Jackson v. Indiana,* 406 U.S. 715 (1972).

16 *Ford v. Wainwright,* 477 U.S. 399 (1986).

17 *Id.* at 417.

18 *See* LaFave & Scott at § 5.3(g).

19 Model Penal Code § 3.04(2)(b)(ii).

20 Model Penal Code § 3.06(d).

21 Model Penal Code § 3.06(5).

22 Model Penal Code § 3.07(2)(b)(ii).

23 *See Vermont v. Tonzola,* 621 A.2d 243 (Vt. 1993).

24 *Sherman v. United States,* 356 U.S. 369 (1958).

25 Model Penal Code § 2.13.

26 Model Penal Code § 2.13(2).

27 *Williams v. Florida,* 399 U.S. 78 (1970)

28 21 Am. Jur. 2d 225 (1990); *State v. Borucki,* 505 A.2d 89 (Me. 1986).

CHAPTER 9

CONSTITUTIONAL DEFENSES

CHAPTER OUTLINE

Introduction

A variety of defenses arise from the United States Constitution. Most of these rights are found in the first nine amendments. You have already learned a few constitutional defenses, such as the protection of expression by the First Amendment. In addition, many rights that are procedural, such as the right to a speedy trial, are discussed later. A few critical defenses have been chosen for discussion here.

Bear in mind that each state has its own constitution, which may provide greater protection than the United States Constitution. During this discussion you may want to refer to the United States Constitution, which is reprinted as Appendix A of this text.

Double Jeopardy

The Fifth Amendment to the United States Constitution provides that "no person shall be subject for the same offense to be twice put in jeopardy of life or limb." The principle of not punishing someone twice for the same act can be found back as far as Blackstone's Commentaries.[1] The **Double Jeopardy** Clause applies only to criminal proceedings.

There are actually two prohibitions in the Double Jeopardy Clause. The clause prevents: (1) a second prosecution for the same offense and (2) a second punishment for the same offense.

Often the question is whether a prior "jeopardy" occurred. It is generally held that a person has been put in jeopardy once a plea of guilty has been entered and accepted by a court. An unapproved plea will not suffice, and a subsequent prosecution will not be prohibited by the Double Jeopardy Clause. In jury trials, jeopardy attaches once a jury has been selected and sworn. States treat bench trials differently, although the prevailing view is that jeopardy attaches once the first witness has been sworn.

Once jeopardy attaches, the defendant may not be tried again. However, there are a few exceptions. A defendant may be retried if the first trial was terminated by a properly declared mistrial. Mistrials may be declared for a variety of reasons. Death of the trial judge or one of the participating attorneys would likely result in a mistrial. If a witness blurts out an answer to a question before the judge has an opportunity

---
BALLENTINE'S
---

double jeopardy   A rule originating in the Fifth Amendment that prohibits a second punishment or a second trial for the same offense. It is sometimes referred to as *former jeopardy* or *prior jeopardy*.

to sustain an objection to the question, and the answer is extremely prejudicial, a mistrial may be declared. The causes of a mistrial are endless. Note that the mistrial must be proper. That is, if an appellate court later determines that a mistrial should not have been declared, the defendant has been put into jeopardy. It is always proper to retry a defendant whose prior trial was declared a mistrial upon the defendant's motion. If a defendant objects to a government motion for a mistrial, there must be a "manifest necessity" (darn good reason) for the mistrial.[2]

It is also not a violation of the Fifth Amendment to prosecute a defendant who was previously charged, but whose charges were dismissed prior to jeopardy attaching. Additionally, if a defendant appeals a conviction and prevails, the defendant may be retried, unless the appellate court finds that insufficient evidence exists to retry the defendant. However, if a defendant is acquitted on a serious charge and convicted on a lesser and then prevails on appeal, he or she may be retried only on the lesser. It is violative of the Fifth Amendment to retry the defendant on the more serious offense.

The Fifth Amendment only forbids retrial for the same offense. Determining whether two acts constitute the same offense is not always an easy task. Two offenses are the same unless one requires proof of a fact that the other does not.[3] This is the "same evidence test."

The Double Jeopardy Clause is fully applicable to the states through the Fourteenth Amendment. However, the clause does not prevent second punishments for the same offense by different sovereigns. For example, a person who robs a federally insured bank may be prosecuted by both the state where the bank resides and the United States. This is true even though the offenses are the same. Although the Double Jeopardy Clause does not prohibit two sovereigns from prosecuting for the same offense, many states prohibit this by statute. In practice, and sometimes by policy, most prosecutors do not pursue a defendant who has been previously prosecuted in another jurisdiction for the same crime. The Model Penal Code incorporates this approach in certain circumstances.[4] Municipalities are not independent beings; they owe their existence not to the Constitution of the United States, but to a state. Accordingly, prosecutions by cities are treated as being brought by the state, and it is a violation of the Double Jeopardy Clause for a state and city to punish one for the same offense.

Self-Incrimination and Immunity

The Fifth Amendment also states that no person "shall be compelled in any criminal case to be a witness against himself." The following passage explains why the framers of the Constitution included a privilege against self-incrimination.

> Perhaps the best-known provision of the Fifth Amendment is the clause against forced "self-incrimination," whose origin goes back to England where persons accused of crimes before ecclesiastical courts were forced to take an ex officio oath. That is, they had to swear to answer all questions even if the questions did not apply to the case at trial. This requirement was later adopted by the Court of Star Chamber. One of the victims of the Court was a printer and book distributor named John Lilburne, charged in 1637 with treason for importing books "that promoted Puritan dissent." Lilburne told his accusers, "I am not willing to answer you to any more of these questions because I see you go about by this examination to ensnare me. For seeing the things for which I am imprisoned cannot be proved against me, you will get other material out of my examination; and therefore if you will not ask me about the thing laid to my charge, I shall answer no more. ... I think by the law of the land, that I may stand upon my just defense." Lilburne was convicted, fined, whipped, pilloried, and gagged, and imprisoned until he agreed to take the oath. ...
>
> One notorious instance of forced self-incrimination in the American colonies occurred in the Salem witch trials. In 1692, Giles Corey, an elderly Massachusetts farmer, was accused of witchcraft. He knew whether he pleaded guilty or not guilty he would be convicted, executed and his property confiscated. So to assure that his heirs inherited his property, he refused to plead and thus could not be convicted. The judges ordered him strapped to a table, and stones were loaded upon his chest to force the plea out of him. Corey's final words were "more weight." Then his chest caved in.[5]

John Bradshaw, John Lilburne's attorney, stated it best when he said that "It is contrary to the laws of God, nature and the kingdom for any man to be his own accuser."

Generally, the Amendment prohibits the government from compelling people to testify when incrimination is possible. Most people have heard of "pleading the Fifth." However, if immunity from prosecution is granted to a witness, he or she may be compelled to testify. If a witness refuses to testify because of the fear of self-incrimination, the government may offer the witness immunity from prosecution so that the testimony may be compelled. There are two types of immunity: transactional and derivative use.

Transactional immunity shields the witness from prosecution for all offenses related to his or her testimony. For example, if a witness testifies concerning a robbery, the government may not prosecute the witness for that robbery, even though the government may have evidence

────────────────BALLENTINE'S────────────────

transactional immunity   A guaranty given a person that if he or she testifies against others he or she will not be prosecuted for his or her own involvement in the crime ... to which his or her testimony relates.

of guilt independent of the witness's testimony. Transactional immunity gives more protection to the witness than required by the Constitution, so when it is granted a witness may be ordered to testify.

The minimum immunity that must be provided a witness to overcome a Fifth Amendment claim is derivative **use immunity**. This prohibits the government from using the witness's testimony or any evidence derived from that testimony to prosecute the witness. However, all evidence that is independently obtained may be used against the witness.

Use immunity only prohibits the government from using the witness's testimony against him or her. Statutes that provide only for use immunity are unconstitutional, as derivative use is the minimum protection required by the Fifth Amendment.

States vary in how immunity is granted. Some permit the prosecutor to give the immunity; others require both the request of the prosecutor and the approval of the trial judge.

A person may also waive the Fifth Amendment privilege against self-incrimination. Generally, once a person testifies freely, the privilege is waived as to the subject discussed during the same proceeding. A witness (or defendant) may not testify selectively concerning a subject. It is often said that testifying to a fact waives to the details. This prevents a witness from testifying only to the information beneficial to one party and then refusing to testify further, even though he or she may have omitted important facts. However, a witness may not be compelled to testify if there is a chance of incriminating himself or herself beyond the original testimony.

The fact that a witness may waive the Fifth Amendment privilege against self-incrimination on one occasion does not mean it is waived forever. First, a defendant (or witness) may speak to the police during the investigative stage and later refuse to testify at trial, provided such testimony may be incriminating. Second, it is generally held that a person who testifies before a grand jury without claiming the Fifth does not waive the right to raise the defense at trial. Third, even within the same proceeding a person may invoke the Fifth Amendment privilege against self-incrimination if the two hearings are separate and distinct. For example, a defendant may testify at a suppression hearing without waiving the privilege not to testify at trial.

Finally, the Fifth Amendment applies to all proceedings, whether civil, criminal, or administrative.[6] Therefore, a person called to testify in a civil proceeding may invoke the Fifth Amendment's privilege and refuse to testify.

BALLENTINE'S

use immunity A guaranty given a person that if he or she testifies against others, his or her testimony will not be used against him or her if he or she is prosecuted for his or her involvement in the crime.

Due Process and Equal Protection

The Fifth Amendment to the United States Constitution prohibits the government from depriving a person of life, liberty, or property without due process of law. This Amendment acts to constrain the power of the federal government. You have previously learned that the Fourteenth Amendment has similar language and constrains the power of state governments.

The Fourteenth Amendment expressly requires the states to extend equal protection of the laws to the people. There is no express equal protection clause in the Fifth Amendment, but the Supreme Court has found it to be implied in the Due Process Clause. Equal protection concerns classifications and discrimination.

Discrimination is not inherently evil. Students discriminate between professors, possibly due to grading policy or teaching skill, when deciding what courses to enroll in. Governments also discriminate and make classifications, most of which are sensible and acceptable. For example, those who commit homicides are divided into groups: murderers, manslaughterers, and those who are excused or justified in killing. When classifications are based upon meaningful criteria (e.g., mens rea), the law is valid. However, our society has decided that certain classifications are improper and violative of equal protection. A classification between those who exercise a constitutional right and those who do not, if it results in prosecution or increased punishment for the former, is unconstitutional. Classifications based on race, religion, gender, and other immutable conditions are suspect and possibly violative of equal protection.

These clauses are important to criminal law and particularly to criminal procedure. Due process requires the government to treat people fairly; therefore, whenever a law or other governmental action appears to be unfair, there is a due process issue. In a sense, due process is a safety net, protecting the individual when another specific constitutional provision does not.

Due process has two aspects, substantive and procedural. The protection of privacy discussed later in this chapter is an example of substantive due process. On the procedural side, due process is the constitutional source of the principle of *legality*, which requires that criminal laws (and punishments) be written and enacted before an act may be punished. This is a notice concept. It would be unfair to announce that an act is illegal, or increase its punishment, after that act has been committed. You will learn later in this chapter that overly broad or vague laws may be violative of due process.

Through the Fourteenth Amendment's Due Process Clause, most of the provisions of the Bill of Rights, which initially applied only against the federal government, have been extended to the states. Today, the Fourth Amendment's right to be free from unreasonable searches and seizures, the Fifth Amendment's right to be free from self-incrimination, the Sixth Amendment's right to counsel at critical stages of criminal adjudications, and the Eighth Amendment's prohibition of cruel and unusual punishment are among the many rights that are now available to defendants in state courts.

In some instances, due process or equal protection increases the scope of a right found in the Bill of Rights. For example, the Sixth Amendment's right to counsel is limited to the critical stages of criminal proceedings. Appeals are not critical stages, and therefore the Sixth Amendment does not mandate counsel. But the Supreme Court has held that if a state provides for felony appeals by right, then the Equal Protection Clause requires that indigent defendants receive appointed counsel. To hold otherwise would unfairly discriminate against the indigent.[7]

Although the Fourteenth Amendment is the source of the incorporation of most of the Bill of Rights, its importance extends beyond this. Any time an issue of fairness surfaces, due process should be examined. If the issue concerns one of improper classifications, equal protection law should be considered. The Supreme Court stated of substantive due process:

> The inescapable fact is that adjudication of substantive due process claims may call upon the Court in interpreting the Constitution to exercise that same capacity which by tradition courts always have exercised: reasoned judgment. Its boundaries are not susceptible of expression as a simple rule. That does not mean we are free to invalidate state policy choices with which we disagree: yet neither does it permit us to shrink from the duties of our office. As Justice Harlan observed: "Due process has not been reduced to any formula: its content cannot be determined by reference to any code. The best that can be said is that through the course of this Court's decisions it has represented the balance which our Nation, built upon postulates of respect for liberty of the individual, has struck between that liberty and the demands of organized society."

Vagueness and Overbreadth

It is a defense that the statute one is charged under is unconstitutionally vague or overbroad. The Due Process Clauses of the Fifth and Fourteenth Amendments to the United States Constitution are the foundation of the void-for-vagueness and overbreadth doctrines.

A statute is void for **vagueness** whenever "men of common intelligence must necessarily guess at its meaning and differ as to its application."[8] As to the meaning of a statute, confusion among lower courts, resulting in varying interpretations, is evidence of vagueness.[9] The Supreme Court has held that uncertain statutes do not provide notice of what conduct is forbidden and are violative of due process. The Court has also found statutes that permit arbitrary or discriminatory enforcement void. That is, if the police or courts are given unlimited authority to decide who will be prosecuted, the statute is invalid.

It was under the void-for-vagueness doctrine that many vagrancy laws have been attacked. If it were not for the doctrine, legislatures could draft statutes so that nearly everyone would be engaged in criminal activity at one time or another, and police and prosecutors would have unfettered discretion to decide who would be arrested and prosecuted.

A closely related doctrine is **overbreadth**. A statute is overbroad if it includes within its grasp not only unprotected activity, but also activity protected by the Constitution. For example, in one case a city ordinance made it illegal for "one or more persons to assemble" on a sidewalk and conduct themselves in an annoying manner. The United States Supreme Court found that the law was unconstitutional not only because it made unprotected activity illegal (fighting words or riotous activity), but it also included activity that is protected by the First Amendment's free assembly and association provisions.[10] It is possible for a statute to be clear and precise (not vague), but overbroad.

Ex Post Facto and Bills of Attainder

Article I of the United States Constitution prohibits the state and federal governments from enacting both ex post facto laws and bills of attainder.

BALLENTINE'S
---

vagueness doctrine   The rule of constitutional law that a statute, particularly a criminal statute, that does not reasonably put a person on notice as to what it is he or she may not do, or what he or she is required to do, violates due process and is therefore unconstitutional.

overbreadth doctrine   The doctrine that a statute is unconstitutional if its language is so broad that it unnecessarily interferes with the exercise of constitutional rights, particularly First Amendment rights, even though the purpose of the statute is to prohibit activities that the government may constitutionally prohibit.

An **ex post facto law** is one that (1) makes an act illegal after the act was taken, (2) increases the punishment or severity of a crime after it occurred, (3) changes the procedural rules so as to increase the chances of conviction after the crime occurs. In short, a government may not make criminal law retroactive, if doing so is detrimental to the defendant. However, changes that benefit a defendant may be applied retroactively. So, if a legislature increases the prosecution's burden of proof after a defendant has committed a crime, but before trial, the legislature may make the change applicable to the defendant. The clause advances the notice theory (due process) and also prevents malicious legislative action from being taken against a particular person.

A **bill of attainder** is a legislative act punishing a person without a judicial trial. This provision reinforces the concept of separation of powers. It is the duty of the legislative branch to make the laws, and it is the duty of the judicial branch to determine who has violated those laws.

In a few instances, however, Congress may act in a judicial role. Congress may punish those who disrupt its functions for contempt. In addition, Congress is authorized by the Constitution to conduct impeachment hearings of the president, federal judges, and other federal officers and to discipline its own members.

First Amendment and Religion

The First Amendment contains a large number of protections, including freedom of the press; to choose and practice a religion; freedom of speech; and freedom to peaceably assemble. Although the First Amendment is only directly applicable against the national government, the Fourteenth Amendment extends its prohibitions to the states.

Concerning freedom of religion, the First Amendment states that "Congress shall make no law respecting an establishment of religion, or prohibiting the free exercise thereof." The free exercise clause is of the most importance in criminal law. The freedom to believe is, of course,

---
BALLENTINE'S

ex post facto law   A law making a person criminally liable for an act that was not criminal at the time it was committed. The Constitution prohibits both Congress and the states from enacting such laws.

bill of attainder   A legislative act that inflicts capital punishment upon named persons without a judicial trial. Congress and the state legislatures are prohibited from issuing bills of attainder by the Constitution.

absolute. Any law prohibiting a certain religious belief is void. However, the Supreme Court has held that some religious practices may be regulated.

To determine whether a specific religious act may be criminalized, the governmental interest in regulating the behavior is balanced against the First Amendment infringement. If the governmental interest is greater than the infringement, then a state may regulate the conduct. For example, it has been held that the Mormon practice of polygamy may be regulated.[11] Also, a parent who depends upon prayer to save a dying child may be charged with manslaughter for failing to seek competent medical care. In this instance the state's interest in protecting the child's life outweighs the parent's interest in practicing his or her religion in such a manner.

On the other side, the California Supreme Court disallowed the conviction of a member of the Native American Church for possession of peyote, a drug made from cactus. The court found that peyote was an important part of worship in the Native American Church, and, as such, California's interest in regulating the use of the drug was outweighed by the drug's religious significance.[12] Note that the United States Supreme Court took the opposite view concerning the use of peyote in *Department of Human Resources v. Smith,* 494 U.S. 872 (1990), wherein the Court stated that

> [T]he right of free exercise does not relieve an individual of the obligation to comply with a valid and neutral law of general applicability on the ground that the law proscribes (or prescribes) conduct that his religion prescribes (or proscribes).

In the *Hialeah* case, the Supreme Court invalidated several ordinances that prohibited the adherents of Santeria from sacrificing animals as part of their religious rites.

CHURCH OF LUKUMI BABALU AYE, INC.
v.
HIALEAH
113 S. Ct. 2217 (1993)

This case involves practices of the Santeria religion, which originated in the nineteenth century. When hundreds of thousands of members of the Yoruba people were brought as slaves from eastern Africa to Cuba, their traditional African religion absorbed significant elements of Roman Catholicism. The resulting syncretion, or fusion, is Santeria, "the way of the saints." The Cuban Yoruba express their devotion to spirits, called *orishas,* through the iconography of Catholic saints, Catholic symbols are often present at Santeria rites, and Santeria devotees attend the Catholic sacraments ... .

The Santeria faith teaches that every individual has a destiny from God, a destiny fulfilled with the aid and energy of orishas. The basis of the Santeria religion is the nurture of a personal relation with the orishas, and one of the principal forms of devotion is an animal sacrifice. ... The sacrifice of animals as part of religious rituals has ancient roots. ... Animal sacrifice is mentioned throughout the Old Testament ... and it played an important role in the practice of Judaism before destruction of the second Temple in Jerusalem ... . In modern Islam, there is an annual sacrifice commemorating Abraham's sacrifice of a ram in the stead of his son. ...

According to Santeria teaching, the orishas are powerful but not immortal. They depend for survival on the sacrifice.

Santeria adherents faced widespread persecution in Cuba, so the religion and its rituals were practiced in secret. The open practice of Santeria and its rites remains infrequent. ... The religion was brought to this Nation most often by exiles from the Cuban revolution. The District Court estimated that there are at least 50,000 practitioners in South Florida today.

Petitioner Church of Lukumi Babalu Aye, Inc. (Church), is a not-for-profit corporation organized under Florida law in 1973. The Church and its congregants practice the Santeria religion. The president of the Church is petitioner Ernesto Pichardo, who is also the Church's priest and holds the religious title of Italero, the second highest in the Santeria faith. In April 1987, the Church leased land in the city of Hialeah, Florida, and announced plans to establish a house of worship as well as a school, cultural center, and museum. Pichardo indicated that the Church's goal was to bring the practice of the Santeria faith, including its ritual of animal sacrifice, into the open.

The Church began the process of obtaining utility service and receiving the necessary licensing, inspection, and zoning approvals. Although the Church's efforts at obtaining the necessary licenses and permits were far from smooth ... it appears that it received all needed approvals by early August 1987.

The prospect of a Santeria church in their midst was distressing to many members of the Hialeah community, and the announcement of the plans to open a Santeria church in Hialeah prompted the city council to hold an emergency public session on June 9, 1987. [The city council enacted ordinance] 87-66, which noted the "concern" expressed by residents of the city "that certain religions may propose to engage in practices which are inconsistent with public morals, peace or safety," and declared that "[t]he City reiterates its commitment to a prohibition against any and

all acts of any and all religious groups which are inconsistent with public morals, peace or safety." Next, the council approved an emergency ordinance, Ordinance 87-40, that incorporated in full, except as to penalty, Florida's animal cruelty laws. ... Among other things, the incorporated state law subjected to criminal punishment "[w]hoever ... unnecessarily or cruelly ... kills any animal."

[In September 1987, the city council adopted three additional ordinances prohibiting owning or possessing an animal for purpose of sacrifice and regulating the slaughtering of animals.] Violations of each of the four ordinances were punishable by fines not exceeding $500 or imprisonment not exceeding 60 days, or both.

Following enactment of these ordinances, the Church and Pichardo filed this action pursuant to 42 U.S.C. § 1983 in the United States District Court for the Southern District of Florida. Named as defendants were the city of Hialeah and its mayor and members of its city council in their individual capacities. [The defendants prevailed at the trial and appellate levels.]

... The city does not argue that Santeria is not a "religion" within the meaning of the First Amendment. Nor could it. Although the practice of animal sacrifice may seem abhorrent to some, "religious beliefs need not be acceptable, logical, consistent, or comprehensible to others in order to merit First Amendment protection. ... Given the historical association between animal sacrifice and religious worship ... petitioners' assertion that animal sacrifice is an integral part of their religion "cannot be deemed bizarre or incredible." ... Neither the city nor the courts below, moreover, have questioned the sincerity of petitioners' professed desire to conduct animal sacrifices for religious reasons. We must consider petitioners' First Amendment claim.

In addressing the constitutional protection for free exercise of religion, our cases establish the general proposition that a law that is neutral and of general applicability need not be justified by a compelling governmental interest even if the law has the incidental effect of burdening a particular religious practice. ... Neutrality and general applicablility are interrelated, and, as becomes apparent in this case, failure to satisfy one requirement is a likely indication that the other has not been satisfied. A law failing to satisfy these requirements must be justified by a compelling governmental interest and must be narrowly tailored to advance the interest. These ordinances fail to satisfy the [constitutional] requirements. ...

There are, of course, many ways of demonstrating that the object or purpose of a law is the suppression of religion or religious conduct. To determine the object of a law, we must begin with its text, for the minimum requirement of neutrality is that a law not discriminate on its face. A law lacks facial neutrality if it refers to a religious practice without a secular meaning discernable from the language or context. Petitioners contend that three of the ordinances fail this test of facial neutrality because they use the words "sacrifice" and "ritual," words with strong religious connotations. ... We agree that these words are consistent with the claim of facial discrimination, but the argument is not conclusive. The words "sacrifice" and "ritual" have a religious origin, but current use admits also of secular meanings. ...

We reject the contention advanced by the city ... that our inquiry must end with the text of the laws at issue. Facial neutrality is not determinative. The Free Exercise Clause, like the Establishment Clause, extends beyond facial discrimination. The Clause "forbids subtle departures from neutrality" ... . The Free Exercise Clause protects against governmental hostility which is masked, as well as overt. "The Court must survey meticulously the circumstances of governmental categories to eliminate, as it were, religious gerrymanders." ...

The record in this case compels the conclusion that suppression of the central element of the Santeria worship service was the object of the ordinances. First, though the use of the words "sacrifice" and "ritual" does not compel a finding of improper targeting of the Santeria religion, the choice of these words is support for our conclusion. ... [One of the ordinances] recited that "residents and citizens of the City of Hialeah have expressed their concern that certain religions may propose to engage in practices which are inconsistent with public morals, peace or safety," and

"reiterate[d]" the city's commitment to prohibit "any and all [such] acts of any and all religious groups." No one suggests, and on this record it cannot be maintained, that city officials had in mind a religion other than Santeria.

It becomes evident that these ordinances target Santeria sacrifice when the ordinances' operation is considered. Apart from the text, the effect of a law in its real operation is strong evidence of its object. To be sure, adverse impact will not always lead to a finding of impermissible targeting. ...

It is a necessary conclusion that almost the only conduct subject to [the ordinances] is the religious exercise of Santeria Church members. The texts show that they were drafted in tandem to achieve this purpose. ... [One of the ordinances] prohibits the sacrifice of animals but defines sacrifice as "to unnecessarily kill ... an animal in a public or private ritual or ceremony not for the primary purpose of food consumption." The definition excludes almost all killings of animals except for religious sacrifice, and the primary purpose requirement narrows the proscribed category even further, in particular by exempting Kosher slaughter ... .

The net result of the gerrymander is that few if any killings of animals are prohibited other than Santeria sacrifice, which is proscribed because it occurs during a ritual or ceremony and its primary purpose is to make an offering to the orishas, not food consumption. Indeed, careful drafting ensured that, although Santeria sacrifice is prohibited, killings that are no more necessary or humane in almost all other circumstances are unpunished.

Operating in similar fashion [is another ordinance] which prohibits the "possess[ion], sacrifice, or slaughter" of an animal with the inten[t] to use such animal for food purposes." This prohibition, extending to the keeping of an animal as well as the killing itself, applies if the animal is killed in "any type of ritual" ... . The ordinance exempts, however, "any licensed [food] establishment" with regard to "any animals which are specifically raised for food purposes," if this activity is permitted by zoning and other laws. This exception, too, seems intended to cover Kosher slaughter. Again, the burden of the ordinance, in practical terms, falls on Santeria adherents but almost no others ... .

We also find significant evidence of the ordinances' improper targeting of Santeria sacrifice in the fact that they proscribe more religious conduct than is necessary to achieve their stated ends. ...

The legitimate governmental interests in protecting the public health and preventing cruelty to animals could be addressed by restrictions stopping far short of a flat prohibition of all Santeria sacrificial practice. If improper disposal, not the sacrifice itself, is the harm to be prevented, the city could have imposed a general regulation on the disposal of organic garbage. It did not do so. Indeed, counsel for the city conceded at oral argument that, under the ordinances, Santeria sacrifices would be illegal even if they occurred in licensed, inspected, and zoned slaughterhouses. ... Thus, these broad ordinances prohibit Santeria sacrifice even when it does not threaten the city's interest in the public health. ...

Respondent claims that [the ordinances] advance two interests: protecting the public health and preventing cruelty to animals. The ordinances are underinclusive for those ends. They fail to prohibit nonreligious conduct that endangers these interests in a similar or greater degree than Santeria sacrifice does. The underinclusion is substantial, not inconsequential. Despite the city's proffered interest in preventing cruelty to animals, the ordinances are drafted with care to forbid few killings but those occasioned by religious sacrifice. Many types of animal deaths or kills for nonreligious reasons are either not prohibited or approved by express provision. For example, fishing ... is legal. Extermination of mice and rats within a home is also permitted. Florida law incorporated by [the ordinances] sanctions euthanasia of "stray,

neglected, abandoned, or unwanted animals ... and the use of live animals "to pursue or take wildlife or to participate in any hunting" ... .

The ordinances are underinclusive as well with regard to the health risk posed by consumption of uninspected meat. Under the city's ordinances, hunters may eat their kill and fisherman may eat their catch without undergoing governmental inspection. ...

A law burdening religious practice that is not neutral or not of general application must undergo the most rigorous of scrutiny. To satisfy the commands of the First Amendment, a law restrictive of religious practice must advance "interests of the highest order" and must be narrowly tailored in pursuit of those interests. ... The compelling interest standard [applies].

... As we have discussed ... all four ordinances are overbroad or underinclusive in substantial respects ... .

Respondent has not demonstrated, moreover, that, in the context of these ordinances, its governmental interests are compelling. ...

The Free Exercise Clause commits government itself to religious tolerance, and upon even slight suspicion that proposals for state intervention stem from animosity to religion or distrust of its practices, all officials must pause to remember their own high duty to the Constitution and to the rights it secures. Those in office must be resolute in resisting importunate demands and must ensure that the sole reasons for imposing the burdens of law and regulation are secular. Legislators may not devise mechanisms, overt or disguised, designed to persecute or oppress a religion or its practices. The laws here in question were enacted contrary to these constitutional principles and they are void. Reversed.

Smith can be distinguished from the *Hialeah* case because *Smith* involved a law of general applicability. That is, use of the drugs, including peyote, was generally prohibited to everyone. Clearly, the laws were not enacted solely to regulate religious worship. However, in the *Hialeah* case, the Court determined that the regulation was intended to target the Santeria's religious practices.

Determining whether an act is truly an exercise of religious beliefs is not always easy. The practices of one religion may appear unusual, or even bizarre, to another. But this is not determinative. The *Hodges* case both illustrates the sensitivity with which our society treats religion and stands as an example of an activity that is not a religion, although the opinion does not contain the latter finding, for reasons you will see.

STATE
v.
HODGES
695 S.W.2d 171 (Tenn. 1985)

In January, 1983, defendant was charged in a multiple count indictment with tampering with utility metering devices. His lawyer appeared before the trial judge on February 22, 1983, asking for a trial date for the misdemeanors with which defendant was charged. The trial judge informed defendant's counsel on that occasion that he would not "put up with [defendant's] foolishness" and if "he comes in here dressed like a chicken, I am going to order him out of here under guard."

On June 28, 1983, defendant appeared for trial, with the same counsel, and to say that he was dressed "like a chicken" as the trial judge had anticipated, is a mild description of the outrageous attire in which defendant barely covered himself. [In a footnote the court described his appearance. The defendant "appeared for trial dressed in a grossly shocking and bizarre attire, consisting of brown and white fur tied around his body at his ankles, loins and head, with a like vest made out of fur, and complete with eye goggles over his eyes. He had colored his face and chest with a very pale green paint for coloring. He had what appeared to be a human skull dangling from his waist and in his hand he carried a stuffed snake. ... [T]he so-called vest consisted of two pieces of fur that covered each arm but did not meet in front and back, leaving defendant's chest and back naked to his waist. His legs were also naked from mid-way between his knee and waist to his ankles. He appeared to be carrying a military gas mask and other unidentifiable ornaments."]

The trial judge first addressed defendant's attorney and asked him to have his client appear in proper clothes. Defendant's attorney responded by informing the court that defendant wished to exercise his right of "freedom of expression." The trial judge then directed his remarks to defendant and ordered him to put on "regular clothes" for the trial scheduled that day. The trial judge sought a yes or no answer, but defendant responded with the following assertion:

"This is a spiritual attire and it is my religious belief and I have never worn anything else in court but this when I am on trial."

Whereupon, the trial judge found him to be in contempt of court, revoked his bond, and ordered him committed to jail for ten days or until he agreed to appear for trial in proper clothes.

Defendant's counsel asked the court to allow him to "build a record for appeal" which was denied. Motions were filed the following day, June 29, 1983, on behalf of defendant for a new trial, for reconsideration of the finding of contempt, and for bail pending appeal. At the hearing held the same day, defense counsel again sought an evidentiary hearing on the issue of defendant's religious belief which was again denied. ... The court of Criminal Appeals reversed the contempt adjudication, holding that the trial judge erred in failing to inquire into the "nature and sincerity of appellant's beliefs, the denomination of his religion, its origin, organization and the length of time which appellant has espoused it."

We agree that the trial judge erred in failing to inquire into the religious belief of defendant and in failing to allow a full record to be developed for appeal. However, we think the intermediate court's instructions on remand, quoted above, may be misleading and not entirely in conformity with United States Supreme Court opinions.

A Rhode Island litigant appeared in court wearing a white, knitted skull cap and the trial judge ordered him to remove it or leave the courtroom and refused to consider the litigant's claim that he was a Sunni Muslim, that he was wearing a prayer cap that was a religious symbol of that sect, that indicted that the wearer was in constant prayer. ... On appeal, the Supreme Court of Rhode Island accurately summarized the first amendment principle enunciated by the United States Supreme Court applicable where a religious belief or practice collides with a state law or regulation, as follows:

> Despite the exalted status so rightly afforded to religious beliefs and activities that are motivated and embody those beliefs, the freedom of an individual to practice his religion does not enjoy absolute immunity from infringement by the state. Individuals have been subject to mandatory inoculations despite religious objections to such medical care. ... Thus while the freedom to hold religious beliefs and opinions is absolute, the freedom to act in harmony with these religious beliefs and opinions is not beyond state regulation where such restriction serves the public interest by promoting public health and safety or preserving order. We must then accommodate the right to exercise the religious freedoms safeguarded by the first amendment with the right of the state to regulate those individual freedoms for the sake of societal interests. The problem is one of balance and degree—the courts are called upon to determine when the societal interest becomes so important as to justify an incursion by the state into religious activity that is otherwise protected by the free exercise clause of the first amendment. ...

After discussion of the United States Supreme Court's application of the balancing test to the

facts ... the Supreme Court of Rhode Island continued as follows:

> We believe that because petitioner claimed that his act was protected by the free exercise clause, in order to justifiably curtail the exercise of the alleged right the trial justice should have first allowed petitioner to display the sincerity of his religious belief, and then should have ... [balanced] petitioner's first amendment right with the interest of the court in maintaining decorum in its proceedings by regulating dress in the courtroom. ...

Thus, the threshold inquiry is whether or not the religious belief or practice asserted qualifies for the protection of the free exercise clause of the first amendment. The record in this case, though meager, clearly indicates that that issue may be decisive, particularly if it proves to be true that defendant is the sole adherent to his asserted religious belief and practice. ...

Although a determination of what is a "religious" belief or practice entitled to constitutional protection may present a most delicate question, the very concept of ordered liberty precludes allowing every person to make his own standards of matters of conduct in which society as a whole has important interests. ...

Paraphrasing an additional observation of the Court that involved Thoreau's isolation at Walden Pond, the Court made it clear that a belief which is philosophical and personal rather than religious, does not rise to the demands of the free exercise clause of the first amendment. ...

Only beliefs rooted in religion are protected by the Free Exercise Clause, which, by its terms, gives special protection to the exercise of religion. ... The determination of what is a "religious" belief or practice is more often than not a difficult and delicate task ... . However, the resolution of that question is not to turn upon a judicial perception of the particular belief or practice in question; religious beliefs need not be acceptable, logical, consistent, or comprehensible to others in order to merit First Amendment protection.

One can, of course, imagine an asserted claim so bizarre, so clearly nonreligious in motivation, as not to be entitled to protection under the First Amendment. ...

This case is clearly illustrative of what Mr. Justice Jackson had in mind when he said, "The price of freedom of religion or of speech or of the press is that we must put with, and even pay for, a good deal of rubbish." ...

The judgment of the Court of Criminal Appeals is affirmed and this case is remanded to the trial court for further proceedings consistent with this opinion.

How does a court distinguish between fraudulent and bona fide religious practices? First, it must be determined that the defendant is asserting a religious belief, not a personal or philosophical belief. Several factors are considered. How well established is the religion in the world? If a defendant is the only adherent, or one of only a few followers, of a religion, it is less likely to be deemed legitimate. How old is the religion? For how long has the defendant practiced the religion? What is the nature of the practice in question? How important is the practice to the religion? Once it is determined that a religious practice is being regulated by the state, then the state's interest in regulating the defendant's conduct must be weighed against the defendant's First Amendment interest. If the state's interest is compelling, then the conduct may be regulated.

First Amendment and Speech

The First Amendment also protects speech. Not all speech is protected. You have already learned that fighting words and those words which create a "clear and present danger" may be regulated. Slanderous and libelous statements also fall outside the protection of the First Amendment. Fighting words, dangerous words, slanderous and libelous words, are all content-based doctrines; that is, the substance of what is being said is regulated.

In some instances, a state may regulate speech, not because of its content, but by its time, place, and manner of being expressed. Here, a balancing of interests is conducted: does the government's interest in enforcing the statute outweigh the First Amendment interest? For example, it is unlawful to stand in the middle of the street to make a speech. The interest in maintaining a safe, consistent flow of traffic outweighs the First Amendment interest. However, the result would be different if a state attempted to prohibit all speeches made in a public place. Such a statute would be overbroad, as it includes not only activity which the state may regulate (standing in traffic), but also lawful activity. Commercial speech is also protected by the First Amendment, but is subject to greater control than other speech.

Not only is the actual spoken word protected: expression of ideas through acts are also protected, although to a lesser degree than pure speech. Picketing is an example of protected expression, as is flag burning.

TEXAS
v.
Gregory Lee JOHNSON
491 U.S. 397 (1989)

After publicly burning the American flag as a means of political protest, Gregory Lee Johnson was convicted of desecrating a flag in violation of Texas law. This case presents the question whether his conviction is consistent with the First Amendment. We hold that it is not.

While the Republican National Convention was taking place in Dallas in 1984, respondent Johnson participated in a political demonstration dubbed the "Republican War Chest Tour." As explained in literature distributed by the demonstrators and in speeches made by them, the purpose of this event was to protest the policies of the Reagan administration and of certain Dallas-based corporations. The demonstrators marched through the Dallas streets, chanting political slogans and stopping at several corporate locations to stage "die-ins" intended to dramatize the consequences of nuclear war. On several occasions they spray-painted the walls of buildings and overturned potted plants, but Johnson himself took no part in such activities. He did, however, accept an American flag handed to him by a fellow protester who had taken it from a flag pole outside one of the targeted buildings.

The demonstration ended in front of Dallas City Hall, where Johnson unfurled the American flag, doused it with kerosene, and set it on fire. While the flag burned, the protesters chanted, "America, the red, white, and blue, we spit on you." After the demonstrators dispersed, a witness to the flag-burning collected the flag's remains and buried them in his backyard. No one was physically injured or threatened with injury,

though several witnesses testified that they had been seriously offended by the flag-burning. ...

Johnson was convicted of flag desecration for burning the flag rather than for uttering insulting words. That fact somewhat complicates our consideration of his conviction under the First Amendment. We must first determine whether Johnson's burning of the flag constituted expressive conduct, permitting him to invoke the First Amendment. ... If his conduct was expressive, we next decide whether the State's regulation is related to the suppression of free expression. If the State's regulation is not related to expression, then the less stringent standard ... for regulations of non-communicative conduct controls. ... If it is, then we are outside of the *O'Brien* test, and we must ask whether this interest justifies Johnson's conviction under a more demanding standard. ...

The First Amendment literally forbids the abridgment only of "speech," but we have long recognized that its protection does not end at the spoken or written word. While we have rejected "the view that an apparently limitless variety of conduct can be labeled 'speech' whenever the person engaging in the conduct intends thereby to express an idea," ... we have acknowledged that conduct may be "sufficiently imbued with elements of communication to fall within the scope of the First and Fourteenth Amendments." ...

In deciding whether particular conduct possesses sufficient communicative elements to bring the First Amendment into play, we have asked whether "[a]n intent to convey a particularized message was present, and [whether] the likelihood was great that the message would be understood by those who viewed it."... Hence, we have recognized the expressive nature of students' wearing of black armbands to protest American military involvement in

Vietnam ... of a sit-in by blacks in a "whites only" area to protest segregation. ...

The expressive, overtly political nature of this conduct was both intentional and overwhelmingly apparent. At his trial, Johnson explained his reasons for burning the flag as follows: "The American Flag was burned as Ronald Reagan was being nominated as President. And a more powerful statement of symbolic speech, whether you agree with it or not, couldn't have been made at that time. It's quite a just position [juxtaposition]. We had new patriotism and no patriotism." In these circumstances, Johnson's burning of the flag was conduct "sufficiently imbued with elements of communication.".…

In order to decide whether the O'Brien test applies here, therefore, we must decide whether Texas has asserted an interest in support of Johnson's conviction that is unrelated to the suppression of expression. If we find that an interest asserted by the State is simply not implicated on the facts before us, we need not ask whether O'Brien applies. … The State offers two separate interests to justify his conviction: preventing breaches of the peace, and preserving the flag as a symbol of nationhood and national unity. We hold that the first interest is not implicated on this record and that the second is related to the suppression of expression. ...

The State's position, therefore, amounts to a claim that an audience that takes serious offense at particular expression is necessarily likely to disturb the peace and that the expression may be prohibited on this basis. Our precedents do not countenance such a presumption. On the contrary, they recognize that a principal "function of free speech under our system of government is to invite dispute. It may indeed best serve its high purpose when it induces a condition of unrest, creates dissatisfaction with conditions as they are, or even stirs people to anger."...

The State also asserts an interest in preserving the flag as a symbol of nationhood and national unity. ...

Johnson was not, we add, prosecuted for the expression of just any idea; he was prosecuted for his expression of dissatisfaction with the policies of this country, expression situated at the core of our First Amendment values. ...

Moreover, Johnson was prosecuted because he knew that his politically charged expression would cause "serious offense." If he had burned the flag as a means of disposing of it because it was dirty or torn, he would not have been convicted of flag desecration under the Texas law; federal law designates burning as the preferred means of disposing of a flag "when it is in such condition that it is no longer a fitting emblem for display." ...

If there is a bedrock principle underlying the First Amendment, it is that the Government may not prohibit the expression of an idea simply because society finds the idea itself offensive or disagreeable. ...

We are tempted to say, in fact, that the flag's deservedly cherished place in our community will be strengthened, not weakened, by our holding today. Our decision is a reaffirmation of the principles of freedom and inclusiveness that the flag best reflects, and of the conviction that our toleration of criticism such as Johnson's is a sign and source of our strength. ...

The way to preserve the flag's special role is not to punish those who feel differently about these matters. It is to persuade them that they are wrong. . . . And, precisely because it is our flag that is involved, one's response to the flag-burner may exploit the uniquely persuasive power of the flag itself. We can imagine no more appropriate response to burning a flag than waving one's own, no better way to counter a flag-burner's message than by saluting the flag that burns, no surer means of preserving the dignity even of the flag that burned than by—as one witness here did—according its remains a respectful burial. We do not consecrate the flag by punishing its desecration, for in doing so we dilute the freedom that this cherished emblem represents. ...

Justice Kennedy, concurring.

I write not to qualify the words Justice Brennan chooses so well, for he says with power all that is necessary to explain our ruling. I join his opinion without reservation, but with a keen sense that his case, like others before us from time to time, exacts its personal toll. This prompts me to add to our pages these few remarks.

The case before us illustrates better than most that the judicial power is often difficult in its exercise. We cannot here ask another branch to share responsibility, as when the argument is made that a statute is flawed or incomplete. For we are presented with a clear and simple statute to be judged against a pure command of the Constitution. The outcome can be laid at no door but ours.

The hard fact is that sometimes we must make decisions we do not like. We make them because they are right, right in the sense that the law and the Constitution, as we see them, compel the result. And so great is our commitment to the process that, except in the rare case, we do not pause to express distaste for the result, perhaps for fear of undermining a valued principle that dictates decision. This is one of those rare cases.

Our colleagues in dissent advance powerful arguments why respondent may be convicted for his expression, reminding us that among those who will be dismayed by our holding will be some who have had the singular honor of carrying the flag into battle. And I agree that the flag holds a lonely place of honor in an age when absolutes are distrusted and simple truths are burdened by unneeded apologetics.

With respect to those views, I do not believe the Constitution gives us the right to rule as the dissenting members of the Court urge, however painful this judgment is to announce. ... It is poignant but fundamental that the flag protects those who hold it in contempt ...

First Amendment free exercise of speech claims also arise in the context of hate crime legislation. Such legislation either makes it illegal to express prejudicial opinions or enhances the penalty for a crime that is motivated by prejudice. The former is unconstitutional. As to the latter, most states enhance the penalties for crimes such as trespass, assault, battery, and harassment if the motive of the crime was the victim's race, religion, color, or other characteristic.

Two Supreme Court opinions, only one year apart, set the limits of hate crime laws. Both are excerpted here. In the first, the Court held an ordinance unconstitutional. In the second, the Court upheld the law.

R.A.V.
v.
City of ST. PAUL
505 U.S. 377 (1992)

In the predawn hours of June 21, 1990, petitioner and several other teenagers allegedly assembled a crudely-made cross by taping together broken chair legs. They then allegedly burned the cross inside the fenced yard of a black family that lived across the street from the house where petitioner was staying. Although this conduct could have been punished under any number of laws, one of the two provisions under which respondent city of St. Paul chose to charge petitioner (then a juvenile) was the St. Paul-Motivated Crime Ordinance, which provides:

"Whoever placed on public property or private property a symbol, object, appellation, characterization or graffiti, including, but not limited to, a burning cross or Nazi swastika, which one knows or has reasonable grounds to know arouse anger, alarm or resentment in others on the basis of race, color, creed, religion or gender commits disorderly conduct and shall be guilty of a misdemeanor."

Petitioner moved to dismiss this count on the ground that the St. Paul ordinance was substantially overbroad and impermissibly content-based and therefore facially invalid under the First Amendment. The trial court granted this motion, but the Minnesota Supreme Court reversed. That court rejected petitioner's overbreadth claim because, as construed in prior Minnesota cases ... the modifying phrase "arouses anger, alarm or resentment in others" limited the reach of the ordinance to conduct that amounts to "fighting words," ... and therefore the ordinance reached only expression "that the first amendment does not protect." ... The court also concluded that the ordinance was not impermissibly content-based because, in its view, "the ordinance is a narrowly tailored means toward accomplishing the compelling governmental interest in protecting the community against bias-motivated threats to public safety and order." ...

Assuming, arguendo, that all of the expression reached by the ordinance is proscribable under the "fighting words" doctrine, we nonetheless conclude that the ordinance is facially unconstitutional in that it prohibits otherwise permitted speech solely on the basis of the subjects the speech addresses. ...

The proposition that a particular instance of speech can be proscribable on the basis of one feature (e.g., obscenity) but not on the basis of another (e.g., opposition to the city government) is commonplace, and has found application in many contexts. We have long held, for example, that nonverbal expressive activity can be banned because of the action it entails, but not because of the ideas it expresses—so that burning the flag in violation of an ordinance against outdoor fires could be punishable, whereas burning a flag in violation of an ordinance against dishonoring the flag is not. ...

Similarly, we have upheld reasonable "time, place, or manner" restrictions, but only if they are "justified without reference to the content of the regulated speech." ... And just as the power to proscribe particular speech on the basis of a non-content element (e.g., noise) does not entail the power to proscribe it on the basis of a content element; so also, the power to proscribe it on the basis of one content element (e.g., obscenity) does not entail the power to proscribe it on the basis of other content elements.

In other words, the exclusion of "fighting words" from the scope of the First Amendment simply means that, for purposes of that Amendment, the unprotected features of the words are, despite their verbal character, essentially a "non-speech" element of communication. Fighting words are thus analogous to a noisy sound truck: Each is, as Justice Frankfurter recognized, a "mode of speech," ... both can be used to convey an idea; but neither has, in and of itself, a claim upon the First Amendment. As with the sound truck, however, so also with fighting words: The government may not regulate use based on hostility—or favoritism—towards the underlying message expressed. ...

Applying these principles to the St. Paul ordinance, we conclude that, even as narrowly construed by the Minnesota Supreme Court, the ordinance is facially unconstitutional. Although the phrase in the ordinance, "arouses anger, alarm or resentment in others," has been limited by the Minnesota Supreme Court's construction to reach only those symbols or displays that amount to "fighting words," the remaining, unmodified terms make clear that the ordinance applies only to "fighting words" that insult, or provoke violence, "on the basis of race, color, creed, religion or gender." Displays containing abusive invective, no matter how vicious or severe, are permissible unless they are addressed to one of the specified disfavored topics. Those who wish to use "fighting words" in connection with other ideas—to express hostility, for example, on the basis of political affiliation, union membership, or homosexuality—are not covered. The First Amendment does not permit St. Paul to impose special prohibitions on those speakers who express views on disfavored subjects. ...

In its practical operation, moreover, the ordinance goes even beyond mere content discrimination, to actual viewpoint discrimination. Displays containing some words—odious racial epithets, for example—aspersions upon a person's mother, for example—would seemingly be usable ad libitum in the placards of those arguing in favor of racial, color, etc. tolerance and equality, but could not be used by the speaker's opponents. One could hold up a sign saying, for example, that all "anti-catholic bigots" are misbegotten; but not that all "papists" are, for that would insult or provoke violence "on the basis of religion." St. Paul has no such authority to license one side of a debate to fight freestyle, while requiring the other to follow Marquis of Queensbury Rules. ...

Let there be no mistake about our belief that burning a cross in someone's front yard is reprehensible. But St. Paul has sufficient means at its disposal to prevent such behavior without adding the First Amendment to the fire. ...

One year after *R.A.V.*, the Supreme Court handed down the *Mitchell* case. *R.A.V.* and *Mitchell* establish that although bigoted expressions themselves may not be prohibited (legislation aimed at content), bigotry as a motive may be considered at sentencing to enhance a penalty (legislation aimed at the motive of content).

WISCONSIN
v.
MITCHELL
113 S. Ct. 2194 (1993)

Respondent Todd Mitchell's sentence for aggravated battery was enhanced because he intentionally selected his victim on account of the victim's race. The question presented in this case is whether this penalty enhancement is prohibited by the First and Fourteenth Amendments. We hold that it is not.

On the evening of October 7, 1989, a group of young black men and boys, including Mitchell, gathered at an apartment complex in Kenosha, Wisconsin. Several members of the group discussed a scene from the motion picture "Mississippi Burning," in which a white man beat a young black boy who was praying. The group moved outside and Mitchell asked them: "Do you all feel hyped up to move on some white people?" ... Shortly thereafter, a young white boy approached the group on the opposite side of the street where they were standing. As the boy walked by, Mitchell said: "You all want to fuck somebody up? There goes a white boy: go get him." ... Mitchell counted to three and pointed in the boy's direction. The group ran towards the boy, beat him severely, and stole his tennis shoes. The boy was rendered unconscious and remained in a coma for four days.

After a jury trial in the Circuit Court for Kenosha County, Mitchell was convicted of aggravated battery. ... That offense ordinarily carries a maximum sentence of two years imprisonment. ... But because the jury found that Mitchell had intentionally selected his victim because of the boy's race, the maximum sentence for Mitchell's offense was increased to seven years under a [Wisconsin statute]. That provision enhances the maximum penalty for an offense whenever the defendant "[i]ntentionally selects the person against whom the crime ... is committed ... because of race, religion, color, disability, sexual orientation, national origin or ancestry of that person." ...

The Circuit Court sentenced Mitchell to four years' imprisonment for the aggravated battery. ...

Mitchell unsuccessfully sought postconviction relief in the Circuit Court. Then he appealed his conviction and sentence, challenging the constitutionality of Wisconsin's penalty-enhancement provision on First Amendment grounds. The Wisconsin Court of Appeals rejected Mitchell's challenge, but the Wisconsin Supreme Court reversed. The Supreme Court held that the statute "violates the First Amendment directly by punishing what the legislature has deemed to be offensive thought." ... It rejected the State's contention "that the statute punishes only the conduct of intentional selection of a victim." According to the court, "[t]he statute punishes the 'because of' aspect of the defendant's selection, the reason the defendant selected the victim, the motive behind the selection." ...

The Supreme Court also held that the penalty-enhancement statute was unconstitutionally overbroad. It reasoned that, in order to prove that a defendant intentionally selected his victim because of the victim's protected status, the State would often have to introduce evidence of the defendant's prior speech, such as racial epithets he may have uttered before the commission of the offense. ...

We granted certiorari because of the importance of the question presented and the existence of a conflict of authority among the states' high courts on the constitutionality of statutes similar to Wisconsin's penalty-enhancement provision. ... We reverse. ...

Mitchell argues (and the Wisconsin Supreme Court held) that the statute violates the First Amendment by punishing offenders' bigoted beliefs.

Traditionally, sentencing judges have considered a wide variety of factors in addition to evidence bearing on guilt in determining what sentence to impose on a convicted defendant. ... [T]he defendant's motive for committing the offense is one important factor. ... Thus, in many states the commission of a murder, or other capital offense, for pecuniary gain is a separate aggravating circumstance under the capital-sentencing statute. ...

But it is equally true that a defendant's abstract beliefs, however obnoxious to most people, may not be taken into consideration by a sentencing judge. ... In [*Dawson v. Delaware*, 503 U.S. _____ (1992)] the State introduced evidence at a capital-sentencing hearing that the defendant was a member of a white supremacist prison gang. Because "the evidence proved nothing more than [the defendant's] abstract beliefs," we held that its admission violated the defendant's First Amendment rights. ... In so holding, however, we

emphasized that "the Constitution does not erect a per se barrier to the admission of evidence concerning one's beliefs and associations at sentencing simply because those beliefs and associations are protected by the First Amendment. ... Thus, in *Barclay v. Florida,* 463 U.S. 939 (1983) ... we allowed the sentencing judge to take into account the defendant's racial animus towards his victim. The evidence in that case showed that the defendant's membership in the Black Liberation Army and desire to provoke a "race war" were related to the murder of a white man for which he was convicted. ... Because "the elements of racial hatred in [the] murder" were relevant to several aggravating factors, we held that the trial judge permissibly took his evidence into account in sentencing the defendant to death. ...

Mitchell suggests that *Dawson* and *Barclay* are inapposite because they did not involve application of a penalty-enhancement provision. But in *Barclay* we held that it was permissible for the sentencing court to consider the defendant's racial animus in determining whether he should be sentenced to death, surely the most severe "enhancement" of all. And the fact that the Wisconsin Legislature has decided, as a general matter, that bias-motivated offenses warrant greater maximum penalties across the board does not alter the result here. For the primary responsibility for fixing criminal penalties lies with the legislature. ...

Mitchell argues that the Wisconsin penalty-enhancement statute is invalid because it punishes the defendant's discriminatory motive, or reason, for acting. But motive plays the same role under the Wisconsin statute as it does under federal and state antidiscrimination laws, which we have previously upheld against constitutional challenge. ... Title VII, for example, makes it unlawful for an employer to discriminate against an employee "because of such individual's race, color, religion, sex, or national origin." ... In [another case] we rejected the argument that Title VII infringed employers' First Amendment rights. Nothing in our decision last Term in *R.A.V.* compels a different result here. That case involved a First Amendment challenge to a municipal ordinance prohibiting the use of " 'fighting words' that

CHAPTER 9 CONSTITUTIONAL DEFENSES **259**

insult or provoke violence, on the basis of race, color, creed, religion or gender." ...

Finally, there remains to be considered Mitchell's argument that the Wisconsin statute is unconstitutionally overbroad because of the "chilling effect" on free speech. Mitchell argues (and the Wisconsin Supreme Court agreed) that the statute is "overbroad" because evidence of the defendant's prior speech or associations may be used to prove that the defendant intentionally selected his victim on account of the victim's protected status. Consequently, the argument goes, the statute impermissibly chills free expression with respect to such matters by those concerned about the possibility of enhanced sentences if they should in the future commit a criminal offense covered by the statute. We find no merit in this contention.

The sort of chill envisioned here is far more attenuated and unlikely than that contemplated in traditional "overbreadth" cases. We must conjure up a vision of a Wisconsin citizen suppressing his unpopular bigoted opinions for fear that if he later commits an offense covered by the statute, these opinions will be offered at trial to establish that he selected his victim on account of the victim's protected status, thus qualifying him for penalty-enhancement. To stay within the realm of rationality, we must surely put to one side minor misdemeanor offenses covered by the statute, such as negligent operation of a motor vehicle ... for it is difficult, if not impossible, to conceive of a situation where such offenses would be racially motivated. We are left, then, with the prospect of a citizen suppressing his bigoted beliefs for fear that evidence of such beliefs will be introduced against him at trial if he commits a more serious offense against person or property. This is simply too speculative a hypothesis to support Mitchell's overbreadth claim.

The First Amendment, moreover, does not prohibit the evidentiary use of speech to establish the elements of a crime or to prove motive or intent. Evidence of a defendant's previous declarations or statements is commonly admitted in criminal trials subject to evidentiary rules dealing with relevancy, reliability, and the like. Nearly half a century ago, ... we rejected a contention similar to that advanced by Mitchell here. Haupt was tried for the offense of treason, which, as defined by the Constitution, may depend very much on proof of motive. To prove that the acts in question were committed out of "adherence to the enemy" rather than "parental solicitude," ... the Government introduced evidence of conversations that had taken place long prior to the indictment, some of which consisted of statements showing Haupt's sympathy with Germany and Hitler and hostility towards the United States. We rejected Haupt's argument that this evidence was improperly admitted. While "[s]uch testimony is to be scrutinized with care to be certain the statements are not expressions of mere proper appreciation of the land of birth," we held that "these statements ... clearly were admissible on the question of intent and adherence to the enemy."...

For the foregoing reasons, we hold that Mitchell's First Amendment rights were not violated by the application of the Wisconsin penalty-enhancement provision in sentencing him. The judgment of the Supreme Court of Wisconsin is therefore reversed, and the case is remanded for further proceedings not inconsistent with this opinion.

Privacy and Other Unenumerated Rights

Unlike some state constitutions, the United States Constitution does not expressly protect privacy. Many of the expressly stated rights in the Bill of Rights effectively protect privacy, such as the Fourth

Amendment, which has been interpreted as applying to searches that encroach upon a person's reasonable expectation to privacy.

The issue is whether the Constitution protects privacy to a greater extent than through its express provisions. Stated another way, is there an independent and inherent privacy right in the Constitution? If so, what is the textual source of that right?

The Supreme Court answered the former question affirmatively in 1965 in *Griswold v. Connecticut*.[13] In that case, a Connecticut statute that prohibited the use of contraceptives, even by married couples, was held unconstitutional as invasive of a right to privacy.

As to the second issue, the source of the right, the Court found that the right to privacy grows out of the First, Fourth, Fifth, Ninth, and Fourteenth Amendments. Justice Douglas, writing for the Court, found the right to privacy to be a penumbra of these expressly protected rights. The Court stressed that the First Amendment's right to association protected the marriage relationship and that the intimate subject sought to be regulated was especially protected. The Court stated that

> [Prior case law] suggests that specific guarantees in the Bill of Rights have penumbras, formed by emanations from those guarantees that help give them life and substance. ... Various guarantees create zones of privacy. The right of association contained in the penumbra of the First Amendment is one, as we have seen. The Third Amendment in its prohibition against the quartering of soldiers "in any house" in time of peace without the consent of the owner is another facet of that privacy. The Fourth Amendment explicitly affirms the "right of the people to be secure in their persons, houses, papers, and effects, against unreasonable searches and seizures." The Fifth Amendment in its Self-Incrimination Clause enables the citizens to create a zone of privacy which government may not force him to surrender to his detriment. The Ninth Amendment provides: "The enumeration in the Constitution, of certain rights, shall not be construed to deny or disparage others retained by the people." ...
>
> The present case, then, concerns a relationship lying within the zone of privacy created by several fundamental constitutional guarantees. ...
>
> We deal with a right to privacy older than the Bill of Rights—older than our political parties, older than our school system. Marriage is a coming together for better or worse, hopefully enduring, and intimate to the degree of being sacred. It is an association that promotes a way of life, not causes; a harmony in living, not political faiths; a bilateral loyalty, not commercial or social projects. Yet it is an association for as noble a purpose as any involved in our prior decisions.

Note that Justice Douglas found that the right to privacy was a penumbra of other fundamental, express rights. He did not find the right to privacy to be an independent constitutional right. This is because he believed that the Fourteenth Amendment was intended to extend the rights found in the Bill of Rights to the states, but that it was not intended to create independent rights. This is known as *total incorporation*.

Privacy has also been an issue in abortion cases. This is complicated by a competing interest that did not exist in *Griswold,* that is, the interest of the state in protecting the fetus. In 1973 the Supreme Court handed down the landmark decision of *Roe v. Wade,*[14] in which the Court declared that the right to privacy protects a woman's right to elect to abort a fetus in some situations.

Specifically, the Court adopted a trimester analysis wherein the state's authority to regulate abortion increases as the pregnancy lengthens. During the first trimester, states could not regulate abortion procedures. During the second trimester, states could regulate abortions insofar as necessary to protect the health and life of the woman. Finally, states could protect the fetus during the third trimester, including proscribing abortion, except in cases in which abortion was necessary to protect the life or health of the mother. The Court decided that governmental interest in protecting fetuses during the third trimester was compelling because fetuses are viable at that time.

The trial court found Roe's right to privacy in the Ninth Amendment, but the Supreme Court refused to rely on the Ninth Amendment alone. Rather, the Court found the right to privacy to stem from the Fourteenth, Ninth, and other amendments.

The *Roe v. Wade* decision was the subject of intense political and legal controversy during the 1980s and early 1990s. *Certiorari* was sought in several abortion-related cases during this period; so-called "right to life" groups believed that, with a more conservative Court than had existed since the *Roe v. Wade* decision issued, the chances of reversing the decision were good. The Court granted *certiorari* in several abortion-related cases, but the cardinal principle announced in *Roe v. Wade* was reaffirmed again and again: the decision on whether to abort a fetus is, in some circumstances, so private and intimate that it is protected by the Constitution from governmental intrusion. This occurred in *Casey v. Planned Parenthood,* wherein the Court also rejected the trimester analysis.[15]

CASEY

v.

PLANNED PARENTHOOD of Southeastern Pennsylvania

112 S. Ct. 2791 (1992)

Liberty finds no refuge in a jurisprudence of doubt. Yet 19 years after our holding that the Constitution protects a woman's right to terminate her pregnancy in its early stages, the respondents as amicus curiae, the United States, as it has

done in five other cases in the last decade, again asks us to overrule *Roe.* ...

At issue in these cases are five provisions of the Pennsylvania Abortion Control Act of 1982 as amended in 1988 and 1989. ... The Act requires that a woman seeking an abortion give her informed consent prior to the abortion procedure, and specifies that she be provided with certain information at least 24 hours before the abortion is performed. For a minor to obtain an abortion, the Act requires the informed consent of one of her parents, but provided for [a] judicial bypass option if the minor does not wish to or cannot obtain a parent's consent. Another provision of the Act requires that, unless certain exceptions apply, a married woman seeking an abortion must sign a statement indicating that she has notified her husband of her intended abortion. ...

Before any of these provisions took effect, the petitioners, who are five abortion clinics and one physician representing himself as well as a class of physicians who provide abortion services, brought this suit seeking declaratory and injunctive relief. Each provision was challenged as unconstitutional on its face. ...

After considering the fundamental constitutional questions resolved by *Roe,* principles of institutional integrity, and the rule of stare decisis, we are led to conclude this: the essential holding of *Roe v. Wade* should be retained and once again reaffirmed.

It must be stated at the outset and with clarity that *Roe's* essential holding, the holding we reaffirm, has three parts. First is a recognition of the right of the woman to choose to have an abortion before viability and to obtain it without undue interference from the State. Before viability, the State's interests are not strong enough to support a prohibition of abortion or the imposition of a substantial obstacle to the woman's effective right to elect the procedure. Second is a confirmation of the State's power to restrict abortions after fetal viability, if the law contains exceptions for pregnancies which endanger a woman's life or health. And third is the principle that the State has legitimate interests from the outset of the pregnancy in protecting the health of the woman and the life of the fetus that may become a child. These principles do not contradict one another; and we adhere to each.

Constitutional protection of the woman's decision to terminate her pregnancy derives from the Due Process Clause of the Fourteenth Amendment. It declares that no State shall "deprive any person of life, liberty, or property, without due process of law." The controlling word in the case before us is "liberty." ... We have held that the Due Process Clause of the Fourteenth Amendment incorporates most of the Bill of Rights against the States. ... It is tempting, as a means of curbing the discretion of federal judges, to suppose that liberty encompasses no more than those rights already guaranteed to the individual against federal interference by the express provisions of the first eight amendments to the Constitution. ... But of course this Court has never accepted that view. It is also tempting, for the same reason, to suppose that the Due Process Clause protects against government interference by other rules of law when the Fourteenth Amendment was ratified. ... But such a view would be inconsistent with our law. It is a promise of the Constitution that there is a realm of personal liberty which the government may not enter. We have vindicated this principle before. Marriage is mentioned nowhere in the Bill of Rights and interracial marriage was illegal in most States in the 19th century, but the Court was no doubt correct in finding it to be an aspect of liberty protected against state interference by the substantive component of the Due Process Clause. ... Neither the Bill of Rights nor the specific practices of States at the time of the adoption of the Fourteenth Amendment marks the outer limits of the substantive sphere of liberty which the Fourteenth Amendment protects. ...

Our law affords constitutional protection to personal decisions relating to marriage, procreation, contraception, family relationships, child rearing, and education. ... These matters, involving the most intimate and personal choices a person may make in a lifetime, choices central to personal dignity and autonomy, are central to the liberty protected by the Fourteenth Amendment. At the heart of liberty is the right to define one's own concept of existence, of meaning, of the universe, and of the mystery of human life. Beliefs about these matters could not define the attributes of personhood were they formed under compulsion of the State.

The consideration begins our analysis of the woman's interest in terminating her pregnancy but cannot end it, for this reason: though the abortion decision may originate within the zone of conscience and belief, it is more than a philosophic exercise. Abortion is a unique act. It is an act fraught with consequences for others: for the woman who must live with the implications of her decision; for the persons who perform and assist in the procedure; for the spouse, family and society which must confront the knowledge that these procedures exist, procedures some deem nothing short of an act of violence against innocent human life; and depending on one's beliefs, for the life or potential life that is aborted. Though abortion is conduct, it does not follow that the State is entitled to proscribe it in all instances. That is because the liberty of the woman is at stake in a sense unique to the human condition and so unique to the law. The mother who carries a child to full term is subject to anxieties, to physical constraints, to pain that only she must bear. ...

No evolution of legal principle has left *Roe's* doctrinal footings weaker than they were in 1973. No development of constitutional law since the case was decided has implicitly or explicitly left *Roe* behind as a mere survivor of obsolete constitutional thinking. ...

We have seen how time has overtaken some of *Roe's* factual assumptions: advances in maternal health care allow for abortions safe to the mother later in pregnancy than was true in 1973 ... and advances in neonatal care have advanced viability to a point somewhat earlier ... . But these facts go only to the scheme of the limits on the realization of competing interests, and the divergences from the factual premises of 1973 have no bearing on the validity of *Roe's* central holding, that viability marks the earliest point at which the State's interest in fetal life is constitutionally adequate to justify a legislative ban on nontherapeutic abortions. The soundness or unsoundness of that constitutional judgment in no sense turns on whether viability occurs at 23 to 24 weeks ... . Whenever it may occur, the attainment of viability may continue to serve as the critical fact, just as it has done since *Roe* was decided; which is to say that no change in *Roe's* factual underpinnings has left its central holding obsolete, and none supports an argument for overruling it. ...

Only where a state regulation imposes an undue burden on a woman's ability to make this decision does the power of the State reach into the heart of the liberty protected by the Due Process Clause ... .

The very notion that the State has a substantial interest in potential life leads to the conclusion that not all regulations must be deemed unwarranted. Not all burdens on the right to decide whether to terminate a pregnancy will be undue. ...

A finding of undue burden is a shorthand for the conclusion that a state regulation has the purpose or effect of placing a substantial obstacle in the path of a woman seeking an abortion of a nonviable fetus. A statute with this purpose is invalid ... .

Although the Court reaffirmed the right to privacy in the abortion context, it also rejected the trimester analysis in favor of an "undue interference" test. That is, a regulation is invalid if it unduly interferes with a woman's choice. Also, the Court reaffirmed the *Roe* holding that until a fetus is viable outside of the mother's womb, a state may not prohibit its abortion. Further, even after viability, abortion is permitted to save the life or health of the mother.

The Court examined the Pennsylvania statute and concluded that:

1. Requiring information concerning abortions and abortion procedures to be distributed to patients before the procedure is performed is not unduly burdensome

2. Mandating twenty-four-hour waiting periods between receipt of the information and performance of the procedure is not unduly burdensome

3. Requiring parental consent (with a judicial bypass) by minor girls is not unduly burdensome

4. Requiring spousal notification by married women is unduly burdensome, and therefore, invalid.

The right to privacy applies outside the abortion context as well. For example, as the Court stated in *Casey,* the right to engage in an interracial marriage is also protected by the Fourteenth Amendment.[16] In *Eisenstadt v. Baird,*[17] the Supreme Court invalidated a statute that prohibited the sale and distribution of contraceptives to unmarried persons. The Court stated in that opinion, "If the right of privacy means anything, it is the right of the individual, married or single, to be free from unwarranted governmental intrusion into matter so fundamentally affecting a person as the decision whether to bear or beget a child."

These are a few examples of how the power of the state to regulate conduct is limited by the right to privacy. Today, courts are likely to rely on the Fourteenth Amendment as the source of the right to privacy. Arguably, the privacy right has its roots in other amendments as well, such as the Ninth Amendment, which declares that the enumeration in the Constitution of certain rights shall not be construed as denying or disparaging others retained by the people. Although this amendment appears to be an independent source of rights, probably with natural rights origins, it has received little attention by the courts, and standing alone has never been relied upon by the Supreme Court to declare an unenumerated right.

The Supreme Court refused to extend the right to privacy to include a right for consenting adults to engage in "deviate sexual" behavior. In *Bowers v. Hardwick,*[18] the Court upheld a Georgia statute that criminalized sodomy.

Finally, be aware that the Court has recognized other unenumerated rights. A right to travel within the United States and abroad is not expressed in the Constitution, but is recognized by the Court. Of course, all rights may be regulated if the government has cause. Most rights may be regulated if the government has a legitimate and compelling interest. The right to travel abroad is subject to reasonable restrictions and regulations,[19] because of national security and foreign affairs concerns.

Any time a statute conflicts with a constitutionally protected activity, the statute will fail unless the government has a compelling interest. The defenses discussed in this chapter are only a few of the many constitutional defenses. Not all, but most criminal constitutional defenses appear in the Bill of Rights.

Nor does this chapter exhaust all the nonconstitutional defenses that may be asserted. Do not forget that each state is free to design its criminal law in any manner it wishes, so long as it is constitutional. The most common factual, legislative, and constitutional substantive law defenses have been discussed.

Review Questions

1. Differentiate overbreadth from vagueness. Give an example of each.

2. Differentiate a bill of attainder from an ex post facto law.

3. May racially derogatory statements be made criminal? May racial motives be used to enhance the punishment for crimes such as assault and battery?

4. Is a right to privacy specifically expressed in the United States Constitution?

5. Through what amendment are rights incorporated and applied against the states?

6. May religious beliefs be regulated by the state? May religious practices be regulated by the state?

7. Which of the following is protected by the First Amendment's free speech clause?
   a. A public flag burning in protest of a recently enacted law.
   b. An advertisement for potato chips found on a billboard.
   c. The placing of a hand over one's heart while the national anthem is played.

Review Problems

1. Senator Bob Kerry of Nebraska was initially outraged by the *Texas v. Johnson* flag-burning decision. However, he later stated, "I was surprised to discover ... [that the decision was] reasonable, understandable and consistent with those values which I believe have made America wonderful." Do you agree with Senator Kerry? Explain your position.

2. State law requires that all children between five years and sixteen years attend an approved school. Defendants have been charged with violating the statute, as they do not permit their children to attend school. The defendants are Mennonites and claim that it would violate their First Amendment right to freely exercise their religion. The defendants teach their children consistent with their religious teachings. Should they be convicted?

3. Do you believe that a person should be subjected to two prosecutions, by different sovereigns, for the same offense? Consider specifically the prosecution of the Los Angeles police officers who arrested and beat Rodney King. They were acquitted of assault and battery in state court. Federal civil rights charges were brought in apparent reaction to the acquittal. In your opinion, is this proper? Support your answer.

4. Do you believe that the federal Constitution implicitly protects privacy? Support your conclusion. If so, name one right not mentioned in this text that you believe should be protected.

Notes

1 21 Am. Jur. *Criminal Law* 243 (1978).

2 *Arizona v. Washington,* 434 U.S. 497 (1978).

3 *Blockburger v. United States,* 284 U.S. 299 (1932).

4 Model Penal Code § 1.10.

5 Passage taken from a 1991 calendar prepared by the Commission on the Bicentennial of the United States Constitution, Washington, D.C.

6 *Pillsbury v. Conboy,* 459 U.S. 248 (1983).

7 *Douglas v. California,* 372 U.S. 353 (1963).

8 *Connally v. General Construction Co.,* 269 U.S. 385 (1926).

9 *United States v. Cardiff,* 344 U.S. 174 (1952).

10 *Coates v. Cincinnati,* 402 U.S. 611 (1971).

11 *Reynolds v. United States,* 98 U.S. 145 (1878).

12 *People v. Woody,* 61 Cal. 2d 716, 394 P.2d 813 (1965).

13 381 U.S. 479 (1965). The Supreme Court noted in *Roe v. Wade,* 410 U.S. 113 (1973) that the right to privacy may have been recognized by the Court as early as 1891, in *Union Pacific Railroad v. Botsford,* 141 U.S. 250 (1891), in which it held that a plaintiff in a tort action could not be compelled to submit to a medical examination because it would have been an invasion of privacy.

14 410 U.S. 113 (1973).

15 *See also Webster v. Reproductive Health Services,* 492 U.S. 490 (1989).

16 *Loving v. Virginia,* 388 U.S. 1 (1967).

17 405 U.S. 438 (1972).

18 478 U.S. 186 (1986).

19 *Zemel v. Rusk,* 381 U.S. 1 (1965).

APPENDIX A

THE CONSTITUTION OF THE UNITED STATES OF AMERICA

We the People of the United States, in Order to form a more perfect Union, establish Justice, insure domestic Tranquility, provide for the common defence, promote the general Welfare, and secure the Blessings of Liberty to ourselves and our Posterity, do ordain and establish this Constitution for the United States of America.

Article I

Section 1 All legislative Powers herein granted shall be vested in a Congress of the United States, which shall consist of a Senate and House of Representatives.

Section 2 (1) The House of Representatives shall be composed of Members chosen every second Year by the People of the several States, and the Electors in each State shall have the Qualifications requisite for Electors of the most numerous Branch of the State Legislature.

(2) No Person shall be a Representative who shall not have attained to the age of twenty-five Years, and been seven Years a Citizen of the United States, and who shall not, when elected, be an Inhabitant of that State in which he shall be chosen.

(3) Representatives and direct Taxes shall be apportioned among the several States which may be included within this Union, according to their respective Numbers, which shall be determined by adding to the whole Number of free Persons, including those bound to Service for a Term of Years, and excluding Indians not taxed, three fifths of all other Persons. The actual Enumeration shall be made within three Years after the first Meeting of the Congress of the United States, and within every subsequent Term of ten Years, in such Manner as they shall by Law direct. The Number of Representatives shall not exceed one for every thirty Thousand, but each State shall have at Least one Representative; and until such enumeration shall be made, the State of New Hampshire shall be entitled to chuse three, Massachusetts eight, Rhode Island and Providence Plantations one, Connecticut five, New York six, New Jersey four, Pennsylvania eight, Delaware one, Maryland six, Virginia ten, North Carolina five, South Carolina five, and Georgia three.

(4) When vacancies happen in the Representation from any State, the Executive Authority thereof shall issue Writs of Election to fill such Vacancies.

(5) The House of Representatives shall chuse their Speaker and other Officers; and shall have the sole Power of Impeachment.

Section 3 (1) The Senate of the United States shall be composed of two Senators from each State, chosen by the Legislature thereof, for six Years; and each Senator shall have one Vote.

(2) Immediately after they shall be assembled in Consequence of the first Election, they shall be divided as equally as may be into three Classes. The Seats of the Senators of the first Class shall be vacated at the Expiration of the second Year, of the second Class at the Expiration of the fourth Year, and of the third Class at the Expiration of the sixth Year, so that one third may be chosen every second Year; and if Vacancies happen by Resignation, or otherwise, during the Recess of the Legislature of any State, the Executive thereof may make temporary Appointments until the next Meeting of the Legislature, which shall then fill such Vacancies.

(3) No Person shall be a Senator who shall not have attained to the Age of thirty Years, and been nine Years a Citizen of the United States, and who shall not, when elected, be an Inhabitant of that State for which he shall be chosen.

(4) The Vice President of the United States shall be President of the Senate, but shall have no Vote, unless they be equally divided.

(5) The Senate shall chuse their other Officers, and also a President pro tempore, in the Absence of the Vice President, or when he shall exercise the Office of the President of the United States.

(6) The Senate shall have the sole Power to try all Impeachments. When sitting for that Purpose, they shall be on Oath or Affirmation. When the President of the United States is tried, the Chief Justice shall preside: And no Person shall be convicted without the Concurrence of two thirds of the Members present.

(7) Judgment in Cases of Impeachment shall not extend further than to removal from Office, and disqualification to hold and enjoy any Office of honor, Trust or Profit under the United States: but the Party convicted shall nevertheless be liable and subject to Indictment, Trial, Judgment and Punishment, according to Law.

Section 4 (1) The Times, Places and Manner of holding Elections for Senators and Representatives, shall be prescribed in each State by the Legislature thereof; but the Congress may at any time by Law make or alter such Regulations, except as to the Places of chusing Senators.

(2) The Congress shall assemble at least once in every Year, and such Meeting shall be on the first Monday in December, unless they shall by Law appoint a different Day.

Section 5 (1) Each House shall be the Judge of the Elections, Returns and Qualifications of its own Members, and a Majority of each shall constitute a Quorum to do Business; but a smaller Number may adjourn from day to day, and may be authorized to compel the Attendance of absent Members, in such Manner, and under such Penalties as each House may provide.

(2) Each House may determine the Rules of its Proceedings, punish its Members for disorderly Behaviour, and, with the Concurrence of two thirds, expel a Member.

(3) Each House shall keep a Journal of its Proceedings, and from time to time publish the same, excepting such Parts as may in their Judgment require Secrecy; and the Yeas and Nays of the Members of either House on any question shall, at the Desire of one fifth of those Present, be entered on the Journal.

(4) Neither House, during the Session of Congress, shall, without the Consent of the other, adjourn for more than three days, nor to any other Place than that in which the two Houses shall be sitting.

Section 6 (1) The Senators and Representatives shall receive a Compensation for their Services, to be ascertained by Law, and paid out of the Treasury of the United States. They shall in all Cases, except Treason, Felony and Breach of the Peace, be privileged from Arrest during their Attendance at the Session of their respective Houses, and in going to and returning from the same; and for any Speech or Debate in either House, they shall not be questioned in any other Place.

(2) No Senator or Representative shall, during the Time for which he was elected, be appointed to any civil Office under the Authority of the United States, which shall have been created, or the Emoluments whereof shall have been encreased during such time; and no Person holding any Office under the United States, shall be a Member of either House during his Continuance in Office.

Section 7 (1) All Bills for raising Revenue shall originate in the House of Representatives; but the Senate may propose or concur with Amendments as on other Bills.

(2) Every Bill which shall have passed the House of Representatives and the Senate, shall, before it become a Law, be presented to the President of the United States; If he approve he shall sign it, but if not he shall return it, with his Objections to that House in which it shall have originated, who shall enter the Objections at large on their Journal, and proceed to reconsider it. If after such Reconsideration two thirds of that House shall agree to pass the Bill, it shall be sent, together with the Objections, to the other House, by which it shall likewise be reconsidered, and if approved by two thirds of that

House, it shall become a law. But in all such Cases the Votes of both Houses shall be determined by Yeas and Nays, and the Names of the Persons voting for and against the Bill shall be entered on the Journal of each House respectively. If any Bill shall not be returned by the President within ten Days (Sunday excepted) after it shall have been presented to him, the Same shall be a Law, in like Manner as if he had signed it, unless the Congress by their Adjournment prevent its Return, in which Case it shall not be a Law.

(3) Every Order, Resolution, or Vote to which the Concurrence of the Senate and House of Representatives may be necessary (except on a question of Adjournment) shall be presented to the President of the United States; and before the Same shall take Effect, shall be approved by him, or being disapproved by him, shall be repassed by two thirds of the Senate and House of Representatives, according to the Rules and Limitations prescribed in the Case of a Bill.

Section 8 (1) The Congress shall have Power To lay and collect Taxes, Duties, Imposts and Excises, to pay the Debts and provide for the common Defence and general Welfare of the United States; but all Duties, Imposts and Excises shall be uniform throughout the United States;

(2) To borrow Money on the credit of the United States;

(3) To regulate Commerce with foreign Nations, and among the several States, and with the Indian Tribes;

(4) To establish an uniform Rule of Naturalization, and uniform Laws on the subject of Bankruptcies throughout the United States;

(5) To coin Money, regulate the Value thereof, and of foreign Coin, and to fix the Standard of Weights and Measures;

(6) To provide for the Punishment of counterfeiting the Securities and current Coin of the United States;

(7) To establish Post Offices and post Roads;

(8) To promote the Progress of Science and useful Arts, by securing for limited Times to Authors and Inventors the exclusive Right to their respective Writings and Discoveries;

(9) To constitute Tribunals inferior to the supreme Court;

(10) To define and punish Piracies and Felonies committed on the high Seas, and Offenses against the Law of Nations;

(11) To declare War, grant Letters of Marque and Reprisal, and make Rules concerning Captures on Land and Water;

(12) To raise and support Armies, but no Appropriation of Money to that Use shall be for a longer Term than two Years;

(13) To provide and maintain a Navy;

(14) To make Rules for the Government and Regulation of the land and naval Forces;

(15) To provide for calling forth the Militia to execute the Laws of the Union, suppress Insurrections and repel Invasions;

(16) To provide for organizing, arming, and disciplining, the Militia, and for governing such Part of them as may be employed in the Service of the United States, reserving to the States respectively, the Appointment of the Officers, and the Authority of training the Militia according to the discipline prescribed by Congress;

(17) To exercise exclusive Legislation in all Cases whatsoever, over such District (not exceeding ten Miles square) as may, by Cession of particular States, and the Acceptance of Congress, become the Seat of the Government of the United States, and to exercise like Authority over all Places purchased by the Consent of the Legislature of the State in which the Same shall be, for the Erection of Forts, Magazines, Arsenals, dockYards, and other needful Buildings;—And

(18) To make all Laws which shall be necessary and proper for carrying into Execution the foregoing Powers, and all other Powers vested by this Constitution in the Government of the United States, or in any Department or Officer thereof.

Section 9 (1) The Migration or Importation of such Persons as any of the States now existing shall think proper to admit, shall not be prohibited by the Congress prior to the Year one thousand eight hundred and eight, but a Tax or Duty may be imposed on such Importation, not exceeding ten dollars for each Person.

(2) The Privilege of the Writ of Habeas Corpus shall not be suspended unless when in Cases of Rebellion or Invasion the public Safety may require it.

(3) No Bill of Attainder or ex post facto Law shall be passed.

(4) No Capitation, or other direct, Tax shall be laid, unless in Proportion to the Census or Enumeration herein before directed to be taken.

(5) No Tax or Duty shall be laid on Articles exported from any State.

(6) No Preference shall be given by any Regulation of Commerce or Revenue to the Ports of one State over those of another; nor shall Vessels bound to, or from, one State, be obliged to enter, clear or pay Duties in another.

(7) No Money shall be drawn from the Treasury, but in Consequence of Appropriations made by Law; and a regular Statement and Account of the Receipts and Expenditures of all public Money shall be published from time to time.

(8) No Title of Nobility shall be granted by the United States: And no Person holding any Office of Profit or Trust under them, shall, without the Consent of the Congress, accept of any present, Emolument, Office, or Title, of any kind whatever, from any King, Prince or foreign State.

Section 10 (1) No State shall enter into any Treaty, Alliance, or Confederation; grant Letters of Marque and Reprisal; coin Money; emit Bills of Credit; make any Thing but gold and silver Coin a Tender in Payment of Debts; pass any Bill of Attainder, ex post facto Law, or Law impairing the Obligation of Contracts, or grant any Title of Nobility.

(2) No State shall, without the Consent of Congress, lay any Imposts or Duties on Imports or Exports, except what may be absolutely necessary for executing its inspection Laws: and the net Produce of all Duties and Imposts, laid by any State on Imports or Exports, shall be for the Use of the Treasury of the United States; and all such Laws shall be subject to the Revision and Controul of the Congress.

(3) No State shall, without the Consent of Congress, lay any Duty of Tonnage, keep Troops, or Ships of War in time of Peace, enter into any Agreement or Compact with another State, or with a foreign Power, or engage in War, unless actually invaded, or in such imminent Danger as will not admit of Delay.

Article II

Section 1 (1) The executive Power shall be vested in a President of the United States of America. He shall hold his Office during the Term of four Years, and, together with the Vice President, chosen for the same Term, be elected, as follows:

(2) Each State shall appoint, in such Manner as the Legislature thereof may direct, a Number of Electors, equal to the whole Number of Senators and Representatives to which the State may be entitled in the Congress: but no Senator or Representative, or Person holding an Office of Trust or Profit under the United States, shall be appointed an Elector.

The Electors shall meet in their respective States, and vote by Ballot for two Persons, of whom one at least shall not be an Inhabitant of the same State with themselves. And they shall make a List of all the Persons voted for, and of the Number of Votes for each; which List they shall sign and certify, and transmit sealed to the Seat of the Government of the United States, directed to the President of the Senate. The President of the Senate shall, in the presence of the Senate and House of Representatives, open all the Certificates, and the Votes shall then be counted. The Person having the greatest Number of Votes shall be the President, if such Number be a Majority of the whole Number of Electors appointed; and if there be more than one who have such Majority, and have an equal Number of Votes, then the House of Representatives shall immediately chuse by Ballot one of them for President; and if no Person have a Majority, then from the five highest on the List the said House shall in like Manner chuse the President. But in chusing the President, the Votes shall be taken by States, the Representation from each State having one Vote; a quorum for this Purpose shall consist of a Member or Members from two thirds of the States, and a Majority of all the States shall be necessary to a Choice. In every Case, after the Choice of the President, the Person having the greatest Number of Votes of the Electors shall be the Vice President. But if there should remain two or more who have equal Votes, the Senate shall chuse from them by Ballot the Vice President.

(3) The Congress may determine the Time of chusing the Electors, and the Day on which they shall give their Votes; which Day shall be the same throughout the United States.

(4) No Person except a natural born Citizen, or a Citizen of the United States, at the time of the Adoption of this Constitution, shall be eligible to the Office of President; neither shall any Person be eligible to that Office who shall not have attained to the Age of thirty five Years, and been fourteen Years a Resident within the United States.

(5) In Case of the Removal of the President from Office, or of his Death, Resignation, or Inability to discharge the Powers and Duties of the said Office, the Same shall devolve on the Vice President, and the Congress may by Law provide for the Case of Removal, Death, Resignation or Inability, both of the President and Vice President, declaring what Officer shall then act as President, and such Officer shall act accordingly, until the Disability be removed, or a President shall be elected.

(6) The President shall, at stated Times, receive for his Services, a Compensation, which shall neither be increased nor diminished during the Period for which he shall have been elected, and he shall not receive within that Period any other Emolument from the United States, or any of them.

(7) Before he enter on the Execution of his Office, he shall take the following Oath or Affirmation:—"I do solemnly swear (or affirm) that I will faithfully execute the Office of President of the United States, and will to the best of my Ability, preserve, protect and defend the Constitution of the United States."

Section 2   (1) The President shall be Commander in Chief of the Army and Navy of the United States, and of the Militia of the several States, when called into the actual Service of the United States; he may require the Opinion, in writing, of the principal Officer in each of the executive Departments, upon any Subject relating to the Duties of their respective Offices, and he shall have Power to grant Reprieves and Pardons for Offenses against the United States, except in Cases of Impeachment.

(2) He shall have Power, by and with the Advice and Consent of the Senate, to make Treaties, provided two thirds of the Senators present concur; and he shall nominate, and by and with the Advice and Consent of the Senate, shall appoint Ambassadors, other public Ministers and Consuls, Judges of the supreme Court, and all other Officers of the United States, whose Appointments are not herein otherwise provided for, and which shall be established by Law: but the Congress may by Law vest the Appointment of such inferior Officers, as they think proper, in the President alone, in the Courts of Law, or in the Heads of Departments.

(3) The President shall have Power to fill up all Vacancies that may happen during the Recess of the Senate, by granting Commissions which shall expire at the End of their next Session.

Section 3   He shall from time to time give to the Congress Information of the State of the Union, and recommend to their Consideration such Measures as he shall judge necessary and expedient; he may, on extraordinary Occasions, convene both Houses, or either of them, and in Case of Disagreement between them, with Respect to the Time of Adjournment, he may adjourn them to such Time as he shall think proper; he shall receive Ambassadors and other public Ministers; he shall take Care that the Laws be faithfully executed, and shall Commission all the Officers of the United States.

Section 4   The President, Vice President and all Civil Officers of the United States, shall be removed from Office on Impeachment for, and Conviction of, Treason, Bribery, or other high Crimes and Misdemeanors.

Article III

Section 1   The judicial Power of the United States, shall be vested in one supreme Court, and in such inferior Courts as the Congress may from time to time ordain and establish. The Judges, both of the supreme and inferior Courts, shall hold their Offices during good Behaviour, and shall, at stated Times, receive for their Services, a Compensation, which shall not be diminished during their Continuance in Office.

Section 2 (1) The judicial Power shall extend to all Cases, in Law and Equity, arising under this Constitution, the Laws of the United States, and Treaties made, or which shall be made, under their Authority;—to all Cases affecting Ambassadors, other public Ministers and Consuls;—to all Cases of admiralty and maritime Jurisdiction;—to Controversies to which the United States shall be a party;—to Controversies between two or more States;—between a State and Citizens of another State;—between Citizens of different States;—between Citizens of the same State claiming Lands under Grants of different States, and between a State, or the Citizens thereof, and foreign States, Citizens or Subjects.

(2) In all Cases affecting Ambassadors, other public Ministers and Consuls, and those in which a State shall be Party, the supreme Court shall have original Jurisdiction. In all the other Cases before mentioned, the supreme Court shall have appellate Jurisdiction, both as to Law and Fact, with such Exceptions, and under such Regulations as the Congress shall make.

(3) The Trial of all Crimes, except in Cases of Impeachment, shall be by Jury; and such Trial shall be held in the State where the said Crimes shall have been committed; but when not committed within any State, the Trial shall be at such Place or Places as the Congress may by Law have directed.

Section 3 (1) Treason against the United States, shall consist only in levying War against them, or in adhering to their Enemies, giving them Aid and Comfort. No Person shall be convicted of Treason unless on the Testimony of two Witnesses to the same overt Act, or on Confession in open Court.

(2) The Congress shall have Power to declare the Punishment of Treason, but no Attainder of Treason shall work Corruption of Blood, or Forfeiture except during the Life of the Person attainted.

Article IV

Section 1 Full Faith and Credit shall be given in each State to the public Acts, Records, and judicial Proceedings of every other State. And the Congress may by general Laws prescribe the Manner in which such Acts, Records and Proceedings shall be proved, and the Effect thereof.

Section 2 (1) The Citizens of each State shall be entitled to all privileges and Immunities of Citizens in the several States.

(2) A Person charged in any State with Treason, Felony, or other Crime, who shall flee from Justice, and be found in another State, shall on Demand of the executive Authority of the State from which he fled, be delivered up, to be removed to the State having Jurisdiction of the Crime.

(3) No Person held to Service of Labour in one State, under the Laws thereof, escaping into another, shall, in Consequence of any Law or Regulation therein, be discharged from such Service or Labour, but shall be delivered up on Claim of the Party to whom such Service or Labour may be due.

Section 3 (1) New States may be admitted by the Congress into this Union; but no new State shall be formed or erected within the Jurisdiction of any other State; nor any State be formed by the Junction of two or more States, or Parts of States, without the Consent of the Legislatures of the States concerned as well as of the Congress.

(2) The Congress shall have power to dispose of and make all needful Rules and Regulations respecting the Territory or other Property belonging to the United States; and nothing in this Constitution shall be so construed as to Prejudice any Claims of the United States, or of any particular State.

Section 4 The United States shall guarantee to every State in this Union a Republican Form of Government, and shall protect each of them against Invasion; and on Application of the Legislature, or of the Executive (when the Legislature cannot be convened) against domestic Violence.

Article V

The Congress, whenever two thirds of both Houses shall deem it necessary, shall propose Amendments to this Constitution, or, on the Application of the Legislatures of two thirds of the several States, shall call a Convention for proposing Amendments, which, in either Case, shall be valid to all Intents and Purposes, as Part of this Constitution, when ratified by the Legislatures of three fourths of the several States, or by Conventions in three fourths thereof, as the one or the other Mode of Ratification may be proposed by the Congress; Provided that no Amendment which may be made prior to the Year One thousand eight hundred and eight shall in any Manner affect the first and fourth Clauses in the Ninth Section of the first Article; and that no State, without its Consent, shall be deprived of its equal Suffrage in the Senate.

Article VI

(1) All Debts contracted and Engagements entered into, before the Adoption of this Constitution, shall be as valid against the United States under this Constitution, as under the Confederation.

(2) This Constitution, and the Laws of the United States which shall be made in Pursuance thereof; and all Treaties made, or which shall be made, under the Authority of the United States, shall be the supreme Law of the Land; and the Judges in every State shall be bound thereby, any Thing in the Constitution or Laws of any State to the Contrary notwithstanding.

(3) The Senators and Representatives before mentioned, and the Members of the several State Legislatures, and all executive and judicial Officers, both of the United States and of the several States, shall be bound by Oath or Affirmation, to support this Constitution; but no religious Test shall ever be required as a Qualification to any Office or public Trust under the United States.

Article VII

The Ratification of the Conventions of nine States, shall be sufficient for the Establishment of this Constitution between the States so ratifying the Same.

ARTICLES IN ADDITION TO, AND AMENDMENT OF, THE CONSTITUTION OF THE UNITED STATES OF AMERICA, PROPOSED BY CONGRESS, AND RATIFIED BY THE SEVERAL STATES, PURSUANT TO THE FIFTH ARTICLE OF THE ORIGINAL CONSTITUTION

Amendment I (1791)

Congress shall make no law respecting an establishment of religion, or prohibiting the free exercise thereof; or abridging the freedom of speech, or of the press; or the right of the people peaceably to assemble, and to petition the Government for a redress of grievances.

Amendment II (1791)

A well regulated Militia, being necessary to the security of a free state, the right of the people to keep and bear Arms, shall not be infringed.

Amendment III (1791)

No Soldier shall, in time of peace be quartered in any house, without the consent of the Owner, nor in time of war, but in a manner to be prescribed by law.

Amendment IV (1791)

The right of the people to be secure in their persons, houses, papers, and effects, against unreasonable searches and seizures, shall not be violated, and no Warrants shall issue, but upon probable cause, supported by Oath or affirmation, and particularly describing the place to be searched, and the persons or things to be seized.

Amendment V (1791)

No person shall be held to answer for a capital, or otherwise infamous crime, unless on a presentment or indictment of a Grand Jury, except in cases arising in the land or naval forces, or in the Militia, when in actual service in time of War or public danger; nor shall any person be subject for the same offence to be twice put in jeopardy of life or limb; nor shall be compelled in any criminal case to be a witness against himself, nor be deprived of life, liberty, or property, without due process of law; nor shall private property be taken for public use, without just compensation.

Amendment VI (1791)

In all criminal prosecutions, the accused shall enjoy the right to a speedy and public trial, by an impartial jury of the State and district wherein the crime shall have been committed, which district shall have been previously ascertained by law, and to be informed of the nature and cause of the accusation; to be confronted with the witnesses against him; to have compulsory process for obtaining witnesses in his favor, and to have the Assistance of Counsel for his defence.

Amendment VII (1791)

In Suits at common law, where the value in controversy shall exceed twenty dollars, the right of trial by jury shall be preserved, and no fact tried by a jury, shall be otherwise re-examined in any Court of the United States, than according to the rules of the common law.

Amendment VIII (1791)

Excessive bail shall not be required, nor excessive fines imposed, nor cruel and unusual punishments inflicted.

Amendment IX (1791)

The enumeration in the Constitution, of certain rights, shall not be construed to deny or disparage others retained by the people.

Amendment X (1791)

The powers not delegated to the United States by the Constitution, nor prohibited by it to the States, are reserved to the States respectively, or to the people.

Amendment XI (1798)

The Judicial power of the United States shall not be construed to extend to any suit in law or equity, commenced or prosecuted against one of the United States by Citizens of another State, or by Citizens or Subjects of any Foreign State.

Amendment XII (1804)

The Electors shall meet in their respective states and vote by ballot for President and Vice-President, one of whom, at least, shall not be an inhabitant of the same state with themselves; they shall name in their ballots the person voted for as President, and in distinct ballots the person voted for as Vice-President, and they shall make distinct lists of all persons voted for as President, and of all persons voted for as Vice-President, and of the number of votes for each, which lists they shall sign and certify, and transmit sealed to the seat of the government of the United States, directed to the President of the Senate;—The President of the Senate shall, in the presence of the Senate and House of Representatives, open all the certificates and the votes shall then be counted;—The person having the greatest number of votes for President, shall be the President, if such number be a majority of the whole number of Electors appointed; and if no person have such majority, then from the persons having the highest numbers not exceeding three on the list of those voted for as President, the House of Representatives shall choose immediately, by ballot, the President. But in choosing the President, the votes shall be taken by states, the representation from each state having one vote; a quorum for this purpose shall consist of a member or members from two-thirds of the states, and a majority of all the states shall be necessary to a choice. And if the House of Representatives shall not choose a President whenever the right of choice shall devolve upon them, before the fourth day of March next following, then the Vice-President shall act as President, as in the case of the death or other constitutional disability of the President—The person having the greatest number of votes as Vice-President, shall be the Vice-President, if such number be a majority of the whole number of Electors appointed, and if no person have a majority, then from the two highest numbers on the list, the Senate shall choose the Vice-President; A quorum for the purpose shall consist of two-thirds of the whole number of Senators, and a majority of the whole number shall be necessary to a choice. But no person constitutionally ineligible to the office of President shall be eligible to that of Vice-President of the United States.

Amendment XIII (1865)

Section 1 Neither slavery nor involuntary servitude, except as a punishment for crime whereof the party shall have been duly convicted, shall exist within the United States, or any place subject to their jurisdiction.

Section 2 Congress shall have power to enforce this article by appropriate legislation.

Amendment XIV (1868)

Section 1 All persons born or naturalized in the United States and subject to the jurisdiction thereof, are citizens of the United States and of the State wherein they reside. No State shall make or enforce any law which shall abridge the privileges or immunities of citizens of the United States; nor shall any State deprive any person of life, liberty, or property, without due process of law; nor deny to any person within its jurisdiction the equal protection of the laws.

Section 2 Representatives shall be apportioned among the several States according to their respective numbers, counting the whole number of persons in each State, excluding Indians not taxed. But when the right to vote at any election for the choice of electors for President and Vice-President of the United States, Representatives in Congress, the Executive and Judicial officers of a State, or the members of the Legislature thereof, is denied to any of the male inhabitants of such State, being twenty-one years of age, and citizens of the United States, or in any way abridged, except for participation in rebellion, or other crime, the basis of representation therein shall be reduced in the proportion which the number of such male citizens shall bear to the whole number of male citizens twenty-one years of age in such State.

Section 3 No person shall be a Senator or Representative in Congress, or elector of President and Vice-President, or hold any office, civil or military, under the United States, or under any State, who, having previously taken an oath, as a member of Congress, or as an officer of the United States, or as a member of any State legislature, or as an executive or judicial officer of any State, to support the Constitution of the United States, shall have engaged in insurrection or rebellion against the same, or given aid or comfort to the enemies thereof. But Congress may by a vote of two-thirds of each House, remove such disability.

Section 4 The validity of the public debt of the United States, authorized by law, including debts incurred for payment of pensions and bounties for services in suppressing insurrection or rebellion, shall not be questioned. But neither the United States nor any State shall assume or pay any debt or obligation incurred in aid of insurrection or rebellion against the United States, or any claim for the loss or emancipation of any slave; but all such debts, obligations and claims shall be held illegal and void.

Section 5 The Congress shall have power to enforce, by appropriate legislation, the provisions of this article.

Amendment XV (1870)

Section 1 The right of citizens of the United States to vote shall not be denied or abridged by the United States or by any State on account of race, color, or previous condition of servitude.

Section 2 The Congress shall have power to enforce this article by appropriate legislation.

Amendment XVI (1913)

The Congress shall have power to lay and collect taxes on incomes, from whatever source derived, without apportionment among the several States, and without regard to any census or enumeration.

Amendment XVII (1913)

The Senate of the United States shall be composed of two Senators from each State, elected by the people thereof, for six years; and each Senator shall have one vote. The electors in each State shall have the qualifications requisite for electors of the most numerous branch of the State legislatures.

When vacancies happen in the representation of any State in the Senate, the executive authority of such State shall issue writs of election to fill such vacancies: *Provided,* That the legislature of any State may empower the executive thereof to make temporary appointments until the people fill the vacancies by election as the legislature may direct.

This amendment shall not be so construed as to affect the election or term of any Senator chosen before it becomes valid as part of the Constitution.

Amendment XVIII (1919)

Section 1 After one year from the ratification of this article the manufacture, sale, or transportation of intoxicating liquors within, the importation thereof into, or the exportation thereof from the United States and all territory subject to the jurisdiction thereof for beverage purposes is hereby prohibited.

Section 2 The Congress and the several States shall have concurrent power to enforce this article by appropriate legislation.

Section 3 This article shall be inoperative unless it shall have been ratified as an amendment to the Constitution by the legislatures of the several States, as provided in the Constitution, within seven years from the date of the submission hereof to the States by the Congress.

Amendment XIX (1920)

The right of citizens of the United States to vote shall not be denied or abridged by the United States or by any State on account of sex.

Congress shall have power to enforce this article by appropriate legislation.

Amendment XX (1933)

Section 1 The terms of the President and Vice President shall end at noon on the 20th day of January, and the terms of Senators and Representatives at noon on the 3d day of January, of the years in which such terms would have ended if this article had not been ratified; and the terms of their successors shall then begin.

Section 2 The Congress shall assemble at least once in every year, and such meeting shall begin at noon on the 3d day of January, unless they shall by law appoint a different day.

Section 3 If, at the time fixed for the beginning of the term of the President, the President elect shall have died, the Vice President elect shall become President. If a President shall not have been chosen before the time fixed for the beginning of his term, or if the President elect shall have failed to qualify, then the Vice President elect shall act as President until a President shall have qualified; and the Congress may by law provide for the case wherein neither a President elect nor a Vice President elect shall have qualified, declaring who shall then act as President, or the manner in which one who is to act shall be selected, and such person shall act accordingly until a President or Vice President shall have qualified.

Section 4 The Congress may by law provide for the case of the death of any of the persons from whom the House of Representatives may choose a President whenever the right of choice shall have devolved upon them, and for the case of the death of any of the persons from whom the Senate may choose a Vice President whenever the right of choice shall have devolved upon them.

Section 5 Sections 1 and 2 shall take effect on the 15th day of October following the ratification of this article.

Section 6 This article shall be inoperative unless it shall have been ratified as an amendment to the Constitution by the legislatures of three-fourths of the several States within seven years from the date of its submission.

Amendment XXI (1933)

Section 1   The eighteenth article of amendment to the Constitution of the United States is hereby repealed.

Section 2   The transportation or importation into any State, Territory or possession of the United States for delivery or use therein of intoxicating liquors, in violation of the laws thereof, is hereby prohibited.

Section 3   This article shall be inoperative unless it shall have been ratified as an amendment to the Constitution by conventions in the several States, as provided in the Constitution, within seven years from the date of the submission hereof to the States by the Congress.

Amendment XXII (1951)

Section 1   No person shall be elected to the office of the President more than twice, and no person who has held the office of President, or acted as President, for more than two years of a term to which some other person was elected President shall be elected to the office of the President more than once. But this Article shall not apply to any person holding the office of President when this Article was proposed by the Congress, and shall not prevent any person who may be holding the office of President, or acting as President, during the term within which this Article becomes operative from holding the office of President or acting as President during the remainder of such term.

Section 2   This Article shall be inoperative unless it shall have been ratified as an amendment to the Constitution by the legislatures of three-fourths of the several States within seven years from the date of its submission to the States by the Congress.

Amendment XXIII (1961)

Section 1   The District constituting the seat of Government of the United States shall appoint in such manner as the Congress may direct:

A number of electors of President and Vice President equal to the whole number of Senators and Representatives in Congress to which the District would be entitled if it were a State, but in no event more than the least populous State; they shall be in addition to those appointed by the States, but they shall be considered, for the purposes of the election of President and Vice President, to be electors appointed by a State; and they shall meet in the District and perform such duties as provided by the twelfth article of amendment.

Section 2   The Congress shall have power to enforce this article by appropriate legislation.

Amendment XXIV (1964)

Section 1   The right of citizens of the United States to vote in any primary or other election for President or Vice President, for electors for President or Vice President, or for Senator or Representative in Congress, shall not be denied or abridged by the United States or any State by reason of failure to pay any poll tax or other tax.

Section 2   The Congress shall have power to enforce this article by appropriate legislation.

Amendment XXV (1967)

Section 1   In case of the removal of the President from office or of his death or resignation, the Vice President shall become President.

Section 2   Whenever there is a vacancy in the office of the Vice President, the President shall nominate a Vice President who shall take office upon confirmation by a majority vote of both Houses of Congress.

Section 3   Whenever the President transmits to the President pro tempore of the Senate and the Speaker of the House of Representatives his written declaration that he is unable to discharge the powers and duties of his office, and until he transmits to them a written declaration to the contrary, such powers and duties shall be discharged by the Vice President as Acting President.

Section 4   Whenever the Vice President and a majority of either the principal officers of the executive departments or of such other body as

Congress may by law provide, transmit to the President pro tempore of the Senate and the Speaker of the House of Representatives their written declaration that the President is unable to discharge the powers and duties of his office, the Vice President shall immediately assume the powers and duties of the office as Acting President.

Thereafter, when the President transmits to the President pro tempore of the Senate and the Speaker of the House of Representatives his written declaration that no inability exists, he shall resume the powers and duties of his office unless the Vice President and a majority of either the principal officers of the executive department or of such other body as Congress may by law provide, transmit within four days to the President pro tempore of the Senate and the Speaker of the House of Representatives their written declaration that the President is unable to discharge the powers and duties of his office. Thereupon Congress shall decide the issue, assembling within forty-eight hours for that purpose if not in session. If the Congress, within twenty-one days after receipt of the latter written declaration, or, if Congress is not in session, within twenty-one days after Congress is required to assemble, determines by two-thirds vote of both Houses that the President is unable to discharge the powers and duties of his office, the Vice President shall continue to discharge the same as Acting President; otherwise, the President shall resume the powers and duties of his office.

Amendment XXVI (1971)

Section 1 The right of citizens of the United States, who are eighteen years of age or older, to vote shall not be denied or abridged by the United States or by any State on account of age.

Section 2 The Congress shall have power to enforce this article by appropriate legislation.

Amendment XXVII (1992)

No law varying the compensation for the services of the senators and representatives shall take effect, until an election of representatives shall have intervened.

APPENDIX B

SELECTED EXCERPTS FROM THE MODEL PENAL CODE

PART I. GENERAL PROVISIONS

Article 1. Preliminary

Section 1.04. Classes of Crimes; Violations.

(1) An offense defined by this Code or by any other statute of this State, for which a sentence of [death or of] imprisonment is authorized, constitutes a crime. Crimes are classified as felonies, misdemeanors or petty misdemeanors.

(2) A crime is a felony if it is so designated in this Code or if persons convicted thereof may be sentenced [to death or] to imprisonment for a term which, apart from an extended term, is in excess of one year.

(3) A crime is a misdemeanor if it is so designated in this Code or in a statute other than this Code enacted subsequent thereto.

(4) A crime is a petty misdemeanor if it is so designated in this Code or in a statute other than this Code enacted subsequent thereto or if it is defined by a statute other than this Code which now provides that persons convicted thereof may be sentenced to imprisonment for a term of which the maximum is less than one year.

(5) An offense defined by this Code or by any other statute of this State constitutes a violation if it is so designated in this Code or in the law defining the offense or if no other sentence than a fine, or fine and forfeiture or other civil penalty is authorized upon conviction or if it is defined by a statute other than this Code which now provides that the offense shall not constitute a crime. A violation does not constitute a crime and conviction of a violation shall not give rise to any disability or legal disadvantage based on conviction of a criminal offense.

(6) Any offense declared by law to constitute a crime, without specification of the grade thereof or of the sentence authorized upon conviction, is a misdemeanor.

(7) An offense defined by any statute of this State other than this Code shall be classified as provided in this Section and the sentence that may be imposed upon conviction thereof shall hereafter be governed by this Code.

Section 1.05. All Offenses Defined by Statute; Application of General Provisions of the Code.

(1) No conduct constitutes an offense unless it is a crime or violation under this Code or another statute of this State.

(2) The provisions of Part I of the Code are applicable to offenses defined by other statutes, unless the Code otherwise provides.

(3) This Section does not affect the power of a court to punish for contempt or to employ any sanction authorized by law for the enforcement of an order or a civil judgment or decree.

Section 1.12. Proof Beyond a Reasonable Doubt; Affirmative Defenses; Burden of Proving Fact When Not an Element of an Offense; Presumptions.

(1) No person may be convicted of an offense unless each element of such offense is proved beyond a reasonable doubt. In the absence of such proof, the innocence of the defendant is assumed.

(2) Subsection (1) of this Section does not:

(a) require the disproof of an affirmative defense unless and until there is evidence supporting such defense; or

(b) apply to any defense which the Code or another statute plainly requires the defendant to prove by a preponderance of evidence.

(3) A ground of defense is affirmative, within the meaning of Subsection (2)(a) of this Section, when:

    (a) it arises under a section of the Code which so provides; or

    (b) it relates to an offense defined by a statute other than the Code and such statute so provides; or

    (c) it involves a matter of excuse or justification peculiarly within the knowledge of the defendant on which he can fairly be required to adduce supporting evidence.

(4) When the application of the Code depends upon the finding of a fact which is not an element of an offense, unless the Code otherwise provides:

    (a) the burden of proving the fact is on the prosecution or defendant, depending on whose interest or contention will be furthered if the finding should be made; and

    (b) the fact must be proved to the satisfaction of the Court or jury, as the case may be.

(5) When the Code establishes a presumption with respect to any fact which is an element of an offense, it has the following consequences:

    (a) when there is evidence of the facts which give rise to the presumption, the issue of the existence of the presumed fact must be submitted to the jury, unless the Court is satisfied that the evidence as a whole clearly negatives the presumed fact; and

    (b) when the issue of the existence of the presumed fact is submitted to the jury, the Court shall charge that while the presumed fact must, on all the evidence, be proved beyond a reasonable doubt, the law declares that the jury may regard the facts giving rise to the presumption as sufficient evidence of the presumed fact.

(6) A presumption not established by the Code or inconsistent with it has the consequences otherwise accorded it by law.

Section 1.13. General Definitions.

In this Code, unless a different meaning plainly is required:

    (1) "statute" includes the Constitution and a local law or ordinance of a political subdivision of the State;

    (2) "act" or "action" means a bodily movement whether voluntary or involuntary;

    (3) "voluntary" has the meaning specified in Section 2.01;

    (4) "omission" means a failure to act;

    (5) "conduct" means an action or omission and its accompanying state of mind, or, where relevant, a series of acts and omissions;

    (6) "actor" includes, where relevant, a person guilty of an omission;

    (7) "acted" includes, where relevant, "omitted to act";

    (8) "person," "he" and "actor" include any natural person and, where relevant, a corporation or an unincorporated association;

    (9) "element of an offense" means (i) such conduct or (ii) such attendant circumstances or (iii) such a result of conduct as

        (a) is included in the description of the forbidden conduct in the definition of the offense; or

        (b) establishes the required kind of culpability; or

        (c) negatives an excuse or justification for such conduct; or

        (d) negatives a defense under the statute of limitations; or

        (e) establishes jurisdiction or venue;

    (10) "material element of an offense" means an element that does not relate exclusively to the statute of limitations, jurisdiction, venue or to any other matter similarly unconnected with (i) the harm or evil, incident to conduct, sought to be prevented by the law defining the offense, or (ii) the existence of a justification or excuse for such conduct;

    (11) "purposely" has the meaning specified in Section 2.02 and equivalent terms such as "with purpose," "designed" or "with design" have the same meaning;

    (12) "intentionally" or "with intent" means purposely;

(13) "knowingly" has the meaning specified in Section 2.02 and equivalent terms such as "knowing" or "with knowledge" have the same meaning;

(14) "recklessly" has the meaning specified in Section 2.02 and equivalent terms such as "recklessness" or "with recklessness" have the same meaning;

(15) "negligently" has the meaning specified in Section 2.02 and equivalent terms such as "negligence" or "with negligence" have the same meaning;

(16) "reasonably believes" or "reasonable belief" designates a belief which the actor is not reckless or negligent in holding.

Article 2. General Principles of Liability

Section 2.01. Requirement of Voluntary Act; Omission as Basis of Liability; Possession as an Act.

(1) A person is not guilty of an offense unless his liability is based on conduct which includes a voluntary act or the omission to perform an act of which he is physically capable.

(2) The following are not voluntary acts within the meaning of this Section:

(a) a reflex or convulsion;

(b) a bodily movement during unconsciousness or sleep;

(c) conduct during hypnosis or resulting from hypnotic suggestion;

(d) a bodily movement that otherwise is not a product of the effort or determination of the actor, either conscious or habitual.

(3) Liability for the commission of an offense may not be based on an omission unaccompanied by action unless:

(a) the omission is expressly made sufficient by the law defining the offense; or

(b) a duty to perform the omitted act is otherwise imposed by law.

(4) Possession is an act, within the meaning of this Section, if the possessor knowingly procured or received the thing possessed or was aware of his control thereof for a sufficient period to have been able to terminate his possession.

Section 2.02. General Requirements of Culpability.

(1) *Minimum Requirements of Culpability.* Except as provided in Section 2.05, a person is not guilty of an offense unless he acted purposely, knowingly, recklessly or negligently, as the law may require, with respect to each material element of the offense.

(2) *Kinds of Culpability Defined.*

(a) *Purposely.*

A person acts purposely with respect to a material element of an offense when:

(i) if the element involves the nature of his conduct or a result thereof, it is his conscious object to engage in conduct of that nature or to cause such a result; and

(ii) if the element involves the attendant circumstances, he is aware of the existence of such circumstances or he believes or hopes that they exist.

(b) *Knowingly.*

A person acts knowingly with respect to a material element of an offense when:

(i) if the element involves the nature of his conduct or the attendant circumstances, he is aware that his conduct is of that nature or that such circumstances exist; and

(ii) if the element involves a result of his conduct, he is aware that it is practically certain that his conduct will cause such a result.

(c) *Recklessly.*

A person acts recklessly with respect to a material element of an offense when he consciously disregards a substantial and unjustifiable risk that the material element exists or will result from his conduct. The risk must be of such a nature and degree that, considering the nature and purpose of the actor's conduct and the circumstances known to him, its disregard involves a gross deviation from the standard of conduct that a law-abiding person would observe in the actor's situation.

(d) *Negligently.*

A person acts negligently with respect to a material element of an offense when he should be aware of a substantial and unjustifiable risk that the material element exists or will result from his conduct. The risk must be of such a nature and degree that the actor's failure to perceive it, considering the nature and purpose of his conduct and the circumstances known to him, involves a gross deviation from the standard of care that a reasonable person would observe in the actor's situation.

(3) *Culpability Required Unless Otherwise Provided.* When the culpability sufficient to establish a material element of an offense is not prescribed by law, such element is established if a person acts purposely, knowingly or recklessly with respect thereto.

(4) *Prescribed Culpability Requirement Applies to All Material Elements.* When the law defining an offense prescribes the kind of culpability that is sufficient for the commission of an offense, without distinguishing among the material elements thereof, such provision shall apply to all the material elements of the offense, unless a contrary purpose plainly appears.

(5) *Substitutes for Negligence, Recklessness and Knowledge.* When the law provides that negligence suffices to establish an element of an offense, such element also is established if a person acts purposely, knowingly or recklessly. When recklessness suffices to establish an element, such element also is established if a person acts purposely or knowingly. When acting knowingly suffices to establish an element, such element also is established if a person acts purposely.

(6) *Requirement of Purpose Satisfied if Purpose Is Conditional.* When a particular purpose is an element of an offense, the element is established although such purpose is conditional, unless the condition negatives the harm or evil sought to be prevented by the law defining the offense.

(7) *Requirement of Knowledge Satisfied by Knowledge of High Probability.* When knowledge of the existence of a particular fact is an element of an offense, such knowledge is established if a person is aware of a high probability of its existence, unless he actually believes that it does not exist.

(8) *Requirement of Wilfulness Satisfied by Acting Knowingly.* A requirement that an offense be committed wilfully is satisfied if a person acts

knowingly with respect to the material elements of the offense, unless a purpose to impose further requirements appears.

(9) *Culpability as to Illegality of Conduct.* Neither knowledge nor recklessness or negligence as to whether conduct constitutes an offense or as to the existence, meaning or application of the law determining the elements of an offense is an element of such offense, unless the definition of the offense or the Code so provides.

(10) *Culpability as Determinant of Grade of Offense.* When the grade or degree of an offense depends on whether the offense is committed purposely, knowingly, recklessly or negligently, its grade or degree shall be the lowest for which the determinative kind of culpability is established with respect to any material element of the offense.

Section 2.03.   Causal Relationship Between Conduct and Result; Divergence Between Result Designed or Contemplated and Actual Result or Between Probable and Actual Result.

(1)   Conduct is the cause of a result when:

(a)   it is an antecedent but for which the result in question would not have occurred; and

(b)   the relationship between the conduct and result satisfies any additional causal requirements imposed by the Code or by the law defining the offense.

(2)   When purposely or knowingly causing a particular result is an element of an offense, the element is not established if the actual result is not within the purpose or the contemplation of the actor unless:

(a)   the actual result differs from that designed or contemplated, as the case may be, only in the respect that a different person or different property is injured or affected or that the injury or harm designed or contemplated would have been more serious or more extensive than that caused; or

(b)   the actual result involves the same kind of injury or harm as that designed or contemplated and is not too remote or accidental in its occurrence to have a [just] bearing on the actor's liability or on the gravity of his offense.

(3) When recklessly or negligently causing a particular result is an element of an offense, the element is not established if the actual result is not within the risk of which the actor is aware or, in the case of negligence, of which he should be aware unless:

(a) the actual result differs from the probable result only in the respect that a different person or different property is injured or affected or that the probable injury or harm would have been more serious or more extensive than that caused; or

(b) the actual result involves the same kind of injury or harm as the probable result and is not too remote or accidental in its occurrence to have a [just] bearing on the actor's liability or on the gravity of his offense.

(4) When causing a particular result is a material element of an offense for which absolute liability is imposed by law, the element is not established unless the actual result is a probable consequence of the actor's conduct.

Section 2.04. Ignorance or Mistake.

(1) Ignorance or mistake as to a matter of fact or law is a defense if:

(a) the ignorance or mistake negatives the purpose, knowledge, belief, recklessness or negligence required to establish a material element of the offense; or

(b) the law provides that the state of mind established by such ignorance or mistake constitutes a defense.

(2) Although ignorance or mistake would otherwise afford a defense to the offense charged, the defense is not available if the defendant would be guilty of another offense had the situation been as he supposed. In such case, however, the ignorance or mistake of the defendant shall reduce the grade and degree of the offense of which he may be convicted to those of the offense of which he would be guilty had the situation been as he supposed.

(3) A belief that conduct does not legally constitute an offense is a defense to a prosecution for that offense based upon such conduct when:

(a) the statute or other enactment defining the offense is not known to the actor and

has not been published or otherwise reasonably made available prior to the conduct alleged; or

(b) he acts in reasonable reliance upon an official statement of the law, afterward determined to be invalid or erroneous, contained in (i) a statute or other enactment; (ii) a judicial decision, opinion or judgment; (iii) an administrative order or grant of permission; or (iv) an official interpretation of the public officer or body charged by law with responsibility for the interpretation, administration or enforcement of the law defining the offense.

(4) The defendant must prove a defense arising under Subsection (3) of this Section by a preponderance of evidence.

Section 2.05. When Culpability Requirements Are Inapplicable to Violations and to Offenses Defined by Other Statutes; Effect of Absolute Liability in Reducing Grade of Offense to Violation.

(1) The requirements of culpability prescribed by Sections 2.01 and 2.02 do not apply to:

(a) offenses which constitute violations, unless the requirement involved is included in the definition of the offense or the Court determines that its application is consistent with effective enforcement of the law defining the offense; or

(b) offenses defined by statutes other than the Code, insofar as a legislative purpose to impose absolute liability for such offenses or with respect to any material element thereof plainly appears.

(2) Notwithstanding any other provision of existing law and unless a subsequent statute otherwise provides:

(a) when absolute liability is imposed with respect to any material element of an offense defined by a statute other than the Code and a conviction is based upon such liability, the offense constitutes a violation; and

(b) although absolute liability is imposed by law with respect to one or more of the material elements of an offense defined by a statute other than the Code, the culpable commission of the offense may be charged and proved, in which event negligence with respect to such elements constitutes sufficient culpability and the classification of the offense and the sentence that may be imposed therefor upon conviction are determined by Section 1.04 and Article 6 of the Code.

Section 2.06. Liability for Conduct of Another; Complicity.

(1) A person is guilty of an offense if it is committed by his own conduct or by the conduct of another person for which he is legally accountable, or both.

(2) A person is legally accountable for the conduct of another person when:

(a) acting with the kind of culpability that is sufficient for the commission of the offense, he causes an innocent or irresponsible person to engage in such conduct; or

(b) he is made accountable for the conduct of such other person by the Code or by the law defining the offense; or

(c) he is an accomplice of such other person in the commission of the offense.

(3) A person is an accomplice of another person in the commission of an offense if:

(a) with the purpose of promoting or facilitating the commission of the offense, he

(i) solicits such other person to commit it; or

(ii) aids or agrees or attempts to aid such other person in planning or committing it; or

(iii) having a legal duty to prevent the commission of the offense, fails to make proper effect so to do; or

(b) his conduct is expressly declared by law to establish his complicity.

(4) When causing a particular result is an element of an offense, an accomplice in the conduct causing such result is an accomplice in the commission of that offense, if he acts with the kind of culpability, if any, with respect to that result that is sufficient for the commission of the offense.

(5) A person who is legally incapable of committing a particular offense himself may be guilty thereof, if it is committed by the conduct of another person for which he is legally accountable, unless such liability is inconsistent with the purpose of the provision establishing his incapacity.

(6) Unless otherwise provided by the Code or by the law defining the offense, a person is not an accomplice in an offense committed by another person if:

(a) he is a victim of that offense; or

(b) the offense is so defined that his conduct is inevitably incident to its commission; or

(c) he terminates his complicity prior to the commission of the offense and

(i) wholly deprives it of effectiveness in the commission of the offense; or

(ii) gives timely warning to the law enforcement authorities or otherwise makes proper effort to prevent the commission of the offense.

(7) An accomplice may be convicted on proof of the commission of the offense and of his complicity therein, though the person claimed to have committed the offense has not been prosecuted or convicted or has been convicted of a different offense or degree of offense or has an immunity to prosecution or conviction or has been acquitted.

Section 2.07. Liability of Corporations, Unincorporated Associations and Persons Acting, or Under a Duty to Act, in Their Behalf.

(1) A corporation may be convicted of the commission of an offense if:

(a) the offense is a violation or the offense is defined by a statute other than the Code in which a legislative purpose to impose liability on corporations plainly appears and the conduct is performed by an agent of the corporation acting in behalf of the corporation within the scope of his office or employment, except that if the law defining the offense designates the agents for whose conduct the corporation is accountable or the circumstances under which it is accountable, such provisions shall apply; or

(b) the offense consists of an omission to discharge a specific duty of affirmative performance imposed on corporations by law; or

(c) the commission of the offense was authorized, requested, commanded, performed or recklessly tolerated by the board of directors or by a high managerial agent acting in behalf of the corporation within the scope of his office or employment.

(2) When absolute liability is imposed for the commission of an offense, a legislative purpose to impose liability on a corporation shall be assumed, unless the contrary plainly appears.

(3) An unincorporated association may be convicted of the commission of an offense if:

(a) the offense is defined by a statute other than the Code which expressly provides for the liability of such an association and the conduct is performed by an agent of the association acting in behalf of the association within the scope of his office or employment, except that if the law defining the offense designates the agents for whose conduct the association is accountable or the circumstances under which it is accountable, such provisions shall apply; or

(b) the offense consists of an omission to discharge a specific duty of affirmative performance imposed on associations by law.

(4) As used in this Section:

(a) "corporation" does not include an entity organized as or by a governmental agency for the execution of a governmental program;

(b) "agent" means any director, officer, servant, employee or other person authorized to act in behalf of the corporation or association and, in the case of an unincorporated association, a member of such association;

(c) "high managerial agent" means an officer of a corporation or an unincorporated association, or, in the case of a partnership, a partner, or any other agent of a corporation or association having duties of such responsibilities that his conduct may fairly be assumed to represent the policy of the corporation or association.

(5) In any prosecution of a corporation or an unincorporated association for the commission of an offense included within the terms of Subsection (1)(a) or Subsection (3)(a) of this Section, other than an offense for which absolute liability has been imposed, it shall be a defense if the defendant proves by a preponderance of evidence that the high managerial agent having supervisory responsibility over the subject matter of the offense employed due diligence to prevent its commission. This paragraph shall not apply if it is plainly inconsistent with the legislative purpose in defining the particular offense.

(6) (a) A person is legally accountable for any conduct he performs or causes to be performed in the name of the corporation or an unincorporated association or in its behalf to the same extent as if it were performed in his own name or behalf.

(b) Whenever a duty to act is imposed by law upon a corporation or an unincorporated association, any agent of the corporation or association having primary responsibility for the discharge of the duty is legally accountable for a reckless omission to perform the required act to the same extent as if the duty were imposed by law directly upon himself.

(c) When a person is convicted of an offense by reason of his legal accountability for the conduct of a corporation or an unincorporated association, he is subject to the sentence authorized by law when a natural person is convicted of an offense of the grade and the degree involved.

Section 2.08 Intoxication.

(1) Except as provided in Subsection (4) of this Section, intoxication of the actor is not a defense unless it negatives an element of the offense.

(2) When recklessness establishes an element of the offense, if the actor, due to self-induced intoxication, is unaware of a risk of which he would have been aware had he been sober, such unawareness is immaterial.

(3) Intoxication does not, in itself, constitute mental disease within the meaning of Section 4.01.

(4) Intoxication which (a) is not self-induced or (b) is pathological is an affirmative defense if

by reason of such intoxication the actor at the time of his conduct lacks substantial capacity either to appreciate its criminality [wrongfulness] or to conform his conduct to the requirements of law.

(5) *Definitions.* In this Section unless a different meaning plainly is required:

(a) "intoxication" means a disturbance of mental or physical capacities resulting from the introduction of substances into the body;

(b) "self-induced intoxication" means intoxication caused by substances which the actor knowingly introduces into his body, the tendency of which to cause intoxication he knows or ought to know, unless he introduces them pursuant to medical advice or under such circumstances as would afford a defense to a charge of crime;

(c) "pathological intoxication" means intoxication grossly excessive in degree, given the amount of the intoxicant, to which the actor does not know he is susceptible.

Section 2.09 Duress.

(1) It is an affirmative defense that the actor engaged in the conduct charged to constitute an offense because he was coerced to do so by the use of, or a threat to use, unlawful force against his person or the person of another, which a person of reasonable firmness in his situation would have been unable to resist.

(2) The defense provided by this Section is unavailable if the actor recklessly placed himself in a situation in which it was probable that he would be subjected to duress. The defense is also unavailable if he was negligent in placing himself in such a situation, whenever negligence suffices to establish culpability for the offense charged.

(3) It is not a defense that a woman acted on the command of her husband, unless she acted under such coercion as would establish a defense under this Section. [The presumption that a woman, acting in the presence of her husband, is coerced is abolished.]

(4) When the conduct of the actor would otherwise be justifiable under Section 3.02, this Section does not preclude such defense.

Section 2.10. Military Orders.

It is an affirmative defense that the actor, in engaging in the conduct charged to constitute an offense, does no more than execute an order of his superior in the armed services which he does not know to be unlawful.

Section 2.11. Consent.

(1) *In General.* The consent of the victim to conduct charged to constitute an offense or to the result thereof is a defense if such consent negatives an element of the offense or precludes the infliction of the harm or evil sought to be prevented by the law defining the offense.

(2) *Consent to Bodily Harm.* When conduct is charged to constitute an offense because it causes or threatens bodily harm, consent to such conduct or to the infliction of such harm is a defense if:

(a) the bodily harm consented to or threatened by the conduct consented to is not serious; or

(b) the conduct and the harm are reasonably foreseeable hazards of joint participation in a lawful athletic contest or competitive sport; or

(c) the consent establishes a justification for the conduct under Article 3 of the Code.

(3) *Ineffective Consent.* Unless otherwise provided by the Code or by the law defining the offense, assent does not constitute consent if:

(a) it is given by a person who is legally incompetent to authorize the conduct charged to constitute the offense; or

(b) it is given by a person who by reason of youth, mental disease or defect or intoxication is manifestly unable or known by the actor to be unable to make a reasonable judgment as to the nature or harmfulness of the conduct charged to constitute the offense; or

(c) it is given by a person whose improvident consent is sought to be prevented by the law defining the offense; or

(d) it is induced by force, duress or deception of a kind sought to be prevented by the law defining the offense.

Section 2.13. Entrapment.

(1) A public law enforcement official or a person acting in cooperation with such an official

perpetrates an entrapment if for the purpose of obtaining evidence of the commission of an offense, he induces or encourages another person to engage in conduct constituting such offense by either:

(a) making knowingly false representations designed to induce the belief that such conduct is not prohibited; or

(b) employing methods of persuasion or inducement which create a substantial risk that such an offense will be committed by persons other than those who are ready to commit it.

(2) Except as provided in Subsection (3) of this Section, a person prosecuted for an offense shall be acquitted if he proves by a preponderance of evidence that his conduct occurred in response to an entrapment. The issue of entrapment shall be tried by the Court in the absence of the jury.

(3) The defense afforded by this Section is unavailable when causing or threatening bodily injury is an element of the offense charged and the prosecution is based on conduct causing or threatening such injury to a person other than the person perpetrating the entrapment.

Article 3. General Principles of Justification

Section 3.01. *Justification an Affirmative Defense; Civil Remedies Unaffected.*

(1) In any prosecution based on conduct which is justifiable under this Article, justification is an affirmative defense.

(2) The fact that conduct is justifiable under this Article does not abolish or impair any remedy for such conduct which is available in any civil action.

Section 3.02. *Justification Generally: Choice of Evils.*

(1) Conduct which the actor believes to be necessary to avoid harm or evil to himself or to another is justifiable, provided that:

(a) the harm or evil sought to be avoided by such conduct is greater than that sought to be prevented by the law defining the offense charged; and

(b) neither the Code nor other law defining the offense provides exceptions or defenses dealing with the specific situation involved; and

(c) a legislative purpose to exclude the justification claimed does not otherwise plainly appear.

(2) When the actor was reckless or negligent in bringing about the situation requiring a choice of harms or evils or in appraising the necessity for his conduct, the justification afforded by this Section is unavailable in a prosecution for any offense for which recklessness or negligence, as the case may be, suffices to establish culpability.

Section 3.03. *Execution of Public Duty.*

(1) Except as provided in Subsection (2) of this Section, conduct is justifiable when it is required or authorized by:

(a) the law defining the duties or functions of a public officer or the assistance to be rendered to such officer in the performance of his duties; or

(b) the law governing the execution of legal process; or

(c) the judgment or order of a competent court or tribunal; or

(d) the law governing the armed services or the lawful conduct of war; or

(e) any other provision of law imposing a public duty.

(2) The other sections of this Article apply to:

(a) the use of force upon or toward the person of another for any of the purposes dealt with in such sections; and

(b) the use of deadly force for any purpose, unless the use of such force is otherwise expressly authorized by law or occurs in the lawful conduct of war.

(3) The justification afforded by Subsection (1) of this Section applies:

(a) when the actor believes his conduct to be required or authorized by the judgment or direction of a competent court or tribunal or in the lawful execution of legal process, notwithstanding lack of jurisdiction of the court or defect in the legal process; and

(b) when the actor believes his conduct to be required or authorized to assist a public officer in the performance of his duties, notwithstanding that the officer exceeded his legal authority.

Section 3.04. Use of Force in Self-Protection.

(1) *Use of Force Justifiable for Protection of the Person.* Subject to the provisions of this Section and of Section 3.09, the use of force upon or toward another person is justifiable when the actor believes that such force is immediately necessary for the purpose of protecting himself against the use of unlawful force by such other person on the present occasion.

(2) *Limitations on Justifying Necessity for Use of Force.*

(a) The use of force is not justifiable under this Section:

(i) to resist arrest which the actor knows is being made by a peace officer, although the arrest is unlawful; or

(ii) to resist force used by the occupier or possessor of property or by another person on his behalf, where the actor knows that the person using the force is doing so under a claim of right to protect the property, except that this limitation shall not apply if:

(1) the actor is a public officer acting in the performance of his duties or a person lawfully assisting him therein or a person making or assisting in a lawful arrest; or

(2) the actor has been unlawfully dispossessed of the property and is making a re-entry or recaption justified by Section 3.06; or

(3) the actor believes that such force is necessary to protect himself against death or serious bodily harm.

(b) The use of deadly force is not justifiable under this Section unless the actor believes that such force is necessary to protect himself against death, serious bodily harm, kidnapping or sexual intercourse compelled by force or threat; nor is it justifiable if:

(i) the actor, with the purpose of causing death or serious bodily harm,

provoked the use of force against himself in the same encounter; or

(ii) the actor knows that he can avoid the necessity of using such force with complete safety by retreating or by surrendering possession of a thing to a person asserting a claim of right thereto or by complying with a demand that he abstain from any action which he has no duty to take, except that:

(1) the actor is not obliged to retreat from his dwelling or place of work, unless he was the initial aggressor or is assailed in his place of work by another person whose place of work the actor knows it to be; and

(2) a public officer justified in using force in the performance of his duties or a person justified in using force in his assistance or a person justified in using force in making an arrest or preventing an escape is not obliged to desist from efforts to perform such duty, effect such arrest or prevent such escape because of resistance or threatened resistance by or on behalf of the person against whom such action is directed.

(c) Except as required by paragraphs (a) and (b) of this Subsection, a person employing protective force may estimate the necessity thereof under the circumstances as he believes them to be when the force is used, without retreating, surrendering possession, doing any other act which he has no legal duty to do or abstaining from any lawful action.

(3) *Use of Confinement as Protective Force.* The justification afforded by this Section extends to the use of confinement as protective force only if the actor takes all reasonable measures to terminate the confinement as soon as he knows that he safely can, unless the person confined has been arrested on a charge of crime.

Section 3.05. Use of Force for the Protection of Other Persons.

(1) Subject to the provisions of this Section and of Section 3.09, the use of force upon or

toward the person of another is justifiable to protect a third person when:

(a) the actor would be justified under Section 3.04 in using such force to protect himself against the injury he believes to be threatened to the person whom he seeks to protect; and

(b) under the circumstances as the actor believes them to be, the person whom he seeks to protect would be justified in using such protective force; and

(c) the actor believes that his intervention is necessary for the protection of such other person.

(2) Notwithstanding Subsection (1) of this Section:

(a) when the actor would be obliged under Section 3.04 to retreat, to surrender the possession of a thing or to comply with a demand before using force in self-protection, he is not obliged to do so before using force for the protection of another person, unless he knows that he can thereby secure the complete safety of such other person; and

(b) when the person whom the actor seeks to protect would be obliged under Section 3.04 to retreat, to surrender the possession of a thing or to comply with a demand if he knew that he could obtain complete safety by so doing, the actor is obliged to try to cause him to do so before using force in his protection if the actor knows that he can obtain complete safety in that way; and

(c) neither the actor nor the person whom he seeks to protect is obliged to retreat when in the other's dwelling or place of work to any greater extent than in his own.

Section 3.06.   Use of Force for the Protection of Property.

(1) *Use of Force Justifiable for Protection of Property.* Subject to the provisions of this Section and of Section 3.09, the use of force upon or toward the person of another is justifiable when the actor believes that such force is immediately necessary:

(a) to prevent or terminate an unlawful entry or other trespass upon land or a trespass against or the unlawful carrying away of

tangible, movable property, provided that such land or movable property is, or is believed by the actor to be, in his possession or in the possession of another person for whose protection he acts; or

(b) to effect an entry or re-entry upon land or to retake tangible movable property, provided that the actor believes that he or the person by whose authority he acts or a person from whom he or such other person derives title was unlawfully dispossessed of such land or movable property and is entitled to possession, and provided, further, that:

(i) the force is used immediately or on fresh pursuit after such dispossession; or

(ii) the actor believes that the person against whom he uses force has no claim of right to the possession of the property and, in the case of land, the circumstances, as the actor believes them to be, are of such urgency that it would be an exceptional hardship to postpone the entry or re-entry until a court order is obtained.

(2) *Meaning of Possession.* For the purposes of Subsection (1) of this Section:

(a) a person who has parted with the custody of property to another who refuses to restore it to him is no longer in possession, unless the property is movable and was and still is located on land in his possession;

(b) a person who has been dispossessed of land does not regain possession thereof merely by setting foot thereon;

(c) a person who has a license to use or occupy real property is deemed to be in possession thereof except against the licensor acting under claim of right.

(3) *Limitations on Justifiable Use of Force.*

(a) *Request to Desist.* The use of force is justifiable under this Section only if the actor first requests the person against whom such force is used to desist from his interference with the property, unless the actor believes that:

(i) such request would be useless; or

(ii) it would be dangerous to himself or another person to make the request; or

(iii) substantial harm will be done to the physical condition of the property which is sought to be protected before the request can effectively be made.

(b) *Exclusion of Trespasser.* The use of force to prevent or terminate a trespass is not justifiable under this Section if the actor knows that the exclusion of the trespasser will expose him to substantial danger of serious bodily harm.

(c) *Resistance of Lawful Re-entry or Recaption.* The use of force to prevent an entry or re-entry upon land or the recaption of movable property is not justifiable under this Section, although the actor believes that such re-entry or recaption is unlawful, if:

(i) the re-entry or recaption is made by or on behalf of a person who was actually dispossessed of the property; and

(ii) it is otherwise justifiable under paragraph (1)(b) of this Section.

(d) *Use of Deadly Force.* The use of deadly force is not justifiable under this Section unless the actor believes that:

(i) the person against whom the force is used is attempting to dispossess him of his dwelling otherwise than under a claim of right to its possession; or

(ii) the person against whom the force is used is attempting to commit or consummate arson, burglary, robbery or other felonious theft or property destruction and either:

(1) has employed or threatened deadly force against or in the presence of the actor; or

(2) the use of force other than deadly force to prevent the commission or the consummation of the crime would expose the actor or another in his presence to substantial danger of serious bodily harm.

(4) *Use of Confinement as Protective Force.* The justification afforded by this Section extends to the use of confinement as protective force only if the actor takes all reasonable measures to terminate the confinement as soon as he knows that he can do so with safety to the property, unless the person confined has been arrested on a charge of crime.

(5) *Use of Device to Protect Property.* The justification afforded by this Section extends to the use of a device for the purpose of protecting property only if:

(a) the device is not designed to cause or known to create a substantial risk of causing death or serious bodily harm; and

(b) the use of the particular device to protect the property from entry or trespass is reasonable under the circumstances, as the actor believes them to be; and

(c) the device is one customarily used for such a purpose or reasonable care is taken to make known to probable intruders the fact that it is used.

(6) *Use of Force to Pass Wrongful Obstructor.* The use of force to pass a person whom the actor believes to be purposely or knowingly and unjustifiably obstructing the actor from going to a place to which he may lawfully go is justifiable, provided that:

(a) the actor believes that the person against whom he uses force has no claim of right to obstruct the actor; and

(b) the actor is not being obstructed from entry or movement on land which he knows to be in the possession or custody of the person obstructing him, or in the possession or custody of another person by whose authority the obstructor acts, unless the circumstances, as the actor believes them to be, are of such urgency that it would not be reasonable to postpone the entry or movement on such land until a court order is obtained; and

(c) the force used is not greater than would be justifiable if the person obstructing the actor were using force against him to prevent his passage.

Section 3.07. Use of Force in Law Enforcement.

(1) *Use of Force Justifiable to Effect an Arrest.* Subject to the provisions of this Section and of Section 3.09, the use of force upon or toward the person of another is justifiable when the actor is making or assisting in making an arrest and the

actor believes that such force is immediately necessary to effect a lawful arrest.

(2) *Limitations on the Use of Force.*

(a) The use of force is not justifiable under this Section unless:

(i) the actor makes known the purpose of the arrest or believes that it is otherwise known by or cannot reasonably be made known to the person to be arrested; and

(ii) when the arrest is made under a warrant, the warrant is valid or believed by the actor to be valid.

(b) The use of deadly force is not justifiable under this Section unless:

(i) the arrest is for a felony; and

(ii) the person effecting the arrest is authorized to act as a peace officer or is assisting a person whom he believes to be authorized to act as a peace officer; and

(iii) the actor believes that the force employed creates no substantial risk of injury to innocent persons; and

(iv) the actor believes that:

(1) the crime for which the arrest is made involved conduct including the use or threatened use of deadly force; or

(2) there is a substantial risk that the person to be arrested will cause death or serious bodily harm if his apprehension is delayed.

(3) *Use of Force to Prevent Escape from Custody.* The use of force to prevent the escape of an arrested person from custody is justifiable when the force could justifiably have been employed to effect the arrest under which the person is in custody, except that a guard or other person authorized to act as a peace officer is justified in using any force, including deadly force, which he believes to be immediately necessary to prevent the escape of a person from a jail, prison, or other institution for the detention of persons charged with or convicted of a crime.

(4) *Use of Force by Private Person Assisting an Unlawful Arrest.*

(a) A private person who is summoned by a peace officer to assist in effecting an un-

lawful arrest, is justified in using any force which he would be justified in using if the arrest were lawful, provided that he does not believe the arrest is unlawful.

(b) A private person who assists another private person in effecting an unlawful arrest, or who, not being summoned, assists a peace officer in effecting an unlawful arrest, is justified in using any force which he would be justified in using if the arrest were lawful, provided that (i) he believes the arrest is lawful, and (ii) the arrest would be lawful if the facts were as he believes them to be.

(5) *Use of Force to Prevent Suicide or the Commission of a Crime.*

(a) The use of force upon or toward the person of another is justifiable when the actor believes that such force is immediately necessary to prevent such other person from committing suicide, inflicting serious bodily harm upon himself, committing or consummating the commission of a crime involving or threatening bodily harm, damage to or loss of property or a breach of the peace, except that:

(i) any limitations imposed by the other provisions of this Article on the justifiable use of force in self-protection, for the protection of others, the protection of property, the effectuation of an arrest or the prevention of an escape from custody shall apply notwithstanding the criminality of the conduct against which such force is used; and

(ii) the use of deadly force is not in any event justifiable under this Subsection unless:

(1) the actor believes that there is a substantial risk that the person whom he seeks to prevent from committing a crime will cause death or serious bodily harm to another unless the commission or the consummation of the crime is prevented and that the use of such force presents no substantial risk of injury to innocent persons; or

(2) the actor believes that the use of such force is necessary to suppress a riot or mutiny after the rioters or

mutineers have been ordered to disperse and warned, in any particular manner that the law may require, that such force will be used if they do not obey.

(b) The justification afforded by this Subsection extends to the use of confinement as preventive force only if the actor takes all reasonable measures to terminate the confinement as soon as he knows that he safely can, unless the person confined has been arrested on a charge of crime.

Article 4. Responsibility

Section 4.01. Mental Disease or Defect Excluding Responsibility.

(1) A person is not responsible for criminal conduct if at the time of such conduct as a result of mental disease or defect he lacks substantial capacity either to appreciate the criminality [wrongfulness] of his conduct or to conform his conduct to the requirements of law.

(2) As used in this Article, the terms "mental disease or defect" do not include an abnormality manifested only by repeated criminal or otherwise anti-social conduct.

Section 4.02. Evidence of Mental Disease or Defect Admissible When Relevant to Element of the Offense; [Mental Disease or Defect Impairing Capacity as Ground for Mitigation of Punishment in Capital Cases].

(1) Evidence that the defendant suffered from a mental disease or defect is admissible whenever it is relevant to prove that the defendant did or did not have a state of mind which is an element of the offense.

[(2) Whenever the jury or the Court is authorized to determine or to recommend whether or not the defendant shall be sentenced to death or imprisonment upon conviction, evidence that the capacity of the defendant to appreciate the criminality [wrongfulness] of his conduct or to conform his conduct to the requirements of law was impaired as a result of mental disease or defect is admissible in favor of sentence of imprisonment.]

Section 4.03 Mental Disease or Defect Excluding Responsibility Is Affirmative Defense; Requirement of Notice; Form of Verdict and Judgment When Finding of Irresponsibility Is Made.

(1) Mental disease or defect excluding responsibility is an affirmative defense.

(2) Evidence of mental disease or defect excluding responsibility is not admissible unless the defendant, at the time of entering his plea of not guilty or within ten days thereafter or at such later time as the Court may for good cause permit, files a written notice of his purpose to rely on such defense.

(3) When the defendant is acquitted on the ground of mental disease or defect excluding responsibility, the verdict and the judgment shall so state.

Section 4.04. Mental Disease or Defect Excluding Fitness to Proceed.

No person who as a result of mental disease or defect lacks capacity to understand the proceedings against him or to assist in his own defense shall be tried, convicted or sentenced for the commission of an offense so long as such incapacity endures.

Section 4.05. Psychiatric Examination of Defendant with Respect to Mental Disease or Defect.

(1) Whenever the defendant has filed a notice of intention to rely on the defense of mental disease or defect excluding responsibility, or there is reason to doubt his fitness to proceed, or reason to believe that mental disease or defect of the defendant will otherwise become an issue in the cause, the Court shall appoint at least one qualified psychiatrist or shall request the Superintendent of the ____ Hospital to designate at least one qualified psychiatrist, which designation may be or include himself, to examine and report upon the mental condition of the defendant. The Court may order the defendant to be committed to a hospital or other suitable facility for the purpose of the examination for a period of not exceeding sixty days or such longer period as the Court determines to be necessary for the purpose and may direct that a qualified psychiatrist

retained by the defendant be permitted to witness and participate in the examination.

(2) In such examination any method may be employed which is accepted by the medical profession for the examination of those alleged to be suffering from mental disease or defect.

(3) The report of the examination shall include the following: (a) a description of the nature of the examination; (b) a diagnosis of the mental condition of the defendant; (c) if the defendant suffers from a mental disease or defect, an opinion as to his capacity to understand the proceedings against him and to assist in his own defense; (d) when a notice of intention to rely on the defense of irresponsibility has been filed, an opinion as to the extent, if any, to which the capacity of the defendant to appreciate the criminality [wrongfulness] of his conduct or to conform his conduct to the requirements of law was impaired at the time of the criminal conduct charged; and (e) when directed by the Court, an opinion as to the capacity of the defendant to have a particular state of mind which is an element of the offense charged.

If the examination can not be conducted by reason of the unwillingness of the defendant to participate therein, the report shall so state and shall include, if possible, an opinion as to whether such unwillingness of the defendant was the result of mental disease or defect.

The report of the examination shall be filed [in triplicate] with the clerk of the Court, who shall cause copies to be delivered to the district attorney and to counsel for the defendant.

Section 4.08.   *Legal Effect of Acquittal on the Ground of Mental Disease or Defect Excluding Responsibility; Commitment; Release or Discharge.*

(1) When a defendant is acquitted on the ground of mental disease or defect excluding responsibility, the Court shall order him to be committed to the custody of the Commissioner of Mental Hygiene [Public Health] to be placed in an appropriate institution for custody, care and treatment.

(2) If the Commissioner of Mental Hygiene [Public Health] is of the view that a person committed to his custody, pursuant to paragraph (1) of this Section, may be discharged or released on condition without danger to himself or to others, he shall make application for the discharge or release of such person in a report to the Court by which such person was committed and shall transmit a copy of such application and report to the prosecuting attorney of the county [parish] from which the defendant was committed. The Court shall thereupon appoint at least two qualified psychiatrists to examine such person and to report within sixty days, or such longer period as the Court determines to be necessary for the purpose, their opinion as to his mental condition. To facilitate such examination and the proceedings thereon, the Court may cause such person to be confined in any institution located near the place where the Court sits, which may hereafter be designated by the Commissioner of Mental Hygiene [Public Health] as suitable for the temporary detention of irresponsible persons.

(3) If the Court is satisfied by the report filed pursuant to paragraph (2) of this Section and such testimony of the reporting psychiatrists as the Court deems necessary that the committed person may be discharged or released on condition without danger to himself or others, the Court shall order his discharge or his release on such conditions as the Court determines to be necessary. If the Court is not so satisfied, it shall promptly order a hearing to determine whether such person may safely be discharged or released. Any such hearing shall be deemed a civil proceeding and the burden shall be upon the committed person to prove that he may safely be discharged or released. According to the determination of the Court upon the hearing, the committed person shall thereupon be discharged or released on such conditions as the Court determines to be necessary, or shall be recommitted to the custody of the Commissioner of Mental Hygiene [Public Health], subject to discharge or release only in accordance with the procedure prescribed above for a first hearing.

(4) If, within [five] years after the conditional release of a committed person, the Court shall determine, after hearing evidence, that the conditions of release have not been fulfilled and that for the safety of such person or for the safety of

others his conditional release should be revoked, the Court shall forthwith order him to be recommitted to the Commissioner of Mental Hygiene [Public Health], subject to discharge or release only in accordance with the procedure prescribed above for a first hearing.

(5) A committed person may make application for his discharge or release to the Court by which he was committed, and the procedure to be followed upon such application shall be the same as that prescribed above in the case of an application by the Commissioner of Mental Hygiene [Public Health]. However, no such application by a committed person need be considered until he has been confined for a period of not less than [six months] from the date of the order of commitment, and if the determination of the Court be adverse to the application, such person shall not be permitted to file a further application until [one year] has elapsed from the date of any preceding hearing on an application for his release or discharge.

Section 4.09. Statements for Purposes of Examination or Treatment Inadmissible Except on Issue of Mental Condition.

A statement made by a person subjected to psychiatric examination or treatment pursuant to Sections 4.05, 4.06 or 4.08 for purposes of such examination or treatment shall not be admissible in evidence against him in any criminal proceeding on any issue other than that of his mental condition but it shall be admissible upon that issue, whether or not it would otherwise be deemed a privileged communication [, unless such statement constitutes an admission of guilt of the crime charged].

Section 4.10. Immaturity Excluding Criminal Conviction; Transfer of Proceedings to Juvenile Court.

(1) A person shall not be tried for or convicted of an offense if:

(a) at the time of the conduct charged to constitute the offense he was less than sixteen years of age [, in which case the Juvenile Court shall have exclusive jurisdiction]; or

(b) at the time of the conduct charged to constitute the offense he was sixteen or seventeen years of age, unless:

(i) the Juvenile Court has no jurisdiction over him, or,

(ii) the Juvenile Court has entered an order waiving jurisdiction and consenting to the institution of criminal proceedings against him.

(2) No court shall have jurisdiction to try or convict a person of an offense if criminal proceedings against him are barred by Subsection (1) of this Section. When it appears that a person charged with the commission of an offense may be of such an age that criminal proceedings may be barred under Subsection (1) of this Section, the Court shall hold a hearing thereon, and the burden shall be on the prosecution to establish to the satisfaction of the Court that the criminal proceeding is not barred upon such grounds. If the Court determines that the proceeding is barred, custody of the person charged shall be surrendered to the Juvenile Court, and the case, including all papers and processes relating thereto, shall be transferred.

Article 5. Inchoate Crimes

Section 5.01. Criminal Attempt.

(1) *Definition of Attempt.* A person is guilty of an attempt to commit a crime if, acting with the kind of culpability otherwise required for commission of the crime, he:

(a) purposely engages in conduct which would constitute the crime if the attendant circumstances were as he believes them to be; or

(b) when causing a particular result is an element of the crime, does or omits to do anything with the purpose of causing or with the belief that it will cause such result without further conduct on his part; or

(c) purposely does or omits to do anything which, under the circumstances as he believes them to be, is an act or omission constituting a substantial step in a course of conduct planned to culminate in his commission of the crime.

(2) *Conduct Which May Be Held Substantial Step Under Subsection (1)(c).* Conduct shall not be held to constitute a substantial step under Subsection (1)(c) of this Section unless it is strongly

corroborative of the actor's criminal purpose. Without negativing the sufficiency of other conduct, the following, if strongly corroborative of the actor's criminal purpose, shall not be held insufficient as a matter of law:

(a) lying in wait, searching for or following the contemplated victim of the crime;

(b) enticing or seeking to entice the contemplated victim of the crime to go to the place contemplated for its commission;

(c) reconnoitering the place contemplated for the commission of the crime;

(d) unlawful entry of a structure, vehicle or enclosure in which it is contemplated that the crime will be committed;

(e) possession of materials to be employed in the commission of the crime, which are specially designed for such unlawful use or which can serve no lawful purpose of the actor under the circumstances;

(f) possession, collection or fabrication of materials to be employed in the commission of the crime, at or near the place contemplated for its commission, where such possession, collection or fabrication serves no lawful purpose of the actor under the circumstances;

(g) soliciting an innocent agent to engage in conduct constituting an element of the crime.

(3) *Conduct Designed to Aid Another in Commission of a Crime.* A person who engages in conduct designed to aid another to commit a crime which would establish his complicity under Section 2.06 if the crime were committed by such other person, is guilty of an attempt to commit the crime, although the crime is not committed or attempted by such other person.

(4) *Renunciation of Criminal Purpose.* When the actor's conduct would otherwise constitute an attempt under Subsection (1)(b) or (1)(c) of this Section, it is an affirmative defense that he abandoned his effort to commit the crime or otherwise prevented its commission, under circumstances manifesting a complete and voluntary renunciation of his criminal purpose. The establishment of such defense does not, however, affect the liability of an accomplice who did not join in such abandonment or prevention.

Within the meaning of this Article, renunciation of criminal purpose is not voluntary if it is motivated, in whole or in part, by circumstances, not present or apparent at the inception of the actor's course of conduct, which increase the probability of detection or apprehension or which make more difficult the accomplishment of the criminal purpose. Renunciation is not complete if it is motivated by a decision to postpone the criminal conduct until a more advantageous time or to transfer the criminal effort to another but similar objective or victim.

Section 5.02. Criminal Solicitation.

(1) *Definition of Solicitation.* A person is guilty of solicitation to commit a crime if with the purpose of promoting or facilitating its commission he commands, encourages or requests another person to engage in specific conduct which would constitute such crime or an attempt to commit such crime or which would establish his complicity in its commission or attempted commission.

(2) *Uncommunicated Solicitation.* It is immaterial under Subsection (1) of this Section that the actor fails to communicate with the person he solicits to commit a crime if his conduct was designed to effect such communication.

(3) *Renunciation of Criminal Purpose.* It is an affirmative defense that the actor, after soliciting another person to commit a crime, persuaded him not to do so or otherwise prevented the commission of the crime, under circumstances manifesting a complete and voluntary renunciation of his criminal purpose.

Section 5.03. Criminal Conspiracy.

(1) *Definition of Conspiracy.* A person is guilty of conspiracy with another person or persons to commit a crime if with the purpose of promoting or facilitating its commission he:

(a) agrees with such other person or persons that they or one or more of them will engage in conduct which constitutes such crime or an attempt or solicitation to commit such crime; or

(b) agrees to aid such other person or persons in the planning or commission of such crime or of an attempt or solicitation to commit such crime.

(2) *Scope of Conspiratorial Relationship.* If a person guilty of conspiracy, as defined by Subsection (1) of this Section, knows that a person with whom he conspires to commit a crime has conspired with another person or persons to commit the same crime, he is guilty of conspiring with such other person or persons, whether or not he knows their identity, to commit such crime.

(3) *Conspiracy With Multiple Criminal Objectives.* If a person conspires to commit a number of crimes, he is guilty of only one conspiracy so long as such multiple crimes are the object of the same agreement or continuous conspiratorial relationship.

(4) *Joinder and Venue in Conspiracy Prosecutions.*

(a) Subject to the provisions of paragraph (b) of this Subsection, two or more persons charged with criminal conspiracy may be prosecuted jointly if:

(i) they are charged with conspiring with one another; or

(ii) the conspiracies alleged, whether they have the same or different parties, are so related that they constitute different aspects of a scheme of organized criminal conduct.

(b) In any joint prosecution under paragraph (a) of this Subsection:

(i) no defendant shall be charged with a conspiracy in any county [parish or district] other than one in which he entered into such conspiracy or in which an overt act pursuant to such conspiracy was done by him or by a person with whom he conspired; and

(ii) neither the liability of any defendant nor the admissibility against him of evidence of acts or declarations of another shall be enlarged by such joinder; and

(iii) the Court shall order a severance or take a special verdict as to any defendant who so requests, if it deems it necessary or appropriate to promote the fair determination of his guilt or innocence, and shall take any other proper measures to protect the fairness of the trial.

(5) *Overt Act.* No person may be convicted of conspiracy to commit a crime, other than a felony of the first or second degree, unless an overt act in pursuance of such conspiracy is alleged and proved to have been done by him or by a person with whom he conspired.

(6) *Renunciation of Criminal Purpose.* It is an affirmative defense that the actor, after conspiring to commit a crime, thwarted the success of the conspiracy, under circumstances manifesting a complete and voluntary renunciation of his criminal purpose.

(7) *Duration of Conspiracy.* For purposes of Section 1.06(4):

(a) conspiracy is a continuing course of conduct which terminates when the crime or crimes which are its object are committed or the agreement that they be committed is abandoned by the defendant and by those with whom he conspired; and

(b) such abandonment is presumed if neither the defendant nor anyone with whom he conspired does any overt act in pursuance of the conspiracy during the applicable period of limitation; and

(c) if an individual abandons the agreement, the conspiracy is terminated as to him only if and when he advises those with whom he conspired of his abandonment or he informs the law enforcement authorities of the existence of the conspiracy and of his participation therein.

Section 5.04. Incapacity, Irresponsibility or Immunity of Party to Solicitation or Conspiracy.

(1) Except as provided in Subsection (2) of this Section, it is immaterial to the liability of a person who solicits or conspires with another to commit a crime that:

(a) he or the person whom he solicits or with whom he conspires does not occupy a particular position or have a particular characteristic which is an element of such crime, if he believes that one of them does; or

(b) the person whom he solicits or with whom he conspires is irresponsible or has an immunity to prosecution or conviction for the commission of the crime.

(2) It is a defense to a charge of solicitation or conspiracy to commit a crime that if the criminal

object were achieved, the actor would not be guilty of a crime under the law defining the offense or as an accomplice under Section 2.06(5) or 2.06(6)(a) or (b).

Section 5.05. Grading of Criminal Attempt, Solicitation and Conspiracy; Mitigation in Cases of Lesser Danger; Multiple Convictions Barred.

(1) *Grading.* Except as otherwise provided in this Section, attempt, solicitation and conspiracy are crimes of the same grade and degree as the most serious offense which is attempted or solicited or is an object of the conspiracy. An attempt, solicitation or conspiracy to commit a [capital crime or a] felony of the first degree is a felony of the second degree.

(2) *Mitigation.* If the particular conduct charged to constitute a criminal attempt, solicitation or conspiracy is so inherently unlikely to result or culminate in the commission of a crime that neither such conduct nor the actor presents a public danger warranting the grading of such offense under this Section, the Court shall exercise its power under Section 6.12 to enter judgment and impose sentence for a crime of lower grade or degree or, in extreme cases, may dismiss the prosecution.

(3) *Multiple Convictions.* A person may not be convicted of more than one offense defined by this Article for conduct designed to commit or to culminate in the commission of the same crime.

Section 5.06. Possessing Instruments of Crime; Weapons.

(1) *Criminal Instruments Generally.* A person commits a misdemeanor if he possesses any instrument of crime with purpose to employ it criminally. "Instrument of crime" means:

(a) anything specially made or specially adapted [sic] for criminal use; or

(b) anything commonly used for criminal purposes and possessed by the actor under circumstances which do not negative unlawful purpose.

(2) *Presumption of Criminal Purpose from Possession of Weapon.* If a person possesses a firearm or other weapon on or about his person, in a vehicle occupied by him, or otherwise readily available for use, it shall be presumed that he had the purpose to employ it criminally, unless:

(a) the weapon is possessed in the actor's home or place of business;

(b) the actor is licensed or otherwise authorized by law to possess such weapon; or

(c) the weapon is of a type commonly used in lawful sport.

"Weapon" means anything readily capable of lethal use and possessed under circumstances not manifestly appropriate for lawful uses which it may have; the term includes a firearm which is not loaded or lacks a clip or other component to render it immediately operable, and components which can readily be assembled into a weapon.

(3) *Presumptions as to Possession of Criminal Instruments in Automobiles.* Where a weapon or other instrument of crime is found in an automobile, it is presumed to be in the possession of the occupant if there is but one. If there is more than one occupant, it shall be presumed to be in the possession of all, except under the following circumstances:

(a) where it is found upon the person of one of the occupants;

(b) where the automobile is not a stolen one and the weapon or instrument is found out of view in a glove compartment, car trunk, or other enclosed customary depository, in which case it shall be presumed to be in the possession of the occupant or occupants who own or have authority to operate the automobile;

(c) in the case of a taxicab, a weapon or instrument found in the passenger's portion of the vehicle shall be presumed to be in the possession of all the passengers, if there are any, and, if not, in the possession of the driver.

Section 5.07. Prohibited Offensive Weapons.

A person commits a misdemeanor if, except as authorized by law, he makes, repairs, sells, or otherwise deals in, uses or possesses any offensive weapon. "Offensive weapon" means any bomb, machine gun, sawed-off shotgun, firearm specially made or specially adapted for concealment or silent discharge, any blackjack, sandbag, metal knuckles, dagger, or other implement for the infliction of serious bodily injury which serves no common lawful purpose. It is a defense under this Section for the defendant to prove by a preponderance of evidence that he possessed or dealt with the weapon solely as a curio or in a dramatic performance, or that he possessed it briefly in consequence of having found it or taken it from an aggressor, or under circumstances similarly negativing any purpose or likelihood that the weapon would be used unlawfully. The presumptions provided in Section 5.06(3) are applicable to prosecutions under this Section.

PART II.   DEFINITION OF SPECIFIC CRIMES

Offenses Involving Danger to the Person

Article 210.   Criminal Homicide

Section 210.0.   Definitions.

In Articles 210–213, unless a different meaning plainly is required:

(1) "human being" means a person who has been born and is alive;

(2) "bodily injury" means physical pain, illness or any impairment of physical condition;

(3) "serious bodily injury" means bodily injury which creates a substantial risk of death or which causes serious, permanent disfigurement, or protracted loss or impairment of the function of any bodily member or organ;

(4) "deadly weapon" means any firearm, or other weapon, device, instrument, material or substance, whether animate or inanimate, which in the manner it is used or is intended to be used is known to be capable of producing death or serious bodily injury.

Section 210.1   Criminal Homicide.

(1) A person is guilty of criminal homicide if he purposely, knowingly, recklessly or negligently causes the death of another human being.

(2) Criminal homicide is murder, manslaughter or negligent homicide.

Section 210.2.   Murder.

(1) Except as provided in Section 210.3(1)(b), criminal homicide constitutes murder when:

(a) it is committed purposely or knowingly; or

(b) it is committed recklessly under circumstances manifesting extreme indifference to the value of human life. Such recklessness and indifference are presumed if the actor is engaged or is an accomplice in the commission of, or an attempt to commit, or flight after committing or attempting to commit robbery, rape or deviate sexual intercourse by force or threat of force, arson, burglary, kidnapping or felonious escape.

(2) Murder is a felony of the first degree [but a person convicted of murder may be sentenced to death, as provided in Section 210.6].[1]

Section 210.3.   Manslaughter.

(1) Criminal homicide constitutes manslaughter when:

(a) it is committed recklessly; or

(b) a homicide which would otherwise be murder is committed under the influence of extreme mental or emotional disturbance for which there is reasonable explanation or excuse. The reasonableness of such explanation or excuse shall be determined from the viewpoint of a person in the actor's situation under the circumstances as he believes them to be.

(2) Manslaughter is a felony of the second degree.

Section 210.4.   Negligent Homicide.

(1) Criminal homicide constitutes negligent homicide when it is committed negligently.

(2) Negligent homicide is a felony of the third degree.

Section 210.5. Causing or Aiding Suicide.

(1) *Causing Suicide as Criminal Homicide.* A person may be convicted of criminal homicide for causing another to commit suicide only if he

---

[1] .... The brackets are meant to reflect the fact that the Institute took no position on the desirability of the death penalty. ...

purposely causes such suicide by force, duress or deception.

(2) *Aiding or Soliciting Suicide as an Independent Offense.* A person who purposely aids or solicits another to commit suicide is guilty of a felony of the second degree if his conduct causes such suicide or an attempted suicide, and otherwise of a misdemeanor.

Section 210.6. *Sentence of Death for Murder; Further Proceedings to Determine Sentence.*

(1) *Death Sentence Excluded.* When a defendant is found guilty of murder, the Court shall impose sentence for a felony of the first degree if it is satisfied that:

(a) none of the aggravating circumstances enumerated in Subsection (3) of this Section was established by the evidence at the trial or will be established if further proceedings are initiated under Subsection (2) of this Section; or

(b) substantial mitigating circumstances, established by the evidence at the trial, call for leniency; or

(c) the defendant, with the consent of the prosecuting attorney and the approval of the Court, pleaded guilty to murder as a felony of the first degree; or

(d) the defendant was under 18 years of age at the time of the commission of the crime; or

(e) the defendant's physical or mental condition calls for leniency; or

(f) although the evidence suffices to sustain the verdict, it does not foreclose all doubt respecting the defendant's guilt.

(2) *Determination by Court or by Court and Jury.* Unless the Court imposes sentence under Subsection (1) of this Section, it shall conduct a separate proceeding to determine whether the defendant should be sentenced for a felony of the first degree or sentenced to death. The proceeding shall be conducted before the Court alone if the defendant was convicted by a Court sitting without a jury or upon his plea of guilty or if the prosecuting attorney and the defendant waive a jury with respect to sentence. In other cases it shall be conducted before the Court sitting with the jury which determined the defendant's guilt or, if the Court for good cause shown discharges that jury, with a new jury empanelled for the purpose.

In the proceeding, evidence may be presented as to any matter that the Court deems relevant to sentence, including but not limited to the nature and circumstances of the crime, the defendant's character, background, history, mental and physical condition and any of the aggravating or mitigating circumstances enumerated in Subsections (3) and (4) of this Section. Any such evidence not legally privileged, which the Court deems to have probative force, may be received, regardless of its admissibility under the exclusionary rules of evidence, provided that the defendant's counsel is accorded a fair opportunity to rebut any hearsay statements. The prosecuting attorney and the defendant or his counsel shall be permitted to present argument for or against sentence of death.

The determination whether sentence of death shall be imposed shall be in the discretion of the Court, except that when the proceeding is conducted before the Court sitting with a jury, the Court shall not impose sentence of death unless it submits to the jury the issue whether the defendant should be sentenced to death or to imprisonment and the jury returns a verdict that the sentence should be death. If the jury is unable to reach a unanimous verdict, the Court shall dismiss the jury and impose sentence for a felony of the first degree.

The Court, in exercising its discretion as to sentence, and the jury, in determining upon its verdict, shall take into account the aggravating and mitigating circumstances enumerated in Subsections (3) and (4) and any other facts that it deems relevant, but it shall not impose or recommend sentence of death unless it finds one of the aggravating circumstances enumerated in Subsection (3) and further finds that there are no mitigating circumstances sufficiently substantial to call for leniency. When the issue is submitted to the jury, the Court shall so instruct and also shall inform the jury of the nature of the sentence of imprisonment that may be imposed, including its implication with respect to possible release upon parole, if the jury verdict is against sentence of death.

Alternative formulation of Subsection (2):

(2) *Determination by Court.* Unless the Court imposes sentence under Subsection (1) of this

Section, it shall conduct a separate proceeding to determine whether the defendant should be sentenced for a felony of the first degree or sentenced to death. In the proceeding, the Court, in accordance with Section 7.07, shall consider the report of the presentence investigation and, if a psychiatric examination has been ordered, the report of such examination. In addition, evidence may be presented as to any matter that the Court deems relevant to sentence, including but not limited to the nature and circumstances of the crime, the defendant's character, background, history, mental and physical condition and any of the aggravating or mitigating circumstances enumerated in Subsections (3) and (4) of this Section. Any such evidence not legally privileged, which the Court deems to have probative force, may be received, regardless of its admissibility under the exclusionary rules of evidence, provided that the defendant's counsel is accorded a fair opportunity to rebut any hearsay statements. The prosecuting attorney and the defendant or his counsel shall be permitted to present argument for or against sentence of death.

The determination whether sentence of death shall be imposed shall be in the discretion of the Court. In exercising such discretion, the Court shall take into account the aggravating and mitigating circumstances enumerated in Subsections (3) and (4) and any other facts that it deems relevant but shall not impose sentence of death unless it finds one of the aggravating circumstances enumerated in Subsection (3) and further finds that there are no mitigating circumstances sufficiently substantial to call for leniency.

(3) *Aggravating Circumstances.*

(a) The murder was committed by a convict under sentence of imprisonment.

(b) The defendant was previously convicted of another murder or of a felony involving the use or threat of violence to the person.

(c) At the time the murder was committed the defendant also committed another murder.

(d) The defendant knowingly created a great risk of death to many persons.

(e) The murder was committed while the defendant was engaged or was an accomplice in the commission of, or an attempt to commit, or flight after committing or attempting to commit robbery, rape or deviate sexual intercourse by force or threat of force, arson, burglary or kidnapping.

(f) The murder was committed for the purpose of avoiding or preventing a lawful arrest or effecting an escape from lawful custody.

(g) The murder was committed for pecuniary gain.

(h) The murder was especially heinous, atrocious or cruel, manifesting exceptional depravity.

(4) *Mitigating Circumstances.*

(a) The defendant has no significant history of prior criminal activity.

(b) The murder was committed while the defendant was under the influence of extreme mental or emotional disturbance.

(c) The victim was a participant in the defendant's homicidal conduct or consented to the homicidal act.

(d) The murder was committed under circumstances which the defendant believed to provide a moral justification or extenuation for his conduct.

(e) The defendant was an accomplice in a murder committed by another person and his participation in the homicidal act was relatively minor.

(f) The defendant acted under duress or under the domination of another person.

(g) At the time of the murder, the capacity of the defendant to appreciate the criminality [wrongfulness] of his conduct or to conform his conduct to the requirements of law was impaired as a result of mental disease or defect or intoxication.

(h) The youth of the defendant at the time of the crime.

Article 211. Assault; Reckless Endangering; Threats

Section 211.0. Definitions.

In this Article, the definitions given in Section 210.0 apply unless a different meaning plainly is required.

Section 211.1 *Assault.*

(1) *Simple Assault.* A person is guilty of assault if he:

    (a) attempts to cause or purposely, knowingly or recklessly causes bodily injury to another; or

    (b) negligently causes bodily injury to another with a deadly weapon; or

    (c) attempts by physical menace to put another in fear of imminent serious bodily injury.

Simple assault is a misdemeanor unless committed in a fight or scuffle entered into by mutual consent, in which case it is a petty misdemeanor.

(2) *Aggravated Assault.* A person is guilty of aggravated assault if he:

    (a) attempts to cause serious bodily injury to another, or causes such injury purposely, knowingly or recklessly under circumstances manifesting extreme indifference to the value of human life; or

    (b) attempts to cause or purposely or knowingly causes bodily injury to another with a deadly weapon.

Aggravated assault under paragraph (a) is a felony of the second degree; aggravated assault under paragraph (b) is a felony of the third degree.

Section 211.2. *Recklessly Endangering Another Person.*

A person commits a misdemeanor if he recklessly engages in conduct which places or may place another person in danger of death or serious bodily injury. Recklessness and danger shall be presumed where a person knowingly points a firearm at or in the direction of another, whether or not the actor believed the firearm to be loaded.

Section 211.3. *Terroristic Threats.*

A person is guilty of a felony of the third degree if he threatens to commit any crime of violence with purpose to terrorize another or to cause evacuation of a building, place of assembly, or facility of public transportation, or otherwise to cause serious public inconvenience, or in reckless disregard of the risk of causing such terror or inconvenience.

Article 212. Kidnapping and Related Offenses; Coercion

Section 212.0. *Definitions.*

In this Article, the definitions given in section 210.0 apply unless a different meaning plainly is required.

Section 212.1. *Kidnapping.*

A person is guilty of kidnapping if he unlawfully removes another from his place of residence or business, or a substantial distance from the vicinity where he is found, or if he unlawfully confines another for a substantial period in a place of isolation, with any of the following purposes:

    (a) to hold for ransom or reward, or as a shield or hostage; or

    (b) to facilitate commission of any felony or flight thereafter; or

    (c) to inflict bodily injury on or to terrorize the victim or another; or

    (d) to interfere with the performance of any governmental or political function.

Kidnapping is a felony of the first degree unless the actor voluntarily releases the victim alive and in a safe place prior to trial, in which case it is a felony of the second degree. A removal or confinement is unlawful within the meaning of this Section if it is accomplished by force, threat or deception, or, in the case of a person who is under the age of 14 or incompetent, if it is accomplished without the consent of a parent, guardian or other person responsible for general supervision of his welfare.

Section 212.2. *Felonious Restraint.*

A person commits a felony of the third degree if he knowingly:

    (a) restrains another unlawfully in circumstances exposing him to risk of serious bodily injury; or

    (b) holds another in a condition of involuntary servitude.

Section 212.3 *False Imprisonment.*

A person commits a misdemeanor if he knowingly restrains another unlawfully so as to interfere substantially with his liberty.

Section 212.4 Interference with Custody.

(1) *Custody of Children.* A person commits an offense if he knowingly or recklessly takes or entices any child under the age of 18 from the custody of its parent, guardian or other lawful custodian, when he has no privilege to do so. It is an affirmative defense that:

(a) the actor believed that his action was necessary to preserve the child from danger to its welfare; or

(b) the child, being at the time not less than 14 years old, was taken away at its own instigation without enticement and without purpose to commit a criminal offense with or against the child.

Proof that the child was below the critical age gives rise to a presumption that the actor knew the child's age or acted in reckless disregard thereof. The offense is a misdemeanor unless the actor, not being a parent or person in equivalent relation to the child, acted with knowledge that his conduct would cause serious alarm for the child's safety, or in reckless disregard of a likelihood of causing such alarm, in which case the offense is a felony of the third degree.

(2) *Custody of Committed Persons.* A person is guilty of a misdemeanor if he knowingly or recklessly takes or entices any committed person away from lawful custody when he is not privileged to do so. "Committed person" means, in addition to anyone committed under judicial warrant, any orphan, neglected or delinquent child, mentally defective or insane person, or other dependent or incompetent person entrusted to another's custody by or through a recognized social agency or otherwise by authority of law.

Section 212.5. Criminal Coercion.

(1) *Offense Defined.* A person is guilty of criminal coercion if, with purpose unlawfully to restrict another's freedom of action to his detriment, he threatens to:

(a) commit any criminal offense; or

(b) accuse anyone of a criminal offense; or

(c) expose any secret tending to subject any person to hatred, contempt or ridicule, or to impair his credit or business repute; or

(d) take or withhold action as an official, or cause an official to take or withhold action.

It is an affirmative defense to prosecution based on paragraphs (b), (c) or (d) that the actor believed the accusation or secret to be true or the proposed official action justified and that his purpose was limited to compelling the other to behave in a way reasonably related to the circumstances which were the subject of the accusation, exposure or proposed official action, as by desisting from further misbehavior, making good a wrong done, refraining from taking any action or responsibility for which the actor believes the other disqualified.

(2) *Grading.* Criminal coercion is a misdemeanor unless the threat is to commit a felony or the actor's purpose is felonious, in which cases the offense is a felony of the third degree.

Article 213. Sexual Offenses

Section 213.0. Definitions.

In this Article, unless a different meaning plainly is required:

(1) the definitions given in Section 210.0 apply;

(2) "Sexual intercourse" includes intercourse per os or per anum, with some penetration however slight; emission is not required;

(3) "deviate sexual intercourse" means sexual intercourse per os or per anum between human beings who are not husband and wife, and any form of sexual intercourse with an animal.

Section 213.1. Rape and Related Offenses.

(1) *Rape.* A male who has sexual intercourse with a female not his wife is guilty of rape if:

(a) he compels her to submit by force or by threat of imminent death, serious bodily injury, extreme pain or kidnapping, to be inflicted on anyone; or

(b) he has substantially impaired her power to appraise or control her conduct by administering or employing without her knowledge drugs, intoxicants or other means for the purpose of preventing resistance; or

(c) the female is unconscious; or

(d) the female is less than 10 years old.

Rape is a felony of the second degree unless (i) in the course thereof the actor inflicts serious bodily injury upon anyone, or (ii) the victim was not a voluntary social companion of the actor upon the occasion of the crime and had not previously permitted him sexual liberties, in which cases the offense is a felony of the first degree.

(2) *Gross Sexual Imposition.* A male who has sexual intercourse with a female not his wife commits a felony of the third degree if:

(a) he compels her to submit by any threat that would prevent resistance by a woman of ordinary resolution; or

(b) he knows that she suffers from a mental disease or defect which renders her incapable of appraising the nature of her conduct; or

(c) he knows that she is unaware that a sexual act is being committed upon her or that she submits because she mistakenly supposes that he is her husband.

Section 213.2. Deviate Sexual Intercourse by Force or Imposition.

(1) *By Force or Its Equivalent.* A person who engages in deviate sexual intercourse with another person, or who causes another to engage in deviate sexual intercourse, commits a felony of the second degree if:

(a) he compels the other person to participate by force or by threat of imminent death, serious bodily injury, extreme pain or kidnapping, to be inflicted on anyone; or

(b) he has substantially impaired the other person's power to appraise or control his conduct, by administering or employing without the knowledge of the other person drugs, intoxicants or other means for the purpose of preventing resistance; or

(c) the other person is unconscious; or

(d) the other person is less than 10 years old.

(2) *By Other Imposition.* A person who engages in deviate sexual intercourse with another person, or who causes another to engage in deviate sexual intercourse, commits a felony of the third degree if:

(a) he compels the other person to participate by any threat that would prevent resistance by a person of ordinary resolution; or

(b) he knows that the other person suffers from a mental disease or defect which renders him incapable of appraising the nature of his conduct; or

(c) he knows that the other person submits because he is unaware that a sexual act is being committed upon him.

Section 213.3. Corruption of Minors and Seduction.

(1) *Offense Defined.* A male who has sexual intercourse with a female not his wife, or any person who engages in deviate sexual intercourse or causes another to engage in deviate sexual intercourse, is guilty of an offense if:

(a) the other person is less than [16] years old and the actor is at least [4] years older than the other person; or

(b) the other person is less than 21 years old and the actor is his guardian or otherwise responsible for general supervision of his welfare; or

(c) the other person is in custody of law or detained in a hospital or other institution and the actor has supervisory or disciplinary authority over him; or

(d) the other person is a female who is induced to participate by a promise of marriage which the actor does not mean to perform.

(2) *Grading.* An offense under paragraph (a) of Subsection (1) is a felony of the third degree. Otherwise an offense under this section is a misdemeanor.

Section 213.4 Sexual Assault.

A person who has sexual contact with another not his spouse, or causes such other to have sexual conduct with him, is guilty of sexual assault, a misdemeanor, if:

(1) he knows that the conduct is offensive to the other person; or

(2) he knows that the other person suffers from a mental disease or defect which renders him or her incapable of appraising the nature of his or her conduct; or

(3) he knows that the other person is unaware that a sexual act is being committed; or

(4) the other person is less than 10 years old; or

(5) he has substantially impaired the other person's power to appraise or control his or her conduct, by administering or employing without the other's knowledge drugs, intoxicants or other means for the purpose of preventing resistance; or

(6) the other person is less than [16] years old and the actor is at least [four] years older than the other person; or

(7) the other person is less than 21 years old and the actor is his guardian or otherwise responsible for general supervision of his welfare; or

(8) the other person is in custody of law or detained in a hospital or other institution and the actor has supervisory or disciplinary authority over him.

Sexual contact is any touching of the sexual or other intimate parts of the person for the purpose of arousing or gratifying sexual desire.

Section 213.5. Indecent Exposure.

A person commits a misdemeanor if, for the purpose of arousing or gratifying sexual desire of himself or of any person other than his spouse, he exposes his genitals under circumstances in which he knows his conduct is likely to cause affront or alarm.

Section 213.6 Provisions Generally Applicable to Article 213.

(1) *Mistake as to Age.* Whenever in this Article the criminality of conduct depends on a child's being below the age of 10, it is no defense that the actor did not know the child's age, or reasonably believed the child to be older than 10. When criminality depends on the child's being below a critical age other than 10, it is a defense for the actor to prove by a preponderance of the evidence that he reasonably believed the child to be above the critical age.

(2) *Spouse Relationships.* Whenever in this Article the definition of an offense excludes conduct with a spouse, the exclusion shall be deemed to extend to persons living as man and wife, regardless of the legal status of their relationship. The exclusion shall be inoperative as respects spouses living apart under a decree of judicial separation. Where the definition of an offense excludes conduct with a spouse or conduct by a woman, this shall not preclude conviction

of a spouse or woman as accomplice in a sexual act which he or she causes another person, not within the exclusion, to perform.

(3) *Sexually Promiscuous Complainants.* It is a defense to prosecution under Section 213.3, and paragraphs (6), (7) and (8) of Section 213.4 for the actor to prove by a preponderance of the evidence that the alleged victim had, prior to the time of the offense charged, engaged promiscuously in sexual relations with others.

(4) *Prompt Complaint.* No prosecution may be instituted or maintained under this Article unless the alleged offense was brought to the notice of public authority within [3] months of its occurrence or, where the alleged victim was less than [16] years old or otherwise incompetent to make complaint, within [3] months after a parent, guardian or other competent person specially interested in the victim learns of the offense.

(5) *Testimony of Complainants.* No person shall be convicted of any felony under this Article upon the uncorroborated testimony of the alleged victim. Corroboration may be circumstantial. In any prosecution before a jury for an offense under this Article, the jury shall be instructed to evaluate the testimony of a victim or complaining witness with special care in view of the emotional involvement of the witness and the difficulty of determining the truth with respect to alleged sexual activities carried out in private.

Offenses Against Property

Article 220. Arson, Criminal Mischief, and Other Property Destruction

Section 220.1. Arson and Related Offenses.

(1) *Arson.* A person is guilty of arson, a felony of the second degree, if he starts a fire or causes an explosion with the purpose of:

(a) destroying a building or occupied structure of another; or

(b) destroying or damaging any property, whether his own or another's, to collect insurance for such loss. It shall be an affirmative defense to prosecution under this paragraph that the actor's conduct did not recklessly endanger any building or occupied structure of another or place any other person in danger of death or bodily injury.

(2) *Reckless Burning or Exploding.* A person commits a felony of the third degree if he purposely starts a fire or causes an explosion, whether on his own property or another's, and thereby recklessly:

(a) places another person in danger of death or bodily injury; or

(b) places a building or occupied structure of another in danger of damage or destruction.

(3) *Failure to Control or Report Dangerous Fire.* A person who knows that a fire is endangering life or a substantial amount of property of another and fails to take reasonable measures to put out or control the fire, when he can do so without substantial risk to himself, or to give a prompt fire alarm, commits a misdemeanor if:

(a) he knows that he is under an official, contractual, or other legal duty to prevent or combat the fire; or

(b) the fire was started, albeit lawfully, by him or with his assent, or on property in his custody or control.

(4) *Definitions.* "Occupied structure" means any structure, vehicle or place adapted for overnight accommodation of persons, or for carrying on business therein, whether or not a person is actually present. Property is that of another, for the purposes of this section, if anyone other than the actor has a possessory or propietory interest therein. If a building or structure is divided into separately occupied units, any unit not occupied by the actor is an occupied structure of another.

Section 220.2. Causing or Risking Catastrophe.

(1) *Causing Catastrophe.* A person who causes a catastrophe by explosion, fire, flood, avalanche, collapse of building, release of poison gas, radioactive material or other harmful or destructive force or substance, or by any other means of causing potentially widespread injury or damage, commits a felony of the second degree if he does so purposely or knowingly, or a felony of the third degree if he does so recklessly.

(2) *Risking Catastrophe.* A person is guilty of a misdemeanor if he recklessly creates a risk of catastrophe in the employment of fire, explosives or other dangerous means listed in Subsection (1).

(3) *Failure to Prevent Catastrophe.* A person who knowingly or recklessly fails to take reasonable measures to prevent or mitigate a catastrophe commits a misdemeanor if:

(a) he knows that he is under an official, contractual or other legal duty to take such measures; or

(b) he did or assented to the act causing or threatening the catastrophe.

Section 220.3. Criminal Mischief.

(1) *Offense Defined.* A person is guilty of criminal mischief if he:

(a) damages tangible property of another purposely, recklessly, or by negligence in the employment of fire, explosives, or other dangerous means listed in Section 220.2(1); or

(b) purposely or recklessly tampers with tangible property of another so as to endanger person or property; or

(c) purposely or recklessly causes another to suffer pecuniary loss by deception or threat.

(2) *Grading.* Criminal mischief is a felony of the third degree if the actor purposely causes pecuniary loss in excess of $5,000 or a substantial interruption or impairment of public communication, transportation, supply of water, gas or power, or other public service. It is a misdemeanor if the actor purposely causes pecuniary loss in excess of $100, or a petty misdemeanor if he purposely or recklessly causes pecuniary loss in excess of $25. Otherwise criminal mischief is a violation.

Article 221. Burglary and Other Criminal Intrusion

Section 221.0. Definitions.

In this Article, unless a different meaning plainly is required:

(1) "occupied structure" means any structure, vehicle or place adapted for overnight accommodation of persons, or for carrying on business therein, whether or not a person is actually present.

(2) "night" means the period between thirty minutes past sunset and thirty minutes before sunrise.

Section 221.1. Burglary.

(1) *Burglary Defined.* A person is guilty of burglary if he enters a building or occupied structure, or separately secured or occupied portion thereof, with purpose to commit a crime therein, unless the premises are at the time open to the public or the actor is licensed or privileged to enter. It is an affirmative defense to prosecution for burglary that the building or structure was abandoned.

(2) *Grading.* Burglary is a felony of the second degree if it is perpetrated in the dwelling of another at night, or if, in the course of committing the offense, the actor:

(a) purposely, knowingly or recklessly inflicts or attempts to inflict bodily injury on anyone; or

(b) is armed with explosives or a deadly weapon.

Otherwise, burglary is a felony of the third degree. An act shall be deemed "in the course of committing" an offense if it occurs in an attempt to commit the offense or in flight after the attempt or commission.

(3) *Multiple Convictions.* A person may not be convicted both for burglary and for the offense which it was his purpose to commit after the burglarious entry or for an attempt to commit that offense, unless the additional offense constitutes a felony of the first or second degree.

Section 221.2. Criminal Trespass.

(1) *Buildings and Occupied Structures.* A person commits an offense if, knowing that he is not licensed or privileged to do so, he enters or surreptitiously remains in any building or occupied structure, or separately secured or occupied portion thereof. An offense under this Subsection is a misdemeanor if it is committed in a dwelling at night. Otherwise it is a petty misdemeanor.

(2) *Defiant Trespasser.* A person commits an offense if, knowing that he is not licensed or privileged to do so, he enters or remains in any place as to which notice against trespass is given by:

(a) actual communication to the actor; or

(b) posting in a manner prescribed by law or reasonably likely to come to the attention of intruders; or

(c) fencing or other enclosure manifestly designed to exclude intruders.

An offense under this Subsection constitutes a petty misdemeanor if the offender defies an order to leave personally communicated to him by the owner of the premises or other authorized person. Otherwise it is a violation.

(3) *Defenses.* It is an affirmative defense to prosecution under this Section that:

(a) a building or occupied structure involved in an offense under Subsection (1) was abandoned; or

(b) the premises were at the time open to members of the public and the actor complied with all lawful conditions imposed on access to or remaining in the premises; or

(c) the actor reasonably believed that the owner of the premises, or other person empowered to license access thereto, would have licensed him to enter or remain.

Article 222. Robbery

Section 222.1 Robbery.

(1) *Robbery Defined.* A person is guilty of robbery if, in the course of committing a theft, he:

(a) inflicts serious bodily injury upon another; or

(b) threatens another with or purposely puts him in fear of immediate serious bodily injury; or

(c) commits or threatens immediately to commit any felony of the first or second degree.

An act shall be deemed "in the course of committing a theft" if it occurs in an attempt to commit theft or in flight after the attempt or commission.

(2) *Grading.* Robbery is a felony of the second degree, except that it is a felony of the first degree if in the course of committing the theft the actor attempts to kill anyone, or purposely inflicts or attempts to inflict serious bodily injury.

Article 223. Theft and Related Offenses

Section 223.0 Definitions.

In this Article, unless a different meaning plainly is required:

(1) "deprive" means: (a) to withhold property of another permanently or for so extended a period as to appropriate a major portion of its economic value, or with intent to restore only upon payment of reward or other compensation; or (b) to dispose of the property so as to make it unlikely that the owner will recover it.

(2) "financial institution" means a bank, insurance company, credit union, building and loan association, investment trust or other organization held out to the public as a place of deposit of funds or medium of savings or collective investment.

(3) "government" means the United States, any State, county, municipality, or other political unit, or any department, agency or subdivision of any of the foregoing, or any corporation or other association carrying out the functions of government.

(4) "movable property" means property the location of which can be changed, including things growing on, affixed to, or found in land, and documents although the rights represented thereby have no physical location. "Immovable property" is all other property.

(5) "obtain" means: (a) in relation to property, to bring about a transfer or purported transfer of a legal interest in the property, whether to the obtainer or another; or (b) in relation to labor or service, to secure performance thereof.

(6) "property" means anything of value, including real estate, tangible and intangible personal property, contract rights, choses-in-action and other interests in or claims to wealth, admission or transportation tickets, captured or domestic animals, food and drink, electric or other power.

(7) "property of another" includes property in which any person other than the actor has an interest which the actor is not privileged to infringe, regardless of the fact that the actor also has an interest in the property and regardless of the fact that the other person might be precluded from civil recovery because the property was used in an unlawful transaction or was subject to forfeiture as contraband. Property in possession of the actor shall not be deemed property of another who has only a security interest therein, even if legal title is in the creditor pursuant to a conditional sales contract or other security agreement.

Section 223.1 Consolidation of Theft Offenses; Grading; Provisions Applicable to Theft Generally.

(1) *Consolidation of Theft Offenses.* Conduct denominated theft in this Article constitutes a single offense. An accusation of theft may be supported by evidence that it was committed in any manner that would be theft under this Article, notwithstanding the specification of a different manner in the indictment or information, subject only to the power of the Court to ensure fair trial by granting a continuance or other appropriate relief where the conduct of the defense would be prejudiced by lack of fair notice or by surprise.

(2) *Grading of Theft Offenses.*

(a) Theft constitutes a felony of the third degree if the amount involved exceeds $500, or if the property stolen is a firearm, automobile, airplane, motorcycle, motorboat or other motor-propelled vehicle, or in the case of theft by receiving stolen property, if the receiver is in the business of buying or selling stolen property.

(b) Theft not within the preceding paragraph constitutes a misdemeanor, except that if the property was not taken from the person or by threat, or in breach of a fiduciary obligation, and the actor proves by a preponderance of the evidence that the amount involved was less than $50, the offense constitutes a petty misdemeanor.

(c) The amount involved in a theft shall be deemed to be the highest value, by any reasonable standard, of the property or services which the actor stole or attempted to steal. Amounts involved in thefts committed pursuant to one scheme or course of conduct, whether from the same person or several persons, may be aggregated in determining the grade or the offense.

(3) *Claim of Right.* It is an affirmative defense to prosecution for theft that the actor:

(a) was unaware that the property or service was that of another; or

(b) acted under an honest claim of right to the property or service involved or that he had a right to acquire or dispose of it as he did; or

(c) took property exposed for sale, intending to purchase and pay for it promptly, or reasonably believing that the owner, if present, would have consented.

(4) *Theft from Spouse.* It is no defense that theft was from the actor's spouse, except that misappropriation of household and personal effects, or other property normally accessible to both spouses, is theft only if it occurs after the parties have ceased living together.

Section 223.3. Theft by Unlawful Taking or Disposition.

(1) *Movable Property.* A person is guilty of theft if he unlawfully takes, or exercises unlawful control over, movable property of another with purpose to deprive him thereof.

(2) *Immovable Property.* A person is guilty of theft if he unlawfully transfers immovable property of another or any interest therein with purpose to benefit himself or another not entitled thereto.

Section 223.3. Theft by Deception.

A person is guilty of theft if he purposely obtains property of another by deception. A person deceives if he purposely:

(1) creates or reinforces a false impression, including false impressions as to law, value, intention or other state of mind; but deception as to a person's intention to perform a promise shall not be inferred from the fact alone that he did not subsequently perform the promise; or

(2) prevents another from acquiring information which would affect his judgment of a transaction; or

(3) fails to correct a false impression which the deceiver previously created or reinforced, or which the deceiver knows to be influencing another to whom he stands in a fiduciary or confidential relationship; or

(4) fails to disclose a known lien, adverse claim or other legal impediment to the enjoyment of property which he transfers or encumbers in consideration for the property obtained, whether such impediment is or is not valid, or is or is not a matter of official record.

The term "deceive" does not, however, include falsity as to matters having no pecuniary significance, or puffing by statements unlikely to deceive ordinary persons in the group addressed.

Section 223.4. Theft by Extortion.

A person is guilty of theft if he obtains property of another by threatening to:

(1) inflict bodily injury on anyone or commit any other criminal offense; or

(2) accuse anyone of a criminal offense; or

(3) expose any secret tending to subject any person to hatred, contempt or ridicule, or to impair his credit or business repute; or

(4) take or withhold action as an official, or cause an official to take or withhold action; or

(5) bring about or continue a strike, boycott or other collective unofficial action, if the property is not demanded or received for the benefit of the group in whose interest the actor purports to act; or

(6) testify or provide information or withhold testimony or information with respect to another's legal claim or defense; or

(7) inflict any other harm which would not benefit the actor.

It is an affirmative defense to prosecution based on paragraphs (2), (3) or (4) that the property obtained by threat of accusation, exposure, lawsuit or other invocation of official action was honestly claimed as restitution or indemnification for harm done in the circumstances to which such accusation, exposure, lawsuit or other official action relates, or as compensation for property or lawful services.

Section 223.5. Theft of Property Lost, Mislaid, or Delivered by Mistake.

A person who comes into control of property of another that he knows to have been lost, mislaid, or delivered under a mistake as to the nature or amount of the property or the identity of the recipient is guilty of theft if, with purpose to deprive the owner thereof, he fails to take reasonable measures to restore the property to a person entitled to have it.

Section 223.6. Receiving Stolen Property.

(1) *Receiving.* A person is guilty of theft if he purposely receives, retains, or disposes of movable property of another knowing that it has been stolen, or believing that it has probably been stolen, unless the property is received, retained, or disposed with purpose to restore it to the owner. "Receiving" means acquiring possession, control or title, or lending on the security of the property.

(2) *Presumption of Knowledge.* The requisite knowledge or belief is presumed in the case of a dealer who:

(a) is found in possession or control of property stolen from two or more persons on separate occasions; or

(b) has received stolen property in another transaction within the year preceding the transaction charged; or

(c) being a dealer in property of the sort received, acquires it for a consideration which he knows is far below its reasonable value.

"Dealer" means a person in the business of buying or selling goods including a pawnbroker.

Section 223.7. Theft of Services.

(1) A person is guilty of theft if he purposely obtains services which he knows are available only for compensation, by deception or threat, or by false token or other means to avoid payment for the service. "Services" includes labor, professional service, transportation, telephone or other public service, accommodation in hotels, restaurants or elsewhere, admission to exhibitions, use of vehicles or other movable property. Where compensation for service is ordinarily paid immediately upon the rendering for such service, as is the case of hotels and restaurants, refusal to pay or absconding without payment or offer to pay gives rise to a presumption that the service was obtained by deception as to intention to pay.

(2) A person commits theft if, having control over the disposition of services of others, to which he is not entitled, he knowingly diverts such services to his own benefit or to the benefit of another not entitled thereto.

Section 223.8. Theft by Failure to Make Required Disposition of Funds Received.

A person who purposely obtains property upon agreement, or subject to a known legal obligation, to make specified payment or other disposition, whether from such property or its proceeds or from his own property to be reserved in equivalent amount, is guilty of theft if he deals with the property obtained as his own and fails to make the required payment or disposition. The foregoing applies notwithstanding that it may be impossible to identify particular property as belonging to the victim at the time of the actor's failure to make the required payment or disposition. An officer or employee of the government or of a financial institution is presumed: (i) to know any legal obligation relevant to his criminal liability under this Section, and (ii) to have dealt with the property as his own if he fails to pay or account upon lawful demand, or if an audit reveals a shortage or falsification of accounts.

Article 224. Forgery and Fraudulent Practices

Section 224.0. Definitions.

In this Article, the definitions given in Section 223.0 apply unless a different meaning plainly is required.

Section 224.1. Forgery.

(1) *Definition.* A person is guilty of forgery if, with purpose to defraud or injure anyone, or with knowledge that he is facilitating a fraud or injury to be perpetrated by anyone, the actor:

(a) alters any writing of another without his authority; or

(b) makes, completes, executes, authenticates, issues or transfers any writing so that it purports to be the act of another who did not authorize that act, or to have been executed at a time or place or in a numbered sequence other than was in fact the case, or to be a copy of an original when no such original existed; or

(c)   utters any writing which he knows to be forged in a manner specified in paragraphs (a) or (b).

"Writing" includes printing or any other method of recording information, money, coins, tokens, stamps, seals, credit cards, badges, trademarks, and other symbols of value, right, privilege, or identification.

(2) *Grading.* Forgery is a felony of the second degree if the writing is or purports to be part of an issue of money, securities, postage or revenue stamps, or other instruments issued by the government, or part of an issue of stock, bonds or other instruments representing interests in or claims against any property or enterprise. Forgery is a felony of the third degree if the writing is or purports to be a will, deed, contract, release, commercial instrument, or other document evidencing, creating, transferring, altering, terminating, or otherwise affecting legal relations. Otherwise forgery is a misdemeanor.

Section 224.5.   Bad Checks.

A person who issues or passes a check or similar sight order for the payment of money, knowing that it will not be honored by the drawee, commits a misdemeanor. For the purposes of this Section as well as in any prosecution for theft committed by means of a bad check, an issuer is presumed to know that the check or order (other than a postdated check or order) would not be paid, if:

(1)   the issuer had no account with the drawee at the time the check or order was issued; or

(2)   payment was refused by the drawee for lack of funds, upon presentation within 30 days after issue, and the issuer failed to make good within 10 days after receiving notice of that refusal.

Section 224.8.   Commercial Bribery and Breach of Duty to Act Disinterestedly.

(1)   A person commits a misdemeanor if he solicits, accepts or agrees to accept any benefit as consideration for knowingly violating or agreeing to violate a duty of fidelity to which he is subject as:

(a)   partner, agent or employee of another;

(b)   trustee, guardian, or other fiduciary;

(c)   lawyer, physician, accountant, appraiser, or other professional adviser or informant;

(d)   officer, director, manager or other participant in the direction of the affairs of an incorporated or unincorporated association; or

(e)   arbitrator or other purportedly disinterested adjudicator or referee.

(2)   A person who holds himself out to the public as being engaged in the business of making disinterested selection, appraisal, or criticism of commodities or services commits a misdemeanor if he solicits, accepts or agrees to accept any benefit to influence his selection, appraisal or criticism.

(3)   A person commits a misdemeanor if he confers, or offers or agrees to confer, any benefit the acceptance of which would be criminal under this Section.

Offenses Against the Family

Article 230.   Offenses Against the Family

Section 230.1.   Bigamy and Polygamy.

(1) *Bigamy.* A married person is guilty of bigamy, a misdemeanor, if he contracts or purports to contract another marriage, unless at the time of the subsequent marriage:

(a)   the actor believes that the prior spouse is dead; or

(b)   the actor and the prior spouse have been living apart for five consecutive years throughout which the prior spouse was not known by the actor to be alive; or

(c)   a Court has entered a judgment purporting to terminate or annul any prior disqualifying marriage, and the actor does not know that judgment to be invalid; or

(d)   the actor reasonably believes that he is legally eligible to remarry.

(2) *Polygamy.* A person is guilty of polygamy, a felony of the third degree, if he marries

or cohabits with more than one spouse at a time in purported exercise of the right of plural marriage. The offense is a continuing one until all cohabitation and claim of marriage with more than one spouse terminates. This section does not apply to parties to a polygamous marriage, lawful in the country of which they are residents or nationals, while they are in transit through or temporarily visiting this State.

(3) *Other Party to Bigamous or Polygamous Marriage.* A person is guilty of bigamy or polygamy, as the case may be, if he contracts or purports to contract marriage with another knowing that the other is thereby committing bigamy or polygamy.

Section 230.2. Incest.

A person is guilty of incest, a felony of the third degree, if he knowingly marries or cohabits or has sexual intercourse with an ancestor or descendant, a brother or sister of the whole or half blood [or an uncle, aunt, nephew or niece of the whole blood]. "Cohabit" means to live together under the representation or appearance of being married. The relationships referred to herein include blood relationships without regard to legitimacy, and relationship of parent and child by adoption.

Section 230.4. Endangering Welfare of Children.

A parent, guardian, or other person supervising the welfare of a child under 18 commits a misdemeanor if he knowingly endangers the child's welfare by violating a duty of care, protection or support.

Section 230.5. Persistent Non-Support.

A person commits a misdemeanor if he persistently fails to provide support which he can provide and which he knows he is legally obliged to provide to a spouse, child or other dependent.

Offenses Against Public Administration

Article 240. Bribery and Corrupt Influence

Section 240.0. Definitions.

In Articles 240–243, unless a different meaning plainly is required:

(1) "benefit" means gain or advantage, or anything regarded by the beneficiary as gain or advantage, including benefit to any other person or entity in whose welfare he is interested, but not an advantage promised generally to a group or class of voters as a consequence of public measures which a candidate engages to support or oppose;

(2) "government" includes any branch, subdivision or agency of the government of the State or any locality within it;

(3) "harm" means loss, disadvantage or injury, or anything so regarded by the person affected, including loss, disadvantage or injury to any other person or entity in whose welfare he is interested;

(4) "official proceeding" means a proceeding heard or which may be heard before any legislative, judicial, administrative or other governmental agency or official authorized to take evidence under oath, including any referee, hearing examiner, commissioner, notary or other person taking testimony or deposition in connection with any such proceeding;

(5) "party official" means a person who holds an elective or appointive post in a political party in the United States by virtue of which he directs or conducts, or participates in directing or conducting party affairs at any level of responsibility;

(6) "pecuniary benefit" is benefit in the form of money, property, commercial interests or anything else the primary significance of which is economic gain;

(7) "public servant" means any officer or employee of government, including legislators and judges, and any person participating as juror, advisor, consultant or otherwise, in performing a governmental function; but the term does not include witnesses;

(8) "administrative proceeding" means any proceeding, other than a judicial proceeding, the outcome of which is required to be based on a record or documentation prescribed by law, or in which law or regulation is particularized in application to individuals.

Section 240.1. Bribery in Official and Political Matters.

A person is guilty of bribery, a felony of the third degree, if he offers, confers or agrees to confer upon another, or solicits, accepts or agrees to accept from another:

(1) any pecuniary benefit as consideration for the recipient's decision, opinion, recommendation, vote or other exercise of discretion as a public servant, party official or voter; or

(2) any benefit as consideration for the recipient's decision, vote, recommendation or other exercise of official discretion in a judicial or administrative proceeding; or

(3) any benefit as consideration for a violation of a known legal duty as public servant or party official.

It is no defense to prosecution under this section that a person whom the actor sought to influence was not qualified to act in the desired way whether because he had not yet assumed office, or lacked jurisdiction, or for any other reason.

Section 240.2. Threats and Other Improper Influence in Official and Political Matters.

(1) *Offenses Defined.* A person commits an offense if he:

(a) threatens unlawful harm to any person with purpose to influence his decision, opinion, recommendation, vote or other exercise of discretion as a public servant, party official or voter; or

(b) threatens harm to any public servant with purpose to influence his decision, opinion, recommendation, vote or pecuniary benefit as consideration for exerting special influence upon a public servant or procuring another to do so. "Special influence" means power to influence through kinship, friendship or other relationship, apart from the merits of the transaction.

(3) *Paying for Endorsement or Special Influence.* A person commits a misdemeanor if he offers, confers or agrees to confer any pecuniary benefit receipt of which is prohibited by this Section.

Article 241. Perjury and Other Falsification in Official Matters

Section 241.0. Definitions.

In this Article, unless a different meaning plainly is required:

(1) the definitions given in Section 240.0 apply; and

(2) "statement" means any representation, but includes a representation of opinion, belief or other state of mind only if the representation clearly relates to state of mind apart from or in addition to any facts which are the subject of the representation.

Section 241.1. Perjury.

(1) *Offense Defined.* A person is guilty of perjury, a felony of the third degree, if in any official proceeding he makes a false statement under oath or equivalent affirmation, or swears or affirms the truth of a statement previously made, when the statement is material and he does not believe it to be true.

(2) *Materiality.* Falsification is material, regardless of the admissibility of the statement under rules of evidence, if it could have affected the course or outcome of the proceeding. It is no defense that the declarant mistakenly believed the falsification to be immaterial. Whether a falsification is material in a given factual situation is a question of law.

(3) *Irregularities No Defense.* It is not a defense to prosecution under this Section that the oath or affirmation was administered or taken in an irregular manner or that the declarant was not competent to make the statement. A document purporting to be made upon oath or affirmation at any time when the actor presents it as being so verified shall be deemed to have been duly sworn or affirmed.

(4) *Retraction.* No person shall be guilty of an offense under this Section if he retracted the falsification in the course of the proceeding in which it was made before it became manifest that the falsification was or would be exposed and before the falsification substantially affected the proceeding.

(5) *Inconsistent Statements.* Where the defendant made inconsistent statements under oath

or equivalent affirmation, both having been made within the period of the statute of limitations, the prosecution may proceed by setting forth the inconsistent statements in a single count alleging in the alternative that one or the other was false and not believed by the defendant. In such case it shall not be necessary for the prosecution to prove which statement was false but only that one or the other was false and not believed by the defendant to be true.

(6) *Corroboration.* No person shall be convicted of an offense under this Section where proof of falsity rests solely upon contradiction by testimony of a single person other than the defendant.

Section 241.2. False Swearing.

(1) *False Swearing in Official Matters.* A person who makes a false statement under oath or equivalent affirmation, or swears or affirms the truth of such a statement previously made, when he does not believe the statement to be true, is guilty of a misdemeanor if:

(a) the falsification occurs in an official proceeding; or

(b) the falsification is intended to mislead a public servant in performing his official function.

Offenses Against Public Order and Decency

Article 250. Riot, Disorderly Conduct, and Related Offenses

Section 250.1 Riot; Failure to Disperse.

(1) *Riot.* A person is guilty of riot, a felony of the third degree, if he participates with [two] or more others in a course of disorderly conduct:

(a) with purpose to commit or facilitate the commission of a felony or misdemeanor;

(b) with purpose to prevent or coerce official action; or

(c) when the actor or any other participant to the knowledge of the actor uses or plans to use a firearm or other deadly weapon.

(2) *Failure of Disorderly Persons to Disperse Upon Official Order.* Where [three] or more persons are participating in a course of disorderly conduct likely to cause substantial harm or serious inconvenience, annoyance or alarm, a peace officer or other public servant engaged in executing or enforcing the law may order the participants and others in the immediate vicinity to disperse. A person who refuses or knowingly fails to obey such an order commits a misdemeanor.

Section 250.2 Disorderly Conduct.

(1) *Offense Defined.* A person is guilty of disorderly conduct if, with purpose to cause public inconvenience, annoyance or alarm, or recklessly creating a risk thereof, he:

(a) engages in fighting or threatening, or in violent or tumultuous behavior; or

(b) makes unreasonable noise or offensively coarse utterance, gesture or display, or addresses abusive language to any person present; or

(c) creates a hazardous or physically offensive condition by any act which serves no legitimate purpose of the actor.

"Public" means affecting or likely to affect persons in a place to which the public or a substantial group has access; among the places included are highways, transport facilities, schools, prisons, apartment houses, places of business or amusement, or any neighborhood.

(2) *Grading.* An offense under this section is a petty misdemeanor if the actor's purpose is to cause substantial harm or serious inconvenience, or if he persists in disorderly conduct after reasonable warning or request to desist. Otherwise disorderly conduct is a violation.

Section 250.4. Harassment.

A person commits a petty misdemeanor if, with purpose to harass another, he:

(1) makes a telephone call without purpose of legitimate communication; or

(2) insults, taunts or challenges another in a manner likely to provoke violent or disorderly response; or

(3) makes repeated communications anonymously or at extremely inconvenient hours, or in offensively coarse language; or

(4) subjects another to an offensive touching; or

(5) engages in any other course of alarming conduct serving no legitimate purpose of the actor.

Section 250.5. Public Drunkenness; Drug Incapacitation.

A person is guilty of an offense if he appears in any public place manifestly under the influence of alcohol, narcotics or other drugs, not therapeutically administered, to the degree that he may endanger himself or other persons or property, or annoy persons in his vicinity. An offense under this Section constitutes a petty misdemeanor if the actor has been convicted hereunder twice before within a period of one year. Otherwise the offense constitutes a violation.

Section 250.6. Loitering or Prowling.

A person commits a violation if he loiters or prowls in a place, at a time, or in a manner not usual for law-abiding individuals under circumstances that warrant alarm for the safety of persons or property in the vicinity. Among the circumstances which may be considered in determining whether such alarm is warranted is the fact that the actor takes flight upon appearance of a peace officer, refuses to identify himself, or manifestly endeavors to conceal himself or any object. Unless flight by the actor or other circumstances makes it impracticable, a peace officer shall prior to any arrest for an offense under this section afford the actor an opportunity to dispel any alarm which would otherwise be warranted, by requesting him to identify himself and explain his presence and conduct. No person shall be convicted of an offense under this Section if the peace officer did not comply with the preceding sentence, or if it appears at trial that the explanation given by the actor was true and, if believed by the peace officer at the time, would have dispelled the alarm.

Article 251. Public Indecency

Section 251.1. Open Lewdness.

A person commits a petty misdemeanor if he does any lewd act which he knows is likely to be observed by others who would be affronted or alarmed.

(1) *Prostitution.* A person is guilty of prostitution, a petty misdemeanor, if he or she:

(a) is an inmate of a house of prostitution or otherwise engages in sexual activity as a business; or

(b) loiters in or within view of any public place for the purpose of being hired to engage in sexual activity.

"Sexual activity" includes homosexual and other deviate sexual relations. A "house of prostitution" is any place where prostitution or promotion of prostitution is regularly carried on by one person under the control, management or supervision of another. An "inmate" is a person who engages in prostitution in or through the agency of a house of prostitution. "Public place" means any place to which the public or any substantial group thereof has access.

(2) *Promoting Prostitution.* A person who knowingly promotes prostitution of another commits a misdemeanor or felony as provided in Subsection (3). The following acts shall, without limitation of the foregoing, constitute promoting prostitution:

(a) owning, controlling, managing, supervising or otherwise keeping, alone or in association with others, a house of prostitution or a prostitution business; or

(b) procuring an inmate for a house of prostitution or a place in a house of prostitution for one who would be an inmate; or

(c) encouraging, inducing, or otherwise purposely causing another to become or remain a prostitute; or

(d) soliciting a person to patronize a prostitute; or

(e) procuring a prostitute for a patron; or

(f) transporting a person into or within this state with purpose to promote that person's engaging in prostitution, or procuring or paying for transportation with that purpose; or

(g) leasing or otherwise permitting a place controlled by the actor, alone or in association with others, to be regularly used for prostitution or the promotion of prostitution, or failure to make reasonable effort to abate such use by ejecting the tenant, notifying law enforcement authorities, or other legally available means; or

(h) soliciting, receiving, or agreeing to receive any benefit for doing or agreeing to do anything forbidden by this Subsection.

(3) *Grading of Offenses Under Subsection (2)*. An offense under Subsection (2) constitutes a felony of the third degree if:

(a) the offense falls within paragraph (a), (b) or (c) of Subsection (2); or

(b) the actor compels another to engage in or promote prostitution; or

(c) the actor promotes prostitution of a child under 16, whether or not he is aware of the child's age; or

(d) the actor promotes prostitution of his wife, child, ward or any person for whose care, protection or support he is responsible.

Otherwise the offense is a misdemeanor.

(4) *Presumption from Living off Prostitutes*. A person, other than the prostitute or the prostitute's minor child or other legal dependent incapable of self-support, who is supported in whole or substantial part by the proceeds of prostitution is presumed to be knowingly promoting prostitution in violation of Subsection (2).

(5) *Patronizing Prostitutes*. A person commits a violation if he hires a prostitute to engage in sexual activity with him, or if he enters or remains in a house of prostitution for the purpose of engaging in sexual activity.

(6) *Evidence*. On the issue whether a place is a house of prostitution the following shall be admissible evidence; its general repute; the repute of the persons who reside in or frequent the place; the frequency, timing and duration of visits by non-residents. Testimony of a person against his spouse shall be admissible to prove offenses under this Section.

Section 251.3. Loitering to Solicit Deviate Sexual Relations.

A person is guilty of a petty misdemeanor if he loiters in or near any public place for the purpose of soliciting or being solicited to engage in deviate sexual relations.

Section 251.4. Obscenity.

(1) *Obscene Defined*. Material is obscene if, considered as a whole, its predominant appeal is to prurient interest, that is, a shameful or morbid interest, in nudity, sex or excretion, and if in addition it goes substantially beyond customary limits of candor in describing or representing such matters. Predominant appeal shall be judged with reference to ordinary adults unless it appears from the character of the material or the circumstances of its dissemination to be designed for children or other specially susceptible audience. Undeveloped photographs, molds, printing plates, and the like, shall be deemed obscene notwithstanding that processing or other acts may be required to make the obscenity patent or to disseminate it.

(2) *Offenses*. Subject to the affirmative defense provided in Subsection (3), a person commits a misdemeanor if he knowingly or recklessly:

(a) sells, delivers or provides, or offers or agrees to sell, deliver or provide, any obscene writing, picture, record or other representation or embodiment of the obscene; or

(b) presents or directs an obscene play, dance or performance, or participates in that portion thereof which makes it obscene; or

(c) publishes, exhibits or otherwise makes available any obscene material; or

(d) possesses any obscene material for purposes of sale or other commercial dissemination; or

(e) sells, advertises or otherwise commercially disseminates material, whether or not obscene, by representing or suggesting that it is obscene.

A person who disseminates or possesses obscene material in the course of his business is presumed to do so knowingly or recklessly.

(3) *Justifiable and Non-Commercial Private Dissemination*. It is an affirmative defense to prosecution under this Section that dissemination was restricted to:

(a) institutions or persons having scientific, educational, governmental or other similar justification for possessing obscene material; or

(b) non-commercial dissemination to personal associates of the actor.

(4) *Evidence; Adjudication of Obscenity.* In any prosecution under this Section, evidence shall be admissible to show:

(a) the character of the audience for which the material was designed or to which it was directed;

(b) what the predominant appeal of the material would be for ordinary adults or any special audience to which it was directed, and what effect, if any, it would probably have on conduct of such people;

(c) artistic, literary, scientific, educational or other merits or the material;

(d) the degree of public acceptance of the material in the United States;

(e) appeal to prurient interest, or absence thereof, in advertising or other promotion of the material; and

(f) the good repute of the author, creator, publisher or other person from whom the material originated.

Expert testimony and testimony of the author, creator, publisher or other person from whom the material originated, relating to factors entering into the determination of the issue of obscenity, shall be admissible. The Court shall dismiss a prosecution for obscenity if it is satisfied that the material is not obscene.

GLOSSARY

accessory   A person who is involved with the commission of a crime but who is not present at the time it is committed.

actus reus   An "answerable act," i.e., an act for which one is answerable; a guilty act. In combination with mens rea ... , actus reus is an essential element of any crime.

affirmative defense   A defense that amounts to more than simply a denial of the allegations in the plaintiff's complaint. It sets up new matter which, if proven, could result in a judgment against the plaintiff even if all the allegations of the complaint are true.

alibi   The defense that the accused was elsewhere at the time the crime was committed.

appellate court   A higher court to which an appeal is taken from a lower court.

arson   The willful and malicious burning of a building. In some jurisdictions, arson includes the deliberate burning of any structure.

assault   An act of force or threat of force intended to inflict harm upon a person or to put the person in fear that such harm is imminent; an attempt to commit a battery. The perpetrator must have, or appear to have, the present ability to carry out the act.

attempt   An act done with the intent to commit a crime, which would have resulted in the crime being committed except that something happened to prevent it. The line between an attempt and mere preparations is often difficult to draw; it is a matter of degree.

battered woman syndrome   A psychological condition in which a woman commits physical violence against her husband or mate as a result of the continued physical or mental abuse to which he has subjected her. The

courts are split with respect to the admissibility of expert testimony ... to prove the psychological effects of continued abuse.

battery   The unconsented-to touching or striking of one person by another, or by an object put in motion by him, with the intention of doing harm or giving offense. Battery is both a crime and a tort.

bill of attainder   A legislative act that inflicts capital punishment upon named persons without a judicial trial. Congress and the state legislatures are prohibited from issuing bills of attainder by the Constitution.

Bill of Rights   The first 10 amendments to the United States Constitution. The Bill of Rights is the portion of the Constitution that sets forth the rights which are the fundamental principles of the United States and the foundation of American citizenship.

breach of the peace   Conduct that violates the public order or disturbs the public tranquility

bribery   The crime of giving something of value with the intention of influencing the action of a public official.

burden of going forward (production)   The duty of a party, with respect to certain issues being tried, to produce evidence sufficient to justify a verdict before the other party is obligated to produce evidence to the contrary. ... [A]lso referred to as the *burden of evidence*, the *burden of proceeding*, and the *burden of producing evidence*. The burden of going forward may shift back and forth between the parties during the course of a trial.

burden of persuasion   The ultimate burden of proof; the responsibility of convincing the jury, or, in a nonjury trial, the judge, of the truth.

burden of proof The duty of establishing the truth of a matter; the duty of proving a fact that is in dispute. In most instances the burden of proof, like the burden of going forward, shifts from one side to the other during the course of a trial as the case progresses and evidence is introduced by each side.

burglary At common law, the offense of breaking and entering a dwelling at night with the intent to commit a felony ... . The crime of burglary has been broadened by statute to include entering buildings other than dwellings, with or without a breaking, and regardless of the time of day or night.

certiorari (Latin) A writ issued by a higher court to a lower court requiring the certification of the record in a particular case so that the higher court can review the record and correct any actions taken in the case which are not in accordance with the law. The Supreme Court of the United States uses the writ of certiorari to select the state court cases it is willing to review. Commonly referred to as "cert."

civil liberties Political liberties guaranteed by the Constitution and, in particular, by the Bill of Rights, especially the First Amendment.

clear and present danger The test of whether speech is capable of creating such a substantial danger to the security of the country that it is not protected under the First Amendment.

coconspirator's rule The rule of evidence that statements made by a person involved in a conspiracy may be used as evidence of the guilt of all the conspirators.

common law 1. Law found in the decisions of the courts rather than in statutes; judge-made law. 2. English law adopted by the early American colonists, which is part of the United States' judicial heritage and forms the basis of much of its law today.

compensatory damages Damages recoverable in a lawsuit for loss or injury suffered by the plaintiff as a result of the defendant's conduct.

Also called actual damages, they may include expenses, loss of time, reduced earning capacity, bodily injury, and mental anguish.

concert of action rule The rule that if one of the elements of a crime is such that it can only be committed by two persons acting together, such mutual action cannot also be a conspiracy. This principle is also referred to as the *Wharton Rule*.

concurrent jurisdiction Two or more courts having the power to adjudicate the same class of cases or the same matter.

consent Agreement; approval; acquiescence; being of one mind. Consent necessarily involves two or more persons because, without at least two persons, there cannot be a unity of opinion or the possibility of thinking alike. ... As a defense to a prosecution for rape, consent is an exercise of one's intelligence in making a choice between resistance and uncoerced assent, based upon knowledge of the significance of the act and of the moral issues involved.

conspiracy An agreement between two or more persons to engage in a criminal act or to accomplish a legal objective by criminal or unlawful means.

constructive Inferred, implied, or presumed from the circumstances.

contempt An act of disrespect toward a court or legislative body; deliberate disobedience of a court order.

contract An agreement entered into, for adequate consideration, to do, or refrain from doing, a particular thing. The Uniform Commercial Code defines a contract as the total legal obligation resulting from the parties' agreement. In addition to adequate consideration, the transaction must involve an undertaking that is legal to perform, and there must be mutuality of agreement and obligation between at least two competent parties.

conversion Control over another person's personal property which is wrongfully exercised; control applied in a manner that violates that person's title to or rights in the property. Conversion is both a tort and a crime.

corporate liability The liability of a corporation for the acts of its directors, officers, shareholders, agents, and employees.

corpus delicti Means "the body of the crime"; the fact that a crime has actually been committed.

court of general jurisdiction Generally, another term for trial court; that is, a court having jurisdiction to try all classes of civil and criminal cases except those which can be heard only by a court of limited jurisdiction.

court of limited jurisdiction A court whose jurisdiction is limited to civil cases of a certain type ... or which involve a limited amount of money ... , or whose jurisdiction in criminal cases is confined to petty offenses and preliminary hearings ... . A court of limited jurisdiction is sometimes called a court of special jurisdiction.

court of record Generally, another term for trial court.

criminal law Branch of the law that specifies what conduct constitutes crime and establishes appropriate punishments for such conduct.

criminal procedure The rules of procedure by which criminal prosecutions are governed.

culpable Blameworthy; blamable; responsible; at fault.

damages The sum of money that may be recovered in the courts as financial reparation for an injury or wrong suffered as a result of breach of contract or a tortious act.

deadly weapon A weapon that is likely to cause death or serious bodily injury when used in the manner in which it was designed to be used.

deter To discourage; to prevent from acting.

diminished capacity The rule that a criminal defendant, although not sufficiently mentally impaired to be entitled to a defense of insanity, may have been so reduced in mental

capacity ... that he or she was incapable of forming the mental state necessary, in law, for the commission of certain crimes.

double jeopardy A rule originating in the Fifth Amendment that prohibits a second punishment or a second trial for the same offense. It is sometimes referred to as *former jeopardy* or *prior jeopardy*.

due process clause Actually a reference to two due process clauses, one in the Fifth Amendment and one in the Fourteenth Amendment. The Fifth Amendment requires the federal government to accord "due process of law" to citizens of the United States; the Fourteenth Amendment imposes a similar requirement upon state governments.

duress Coercion applied for the purpose of compelling a person to do, or to refrain from doing, some act. ... Duress may be a defense ... to a criminal prosecution if the defendant committed the crime out of a well-grounded fear of death or serious bodily harm.

Durham rule A test for establishing insanity for the purpose of a defense to criminal prosecution, in some jurisdictions. Under this test, a defendant's criminal responsibility is determined on the basis of whether his or her unlawful act was the result or "product" of "mental disease or mental defect."

element A component or essential part of something.

embezzlement The fraudulent conversion of property, including but not limited to money, with which a person ... has been entrusted.

entrapment Inducing a person to commit a crime he or she is otherwise not inclined to commit, in order to bring a criminal prosecution against him or her. Such conduct by law enforcement authorities is an affirmative defense to a prosecution for the crime into which the defendant was entrapped.

ex post facto law A law making a person criminally liable for an act that was not criminal at the time it was committed. The

Constitution prohibits both Congress and the states from enacting such laws.

extortion The criminal offense of obtaining money or other thing of value by duress, force, threat of force, fear, or color of office.

false imprisonment The unlawful restraint by one person of the physical liberty of another.

false pretenses The crime of obtaining the money or property of another by fraudulent misrepresentation. The essential elements of the offense are an intentional false statement concerning a material fact, in reliance on which title or possession is surrendered.

federalism The system by which the states of the United States relate to each other and to the federal government.

felony murder rule The rule that a death which occurs by accident or chance during the course of the commission of a felony is first-degree murder. The felony murder rule, which is a common law doctrine, has been modified by statute in most states.

fighting words Words which tend to incite a breach of the peace; a category of speech that the Supreme Court has declared is not protected by the First Amendment guaranty of freedom of speech.

first-degree murder Murder committed deliberately with malice aforethought, that is, with premeditation.

foreseeable That which may be anticipated or known in advance; that which a person should have known.

forfeiture A deprivation of money, property, or rights, without compensation, as a consequence of a default or the commission of a crime; civil forfeiture.

forgery The false making, material alteration, or uttering, with intent to defraud or injure, of any writing that, if genuine, might appear to be legally effective or the basis for legal liability.

hearsay The testimony of a witness as to a statement made to him or her outside of court, or made to someone else who told him or her what was said, that is offered in court to prove the truth of the matter contained in the statement.

inference That which may be reasoned from the evidence as being true or proven; a conclusion of fact.

inferior court 1. A court of original jurisdiction, as distinguished from an appellate court; a trial court. 2. A court of limited jurisdiction.

injunction A court order that commands or prohibits some act or course of conduct. It is preventive in nature and designed to protect a plaintiff from irreparable injury to his or her property or property rights by prohibiting or commanding the doing of certain acts. ... [A] form of equitable relief.

intentional Done with intent or with an intention; knowingly.

interpret To construe; to explain; to draw out meaning.

intervening cause A cause that intrudes between the negligence of the defendant and the injury suffered by the plaintiff, breaking the connection between the original wrongful act or omission and the injury, and itself becoming the proximate cause of the injury.

irresistible impulse An impulse to commit an act that one is powerless to control. "Irresistible impulse" is the test used in some jurisdictions to determine insanity for purposes of a criminal defense. This test asks: Although the defendant is able to understand the nature and consequences of his or her act, and to understand that it is wrong, is he or she unable because of mental disease to resist the impulse to do it?

judicial review Review by an appellate court of a determination by a lower court.

jurisdiction In a general sense, the right of a court to adjudicate lawsuits of a certain kind. In a specific sense, the right of a court to determine a particular case; ... the power of the court over the subject matter of, or the property involved in, the case at bar. In a geographical sense, the power of a court to hear cases only within a specific territorial area.

kidnapping   The crime of taking and detaining a person against his or her will by force, intimidation, or fraud.

knowingly   With knowledge; deliberately; consciously; intentionally. As used in the criminal law and applied to a criminal defendant, "knowingly" means that the accused possessed intent, a necessary element of most crimes; in other words, that he or she knew what he or she was doing and understood the probable results.

larceny   The crime of taking personal property, without consent, with the intent to convert it to the use of someone other than the owner or to deprive the owner of it permanently. Larceny does not involve the use of force or the threat of force.

legal cause   1. The proximate cause of an injury. 2. Probable cause. 3. Cause that the law deems sufficient.

legal impossibility   A person who is unable to commit a crime because of legal impossibility cannot be convicted of a crime he or she intends or attempts. By contrast, a person who is unable to complete a criminal act because of factual impossibility may nonetheless be criminally responsible.

legislative history   Recorded events that provide a basis for determining the legislative intent underlying a statute enacted by a legislature. The records of legislative committee hearings and of debates on the floor of the legislature are among the sources for legislative history.

malicious (criminal) mischief   The willful destruction of the property of another. It is a tort and, in most jurisdictions, a crime as well.

manslaughter   The killing of a human being, without premeditation or malice and without legal excuse or justification. Voluntary

manslaughter occurs when a homicide is intentional but the result of sudden passion or great provocation. Involuntary manslaughter is an unintentional killing in the course of doing an unlawful act not amounting to a felony or while doing a lawful act in a reckless manner. There are various degrees of manslaughter, which are not consistent from jurisdiction to jurisdiction.

mayhem   A form of aggravated assault, the crime of maliciously disabling or disfiguring a person.

mens rea   An "answerable intent," i.e., an intent for which one is answerable; an evil intent; a guilty mind; a criminal intent. In combination with actus reus (a guilty or criminal act), mens rea is an essential element of any crime except regulatory crimes or strict liability crimes and some petty offenses and infractions. Mens rea may be inferred or presumed.

merger of offenses   The doctrine that when a lesser offense is a component of a more serious offense, prosecution can be only for the greater offense.

M'Naghten rule   A test employed in a number of jurisdictions for determining whether a criminal defendant had the capacity to form criminal intent at the time he or she committed the crime of which he or she is accused. Specifically, the M'Naghten rule is that an accused is not criminally responsible if he or she was laboring under such a defect of reason from disease of the mind that he or she either did not know the nature of his or her act or, if he or she did, that he or she did not know it was wrong. The M'Naghten rule is also referred to as the *right and wrong test.*

Model Penal Code   A proposed criminal code prepared jointly by the Commission on Uniform State Laws and the American Law Institute.

motive   The reason that leads the mind to desire a result; that which leads the mind to engage in a criminal act; that which causes the mind to form intent; the reason for an intention.

National Crime Information Center (NCIC)
[A] computerized network used by police departments across the country to determine if there are outstanding warrants on a suspect or an arrestee, to locate missing persons, and to trace stolen vehicles, guns, and the like.

necessity That which is compelled by natural forces and cannot be resisted. Necessity is a defense in a criminal prosecution if the defendant committed the crime to prevent a more serious harm from occurring.

negligence The failure to do something that a reasonable person would do in the same circumstances, or the doing of something a reasonable person would not do. Negligence is a wrong generally characterized by carelessness, inattentiveness, and neglectfulness rather than by a positive intent to cause injury.

omission Not doing something required by the law.

ordinances A law of a municipal corporation; a local law enacted by a city council, town council, board of supervisors, or the like.

overbreadth doctrine The doctrine that a statute is unconstitutional if its language is so broad that it unnecessarily interferes with the exercise of constitutional rights, particularly First Amendment rights, even though the purpose of the statute is to prohibit activities that the government may constitutionally prohibit.

perjury Giving false testimony in a judicial proceeding or an administrative proceeding; lying under oath as to a material fact; swearing to the truth of anything one knows or believes to be false. Perjury is a crime. A person who makes a false affirmation is equally a perjurer.

police power The power of government to make and enforce laws and regulations necessary to maintain and enhance the public welfare and to prevent individuals from violating the rights of others.

precedent Prior decisions of the same court, or a higher court, which a judge must follow in deciding a subsequent case presenting similar facts and the same legal problem, even though different parties are involved and many years have elapsed.

presumption A rule of law that, on the basis of reason and human experience, accords probative value to specific facts in evidence or draws a particular inference as to the existence of a fact that is not actually known but which arises from other facts that are known or proven. A presumption is distinguished from an inference in that a judge or jury may or may not, as it chooses, infer that a thing is true, whereas a presumption requires the inference to be drawn. Some presumptions are rebuttable; others are irrebuttable.

principal A principal in the first degree is a person who commits a crime, either in person or through an innocent agent; a principal in the second degree is a person who is present at the commission of a crime, giving aid and encouragement to the chief perpetrator.

prostitution Engaging in sexual intercourse or other sexual activity for pay. A man as well as a woman may be a prostitute.

provocation Words or conduct that incite anger or passion or that cloud judgment and the ability to reason.

proximate cause As an element of liability in a tort case, that cause which, unbroken by any intervening cause, produced the injury, and without which the result would not have occurred; the primary cause; the efficient cause. Note that the proximate cause of an injury is not necessarily the final cause or the act or omission nearest in time to the injury.

punitive damages Damages that are awarded over and above compensatory damages or actual damages because of the wanton, reckless, or malicious nature of the wrong done by the plaintiff. Such damages bear no relation to the plaintiff's actual loss and are often called exemplary damages, because their purpose is to make an example of the plaintiff to discourage others from engaging in the same kind of conduct in the future.

purposely   Intentionally; knowingly.

Racketeer Influenced and Corrupt Organizations Act   A federal statute, commonly referred to as RICO, which criminalizes racketeering that affects interstate commerce or persons or businesses engaged in interstate commerce.

rape   Sexual intercourse with a woman by force or by putting her in fear or in circumstances in which she is unable to control her conduct or to resist … . Under the common law definition of the crime, only a female can be raped and only a male can perpetrate the crime. In recent years, however, courts in several states have held that the rape statutes of their jurisdictions are gender-neutral and apply equally to perpetrators of either sex.

receiving stolen property   Receiving property with the knowledge that it is stolen property, and with fraudulent intent. Although receiving stolen property is a crime separate and distinct from the crime of stealing the property, if the theft was recent there is a rebuttable presumption that the theft was committed by the person in possession of the property.

recklessness   Indifference to consequences; indifference to the safety and rights of others. Recklessness implies conduct amounting to more than ordinary negligence.

record on appeal   The papers a trial court transmits to the appellate court, on the basis of which the appellate court decides the appeal. The record on appeal includes the pleadings, all motions made before the trial court, the official transcript, and the judgment or order appealed from.

regulation   A rule having the force of law, promulgated by an administrative agency.

retreat to the wall   A term referring to the doctrine, in effect in some jurisdictions, that before a person is entitled to use deadly force in self-defense he or she must attempt to withdraw from the encounter by giving as much ground as possible.

robbery   The felonious taking of money or any thing of value from the person of another or from his or her presence, against his or her will, by force or by putting him or her in fear.

rules of court   Rules promulgated by the court, governing procedure or practice before it.

scienter   (Latin) Knowledge, particularly guilty knowledge; i.e., knowledge a person has that, as a matter of law, will result in his or her liability or guilt.

second-degree murder   A murder that does not fall into the category of first-degree murder; a murder committed with intent to kill, but without premeditation or deliberation.

self-defense   The use of force to protect oneself from death or imminent bodily harm at the hands of an aggressor. A person may use only that amount of force reasonably necessary to protect himself or herself against the peril with which he or she is threatened; thus, deadly force may be used in self-defense only against an aggressor who … uses deadly force.

separation of powers   A fundamental principle of the Constitution, which gives exclusive power to the legislative branch to make the law, exclusive power to the executive branch to administer it, and exclusive power to the judicial branch to enforce it. The authors of the Constitution believed that the separation of powers would make abuse of power less likely.

shield laws   Statutes that, in cases involving forcible sex crimes, prohibit the prosecution from introducing the victim's sexual history (especially alleged promiscuity or immorality) into evidence.

sodomy   A term whose definition varies from state to state, but which, at its broadest, criminalizes sexual relations between persons of the same sex, sexual contact per anus or per os between unmarried persons, and sexual intercourse with animals. Sodomy is also referred to as "the crime against nature" or *buggery.*

solicitation The crime of encouraging or inciting a person to commit a crime.

specific intent The intent to commit the very act with which the defendant has been charged. General criminal intent (mens rea) is an essential element of virtually all crimes. Specific intent is an additional requirement with respect to certain crimes.

stalking The crime of willfully, maliciously, and repeatedly following or harassing another and making threats intended to put the person in imminent fear of death or serious bodily injury.

stare decisis (Latin) Means "standing by the decision." Stare decisis is the doctrine that judicial decisions stand as precedents for cases arising in the future. It is a fundamental policy of our law that, except in unusual circumstances, a court's determination on a point of law will be followed by courts of the same or lower rank in later cases presenting the same legal issue, even though different parties are involved and many years have elapsed.

statute A law enacted by a legislature; an act.

statutes of limitations Federal and state statutes prescribing the maximum period of time during which various types of civil actions and criminal prosecutions can be brought after the occurrence of the injury or the offense.

statutory construction Determining the meaning of a statute.

statutory rape Sexual intercourse with a female under the age of consent, with or without her consent.

strict liability Liability for an injury whether or not there is fault or negligence; absolute liability.

strict liability crimes Crimes or offenses in which mens rea or criminal intent is not an element. Such offenses include regulatory crimes, petty offenses, and infractions.

subornation of perjury The crime of persuading or inducing another person to commit the crime of perjury.

tax evasion Willfully avoiding payment of taxes legally due ... .

tax fraud The crime of tax evasion. Tax evasion which is intentional but not willful is civil fraud.

tort A wrong involving a breach of duty and resulting in an injury to the person or property of another. A tort is distinguished from a breach of contract in that a tort is a violation of a duty established by law, whereas a breach of contract results from a failure to meet an obligation created by the agreement of the parties. Although the same act may be both a crime and a tort, the crime is an offense against the public which is prosecuted by the state in a criminal action; the tort is a private wrong that must be pursued by the injured party in a civil action.

transactional immunity A guaranty given a person that if he or she testifies against others he or she will not be prosecuted for his or her own involvement in the crime ... to which his or her testimony relates.

transferred intent The doctrine that if a defendant who intends to injure ... one person unintentionally harms another, the intent is transferred to the person who is unintentionally harmed. This doctrine permits the defendant to be prosecuted as if he or she had intended to harm the person injured.

trial court A court that hears and determines a case initially, as opposed to an appellate court; a court of general jurisdiction.

use immunity A guaranty given a person that if he or she testifies against others, his or her testimony will not be used against him or her if he or she is prosecuted for his or her involvement in the crime.

vagueness doctrine   The rule of constitutional law that a statute, particularly a criminal statute, that does not reasonably put a person on notice as to what it is he or she may not do, or what he or she is required to do, violates due process and is therefore unconstitutional.

vicarious liability   Liability imposed upon a person because of the act or omission of another.

INDEX